Cultural Memory
in
the
Present

Mieke Bal and Hent de Vries, Editors

Let us lend them two names that are still "historical,"
there where a certain concept of history itself
becomes inappropriate.
—Jacques Derrida

It is therefore the being-together of these two brothers,
of these two modalities of the origin,
that is unbearable, as if their reunion threatened
monotheistic reason in its fundamental concepts.
—Fethi Benslama

THE JEW, THE ARAB

THE JEW, THE ARAB

A History of the Enemy

Gil Anidjar

STANFORD UNIVERSITY PRESS

STANFORD, CALIFORNIA 2003

Stanford University Press
Stanford, California

Sections of Chapters 2 and 5 © 2002 from *Jacques Derrida: Acts of Religion*,
edited by Gil Anidjar. Reproduced by permission of Routledge, Inc., part of
the Taylor & Francis Group.

Printed in the United States of America
on acid-free, archival-quality paper

Library of Congress Cataloging-in-Publication Data

Anidjar, Gil.
The Jew, the Arab : a history of the enemy / Gil Anidjar.
    p. cm.—(Cultural memory in the present)
    Includes bibliographical references.
    ISBN 0-8047-4823-3 (cloth : alk. paper)—
    ISBN 0-8047-4824-1 (pbk. : alk. paper)
    1. Christianity and antisemitism—Europe—History.
2. Christianity and other religions—Islam.   3. Enemies
(Persons)—Europe—History.   I. Title.   II. Series.
BT93.A45 2003
940'.04924—DC21

                                    2002155101

Original printing 2003

Last figure below indicates year of this printing:
12   11   10   09   08   07   06   05   04   03

Typeset by Tim Roberts in 10/13.5 Adobe Garamond

Contents

As he draws away

The enemy who drinks tea in our shack
Has a horse in smoke, and a daughter with
Thick eyebrows and brown eyes. And her long hair
Is as long as the night of songs over her shoulders. And her picture
Never leaves him when he comes to drink our tea. But he
Does not tell us what she does in the evening, nor does he tell of
a horse abandoned by the songs on the hilltop . . .

    . . . In our shack, the enemy rests from his gun,
Lays it on my grandfather's chair, and eats our bread
As any guest would. He dozes off a little
On the wicker chair. And caresses the fur
Of our cat. He always says:
Don't blame the victim!
We ask him: Who is it?
He says: Blood that night cannot dry . . .

    . . . His coat buttons flash as he draws away (*'indama yabta'id*).
Good evening to you! Greet our well.
Greet the side of the fig. Step gently on our shadows
In the barley fields. And greet our pines
above. And do not forget to lock the door of the house
At night. And do not forget the horse's fear
From airplanes.
And greet us there, if there is time . . .

These words, which it was our intention
To say at the doorstep . . . he hears very well,
Very well, and covers them with a quick cough,
And waves them aside.
But why does he visit the victim every evening?
Memorize our proverbs, as we do,
And repeat our own canticles
About our very own appointments in the holy place?
Were it not for the gun,
Our flutes would have merged . . .

    . . . The war will not end as long as the earth
turns around itself within us!
So let us be good then. He asked us
To be good here. He recites a poem
To Yeats' Irish Airman: Those that I fight

I do not hate / Those that I guard
I do not love . . .
And he leaves our wooden shack
And walks eighty meters to
Our old stone house, there, on the edge of the plain . . .

Greet our house, stranger.
Our coffee cups
Have remained as we left them. Can you still smell
Our fingers on them? Will you tell your own daughter
With the braids and thick eyebrows that she has
An absent friend
Who wishes to visit her, for no reason really, all for nothing . . .
Only to enter her mirror and see his secret:
How she follows the course of his life after him,
In his place? Greet her,
If there is time . . .

These words, which it was our intention
To tell him, he hears very well,
Very well,
And covers them with a quick cough,
And waves them aside. His coat buttons flash
As he draws away . . .
   —Mahmoud Darwish

Acknowledgments

I would like to acknowledge the support of Columbia University (Faculty Summer Research Grant, 2001, 2002) and of my colleagues in the Department of Middle East and Asian Languages and Cultures. I am grateful to Helen Tartar for the integrity of her vision and for keeping all promises, to Larry Schehr and Bud Bynack for their readings, and to Stanford University Press for doing it again.

My friends Nina Caputo, Gérard Cohen, Mitch Hart, Joseph Massad, Marc Nichanian, Amnon Raz-Krakotzkin, Andrew Rubin, Peter Szendy, and Ruth Tsoffar for teaching me, Helen Brackett for more than I know, Eduardo Cadava for Emerson and for much more, Steven Miller for his "Open Letter to the Enemy," Lecia Rosenthal for the future, and Avital Ronell, once again, for everything.

Preface

It should become clear that *The Jew, the Arab* is about Europe: Europe is its limit and its limitations.

Europe, then, and, concerning it, the following questions. Is there a concept of the enemy? And, if there is such a concept, to what discursive sphere (politics, theology, law, philosophy, psychoanalysis—but there are others) does it belong? Which does it determine? Or—and in the oscillation of this "or," hovers everything that follows—if there is no concept of the enemy, if the concept of the enemy remains yet to be formulated (or simply to be thought), what, then, are the factors that could have prevented such a formulation? One answer to this last question (and some engagement with the former) as it will be offered here is that the enemy—as a concrete, discursive, vanishing field, "the shadow of an ageless ghost," as Derrida puts it—is structured by the Arab and the Jew, that is to say, by the relation of Europe to *both* Arab *and* Jew. A second answer is that this structuring has, in turn, everything to do with religion and politics. The challenge of these two no doubt insufficient answers to what are already too numerous questions will be to demonstrate that, in Europe, in "Christian Europe," they—the Jew, the Arab on the one hand, religion and politics, on the other—are distinct, but indissociable. Stated in a different idiom: The Jew, the Arab constitute the condition of religion and politics.

Introduction: Moments of the Theologico-Political

mo•ment

Noun. Pronunciation: \'mō-mənt\. Etymology: Middle English, from Middle French, from Latin *momentum*, movement, particle sufficient to turn the scales, moment, from *movere*, to move. Date: Fourteenth century. 1 a: a minute portion or point of time: INSTANT b: a comparatively brief period of time 2 a: present time <at the moment she is working on a novel> b: a time of excellence or conspicuousness <he has his moments> 3 : importance in influence or effect <a matter of great moment> 4 *obsolete*: a cause or motive of action 5 : a stage in historical or logical development 6 a: tendency or measure of tendency to produce motion especially about a point or axis b: the product of quantity (as a force) and the distance to a particular axis or point 7 a: the mean of the nth powers of the deviations of the observed values in a set of statistical data from a fixed value b: the expected value of a power of the deviation of a random variable from a fixed value *synonym*: see IMPORTANCE
  —*Merriam-Webster's Dictionary*

We must now decide what incidents seem dreadful or rather pitiable. Such must necessarily be the actions of friends to each other or of enemies, *echthroi*, or of people that are neither. Now if an enemy does it to an enemy, there is nothing pitiable either in the deed or in the intention, except so far as the actual calamity goes.
  —Aristotle, *Poetics*

In this book, I am engaging how the enemy becomes enemy, the history of the enemy that is inscribed within and between the polarized identities of Jew and Arab. If it constitutes a history, it is one that is longer than a colonial one, although colonial dimensions—the implication, indeed, the founding and continuing role of British colonialism and American imperialism, to mention only two prominent actors, in the creation and the continuation of the "Middle East conflict"—are perhaps better known and better studied, if not necessarily better understood. But *The Jew, the Arab: A History of the Enemy* is also less than a history—less a history, that is, than a preliminary account of why that history has not been written.

Beyond a horridly all too familiar and inescapable "cycle of violence," what is it that maintains the distance and kindles the enmity between the Arab and the Jew? What purposes are served by, what are the reasons for, the naturalization of this distance, the naturalization of the opposition, of the enmity between Arab and Jew, one that, as prominent narratives would have us believe, goes back to ancient biblical times, the ineluctable legacy of "the Middle East," a region and a land eternally ravaged by war and conflict? How did the ostensible markers of Arab (an "ethnic" marker) and Jew (a "religious" one) come to inscribe themselves so forcefully on modern discourses of the most varied kind—political, religious, cultural, and so forth—even when accompanying distinct or even opposed political agendas, caveats and sophisticated critiques and debunkings?[1]

Law is perhaps the single most important apparatus by way of which, in the course of the nineteenth and twentieth centuries, the colonial state ruled over its populations. As Mahmood Mamdani puts it, "one single claim defined a shared civilizational project: whether rulers or ruled, Westerners or non-Westerners, all those subjects to the power of the state would be governed through imported Western law."[2] Within this legal system, the state deploys "repressive and productive mechanisms" that participate in formulating "the new as that which has always been."[3] One of these mechanisms, and the basis for distinguishing and indeed discriminating between colonizer and colonized, was race. Such discrimination, however, was not enough, and further distinctions were introduced, sometimes even prior to the official establishment of Western law, prior to the full institution of colonial rule. The temporality of these distinctions is thus less important than the structures they put in place. At one level, then, one finds "a *racial* separation in civil law between natives and nonnatives," between colonizers and colonized. At another level, however, natives themselves are "divided . . . into separate groups and governed each through a different set of 'customary' laws."

In addition to race, law thus constituted another, distinct category—ethnicity. "The very category 'native' was legally dismantled as different groups of natives were set apart on the basis of ethnicity. From being only a cultural community, the ethnic group was turned into a political community." By invoking "local customs," a sphere was created within (Western) law that was outside the law, within the law, yet outside of its jurisdiction, a sphere governed by distinct cultural and political imperatives. "Within a single legal order" there emerged distinct *ethnic* differences, that is to say, naturalized political differences. "The language of the law tried to *naturalize* political differences in the colony by mapping these along a civilizational ladder. As the litmus of a civilizational test, the law separated the minority of civilized from the majority of those yet-to-be-civilized, incorporating the minority into a regime of rights while excluding the majority from the same regime."[4]

What is important to consider, therefore, is the history whereby the distinction between race and ethnicity is here primarily a legal distinction by means of which a population is both included (ruled by Western law) and excluded (deemed to be exterior to the law by the law) and falling under a different set of laws named "customary." The colonial state and Western law produced political differences *within* the colonized, but it also naturalized these political differences as cultural, and indeed ethnic. Within one legal system, within one colonized population, there emerged internal differences between ethnicity and race, between majority and minority, between indigenous and nonindigenous (26–27).

As Mamdani accounts for the regime of divisions that was established in Africa, he explains that the racialized minorities that were lifted above the majority of the colonized were defined as "subject races." They came to be identified as distinct from the majority of the colonized as nonindigenous and became "virtual citizens." They were

deprived of rights of citizenship, yet considered to have the potential of becoming full citizens. Though colonized, they came to function as junior clerks in the juggernaut that was the civilizing mission. Without being part of the colonial rulers, they came to be integrated into the machinery of colonial rule, as agents, whether in the state apparatus or in the marketplace. As such they came to be seen as both instruments and beneficiaries of colonialism, however coerced the instrumentality and petty the benefits. Though part of the colonized population, the subject races received preferential treatment under the law. In contrast, subject ethnicities were set apart and literally sat upon, legally. (27)

In Africa, Mamdani explains, the subject races were many. The list extends to the Asians of East Africa, the Indians and "Coloured" of South Africa, the Arabs of Zanzibar, and, of course, to the Tutsi of Rwanda and Burundi (28). The terrible history of the political divisions that, naturalized by colonial rule, sedimented as cultural distinctions that were later to lead to what has been called "ethnic violence" in Rwanda, is what Mamdani describes and, more importantly, explains and interrogates. Colonial rule produced political identities, identities that it proceeded to naturalize. In a process that has remained for the most part invisible, "the Tutsi were constructed by colonial ideology as well as law as nonindigenous Hamites," a distinct "*race . . .* both *civilizing and alien*" (28, 89).

The so-called Hamitic hypothesis served as part of an extended ideological apparatus meant to "turn the Tutsi, the 'born rulers' of Rwanda, into an elite 'capable of understanding and implementing progress,' and thus functioning as auxiliaries to both the missionaries and the colonial administration." A school system was created "that could act as a womb of racial ideology." Thus, the Tutsi "were given a 'superior' education, taught in French in a separate stream. The *assimilationist* education prepared them for administrative positions in government and testified to their preparation for citizenship, even if at the lowest orders" (90). Much like the Jews of Algeria—who, uniquely, were granted French citizenship in 1870,[5] thus becoming the embodiment of a distantly shimmering promise extended to Jews of the entire Arab world, a promise that was dutifully maintained, if not quite realized, by the *Alliance Israélite Universelle*—the Tutsi became nonnative outsiders, a political minority that did not belong to the native community. They became internal enemies.

In order to understand the Rwanda genocide, "whereby it became possible not only to set a group apart as an enemy, but also to exterminate it with an easy conscience" (13), Mamdani proposes to attend to the ways in which both race and ethnicity are legal and political inventions, the sedimented result of a complex legal process. He proposes to "understand the dynamic that polarizes political identities" (23), identities that are "legally enforced and institutionally reproduced" (15) and that had not existed (not in any comparable way) prior to colonial rule. Although distinctions were and are always operative within any given cultural system, they could always fluctuate and change, "shade into one another, with plenty of middle ground to nurture hybridity and ambiguity" (23). Yet, with the kind of polarization that is produced under colonial rule, "there is no middle ground, no continuum, between polarized identities. Polarized identities give rise to a kind of political difference where you must be either one or the other. You cannot partake of both. The difference becomes binary, not simply in law but in political life. It sustains no ambiguity" (23).

Thanks to Mamdani's magisterial demonstration, the polarization of Hutu and Tutsi along political, racial, and ethnic lines is now well known. But Mamdani suggestively opens a different area of reflection when he asks about the possible futures that are facing Rwanda after the genocide. Introducing a somewhat enigmatic parallel, Mamdani raises the following questions: "Will Rwanda follow the example of Israel, and create a separate community of Tutsi, alongside another of Hutu?[6] Will it follow the example of Zanzibar and merge in a larger union with the tendency to dissolve bipolar political identities . . . in a wider arena with multiple political identities? Or will it charter a third course . . . by trying to forge a political identity that transcends Hutu and Tutsi?" (265) Despite the enormous difficulties involved with generalizations and, most particularly, with comparisons such as these (and suspending, for now, the violent processes whereby European Jews *became* colonizing settlers, as well as the continuities between anti-Semitism and Zionism and the identifications and complicities that link Europe's colonial history to the colonization of Palestinian Arabs by European Jews), they pose troubling yet necessary questions. Who, in Israel and Palestine, are the Hutu, and who the Tutsi? And what are the historical, legal, religious, and political processes that have come to naturalize the Jew and the Arab as polarized identities? Though he does not take the term as a dominant marker of his inquiry, Mamdani does make clear that any answer to these queries has to engage the question—and the history—of the enemy: "Before you can try and eliminate an enemy," Mamdani writes, "you must first define that enemy. The definition of the political self and the political other has varied throughout history. The history of that variation is the history of political identities, be these religious, national, racial or otherwise" (9). The question of the enemy emerges and recurs here as the history of political identities, as the history, perhaps, of the political. How, for example, did it become possible in this particular case "not only to set a group apart as an enemy, but also to exterminate it with an easy conscience" (13)? And how did the killings in Rwanda "remain directed in the main at those identified as the political enemy, not the class enemy" (194)? What were the conditions that brought about a "truly disturbing aspect of the genocide," namely, that "the definition of the enemy appeared credible to many ordinary Hutu" (202)? What is the history that led to the emergence of an "internal enemy," an enemy who was quickly turned into an outsider to be fought with, expelled, and later exterminated? And how did the sedimentation of political identities produce such chillingly effective results? Much like the Hutu Presidential Guard, the Hutu moved "from confronting the enemy that seemed to advance relentlessly on the battlefield or on the diplomatic frontier" and "turned around to face the enemy within" (207). Yet that enemy had not simply been there to be faced. It had to be found and, indeed, searched for. They turned "away from the enemy on the battlefield . . . [and] looked for an enemy within" (215).

Early on in his argument, Mamdani recalls that "Europe 'solved' its political crisis by exporting it to the Middle East" (39). This is undoubtedly true. But what was Europe—what is it still—that it had this particular crisis to export? And what does that have to do with the Jew, the Arab? Most analyses so far have focused on this export of the "Jewish question," considering the choice of Arab Palestine as a contingency of European colonialism or as a result of Zionist aspirations. Other important analyses attend to the transformations of another history, the history of the opposition between "Islam and the West." To put it schematically, the first analyses attend to anti-Semitism, the latter to Orientalism. Without diminishing the accuracy of these accounts or the injustice involved in making Palestinians pay for the guilt of Europe vis-à-vis the Jews, one must nonetheless consider that these accounts entirely take for granted distinct states of enmity (between Jews and Arabs, between Europe and the Arabs, between Europe and the Jews, compounded in this last case by some eternally irreparable guilt) while ignoring the possibility of hidden links and explicit associations between these pairings.[7] They forego explanation of the historical problem that enmity poses, failing to engage the three "elements" at once (Europe, the Jew, the Arab).

They presuppose, for example, and without interrogating it, the separation of two groupings, "Europe and the Jews" and "Islam and the West" (to quote two celebrated subject headings) and reinscribe the stability of an "idea" of Europe (one that continues to be as fragile today as it ever was, even at its most violent moments of enforced identity), an idea that would exist without necessary relation to the Jew and/or the Arab. These accounts also take for granted the distinction of Arab and Jew as two polarized identities having been constituted independently of each other. There is, of course, no point in denying that such perspectives are quite plausible, even valid and necessary to pursue. They can moreover be complemented, if still insufficiently, by corrective studies that attend to Mediterranean culture or to the three monotheistic religions as a unit of one kind or other. Yet one cannot help but wonder at the absence of any consideration, any sustained analysis, or even any history of "Europe" in its relation to *both* Jew *and* Arab.

By suggesting that only the "Jewish question"—and not an "Arab" one—has been exported by and out of Europe, one foregoes such account of Europe. Moreover, one naturalizes and separates anti-Semitism and Orientalism in their distinct and anachronistic historical garbs, and, more importantly, one treats both Jew and Arab as simply existing categories that would have, except for few exceptions, not to say aberrant instances ("Medieval Spain," "Bosnia-Herzegovina"), thoroughly and hermetically distinct histories. There is more at stake here than a correction of the historical record on Arabs and Jews vis-à-vis or outside of the "Christian West." (Did they really get along? Could they? Why did/do they hate each other? And why do they hate us? Was it peaceful coexistence? What was their true contribution to philosophy, to science, to civilization? And then what happened? And so forth.) Nor—does this really need to be said?—is it a matter of asserting that this wrestling match is not of two (or three) parties, but of one, that there are no differences or distinctions to be made and maintained. The very framing of the question, and, more importantly, the reflection on its constitutive elements persists in considering either Jew or Arab and their "place" in Europe independently of each other. (If it is us and them, for example, then the com-pearance, not the identity, of both us and them is what continues to be at issue.) Such an approach is neither sufficient to account for the current state of affairs (the so-called "peace efforts" of the Western powers in the Middle East, as well as their "failures") nor does it recognize the ways in which these two political identities—the Jew, the Arab—have been coconstituted by and most importantly *with and within* Europe. The question that this book attempts to raise, then, is: What is Europe? What is Europe such that it has managed to distinguish itself from both Jew and Arab and to render its role in the distinction, the separation, and the enmity of Jew *and* Arab invisible—invisible, perhaps most of all to itself? Otherwise put, how has the history of the enemy become an impossible history?

Europe

The banality, in Hannah Arendt's sense, of yet another division: Europe—so-called "Christian Europe"—divides itself, from the beginning, between an enemy within and an enemy without. "Christianity is coextensive with the West," writes Jean-Luc Nancy, "with a certain process of Westernization that consists in a form of self-reabsorption and self-overcoming."[8] In other words, Christianity as Europe is affected by an internal conflict, a conflict that "takes the form of a schizophrenia or an internal division" (117). It is this Christianity, this Europe, about which Nancy wonders "why our gaze appears always to be turned systematically away from [it] . . . almost as if we *did not want* to look the Christian in the face," and it is this Europe, this Christianity, that Nancy defines as "the very thing— *the thing itself*—that has to be thought" (113).

Nancy illuminates Europe's division by undoing its exteriority, attending to the history of its "becoming internal." Thus, Europe's "internal conflict (one that is today becoming internal to Judaism and Christianity, albeit in entirely different ways) has nothing to do with the conflict . . . between Christianity and Judaism, nor with the conflicts that exist between all great religions." This is why Nancy defines the task as a reflection on an "*internal* division." As he makes clear, however, this interiority is the result of a history—what Nancy refers to as "the possibility of its becoming"—a becoming-internal of Europe's conflict and the preservation of a certain integrity. "At the heart of Christianity lies a specific type of conflict that is best defined as the conflict between an *integrity* and its disintegration" (117). This task of thinking, as Denis Guénoun puts it, "to think Europe in a double manner," has to attend, therefore, to the division of Europe, to its double alterity—if alterity is what is at stake here. This internal division of a space (Europe) between exteriority and interiority is constitutive of Europe, of the "possibility of its becoming," which always deconstitutes itself.[9]

Europe is a name. And the common name that is Europe, Guénon suggests in his striking book *Hypothèses sur l'Europe*, is constituted as a commonplace, a place in common that is also the site of a division, the site of a separation. Guénoun deploys a logic that, formalized by Jacques Derrida in *The Other Heading*, is structured by two "axioms." First, Europe rests on a "feeling" that, says Derrida, "we are younger than ever, we Europeans, since a certain Europe does not yet exist. Has it ever existed?"[10] And second, "what is proper to a culture is to not be identical to itself" (9/F16). What must be retained from this logic of separation and distance—if it is a logic— is that the feeling that is Europe remains at bay, separated from the Europe toward which it is heading, a Europe the existence of which is therefore in doubt, suspended. Europe—that is, also, "we Europeans"—is thus distanced from itself by virtue of a feeling that fails to ascertain the existence of its object. Over against the "idea of Europe," which, for Edmund Husserl, for example, is "a cognitive certitude, apodictably intuitable,"

Derrida's invocation of a feeling asserts that Europe is "not an assured cognitive truth."[11] Europe's existence is and has been quite uncertain, its identity, like that of any culture, being constituted—as condition of possibility and impossibility—by its nonidentity with itself.

Rodolphe Gasché comments that this nonidentity is itself doubled, is "double in kind."[12] First, the identity of a culture—here, Europe—presupposes "an external difference. This is a difference with itself that derives from identity's continual reference to the identity of other cultures over and against whom any self-identity is established. These other cultural identities, as identities of the Other, can simply be different from the one of European culture, but they can also be identities that stand in relation of opposition to European identity."[13] The second necessary condition of any cultural identity is that this identity "must be further divided by an internal difference, a self-difference," which is "the difference of any identity not from the state of non-identity from which it had to be wrenched, but with a 'state' anterior to the difference of identity and non-identity."[14] As Derrida puts it, "there is no self-relation, no relation to oneself, no identification with oneself, without culture, but a culture of oneself *as* a culture *of* the other, a culture of the double genitive and of the *difference to oneself*. The grammar of the double genitive also signals that a culture never has a single origin. Monogenealogy would always be a mystification in the history of culture."[15]

It is between these two violent openings, these two conditions of possibility and impossibility, which one could also somewhat simplistically and quite unfaithfully recast as the distinction between empirical conditions and transcendental ones, that Guénoun situates Europe, the common name and common site that is Europe, which produces and reproduces, as coconstitutive, the distinction and indeed the opposition between the theological and the political. "The theologico-political," writes Guénoun, "is decisively the *site of the theologico-political difference*."[16] He thus attends to the complex history whereby what was never a unity comes to be constituted and reconstituted as the institutionalization of a cut ("the Emperor will not be the bishop, Cesar will not be the Pope," 52), which "simultaneously posits a space *and* a separation, a separation inscribed in the topical community, as an internal incision without scar" (52), the "mimetic rivalry of Church and Empire" (58) as well as the desire for and against a "reunification" of the theological with the political (108). Guénoun explores the internal difference of each of the terms, insisting, for example, that the theological as well as the religious occur as difference, that is, as internal and external differences whereby "religion is constituted as the difference between religions" (117).

Simultaneously, Guénoun adds, the political in its internal difference is constituted out of religious division (117 n. 33).[17] Guénoun thus links the history of political change in Europe to this particular division, to what he calls the "theologico-political difference." In this history, the nation that begins to emerge with the French Revolution is "the (theologico-political) figure of the inverted kingdom," as well as the "inverted figure of the king-dom" (136). In it, one can witness an attempt at reunification, the production of a body politic that is "at once political and mystical," a recasting of sovereignty as the sovereignty of the people, of the assembly, and no longer of the king: "the nation comes to occupy a very singular place in the 'theologico-political' apparatus of which we are trying to write the history. Constituted as *what assembles itself* (as what brings about the *common, the being of what is in common*), it occupies precisely the place of the church, if one is willing to recall that the church is nothing else than the transposed name of the assembly as such" (143). What is perhaps one of the most forceful illustrations of secularization—the French Revolution as the de-theologization of politics— however, fails to erase the division, the constitutive theologico-political structure of politics. In "the Jewish Question," Marx made that failure limpid in terms that remain relevant to this day. "The nation," writes Guénoun, "is a theological idea" (156).

But earlier in the book, Guénoun adds another "axiom" to those we have been exploring. "Europe," he writes, "figures itself facing Islam" (62). Europe gives itself a face, a *figure*, by way of Islam. Europe fabricates for itself a site where it will be able to protect itself from itself, protect itself from what it projects and imagines as and at its end, the end of Europe. This is to say that, for Europe, Europe and Islam are intimately involved in a "specular formation of mirror images" that is "the primordial identitarian rapport, constitutive of Europeanness" (63). This rapport, an originary structure of Europe, has been very much studied from a variety of perspectives, and we will return to it in the chapters that follow.[18] What Guénoun here emphasizes and interrogates, even if briefly, is the way in which Islam is historically constituted as exteriority, that is to say, exteriorized. ("At bottom, what we would have to say is this: Islam is not extraneous to our history. Or it is so in a singular fashion: from the inside," 287.) Islam would thus be the becoming-exterior of what is within "our" world—"we,

Europeans." ("The exteriority of Islam marks its proximity. Islam in *our* history is the name of this exteriority rising on the internal edge of our world, rushing in and within it," 288.) Nowhere is this clearer, perhaps, than in the modern construction of Islam as "religious fanaticism," which coincides historically with what is still called "secularization." Islam thus becomes an "internal exteriority," an included exclusion, according to the structure of the exception formalized most famously by Carl Schmitt and that will occupy us throughout what follows: If the name of this exclusion, this exteriorization, is "Islam," then in naming itself as what faces Islam, "Europe" hides itself from itself by claiming to have a name and a face independently of Islam. This self-constitution is not only fundamentally related to the question of "religion" in its divisions. It carries with it in unavoidable ways the division between Judaism and Islam, the distinction of Jew from Arab.

Except for a quickly vanishing autobiographical moment, however, Guénoun never links the two figures of Arab and Jew to each other vis-à-vis Europe. Thus, under the isolated figure of an excluded inclusion, he leaves Islam aside in order to attend to the "Jewish contribution" to Europe, never explicitly addressing the historical link of Judaism to the figure of Islam and of Islam to the figure of Judaism, within and without Europe. And yet, it is the figure of the "Arabized Jews" (as Guénoun describes his own genealogy) and the Arabic language spoken by his Jewish ancestors that raise more than a historical question regarding the conditions of Guénoun's own writing, of his "hypotheses on Europe." If, according to his acute analyses, Islam is the "external enemy" (that is, if it has *become* such—becoming enemy as well as becoming external), and Judaism is the "internal enemy," the question that remains, covert and untreated, is indeed the question of a relation, the relation between Europe and the Jew, the Arab. This question would be "more radical," articulating itself, as we will see, around "a reflection upon the constitution of the political out of a religious division" (117 n. 33). It is both a philosophical and an empirical question, and it constitutes itself as the unwritten history of the theologico-political, a history of the enemy.

The Enemy, the Jew, the Arab

He who, for example, laughs at the racist joke . . . won't have assented to a thesis, which, in this register was not even enunciated, but he will have recognized the essential, which follows no argument and is oblivious to any: that the Jews or the Arabs . . . are the index of a major risk, the destruction of all present.
—Alain David, *Racisme et antisémitisme*

A note on terminology. First, as I attempted to access various and no doubt limited, not to say insufficient pathways that would assist and lead me toward accounts of the term "enemy" within the discourse of philosophy, political philosophy, and political science, I was surprised to find only rare and occasional, quantitatively limited discussions. I had to confront, then, something like the disappearance of the enemy, its having vanished from philosophical and political reflections almost from the start, rather than in modern times, as Carl Schmitt argues.[19] To the extent that one could subsume the question of the enemy under that of war, one would have to acknowledge that the modern discourse on war identified by Michel Foucault and others is always articulated as historico-political (in a narrow sense of these terms), no longer as philosophico-juridical. The claim to "decipher the permanence of war in society" was thus never simply a philosophical claim.[20] Nor does it engage the fundamental difference between war and the enemy, the excess of the question of the enemy in relation to war.[21]

To the extent that this question—the question of the enemy—does, on occasion, emerge, it does so mainly as an institutional issue, made to attend to modes of behavior ("How to treat the enemy"), or modes of engagement ("How to fight, vanquish, or annihilate the enemy"), and finally, to modes of appearance ("faces of the enemy") and identification ("Who is the enemy?"). The question of ontology—"What is the enemy?"—hardly surfaces, and when it does, as we will briefly consider in Chapter 3 ("De inimicitia"), it is only too quickly rendered almost ephemeral and a testimony to the vanishing, the drawing away of the enemy.

A cursory reading of Western philosophical and political reflections (what is called today political science and/or political theory, as well as political philosophy) quickly reveals that, over against the friend or the beloved, love or friendship (which have been claimed by the expert discourses of philosophy and politics, but also of ethics, psychology, and others), "the enemy" never becomes a basic concept, barely even a significant operative term.[22] Reasons for the discursive operations of the enemy, the generalization and simultaneous lack of conceptualization of the enemy, may be found in philosophy ("philosophy, when thinking about war, does nothing else than think about peace. It mistakes its objects. . . . Thus, the discourse of peace becomes, at the philosophical level, the departure point of the discourse of war. It becomes the founding underground of political philosophy in general."),[23] or they may be found in political reflections that do engage war, but not the enemy, or, alternatively, that address (and even seem to answer) but fail to ask the question of the enemy. [24]

At any rate, reasons for the state of affairs exemplified here (the state of the question of the enemy) may be numerous, and it remains difficult, if not impossible, to sustain a claim aiming to establish a continuity of the enemy, of the concept of enemy, much less to argue for or demonstrate epistemic shifts or ruptures, strategic developments or secularizing mutations, in the history of the enemy.[25] More importantly, it remains unclear to what extent the very term "enemy," in the various languages in which it is made to appear here (English, German, French, for the most part, and to some extent, Greek, and Latin) could ever be justified by some alleged semantic identity.

What may be no more than philological vagueness, and even a lack of philosophical rigor, remains dictated, perhaps even governed, by a vanishing, the insistence of a drawing away (which is not quite the absence) of the enemy from any, privileged, discursive sphere. Is the question of the enemy a philosophical, legal, or psychological question? Is it a culturally contained, even a historical and (finally?) a political one? Aside from Carl Schmitt's attempt not so much to revive as to virtually establish the concept of the enemy and to locate the decision concerning the distinction between friend and enemy as the condition of the political, aside from Jacques Derrida's groundbreaking reflections on the enemy in *Politics of Friendship*, there is very little to authorize or even enable the claim that one could ever write a history of the enemy.[26] Thus, again, the enemy draws away, leaving behind the question "Why?" and perhaps also, "How?"

According to what protocols, then, and in what modalities, has a history of the enemy become impossible? This book will try to show that this historical impossibility is contingent upon the condition of religion and politics in "Europe," a condition that Derrida has elaborated in his writings on the Abrahamic.[27] Nothing authorizes the collapse of religious (and

historically dubious) markers such as Judaism and Islam with ethnic or political markers such as Arab and Jew. Yet already the dissymmetries inherent to the terms ("Jew" and "Muslim," "Jew" and "Arab") are carried by the
history that seeks to account for their sedimentation as polarized identities.
What appeared to be a lexical choice was not, therefore, ever quite one
(even if the use of the term "Arab," with its emphasis on a linguistic dimension, makes it paradoxically more difficult to simply oppose it to
"Jew," a term whose religious history or inflection remains slightly more
visible). To have followed a restricted tradition that speaks so obscurely, if
also so strangely, of a "Judeo-Muslim symbiosis" (away—always far
away—from Europe, as if the latter had nothing to do with the former),
would already have been to decide to locate the issue in the sphere of religion, however broadly defined. It would have been to ignore that aside
from more or less limited syncretistic areas, the two "religions"—if that is
what they are—as two bodies of law (Hebrew: *dat*, Arabic: *din*), must remain distinct, or at least must claim to remain so for purposes of safety or,
as one says, for security reasons. It is by now banal, if also not entirely adequate, to single out and contrast the example of Arab Christians who (aside
from, and in excess of, religious differences) constitute well-recognized
groups that are, in a variety of ways that differ from one area to another,
both distinct and not distinct from the Arab Muslim populations and
linked in a manner for which no "Christian-Muslim symbiosis" could ever
account. "The Jew, the Arab," then, because things are complicated, multi-
layered, and many tools of analysis are required to account for terminological possibilities and impossibilities.[28]

But there is another reason to invoke "the Jew, the Arab" in the wide
range of historical contexts to which this book appeals. This is a historical
reason: that "Europe," which can be said to have long confused the terms,
to have collapsed Arab and Muslim, Orientals and Semites, Turks and
Saracens, and continues to do so to this day, Europe provides here the
site, uncertain and fragmented as it is, from which the two figures emerge
as enemies. Enemies of Europe and enemies of each other, "the Jew," "the
Arab" are undoubtedly arbitrary names. Yet, they are also old names that
have strategically and insistently inscribed themselves with an as of yet
unaccounted-for necessity in the history—a history of the present if there
ever was one—of Europe and of the West. "The Jew, the Arab," then.
And—as if it were possible—a history of the enemy.

THE JEW, THE ARAB

PART I

The Theological Enemy

"Does not lucidity, the mind's openness upon the true, consist in catching sight of the permanent possibility of war? The state of war suspends morality; it divests the eternal institutions and obligations of their eternity and rescinds ad interim the unconditional imperatives."[1] Thus Emmanuel Levinas who, from the beginning of *Totality and Infinity*, describes the violent opening of a space within which the question of the enemy at once emerges and vanishes. In this space of suspended morality—the space and state of war, in which the enemy may be subject or object, presupposed or produced—the enemy has already drawn away, having traversed the distance opened, the *éloignement* produced by a rupture that does not signify alterity. The enemy is not the other—and the movement by which the enemy vanishes into the distance (something that, neither recoil nor retreat, exceeds all strategy) is a movement that remains within the space of the same, there where what there is, what one catches sight of, is the permanent possibility of war.

The movement of the enemy thus has to be distinguished from that of the other who comes from afar, the neighbor or *prochain* who, before the subject, comes. Symmetrically opposed—rather than asymmetrically approaching—the enemy departs and vanishes, which is to say that the enemy also *remains* as departing and vanishing. The space within which this movement takes place is defined by Levinas as the space of the political, as the space of war. This (that is to say, war) is what philosophy—the exercise of reason—thinks. "The art of foreseeing war and of winning it by every means," which is to say, "politics," is "the very exercise of reason."[2] Politics is philosophy, and its thinking is a thinking of war, and a thinking at war. Echoing Carl Schmitt, who defined the political as the "ever present possibility of conflict . . . the ever present possibility of combat,"[3] Levinas insists that philosophy is a response to the "permanent possibility of war."[4] "We do not need obscure fragments of Heraclitus," Levinas continues, "to prove that being reveals itself as war to philosophical thought."[5] Thus, "does not the experience of war and totality coincide, for the philosopher, with experience and evidence as such?"[6] Thought as totality, being constitutes the space of the same as the permanent possibility of its own destruction.[7]

But being—that is, war ("war is produced as the pure experience of pure being")—is not a lawless space, not a space without order.[8] Rather, being is the order of the same, a world order that, however shattered, allows for no exteriority, leaves no room for alterity. Being—that is, war— "establishes an order from which no one can keep his distance; nothing henceforth is exterior. War does not manifest exteriority and the other as other; it destroys the identity of the same."[9] It is an order that places (or violently throws) law into a state of suspension, a temporal suspension or a suspension in time. In this time and at this time, law is not destroyed, nor is it abolished. Rather, law moves into a different time. In the permanent possibility of war, in what Freud calls "wartime," law is suspended, divested, and stripped of its eternity (Levinas uses the verb *dépouiller*), provisionally cancelled, annulled "in the provisional." In war, then, in the permanent possibility of war, we find ourselves in a space and a time where law is both nullified and maintained and where the enemy cannot be other.[10] In war, there are no others, only enemies.

It was Jacob Taubes who strikingly suggested that this space where law is suspended, upheld but not abolished ("Do we then overthrow the law by this faith? By no means! On the contrary, we uphold the law"), this space of war, is the space of Paul's Letter to the Romans.[11] Romans, Taubes claims, is "a political declaration of war." That is to say, it is a political theology.[12] For Taubes, Paul makes himself into an enemy of Rome, but, more importantly, he becomes a thinker of enmity. Like Levinas's philosopher, Paul's ontology (which is also the end of ontology, even an anti-ontology, a concern for "the things that do not exist," Rom. 4:17) is an ontology of war and wrath, the obviousness of which makes it, perhaps, as invisible as being itself. Much like Levinas's assertion that war is the suspended space of indifference, where alterity has no place—the enemy is not the other—Paul's thought is famously one of *adiaphora*, in-difference. It is only within that space of indifference as the suspension of all obligations that we can recognize the state of war within which Paul writes and out of which he too ambivalently enjoins his followers to care for their enemies. Paul cites Proverbs and recasts a love of enemy that leaves room for the wrath of God.[13] Shower your enemies with love, Paul says, a love that would bury them under a pile of burning coals. "Beloved, never avenge yourself, but leave room for the wrath of God . . . if your enemies are hungry, feed them; if they are thirsty, give them something to drink; for by doing this you will heap burning coals on their heads" (Rom. 12:19–20). If being is the permanent possibility of war, if being is being-at-war and being-as-war, then Romans is also a theory—and a history—of the enemy.

> Have I now become your enemy, *echthros*, by telling you the truth?
> —Gal. 4:16

Taubes, like Carl Schmitt, his main interlocutor ("I am a Jew and I have been elevated by Carl Schmitt to the rank of hereditary enemy") was a formidable reader of Paul.[14] (As for Levinas, we will leave him aside for now, much as he himself would leave war behind or, more precisely, below: "Only beings capable of war can rise to peace").[15] But whereas Schmitt underplayed the political meaning of the enemy in the New Testament (contrasting it with the "private enemy" alone),[16] Taubes raised the question of the theological enemy—the enemy of God—and emphasized its momentous function. Taubes narrates how he inflicted the "gewaltige Satz," the powerful phrase of Rom. 11:28 upon Carl Schmitt himself in a unique and all but peaceful meeting (*Auseinandersetzung*) that took place at Schmitt's house before Schmitt's death, during which the two read Romans together. "As regards the gospel," says Paul, as enthusiastically quoted and punctuated by Taubes, "they are enemies—enemies of God!"[17] My questions, therefore, emerge out of Taubes's quote: Is there a history of the enemy—Taubes explicitly links the enemy of God to history as *Heilsgeschichte*, as history of salvation—and if there is such a history, where does the "theological enemy" figure in it? Who or what is the "enemy of God"?

It is possible to follow a significant thread or a path in Romans—one could even call it a warpath— whereby the figure of the theological enemy emerges as an uncertain preview or repetition of what Paul elsewhere calls "the last enemy," death (1 Cor. 15:26: "the last enemy to be destroyed is death").[18] In Romans, they—for it is a "they,"[19] who is seldom named—are "god-haters," *theostuges*,[20] and "inventors of evil" (Rom. 1:30), and they know that God's law regarding what they do is to "deserve to die" (1:32). They have been abandoned by God, given or passed over, displaced and even betrayed by him (the Greek is *paredoken*, the Latin gives *tradidit*): "God gave them up" (1:24, 26, 28).[21] "Their throats are open graves" (3:13), and they are "slaves of sin" (6:20). It is well known that the "wages of sin is death" (6:23), and it is quite possible that they are, in fact, dead (11:15).[22] It is something even "we"—we who were "enemies," *echthroi*, (5:10)—knew: "While we were living in the flesh, our sinful passions, aroused by the law, were at work in our members to bear fruit for death. But now we are discharged from the law, dead to that which held us captive, so that we are slaves not under the old written code but in the new life of the Spirit" (7:5–6). This captivity in death is one that resonates with that of a prisoner of war (*aikhmalotos, captivus*),[23] and testifies further to the fact that, for Paul, there is indeed a war on.[24]

Paul's own call to arms resonates twice in Romans, first in 6:13 ("No longer present your members to sin as weapons of wickedness, but present . . . your members to God as weapons of righteousness"), and second in 13:12 ("let us lay aside the works of darkness, but let us put on the weapons of light"). The permanent possibility of war in which body parts can always become weapons and in which they can be put on like armor proclaims that being is being at war: "I see in my members another law at war," *antistrateumenon, repugnantem* "with the law of my mind, making me captive to the law of sin that dwells in my members" (7:23).[25] Furthermore, in this war that makes one at once into a "battlefield," as Theodor Zahn puts it,[26] and into a prisoner of war, activity and agency are anything but granted. War, then, is also an experience in subjection. Commenting upon it, Ernst Käsemann observes that the war is on, but in it, the self is not fighting. The self is the "I see" that witnesses the war, no more than an "impotent spectator."[27] One might say that the self is a good theoretician—indeed, a philosopher.

One should not presume to understand the different laws, the different modes of being and existence under or before the law such as those called "life" and "'death" that appear in Paul's letter, especially when they have been the object of much exegetical and critical attention, and for good reasons. For my purpose here, what is more important is to consider that the relation between these different modes is described as one of open hostilities, for "the mind that is set on the flesh is hostile to God," *echthra eis theon, inimicitia est in Deum*. It does not submit to God's law—indeed, it cannot (8:7). Those who remain with the flesh therefore remain, and must remain hostile to God. And although Paul himself wishes that he could stay with them—"I could wish that I myself were accursed and cut off from Christ for the sake of my own brothers, my kindred according to the flesh" (9:3)—he cannot. In complicated ways, he is and he is not their brother, much in the same way that they belong and do not belong to God. There is thus a perspective according to which they are still God's and God's beloved—Israel and not Israel—and another perspective according to which they are God's enemies: "As regards the gospel, they are enemies," *echthroi*, "of God for your sake; but as regards election they are beloved, for the sake of their ancestors; for the gifts and the calling of God are irrevocable" (11:28–29).[28]

"Paul never wrote a sentence that he crafted more carefully, and it sums up all that has gone before," writes Christopher Bryan.[29] Indeed, 11:28 is justifiably at the center of a long controversy, if not at the center of the letter itself. What it highlights is more than Paul's writing skills. As Taubes recognized (and ultimately, it would seem, as Schmitt realized, as well), it is a momentous verse in which the question of enmity is brought to the foreground of Paul's entire doctrine and where it is tied to and divided by the question of subjection.

Just as *theostuges* may mean "god-hater" as much as "god-hated" (1:30)[30] and the "enemy" in "we were enemies" (5:10),[31] the word for enemy, *echthros*, can, in this context, equally be read as active or passive. In other words, enemies—and enemies *of* God, with a double genitive—might be those who actively hate God, or they might be those who are subjected to God's hate.[32] Paul suggests as much when he establishes a parallel between being weak or powerless ("while we were still weak," 5:6) and being an enemy ("while we were enemies," 5:10).[33] There is a crucial distinction to be made, of course, between and within these terms, but it nonetheless remains an undecidable one. Most scholars simply ignore the controversy here and maintain that the word is to be read as passive (in other words, Paul would have "in view the attitude of God rather than man"),[34] while others affirm the oscillation inherent to the text, asserting, for example, that "Israel's situation is distinguished from that of others by ambivalence."[35]

If so, this "ambivalence" is far from limited to Israel. The kind of relation without relation to God's law ("God gave them up") described in Romans as "proper" to the enemy is repeatedly figured as one of hostility, as a "state of war," as the permanent possibility of war between God and (a part of) humanity. But the question of the enemy also figures a peculiar, and ambivalently marked kind of subjection. It is this ambivalence of the enemy as enemy or the enemy as subject (who submits to another law, or must be subjected to the will of God) that links the question of war and enmity to the question of law and subjection. The state of war, the permanent possibility of war, is precisely the situation that Paul describes, one whereby law is suspended, not abolished. In the context of this ongoing war, Paul's assertion—"Do we then overthrow the law by this faith? By no means! On the contrary, we uphold the law" (3:31)—echoes quite precisely Levinas's formulation with which I began: "The state of war suspends morality; it divests the eternal institutions and obligations of their eternity and rescinds ad interim the unconditional imperatives."[36] Insofar as he is *of* God, belonging to God while having been abandoned, given up, and betrayed by him, insofar as he is under God's law while refusing to submit to it, insofar as he is at war with God's law, at once under the law and excluded from it, the theological enemy—at once enemy and beloved—is at the center of Romans.[37] Having been put aside (*paredoken*) by God, he is both under the law and outside of it. He is the exception to the sovereign whom God also gave away and put aside (*paredoken*), the Messiah himself, Jesus, son of God.[38]

Jacques Derrida has furthered this understanding of the messianic as a structural possibility, the permanent possibility of a state of war as the suspended state of the law, by suggesting that it bears the structure of a rapport with law as exception, dividing the law and the subject of the law under what one could call a "generalized messianicity." In "Before the Law," Kafka narrated this divided, interrupted relation to the law. Commenting upon Kafka's text, Derrida argues that its elaborations require a reading of Paul's Letter to the Romans. In talking to his "brothers," Paul was explaining that "in order to have a *rapport* of respect with [the law], *one must not* have a rapport with the law, *one must interrupt the relation*."[39] Before the law one is therefore "both a subject of the law and an outlaw."[40] This has everything to do with the messianic, as becomes clear in a striking passage from *Politics of Friendship*. "Who has ever been sure," Derrida asks, "that the expectation of the Messiah is not, from the start, by destination and invincibly, a fear, an unbearable terror—hence the hatred of what is thus awaited?"[41] "The messianic sentence," Derrida continues, articulates a structural contradiction that "converts a priori . . . the friend into the enemy."[42]

The appearance of a division within and between the Jews and Jesus, within and between the Messiah and the enemy, and finally within and between the enemy (as subject and object of hatred, as object—and subject?—of love) is not simply another case of God's ambivalence. Rather, as Giorgio Agamben shows in his own book on Paul, it is an effect of the messianic as "a theory of the rapport between the messianic and the subject, that settles once and for all the account with identitarian pretensions and with the properties of a subject."[43] The messianic is an "operation" that cuts and "divides the very divisions that the law institutes, making them inoperative."[44] It operates a cut within the identity of any subject, at once producing and eradicating the space of sameness according to the law.[45] Much as the way in which "not all of those from Israel are Israel" (Rom. 9:6), the subject of Paul's letter is at war with itself, making it impossible to sustain the division suggested by Schmitt and maintained for the most part in New Testament scholarship that would posit either a "personal" or a "political" enemy to the exclusion of others and of other enemies.[46] What the messianic constitutes and deconstitutes, beginning with Paul, is at once the theological enemy as *both* personal and political *and* as neither personal nor political. The divided subject of Paul is both enemy and beloved, slave and sovereign, "subject and subject,"[47] Israel and not Israel.

This internal division—which continues to operate within each of the terms—is a temporally extended state of war, the permanent possibility of a war of subjection, where law, institutions, and obligations are suspended, stripped of their eternity. But this narrative, which would give away—carry over, give up, and betray, *paredoken*—its subject from enmity to subjection, is also the structural division that affects enmity as undecidably active or passive. What fails to come together, but offers itself to a reading here is a history of the enemy as the internal division of a subject that is first active, then passive, and both active and passive. The narrative version echoes throughout Romans and in 1 Corinthians, but maintains a nonnarrativized, structural link between subjection and enmity, activity and passivity: "for the creation was subjected to futility, not of its own will but by the will of the one who subjected it, in hope that the creation itself will be set free from its bondage to decay" (8:20). Even emancipation remains an experience in passivity. It is war.

For he must reign until he has put all his enemies under his feet. The last enemy to be destroyed is death. For "God has put all things in subjection under his feet." But when it says, "All things are put in subjection," it is plain that this does not include the one who put all things in subjection under him. When all things are subjected to him, then the Son himself will also be subjected to the one who put all things in subjection under him, so that God may be all in all. (1 Cor. 15:25–28)

What begins to appear here is Paul's own link between enmity and the messianic—more precisely, we witness a doubling of the messianic as what divides the subject (here, the son) in his subjection ("Therefore one must be subject, not only because of wrath but also because of conscience," Rom. 13:5), as what divides the enemy as beloved ("love your enemies"). We will have to attend to these divisions and to the history of their elaborations, for in them and through them, the Messiah has become hated and beloved. (And, in the shadows of that link, another thread will have begun to guide our reading of the enemy: absolute subjection.)[48] The Messiah, "who came and, as one says, became the neighbor," the Messiah, then, has become the enemy.[49] Such would be one of civilization's great discomforts.

Inter-diction 1: Absolute Subjection

"My power," said Jesus, quoted by Paul (in older versions of 2 Corinthians), "my power is made perfect in weakness" (2 Cor. 12:9). Weakness, then, unlike power, and certainly unlike revenge, is not mine. If the subject is the subject *of* power—double genitive— weakness seems to precede the subject as what is not owned, indeed, as what disowns and dispossesses it. As Judith Butler puts it, "the subject is initiated through a primary submission to power," a power that can—if it *can*—then, and perhaps infinitely later and after many turns, become "mine."[50] We have been awakened anew to the weakness that precedes and follows power, to subjection in and after submission, and to subjection *as* submission, by Foucault's work. But Foucault did not "elaborate on the specific mechanisms of how the subject is formed in submission" (2). Butler's book, subtitled *Theories in Subjection*, is an attempt to address the *formation*, the making of the subject by answering the "how" of submission, by "thinking the theory of power together with a theory of the psyche" (3). Butler's work, then, is precisely that—a "work," a "making work" that asks how "we might *make* such a conception of the subject *work* as a notion of political *agency*" (18).

It is remarkable that the importance of subjectivity and sub-jection, as well as the reflections on agency that continue to domi-nate the field of cultural studies, have not brought about more con-siderations of what submission might mean, or more precisely, what its sense and meaning might be. If, as Butler also argues, "power as-sumes this present character" by performing "a break with what has come before" and by dissimulating "as a self-inaugurating agency" (16), if, in other words, power dissimulates *as* agency, then what of "what has come before" as another power, as the other of power? If the agenda continues to be to articulate a theory of agency and free-dom, to articulate a theory of formation, the making and the giving of form to the matter at hand, it would seem unsurprisingly neces-sary to address as well the question of passivity and of submission, perhaps of absolute submission, if only to determine what it is that we—and power itself, in its dissimulation—appear to want to es-cape, to emancipate ourselves from, by way of acts, action, forma-tion, production, labor, *praxis* and work. "Is it useless to revolt?"—as Foucault's title had it—remains the question: Is agency possible?

In other words, and these are Paul's words, in contemporary theory, we are given *the works, ta erga.* And it becomes possible to consider that the lexicon of action, the "syntax of doing," as Avital Ronell calls it, "subjected" as it is "to procedures of legitimation" is, like work, evocative of a "reduction of the human figure" that ren-ders "the human equal to the laboring animal."[51] As Ronell puts it further, "servile by nature and affecting docility, work, at the core of the modern experience of alienation, is inhumane and antisocial."[52] Subjectivity and subjection, agency and submission, cannot, there-fore, be understood apart from each other. Yet the question emerges: Is there a history of absolute subjection, an account of ab-solute submission? In what follows, I want to argue that a reflection on submission and on absolute subjection—a constellation that in-cludes, in ways yet to be clarified, subjectivity and subjection, pas-sivity and submission—constitute an essential, if insufficiently ac-knowledged moment of the renewed reception of Paul.

A self-defined "slave of God," possibly even a "super slave," *hypér doulon*,[53] and beginning with the opposition of faith to works, with a body that "has its place, albeit *subordinated* to the spirit," Paul could be said to reappear on the "European" scene as a thinker of absolute subjection.[54] Jacques Derrida's most extensive discussion of Paul occurs as a reading of Galatians, where Paul's paralyzing blindness—a blindness and a madness to which Paul's body is helplessly subjected—is both a model of the self-portrait and of what strikes its ruin at the very beginning, ruin as the very beginning ("Au commencement, il y a la ruine").[55] After *The Experience of Freedom*, Jean-Luc Nancy's exhilarating "deconstruction of Christianity" concludes, for now, by recalling—and opposing—"servility."[56] Before his death, Jean-François Lyotard became particularly interested in Paul and turned his attention most importantly to the slave (and the child) as defined by a "regime of belonging and not of servitude."[57] Lyotard wondered about emancipation and the permanent possibility of a *mancipium*.[58] He reread Paul and included him (and Augustine) among "the moderns" who promised emancipation (5/F11), calling attention to what was, for Paul, "unsubmissive flesh" (19/F33) as opposed, perhaps, to "God's slavery" (8/F15). Giorgio Agamben, who has relentlessly attended to the extreme powerlessness of "bare life," points out that we owe Paul a third of all occurrences of the word *doulos*—slave—in the New Testament (47 times out of 127).[59] Finally, Alain Badiou begins (and ends) his own book on Paul by arguing that what is at stake in Paul is a theory of subjection and of subjectivity in which the subject's existence is placed under, placed under order and ordainment, sub-ordinated and submitted to the event: "a theory of the subject that subordinates its existence to the hazardous dimension of the event."[60] Badiou's Paul is, in fact, one of the most striking Pauls who lies—if not acts—throughout the renewed Continental reception of his letters, so I will linger with it for a moment.

Of Paul's life, Badiou will say that although we know very little, we do know "what he does not do" (19). A nondoer who cared little about "what Jesus had said and done" (35), Paul was the theoretician of a nonaction that orients a different history, a history of submission. It is a history that refigures freedom as, "in the last resort," as Badiou puts it, the question of a relation between the law and the subject: "Is any subject found in the figure of a legal subjection?" (26). Even when (in the spirit of a Deleuzian becoming-woman, becoming-animal) he answers that Paul's discourse situates itself as that of one "becoming son" in opposition to being a slave ("For Paul, either one is a slave, or one is a son," 51; and see Galatians 4:7: "So through God you are no longer a slave but a son"). It presents itself as an emancipation from a "figure of knowledge that is itself a figure of slavery," (63), Badiou thus strikingly illustrates that the questions of freedom, subjection, submission, and subjectivity are crucial to a reading of Paul.

Yet it is remarkable that Badiou appears to dismiss a slavish submission as what would have to be left behind when Paul himself reinscribes it. "Certainly," Badiou writes, "Jesus is 'lord' (κυριος), and Paul is his 'servant (δουλος)'" (66). No doubt "certainly," yet there is a "but" that must carefully be asserted and that protects from and prevents confusion: "that we have to *serve* the process of truth must not be confused with slavery" (67). Badiou goes on to buttress the distinction by eradicating the risk of confusing emancipation with passive submission. He does so by affirming work and labor: the operation of the "but" is to indicate a "task," a "faithful labor" in which the subjects are the "coworkers" (68). Yet the confusion of the two, so quickly passed and labored over, may still have to be taken into account if, as Badiou himself puts it a few pages later, "what saves us is faith, not works" (79).

Badiou's Paul is a subject of power, one that opposes the works of law as "what constitutes the subject as the powerlessness of thought" (87) and that seeks to unify thought and action, which law had separated. Badiou's Paul is a subject of power that is no longer under orders, no longer sub-ordinated, but rather a subject that "sustains thought in the power of action" (88). This "living unity "(92) of thought and action is a power, that Badiou calls the "universal power of subjectivation," which gives power to truth and "force to salvation" (95). It is a work and a labor—it is love as labor and the labor of love: "Love," writes Badiou, "is the name of this labor" (96). And universalism, too, is a "production" (117). Is there hope of a break? Of a vacation from the discourse of work? There is hope, although perhaps not for us, as Kafka said, not for us as the working subjects of power, but hope, nonetheless. Indeed, it is with a surprising Levinasian echo that Badiou writes of this hope that it is "pure patience" (106). Patience reverses the syntax within which the subject of power found itself. No longer the subject *of,* the subject is preceded by a patience, submitted into existence prior to its coming to language.

Freud's Jesus

For how will it be possible for anyone to be a friend to a man who, he believes, may be his foe?
        —Cicero, *On Friendship*

One is tempted to admit that all Christianization is at war with its contrary.
        —Jacques Derrida, "Above All, No Journalists!"

Won't you be my neighbor?
        —Mr. Rogers

"Every individual," Freud writes in *The Future of an Illusion*, "is virtually an enemy of civilization."[61] But what is it that "disturbs our relations with our neighbor"? And how is it that civilization produces such discomfort, such internal discord and enmity, even between neighbors? How is it that civilization is "perpetually threatened with disintegration," under the looming threat of what appears as a "primary mutual hostility of human beings"?[62] With this distinct, but no less permanent possibility of war, under the threat of a virtual enemy—every individual—civilization is forced or made to open the hostilities. Civilization becomes an enemy, itself an adversary violently opposed to alterity—be it that of neighbors, enemies, or of sexuality. What is "the necessity" that causes this opposition, that "causes [civilization's] antagonism to sexuality"?[63]

Seeking to answer these questions, Freud proposes a return to the origins of "our" civilization, that is to say, to the beginnings of Christian civilization—the foundational "universal love between men." It is from this universal love that there follows as "an inevitable consequence" the "extreme intolerance on the part of Christendom towards those who remained outside it."[64] Seeking to account for civilization and its discontents, Freud proposes a return to Paul and to Jesus.

The answer to civilization's discord and discomfort lies in a "disturbing factor," the "ideal demand" that has begun to occupy us and that runs: "Thou shalt love thy neighbor as thyself." Freud is taken aback, but as always, he is not holding back. Freud thus articulates his own "surprise and bewilderment," as well as the difficulty ("it will be hard for me"), the deep ambivalence ("but if I am to love him [with this universal love] merely because he, too, is an inhabitant of this earth, like an insect, an earth-worm or a grass-snake"), outright resistance ("what is the point of a precept enunciated with so much solemnity if its fulfillment cannot be recommended as reasonable?"), and "further difficulties "that plague him when confronting this foundational imperative.[65] And there is more. Acknowledging what appears like a resistance, or at least an opposition and a struggle, Freud writes: "And there is a second commandment, which seems to me even more incomprehensible and arouses still stronger opposition in me. It is 'Love thine enemies.'"[66]

As in so many instances, Freud here opens the door to an enormous, if covert history. Indeed, the history of that second commandment, the paradigmatic way in which, even more than the love of neighbor, it articulates the incomprehensible, indeed, the impossible ("it is something that is impossible," Aquinas had written),[67] the impossibility of a relation of love to the enemy, is a history that remains to be written. And if it is true that the love of neighbor is a commandment that is "known throughout the world and is undoubtedly older than Christianity, which puts it forward as its proudest claim," the resounding echoes of the commandment to love one's enemies nonetheless appear more deafeningly Christian, constituting one of the most striking legacies of Jesus of Nazareth.[68] The difference between the two commandments—love of neighbor, love of enemies—is quantitatively marked: singular neighbor, plural enemies, and the question of number, as Jacques Derrida demonstrates, is of the essence. It also indicates an increased intensity, because the second commandment "arouses still stronger opposition." Yet the dissymmetry signals, or, perhaps, promises a qualitative difference, the difference, in fact, between neighbor and enemy. It is at this point that we, too, might be unable "to suppress a feeling of surprise and bewilderment" at Freud's gesture, a gesture that consists of closing the door he had himself opened. There will be no history, no account of this second commandment. It deserves no history of its own. Freud writes: "If I think it over, however, I see that I am wrong in treating it as a greater imposition. At bottom it is the same thing."[69]

Freud does not provide much by way of an explanation for this equal, even identical state of affairs, nor does he account for the surprising gesture by which he cuts the struggle short, putting up what does not quite appear as resistance. Freud simply and abruptly puts an end to hostility, to hostilities, understandingly sweeping them under the rug of a history of faith ("I then understand that the case is one like that of *Credo quia absurdum*").[70] One may consider that he obscured things further when, in a footnote on Heine (and in the subsequent citation of a dignified and admonishing voice), Freud illustrates the love of neighbor (or what is now the

same thing, the love of enemy) with and as a murderous wish. Giving expression to "psychological truths that are severely proscribed," Heine puts
it clearly: "one must, it is true, forgive one's enemies—but not before they
have been hanged."[71] Freud further ventriloquizes the voice of undiscrim-
inating recognition, stating that "your neighbor is not worthy of love." He
is, "on the contrary, your enemy."[72] The neighbor is the enemy. This, then,
would be Freud's Jesus.

"You have heard the commandment, 'You shall love your country-
man but hate your enemy.' My command to you is: love your enemies,
pray for your persecutors."[73] To the extent that it is a distinct commandment, this "second commandment" is second to what are already two commandments—famously known as the double love commandment: to love
God and to love the neighbor. Were we to follow Freud's guidance, who,
when approaching the first commandment ("love your neighbor") suggested we comport ourselves naively, as if we were hearing of it for the first
time, we could be inclined to grant the second commandment a certain,
even if provisional, singularity.[74] Yet, Freud tells us, the second commandment is the same as its predecessor. What, then, is the reading that Freud
advocates? More precisely, perhaps, the question is: What is there to read
in the second commandment that has brought Freud to his conclusion?

> "Love your enemies!" Mark you, not simply those who hap-
> pen not to be your friends, but your *enemies*, your positive
> and active enemies. Either this is a mere Oriental hyperbole, a
> bit of verbal extravagance . . . or else it is sincere and literal.
> —William James, *The Varieties of Religious Experience*

The commandment to love one's enemies remains forbidding and
impressive, the most mad of commandments, and "has never been considered a basic part of Christian theology and never been seen as belonging to
the kernel of the New Testament kerygma."[75] One of Jesus' peculiar and
difficult sayings, it "was the most frequently cited" in the second century.
And yet from that time on and up "to modern times, the idea has been either relegated to the personal realm or more frequently confined to a select
group of Christians in religious communities, either in monastic orders, or,
since the Reformation, to people generally dismissed as 'enthusiasts.'"[76]
This cannot fail to be somewhat surprising, given the striking place of
love—and of enemy love, in particular—in Jesus' teachings, its role in Au-

gustine's definition of "true religion" or in the first book of *On Christian Doctrine*, and the well-known representation and self-presentation of Christianity as the religion of love.[77]

The commandment to love one's enemies, moreover, installs a peculiar logic of momentous consequences. As Derrida explains, "where there can be an enemy, the 'there must be the enemy,' or the 'one must love one's enemies' (*seine Feinde lieben*) transforms without delay enmity into friendship, etc. The enemies I love are my friends. So are the enemies of my friends. As soon as there is need or desire for one's enemies, one can count only friends. Including the enemies, and *inversely*, here is the madness that threatens us."[78] Jesus' mad commandment, the madness of a commandment to love one's enemies indiscriminately, is already at work and "reverses, perverts and converts (good) sense, makes opposites slide into each other and 'knows' very well, in its own way, how the best of friends are the best of enemies . . . hence the worst."[79] Jesus' commandment thus places us on the brink of madness, or, as Derrida puts it later, it places us "on the brink of a work of infinite reading."[80]

To love the enemy—what could it mean? What is the obligation that Jesus' commandment imposes? To love the enemy as one loves one's neighbor would at least begin with a generalized ambivalence.[81] Indeed, in another striking account of enmity, Freud argues for this generalized "law of ambivalence of feeling," which makes one rejoice at the death of the beloved one who, "since in each of the loved persons there was also something of the stranger," had, therefore, "also been an enemy." We "rejoice," then, even at the death of loved ones, "for they were in part still *others*, and as others, they appear to confirm by their disappearance the persistence and survival of the self."[82] Thus, "these beloved dead had also been enemies and strangers who had aroused . . . some degree of hostile feeling."[83] To love the enemy would thus mean not to rejoice, not to deny a relationship to the other, not to remain in the "denial of death," which maintains itself by attributing death "to an other that is definitely separated from the self." As Samuel Weber explains, "the denial of death—through its attribution to an other that is definitely separated from the self—is, like all denial, first and foremost the denial of a relationship."[84] To love the enemy would thus mean not to distinguish, not to separate "things that once belonged together," not to *isolate* the self from the enemy. Instead of isolation, to love the enemy means that "what most belongs together and has been torn apart is the inseparability of self and other."[85] This lack of separation, what one might call an in-difference, the irrelevance of distinction, is at the core of the commandment to love one's enemies.

With this commandment, Jesus explicitly cites and recites the old law, offering a new law and raising—for centuries to come—the question of the rapport between the two. Does the new law include the old law or does it radically alter it, perhaps to the point of breaking and doing away with it? Here, at the very least, the new emends the old in four ways. First, it cites the old commandment ("Love your neighbor as thyself") and adds to it ("and hate your enemy"). Second, it shortens what now appears as a double commandment. Whereas the old mentions both neighbor and enemy, the new mentions only the enemy. Third, the new telescopes the old. "You shall love . . . your enemies." Finally, the new adds and multiplies: out of one neighbor, and one enemy, it makes a plural, "enemies." By way of this fourfold emendation, the new law asks for the abolition of a difference, the difference between neighbor and enemy.[86] The law substitutes the enemy for the neighbor (thus suggesting that their substitution is possible according to a rhetorical equivalence, rendered possible through the one commanded affect: love), but it also *generalizes* enmity by subsuming, as objects of the same love, neighbors and enemies. A complex rhetorical gesture of condensation and displacement, of analogy and substitution, maintains and transforms the neighbor as one object of love among many, following which, neighbor and enemy are to be loved equally.[87] Both enemy and neighbor become, as Paul has it, "one in Christ." The name that remains, the name of what (or who) remains to be loved has also (not) changed. It is "enemies" as the one (plural) object of love. The new law thus includes and alters, it resignifies and renames, it generalizes the old. With it, the neighbor has become (like) the enemy in that he will have to be loved along with the enemy, like the enemy, and *as* an enemy.[88] The neighbor has thus become an enemy, a member of the new and extended group now deserving of the same love. Like the (singular) enemy, the neighbor and the enemy have both been subsumed under a new heading: they are both enemies, that is, they are both to be loved.

But the new law does not put an end to what Freud calls "isolation," whereby an "experience is not forgotten, but instead, it is deprived of its affect, and its associative connections are suppressed and interrupted so that it remains as though isolated."[89] Rather, the new law sets up quite precisely an idea, an ideal demand and an ideal of perfection ("you must be made perfect as your heavenly Father is perfect") as the promise that isolation *should* come to an end—were love to be achieved. Failing love, and love of the enemies, in particular, the enemies remain. Having generalized the notion of the enemy as the name of an analogy and of an inclusion, having made the neighbor and the object of Christian love into an enemy, Jesus may have failed to abolish the distinction between self and other, may have failed to put an end to enmity. But Jesus did succeed in creating a new kind of enemy by establishing a new zone of indistinguishability: the enemy as neighbor and the neighbor as enemy. More precisely put, with the commandment to love the enemy, the neighbor, the fellow man, *becomes* the enemy. With Jesus, then, we witness the becoming-enemy of the neighbor.

The Enemy is a Thing

> This is no doubt what Freud was getting at when he spoke of the neighbor qua Thing.
> —Eric L. Santner, *The Psychotheology of Everyday Life*

War is the task that Augustine took upon himself to engage and, in a way, to conduct, "the task of defending the glorious City of God against those who prefer their own gods."[90] This confrontation is repeatedly inscribed throughout *The City of God*, a book written unequivocally "against the Pagans." "In embarking on this treatise of the City of God, I have thought it right to begin by replying to its enemies," *inimicis*, "who, in their pursuit of earthly joys and their appetite for fleeting satisfactions, blame the Christian religion" (4.1). And although enemies appear to be the occasion for writing, enemies arise without ground or reason, and from the beginning ("From this world's city there arise enemies," *inimici*, "against whom the City of God has to be defended," 1.1). These enemies are not necessarily one with the barbarians ("the enemies of Christianity," *adversariis nominis Christi*, "were spared by the barbarians at the sack of Rome, out of respect for Christ," 1.1). The enemies are, one could say, legion:[91] "the adversary and enemy of piety," and that "hostile power" who cannot "vanquish or subdue a man unless that man become associated with the enemy in sin" (10.22), and the "enemies of God," *inimici Dei* who "oppose God's sovereignty not by nature, but by their perversion. They are his enemies because of their will to resist him, not because of their power to hurt

him" (12.3). They testify to the "permanent possibility of war," to the ubiq-
uitous operations of enmity. It is enmity that tore Rome apart at its beginnings, testifying to "the division of the earthly city against itself," while at
that other beginning, "the conflict between Cain and Abel displayed the
hostility between the two cities themselves, the City of God and the city of
men" (15.6). "Enmities," *inimicitiae*, "and war," then, fill "the story of
mankind" (19.5). "Have they not everywhere filled up the story of human
experience? Are they not of frequent occurrence, even in the honorable love
of friends?" Beyond the location of the theological, political, and social enemy—or rather, prior to it, as the very condition of identifying these
spheres—it is in the proximate (the human, the friend) that Augustine locates enmity. He thus goes on to point to the *oikos* as a site of enmity,
praising "that inspired utterance, 'A man's enemies are those of his own
household' [Matt. 10, 36]" (19.5).

Much like the household and the City of God, the bonds of friendship—and particularly the bonds of friendship between good men—are
always fragile and endangered, first of all by ignorance, itself a major source
of enmity ("the friendship of good men can never be carefree"). Ignorance,
ignorantia, is what "leads men to believe an enemy to be a friend, or a
friend an enemy" (19.8). Friendship is thus mixed with fear, which often
turns into murderous desires. Hence, we fear that our friends' affection "be
changed into treachery, malice and baseness," but "certainly we would
rather hear that our friends were dead" (ibid.). Still, Augustine is more preoccupied with the public or the foreign enemy: "there has been, and still is,
no lack of enemies," *hostes*, "among foreign nations" (19.7). It is in this context that Augustine begins to articulate his notion of a "just war."

There is no sustained discussion of the love of enemies in *The City of
God*, no discussion of enemies in the context of Christian love (10.3, 14.7,
19.14), nor a discussion of love in the context of enmity and war. Augustine
does mention the love of enemies in order to differentiate between demons
("who hate some men and love others") and "us" (we who "have the in-
struction of the true religion that we should love even our enemies," 8.17),
but he never deploys such discriminating gestures regarding enemies in the
rest of a book that offers itself as a polemical treatise "against the Pagans."
Insofar as the book also constitutes a political treatise, we will see that there
is nothing exceptional about it. As one among many medieval Christian
polemical treatises, there is nothing exceptional, either, in regard to the issue that occupies us here, the enemy. And yet, given the importance of

love, of Christian love, in Augustine, given the status of *The City of God* as a founding text of Western political theory, as well as a founding text of the theory of "just war,"[92] and finally, given the prominent place Augustine himself makes for various enemies in the book, it is imperative to consider the significance of the absence of the enemy (*inimicus*) from his reflections on love and war. By turning to Augustine's more extended treatment of the commandment to love one's enemies, I hope to be able to offer the rudiments of an explanation for this state of affairs.

"In the principle of loving God and neighbor," Augustine writes in his unfinished commentary on Paul's Letter to the Romans, the will of God is "concisely introduced to all believers, since from these two precepts hang the whole law and all the prophets [cf. Matt. 22:37–40]—that is, the love of our neighbor which the Lord himself commends to us even to the point of loving our enemies," *ad inimici dilectionem.*[93] Augustine makes clear how important the love commandment is by dedicating most of the first book of *On Christian Doctrine* to a discussion of it.[94] From the beginning, Augustine's purpose is to establish distinctions that will enable a better understanding of Scripture and of love. Augustine proceeds by dividing wholes into two parts: "There are two things on which all interpretation of Scripture depends, the process of discovering what we need to learn, and the process of presenting what we have learnt" (1.1). "All teaching is teaching of either things or signs" (1.2). By the first major distinction, we are ready for love: "There are some things which are to be enjoyed, some which are to be used, and some whose function is both to enjoy and use" (1.3). Both enjoyment and use are variations on love: "To enjoy something is to hold fast to it in love for its own sake. To use something is to apply whatever it may be to the purpose of obtaining what you love" (1.4). And yet not everything should be enjoyed, that is to say, not everything should be loved for its own sake: "the things which are to be enjoyed, then, are the Father and the Son and the Holy Spirit, and the Trinity that consists of them" (1.5). Augustine goes on to explain further what the love of God means, summarizing it by stating that "it is only the eternal and unchangeable things which I mentioned that are to be enjoyed" (1.22).

At this point it is clear that the love of neighbor will have to be understood in the light of the division between enjoyment and use. Augustine is unequivocal about what the proper way is. "We have been commanded to love one another but the question is whether one person should be loved by another on his own account or for some other reason. If on his own account, we enjoy him; if for some other reason, we use him. In my opinion, he should be loved for another reason" (1.22). The love of neighbor, then, a love that includes the love of self, should be strictly used for the purpose of a later enjoyment of things eternal. One "should not love himself on his own account," nor should another person "be angry if you love him on account of God" (ibid.).

By the time he comes to discuss the enemy, it will be clear that it, too, will have to be submitted to the same requirement. Like "any other object of love that enters the mind," it, too, "should be swept towards the same destination as that to which the flood of our love is directed" (ibid.). Insofar as the love of neighbor includes the love of self as much as the love of enemy, what has become crucial in Augustine's account is that the distinctions he began with *should not apply*. As Jill Robbins puts it, "by insisting on a third term—*God, truth, the universal*—that regulates the relationship to the other in Christian friendship, such a model threatens to neutralize that which in the other is radically singular and resistant to all categories."[95] There is then no distinction (only, and at best, the vanishing of distinctions) to be made between self, neighbor, and (as we will see) enemy, because they are subsumed under one and the same goal —the love of God. Hence their common status as objects of use, and not of enjoyment: "So a person who loves his neighbor properly should, in concert with him, aim to love God with all his heart, all his soul, and all his mind. In this way, loving him as he would himself, he relates his love of himself and his neighbor entirely to the love of God, which allows not the slightest trickle to flow away from it and thereby diminish it" (1.22).

It is clear, then, why Augustine then proceeds to state that "all people should be loved equally" (1.28). Augustine remains true to the spirit of Jesus and of Paul in that he affirms distinctions—differences—while asserting at the same time that they are of no consequence. This explains why "the person who lives a just and holy life" is nonetheless one who understands differences, one who "does not love what it is wrong to love, or fail to love what should be loved, or love too much what should be loved less" (1.27). It also explains why "no sinner, *qua* sinner, should be loved" whereas "every human being, *qua* human being, should be loved on God's account" (ibid.).

There are, then, important distinctions to be made, differences to uphold, and yet love conquers all. Everybody should be loved, all the same, and there are no exceptions to the love of neighbor ("the commandment to love our neighbor excludes no human being," 1.30). More precisely, perhaps, the exception has become the rule, and a decision should be made to ignore the rule of distinctions such as have been established from the very beginning of Augustine's text. One must ignore the rule of distinctions, one must relate to love as what makes no difference, and one must love the neighbor—that is to say, only the *human* neighbor, of course—as oneself. One must love the neighbor as a person who may always be in need (something like the permanent possibility of need) and whose need is our permanent duty. One must also love the neighbor as the impossible, the impossible to love, as he who is not to be loved (if he is a sinner), because it is wrong to love him, or because he should be loved more, or, more often, less.

So it is clear that we should understand by our neighbor the person to whom an act of compassion is due if he needs it or would be due if he needed it. It follows from this that a person from whom an act of compassion is due to us in our turn is also our neighbor. For the word "neighbor" implies a relationship: one can only be a neighbor to a neighbor. Who can fail to see that there is no exception to this, nobody to whom compassion is not due? The commandment extends even to our enemies, *ad inimicos . . .* it is clear that all people must be reckoned as neighbors, because evil must not be done to anyone. (1.30)

Because distinctions between self, neighbor, and enemy are, for the love of God, abolished, Augustine can develop his complex doctrine of the just war without contradicting himself, without even mentioning, or needing to mention, the love of enemies. From the perspective of his Christian doctrine, that is to say, from the perspective of love, the enemy and the commandment to love the enemy exceed any particular sphere of the city (political—and therefore, military—social, or domestic) and encompass all of them. Like "any other object of love that enters the mind," the enemy is not particularly bound to the sphere of war, nor is he bound to the private sphere. Rather, the enemy relates, refers, and is defined in relation to God and the love of God.[96] As such (which is to say, precisely not "as such"), the enemy cannot be the occasion for a *particular* kind of love, but only a step or a moment toward the enjoyment of divine love. He, too, "should be swept towards the same destination as that to which the whole flood of our love is directed" (1.22).

Unlike God, then, but much like the neighbor and the self, the enemy is not to be enjoyed, that is, not to be loved for his own sake, on his own account. Rather, like the neighbor and the self, the enemy is what through which God is loved, a means toward a divine end.[97] Only one among other paths to enjoyment of things eternal and divine, the enemy must, much like the neighbor and the self, always be loved, but never as such, never as enemy. Thus, it is not that the love of the enemy dissociates between public and private, nor does it dissociate between a spiritual love and a physical behavior, constituting an abstract object stripped of concrete and material attributes, an essence void of accidents (although such distinctions are perhaps likely to be invoked subsequently). Rather, for Augustine, the crucial point is that the enemy is not to be loved any differently from anyone else. Just like anyone else, the enemy is to be used, rather than enjoyed. The enemy is therefore just like us.[98] He is just as we are—"we ourselves who enjoy and use other things are things" (1.22). The enemy is a thing.

Enemies: A Love Story

I have become the enemy of the multitude.
—John of Salisbury, *Policraticus*

But our enemy is our neighbor.
—Thomas Aquinas

Attending to what, in medieval Christian writings, had otherwise remained two distinct and separate discursive spheres, the love of enemies on the one hand, and the question of war on the other, Thomas Aquinas makes the link between them. Considering that just-war theory was developed in almost complete isolation from the commandment to love one's enemies,[99] how did this link become possible? In order to answer this question, we need to consider the shift that occurred between Augustine and Aquinas (here, no more and perhaps no less than celebrated markers of historical and exegetical shifts) in the understanding of the enemy—the commandment to love the enemy and the conception of the enemy at war.

In his commentary on the commandment to love one's enemies, Aquinas multiplies distinctions—he multiplies enemies—and ways of understanding the obligation.[100] Among the objections raised in this particular *quaestio*, one considers that "loving one's enemies," *inimicos*, "seems as perverse as hating one's friends." In the *responsio*, Aquinas engages Matthew 5:44, and attempts to soften the perversity of the commandment by proposing yet other ways of understanding it, different conceptions of the object and of the love it commands. First, the commandment "can mean loving our enemies precisely as enemies." Second, "it can be taken as loving them as human beings." Third, "we can take it as applied to particular cases; in the sense of a special act of love toward an enemy."

In the first of these interpretations, loving the enemy as enemy, *inquantum sunt inimici*, he is already introducing an inner distinction (plausibly a distinction between essence and accident) that will be buttressed later on. Although Aquinas never directly defines the attributes of enmity, in this distinction, the being of the enemy is or not coextensive with his being a human being, with his nature. "Enemyness" can be contingent, the enemy may also be other than enemy, and therefore loving the enemy as enemy, insofar as he is enemy, is, again, perverse. Moreover, Aquinas explains, such love would have nothing to do with *caritas*, but would fall short of and even be opposed to *caritas* "because it means loving evil in another." Such would be the quality of the enemy, then: It is what is evil in the other. Being the enemy is therefore not natural, nor does it signal an essential difference between the one who loves and the enemy. Rather, it appears to be an appended part, an evil part added to one's nature.

The second interpretation performs the abstraction of enmity from the enemy, taking him *quantum ad naturam*. Here, the enemy is considered under the general heading of "neighbor," *proximus*, and the love directed toward him is a "general kind of love," indeed, *caritas*, for "this is what charity of necessity demands." True *caritas* thus considers the enemy simply as one among other objects of love that include "God and his neighbor."[101] Finally, the third interpretation points to another love beyond *caritas*, since it speaks of a love that "absolutely speaking, charity does not of necessity demand." Here, Aquinas reverts to the enemy as such, but one toward whom is demanded only a specific and limited act of love, "a special act of love towards an enemy," something that may mean loving behavior toward a particular enemy, or a particular kind of attitude, in particular circumstances, toward any potential enemy. Such an act exceeds the requirements of *caritas*. It is not required simply because "it is impossible." What is, however, required, is that one prepares one's soul, *anima*, "in the sense that we should be prepared to love even a particular enemy if real necessity arises."

A few pages earlier, Aquinas had explained that "man leads a double life" (23, art. 1). "One [life] is outward according to the world and body and senses . . . the other is inward, according to the life of mind and spirit; it is here that we have intercourse with God and the angels, though imperfectly in our present state." Hence, when it is made clear that the love of enemy "belongs rather to the perfection of charity" (25, art. 8) one may easily deduce that there is no expectation, no obligation to show external signs of love.(This position is in fact defended in the *Quaestio* of art. 9: "It is not therefore necessary to show outward marks and proofs of love toward enemies.") The distinction between body and soul is here fully operative, and it corresponds to different "conversations" with the earthly and with the divine. It also corresponds to different conceptions of the enemy. In short, the enemy as enemy is not to be loved, and "love thy enemies" does not mean what it says. In fact, in this case, what the commandment says (with a little help from Augustine, upon whom a perhaps less than friendly exegetical pressure is applied here) is that we *ought* to hate them: "enemies are contrary to us precisely as enemies," *inquantum sunt inimici*, "and it is this that we ought to hate in them" (and immediately after: "to love an enemy as such," *quod diligere inimicos inquantum sunt inimici*, "this is blameworthy," 25, art. 8). The enemy as human being, however, should be loved: "as men capable of eternal happiness, we should love them." (This, of course, leaves open the question of what to do with human beings who are not capable of eternal happiness, human beings who are not part of salvation history.) And that love includes acts of kindness, though this, too, "is a matter of perfection." Nonetheless, the Christian should try "by kindness to induce his enemy to love him" (art. 9).

What is perhaps most striking about Aquinas's recasting of the commandment to love the enemy and about the distinctions he makes is that it all says very little about the enemy. It is as if theological reflection had nothing to do with the enemy, nothing to do with thinking the enemy. Aside from uncertain hints regarding enmity as a contingent part of one's nature, the distinctions Aquinas proposes are not located in the enemy "himself," but in the love that is directed (if not necessarily expressed) toward the enemy. We are told of the distinction between internal and externally manifested love: "Now the commandment absolutely insists that we have this interior love for our enemies in general, though it does not absolutely demand that we love them as individuals, but only that we be ready to do so, as explained earlier. It is the same with love's outward expressions or signs" (art. 9). We are told of the distinction between general and particular love: it remains possible to love one's enemies with a "general kind of love," whereas "it is impossible" to love any one of them specifically. We are told of the distinction between general love and particular acts of kindness (Aquinas writes of "a special act of love"), between ability or readiness and actuality (loving the enemy may be impossible, but we should be *ready* to do so, which is a matter of "attitude of mind": "we should be prepared to love even a particular enemy if real necessity arise"). Finally, we are told of the distinction between perfection and imperfection: "apart from the case of necessity, to do this actually and to love one's enemy for God's sake, belongs rather to the perfection of charity." Perfection, however, is located outside of the case of necessity. Perfect charity does not love the enemy as enemy, or as human being, or as a particular individual—instead, it loves the enemy as all of the above.

Love—*caritas*—has therefore little to say about the enemy, paradoxically showing little concern for the enemy as enemy. As perfection, as perfect love, love abolishes (or perhaps fulfills) the divisions that affect the possibility and impossibility of sense, the sense of the commandment to love one's enemies. In its imperfection, however, love's internal divisions, from internal to external, from particular to general, from imperfect to perfect, conduct "conversations" that either do not necessitate or simply disable a reflection on the nature, that is, the place, of the enemy. In other words, to think theologically (to love perfectly) is to erase the very distinctions that love makes. To think imperfectly (to love imperfectly) is to maintain these distinctions. In either case, what is disabled is thinking (as loving) of the enemy as enemy. Insofar as love is always love of God (Peter Lombard, Aquinas reports, went so far as to assert that love "is not something created in the soul but the Holy Spirit himself dwelling there," 23, art. 2), insofar as "the motion of charity springs from the Holy Spirit," it will leave little room for the enemy.

On the other hand, because he is otherwise impossible to love (and, as enemy, even forbidden to love), the enemy whom we love is thus of necessity abstracted, theorized, imagined. Imperfect *caritas* has no interest in the enemy, but only insists on differences of its own, understandably discriminating between distinct love objects, between human beings and enemies, for example, and even between enemies. Thus, one may put "love of neighbor before love of God," as Saint Paul did (27, art. 8). Thus, also, love, the earthly fire of love, "affects nearby objects more than distant ones, so charity, too, loves those nearest most fervently. From this angle, love of friends, taken just in itself, is warmer and better than love of enemies" (27, art. 7).

Thus the enemy draws away. This is not to say that a particular enemy cannot be loved—a matter of the soul, if not of the body—but rather that love, perfect or imperfect, cannot approach, does not have to approach or perhaps even imagine the enemy. Love, in other words, cannot think the enemy. In the "double life" that he leads, "man" can think the enemy as enemy only in its concrete figures, "from the point of view of the persons who are loved" or hated, that is to say, man can think the enemy only as enemies, *inquantum sunt inimici.*

Schematizing the changes to which we have been trying to attend, one could say that whereas Augustine abolished the differences between God, neighbor, and enemy from the perspective of love (thereby generalizing love—as love of God—to include all spheres of life, whether hostile or not, and thus dispensing with the need to discuss the enemy and the love of the enemy as a concrete or particular issue), Aquinas divorced love, that is to say, perfect love, from the realm of concrete possibility. For him, *caritas* as a set of obligations demands that one make distinctions and consider different perspectives. Aquinas recasts distinctions that are inscribed in Augustine, but inscribed there as no longer operative, and reactivates them. (As we saw, Augustine was closer to Paul, recognizing differences to make away with their relevance.) Thus, the distinctions between neighbor and enemy, between self and enemy, which Augustine had discussed in order to dismiss their relevance under the general heading of love of God, are now reaffirmed, and enemies qua enemies ought to be hated ("enemies are contrary to us precisely as enemies, and it is this that we ought to hate in them, for we should grieve to see them so," 25, art. 8). Thus, the distinction between "interior love" and "outward marks and demonstrations" (25, art. 9) is renewed as well, and the commensurability between inside and outside is reaffirmed. The commandment to love one's enemies is all but dismissed, recast as a call to uphold hierarchical distinctions ("but there are other [outward signs] which we reserve for certain people, and which it is not necessary for salvation that we display towards our enemies," ibid.). Aquinas thus turns Augustine on his head and restores differences that had been all but dismissed, abstracted. Differences are made concrete—one would almost say that they are made carnal. It is these renewed distinctions between body and spirit, between neighbor and enemy, between divine love and human (or inhuman) love that are constitutive of a new discourse on the enemy. Although he never quite belonged to any particular sphere, the enemy can now be subjected to his "own" distinctions. With Paul and Jesus, the enemy could be personal, political, theological, but he was to be equally loved. Augustine theologized the enemy, made it into an abstract "thing." With Aquinas, the enemy becomes legion again. Disseminated anew into these different (if not entirely distinct) discursive spheres, enter the enemies.

It is in his famous discussion of war that Aquinas invokes the term that, recalling Jesus' commandment, has otherwise tended to vanish from discussions of war, and of just war in particular: *inimicus*.[102] A few pages before, Aquinas himself, as if careful not to collapse the distinctions between different terms of enmity, had invoked words that are commonly associated with war, conflict, and the military (*hostis, pugnator*, etc.). Hence, when he summarizes his position as to whether wars are, in fact, licit according to Christian law, Aquinas writes: "we have just agreed that wars are licit and just, insofar as they protect the poor and the whole commonweal from an enemy," *ab hostium injuriis* (40, art. 2). But is it licit, Aquinas then asks, to use subterfuge in war? Is it possible, in other words, to lie to the enemy? After all, "the enemy is our neighbor."[103]

The objection as to the proximity of the enemy, his being our neighbor, is fundamentally in line with the abolition of differences, their irrelevance, as we have observed them in Jesus, in Paul, and to some extent, in Augustine. Here, however, it is an argument that Aquinas uses as a foil. Much as in what we saw earlier, the focus is not quite on the object of the deception, its addressee (here, the enemy), but on the issue of deception. The enemy is still not Aquinas's object. Rather, Aquinas confronts and opposes the claim that there is any deception involved ("Properly speaking this is not deception") distinguishing between kinds of deception by collapsing the semantic distinctions between different kinds of enemies, between *inimicos* and *hostes*. Hence, in the case of uttering a falsehood or giving a false promise, "no one should fool an enemy," *hostes*, "like that." Quoting Ambrose, Aquinas states that "rights of war and agreements even with the enemy," *hostes*, "do exist and should be kept." Concealing from the enemy, however, is another matter: it is not a deception, and it is therefore permitted. Much as we should prevent the infidel from learning the sacred teachings "lest they ridicule them," we should all the more "hide from the enemy," *inimicos*, "our plans against him." And yet by referring to the enemy as neighbor, Aquinas reinforces the unsettling association of the military enemy, *hostes*, with the term *inimicus*, raising the possibility, indeed, the obligation, to love him. Aquinas thus weakens the boundary between two spheres that, until now, seemed to belong or at least to be confined to distinct spheres, war and the military (*hostis*) on the one hand, and the ethico-theological *caritas* (*amicus/inimicus*) on the other.

We go to war, then, with the enemies, *hostis* or *inimicus*, each divided between a theological failure to think these peculiar love objects and the political and strategic obligation to fight (and even hate) them. With Aquinas, the question of the enemy becomes thoroughly sedimented as a theologico-political question, as the question of the theologico-political.

But Where Are the Enemies?

> If Muhammad, for instance, who at the outset was all alone, entirely uneducated, utterly impoverished, hated by his own kinsmen and foreigners alike, so far removed from our borders, and so obvious in his falsehood, could introduce so much corruption into the world on behalf of the devil—what do you think the devil can accomplish through the Jews, who are so numerous, almost all educated and most adept at trickery, so well endowed with the good life and the usuries allowed them by Christians, so loved by our princes on account of the services they provide and the flatteries they spew forth, so scattered and dispersed throughout the world, so secretive in their deceptions that they display a remarkable appearance of being truthful?!
> —Friar Raymond Martin

Stating the obvious, one could say that, in the Middle Ages, between the eleventh and thirteenth centuries, "the enemy" was fully constitutive of political and theological discourse.[104] The dynamics of medieval confrontations imply "the conscious rejection of values and claims of the other," as Amos Funkenstein explains, something that "remained a constitutive element in the ongoing construction of the respective identity" of all parties involved.[105] It is not just that here, too, the political community continued to be oriented toward war at a fundamental level, that a significant number of the dominant values were martial values, and that the link between social and military organization remained tight.[106] Nor is it merely the case that the enemy increasingly appeared as a privileged target of what R. I. Moore has called "the persecuting society," a society in which "persecution became habitual. That is to say not simply that individuals were subject to violence, but that deliberate and socially sanctioned violence began to be directed, *through established governmental, judicial and social institutions*, against groups of people defined by general characteristics such as race, religion or way of life."[107] Nor is it simply that "the origins, the character, and the role of the hermeneutical Jew derive from a theological agenda encompassing much more than the Jews themselves."[108] Nor, finally, is the question of the enemy reducible to the fundamental change undergone by the *pax ecclesiae*, what Tomaz Mastnak has demonstrated as "the succession of the *pax Dei* by the *treuga Dei*," the truce of God.[109]

All this is true enough and has been increasingly studied and scrutinized, though, significantly, in highly isolated ways. There is, moreover, no doubt that with and beyond the development of a new warring discourse and beyond "changes in the concept of war,"[110] the question of the enemy did, in turn, receive novel determinations. Between the eleventh century and thirteenth, "fresh ground was broken." The change was momentous, including both "the creation of a common enemy: the construction of the Muslims as the normative enemies of Christianity and Christendom"[111] *and* parallel developments in Christian anti-Jewish polemics, which "changed radically in the twelfth century, reflecting historical events and changes in the methods and contents of theology,"[112] as well as the transformation (what some have called the demonization) of the Jews from witness to heresy.[113] Jeremy Cohen succinctly describes these new developments in the following terms:

Even before the First Crusade and the anti-Jewish violence that accompanied it, portents of change loomed on the horizon. Apocalyptic generated by the turn of the millennium, the rhetoric of papal reform, and the Investiture Controversy generated a polarized view of society, allowing the proponents of reform more readily to identify the allies and foes of the ideal Christian *respublica*. As the only religious minority officially present in Christendom,[114] the Jews provided the most accessible examples of who or what such enemies might be like; from the first decade of the eleventh century, popular violence struck at Europe's Jews in conjunction with other dissidents.[115]

But the question raised by these events—the question of the enemy—is a discursive question that exceeds each of the particular spheres to which it has largely been confined (the Jew, the Arab, theology, medieval polemics, the history of war, and the Middle Ages in general, as well, for that matter). Where is the enemy spoken of, and, more importantly, not spoken of? What is the discursive specificity of the discourse of enmity, and what are its modes and, most importantly, its relations? What are the links—exegetical, theological, political, and more—that are affirmed between discursive spheres (which may or may not have a relative autonomy), what are those denied, and what are those that have become invisible?

Although we have begun here with a discussion of war—and war already takes place in a number of spheres from the civil and the political to the philosophical and theological—the enemy exceeds its determinations as a martial enemy. Minimally, as we have seen, the commandment to love one's enemies raised difficult questions that were not, that could not be avoided by theologians and that structured many a response to the phenomenal, empirical enemy, indeed, that constituted such an enemy in the first place. And yet the discursive boundaries that have been established (and at times also weakened, as we saw) around the question of the enemy appear to have been all too successful and all too hermetic. To put it simply, discussions of war, if they even address the question of the enemy, make no reference to the commandment to love one's enemies,[116] discussions of the commandment to love the enemies make no reference to specific enemy figures against whom Christendom considered itself at war, and although discussions of the enemy tend to amalgamate distinct groups into one, there are crucial distinctions made between different enemies.

There is more at stake here than apparent contradictions (as if love and war were simply opposites). What is at stake is the integrity of the concept "enemy," which is to say, in this case, its lack of integrity. The enemy is not one, as we saw (hence, love your *enemies*). The enemy must be legion, and it is this becoming-plural of the enemy that gives it a productive and dynamic dimension. The enemy which is not one must henceforth and in fact does come to belong to different spheres, which will increasingly have to be kept separate, that is to say, they will have to be actively separated—the difference between them affirmed or performed precisely because of an otherwise unacknowledged proximity. This is no empirical "error," therefore, but the sedimentation of conditions that have brought about what appears to be an unbreachable (if ever-weakened) separation. The *constat* I want to make here is double. If, as Aquinas's text would seem to show, there is no lexical integrity to the different terms used to refer to enemies, how are we to understand the success of the distinction between theological issues ("love thy enemies") and political ones (war—just or not, holy or not—against politically and legally defined enemies)? At stake is the crucial distinction between the theological and the political, between *jus divinus* and civil or natural law, *jus naturale*, which articulates itself within the concept of the enemy.[117] Perceptions of the enemy, distinctions between enemies, cannot therefore be treated as an epiphenomenon of the distinction between theological and political, but are instead constitutive of it. The textual divisions that separate doctrine from polemics and theological from political treatises, the historical division that distinguishes between exegesis and practice, and last but not least, the dominant and structuring division that distances the Jew from the Arab are rendered porous by "the enemy," a term—if it is one—that, undecidably conceptual and practical, theological and political, traverses discourses and practices, encompassing within an enormously differential, that is, relational field, Jews and Arabs and others.

What good is it to pursue and persecute the enemies of the Christian faith in far and distant lands if the Jews, vile blasphemers and far worse than the Saracens, not far away from us but right in our midst, blaspheme, abuse, and trample on Christ and the Christian sacraments so freely and insolently and with impunity? How can zeal for God nourish God's children if the Jews, enemies of the supreme Christ and of the Christians, remain totally unpunished?[118]

Over the course of the Middle Ages, answers multiplied as to the question "who is the enemy?" And the sheer number of terms, the apparent consistency with which the commandment to "love your enemies" was confined to discussions of *caritas*, as in Aquinas, as opposed to the elaborate debate on the "just war," would seem to indicate that different spheres of enmity did not merge or necessarily even inform each other. That this state of affairs, this state of war, was rendered possible—that is to say, impossible—by the commandment to love one's enemies should be clear by now. And yet there is more at work than an empirical consequence, more than a historical effect, in, say, Pope Alexander II's statement, in his *Dispar nimirum est* of 1063, that although they are both "enemies of the church," *inimica ecclesia*, "surely, the case of the Jews and that of the Saracens are different."[119] It is the lines along which this difference runs that have remained largely unexplored.[120] This is the case for essential reasons that we must continue to interrogate.

Inter-diction 2: Jews and Arabs

Jews and Arabs—the latter serving here as the archival depository of multifarious terms such as "Saracens," "Mohammedans," "Muslims," "Agarenes,"[121] "Ishmaelites," "pagans," and later even "Turks"—were repeatedly associated, lumped, and even collapsed together. This occurred in part because, as Richard Southern writes, in order to understand the novelty that Islam was, the West needed help. But it "could get no help from antiquity, and no comfort from the present. For an age avowedly dependent on the past for its materials, this was a serious matter. Intellectually the nearest parallel to the position of Islam was the position of the Jews. They shared many of the same tenets and brought forward many of the same objections to Christianity."[122]

The Christian imagination proved more than willing to provide the help needed. Examples of repeated associations thus abound, perhaps enabled by Paul's momentous, if figurative association of Hagar with the Jews and with Arabia ("Now this is an allegory: these women are two covenants. One woman, in fact, is Hagar, from Mount Sinai, bearing children for slavery. Now Hagar is Mount Sinai in Arabia and corresponds to the present Jerusalem for she is in slavery with her children." Gal. 4:24–25).[123] Agobard (ca. 779–840), for example, would confirm that Muslims, too, are descendants of Abraham.[124] From the eighth century on, Christian writers would begin to refer to Muslims as being "new Jews" or "consistently characterize Islamic belief and practice as Jewish, or at least as Jewishly influenced."[125] Numerous rumors and stories constitute as fact that the Jews had repeatedly assisted the Muslim conquerors into Spain, their "having betrayed Visigothic Spain to the Arabs in the eighth century."[126] Early in the ninth century, the *Gesta Dagoberti* reconstructs an early prophetic claim concerning the threat by the hand of "circumcised peoples"—"but this was not said about the Jews."[127] In a variant to Ademar of Chabannes's chronicle, both "pagans" and Jews are said to have desecrated the Holy Sepulcher.[128] *La chanson de Roland* has Charlemagne destroy "synagogues and mosques" *les sinagoges e les mahumeries*,[129] to avenge Roland's death at the hands of the Muslim enemy. Artists joined in and had Jews and Muslims associated in yet another way, depicting "Christ being tormented in scenes of the Passion in public altarpieces and sculptures" that "commonly included hideously deformed and dark-skinned Saracens alongside the usual Jews," thus recasting Muslims as Christ killers.[130] English passion plays also have Jewish characters swearing by "almighty Machomet."[131] After the Third Lateran Council (1179), "linkage of Jews and Muslims became a common feature in the ecclesiastical legislation,"[132] while the fourth council (1215) "decreed that both Jews and Saracens under Christian rule wear distinguishing marks on their clothing."[133]

Christendom had thus developed an array of narratives, categories, and classifications that made it easier to collapse the distinction between the Jew and the Arab, and it continued doing so for a very, very long time.[134] As Jeremy Cohen describes this situation, albeit somewhat anachronistically, "inasmuch as Muslims and Jews shared ethnic, linguistic, and presumably religious characteristics, one could logically conclude that they harbored similar hostility toward Christendom."[135] Yet one of the dominant ways in which this association was reinscribed and made operative was precisely by insisting on the difference, even the opposition, between Arab and Jew, by locating each of them in distinct discursive spheres.[136] The specific, if not always stable terms in which the complex web of associations and dissociations that organized this opposition was cast became constitutive of the theologico-political.

It was thought of *as* theologico-political and as separating the theological from the political. "Christian theological discourse came to discern a qualitative parity between the Jews and other outsiders,"[137] yet invested an enormous energy in disrupting or erasing such parity, buttressing the fragile borders that separated theology from politics. Hence, when Bernard of Clairvaux (1090–1153) condoned fighting "the Ishmaelites" who, with the Jews, constituted "our enemies," he insisted precisely on this crucial distinction: "It is good that you go against the Ishmaelites. But whosoever touches a Jew to take his life, is like one who harms Jesus himself . . . for in the book of Psalms it is written of them 'Slay them not, lest my people forget.'"[138] Enemies both, the Jew and the Arab receive distinct determinations, one military and political, the other theological. This is not to say that other, indeed, even the very same determinations were to disappear entirely from view—and we have seen that in regard to enemies, the distinction between them always was a weak distinction structurally, one that tended toward its own vanishing. "Saracens" were undoubtedly thought of by way of theological categories, and no discourse on the enemy could free itself from such categories. Yet within this theological frame, the association between Jew and Arab was traversed by a growing distance— topographies of inside and outside—the growing traits of an opposition arbitered, as it were, and indeed staged and produced by a Christian judge.

"Renowned lover, correspondent, dialectician, teacher, and monk, Peter Abelard (1079–1142) captures the singular spirit of the twelfth century more than do most of his European contemporaries."[139] A towering figure of Western love, along with his famous and beloved mistress Heloise, Abelard has yet to gain renown for what he had to say about enemies.[140] Yet in his famous *Collationes* (Comparisons), otherwise known as "Dialogue between a philosopher, a Jew, and a Christian," Abelard stages the scene of encounter between the Christian, the Jew, and the Arab, a staging that does provide a significant account of the enemy.[141] One must, of course, immediately consider that the text does not quite say that there is an Arab involved, and the scholarly debate on this issue remains in fact open.[142] By suggesting that the *Collationes* stages the enemy (the Jew, the Arab), I do not therefore mean to resolve the controversy, but rather to consider that the indications to that effect—to the effect, that is, that the philosopher would be an Arab—and the way in which the dialogue proceeds testify to the structural distinctions that emerge within the enemy as we have begun to explore them.

Much like Othello's, the philosopher's religious identification is, if not erased, then vanishing. The narrator and speaker, presumably Abelard himself, opens the dialogue and promises to judge the validity of the distinct claims of the participants in the debate. At the very beginning, he inquires after their faith ("I asked them immediately what their religion," *professionis*, "was," 3), a question with which they are happy to comply ("We are men, they said, who belong to different faiths and ways of life"). In his response, the philosopher calls himself a "pagan," *gentiles*—a name that would remain associated, throughout the Middle Ages, with the Muslims.[143] Indeed, in one of his tirades against the philosopher, the Jew elaborates on what the two of them have in common:

For just as it is clear that Ishmael was circumcised by Abraham according to the Lord's command, so Esau was circumcised by Isaac and the wicked sons by the patriarchs in the same way as the chosen sons, so that from this their descendants would also follow the example of circumcision if they remained God's followers, just as you yourselves still do even today—you who undergo circumcision at the age of twelve, following the example of your father Ishmael. (49)

The controversy that still surrounds the identification of the philosopher with Arabs may appear surprising at this point, but I would argue that it is not arbitrary, not simply the result of strange, if persistent, biases. Quite the opposite, it is the result of a consistent logic that we can now understand, a logic whereby the text refrains from securing a religious (or in that case even an "ethnic") affiliation for this character. From the very beginning, the philosopher is thus insistently identified by the might of his weapons—be they discursive or metaphorical—rather than by his religious affiliation or his grounding in sacred texts ("We all, indeed, equally profess ourselves to be worshippers of the one God, but we serve him by different faiths and ways of life: one of us—who is a pagan, one of what they call the 'philosophers'—is content with natural law, whereas the other two—one is called a 'Jew', the other a 'Christian'—have sacred texts," 3).[144] Summarizing the dissymmetry of the encounter between the philosopher, on the one hand, and the Christian and the Jew, on the other, the speaker all but erases any religious affiliation on the part of the philosopher, declaring him to be lawless, that is to say, without religion.

But you, Philosopher, who profess no law and yield only to reasoning, should not consider it anything great if you appear to be the strongest in this contest, since you have two swords for the fight, but the others battle against you with only one. You are able to use both written authority and reasoning against them, but they cannot base any objects to your position on a written law, since you follow no law; and also the fact that you, being more accustomed to reasoning, have a fuller philosophical armoury. (7)

There is a war on, and this enemy ("the life of triumph is no better than the life of fighting, though it is sweeter") may be winning.[145] The particular staging of conflict, the polemical encounters that are performed in the text as a whole, are therefore important to consider as testifying to the intensity and to the terms of enmity. The dialogue as a whole stages two battles under the eyes of the Christian observer: first, between the Jew and the philosopher—that is, plausibly enough, between the Jew and the Arab—and second, between the philosopher and the Christian. The first battle is concluded with what appears as the failure of the Jew to convince the philosopher ("I have had sufficient discussion with you about your faith and mine. My considered judgment of what has taken place in our debate is this. Even granting that you were given your law as a gift from God, you cannot compel me on its authority to admit that I should submit to its burden," 75). At this point, the arbiter reserves his judgment ("Both of them said that they were ready to hear my judgment. But I, desiring more to learn than give judgment, said that I first wish to hear the reasonings of them all," 77). As is well known, he will never deliver one in the version of the *Collationes* that has reached us. Yet the philosopher does pass judgment on the Jew. It becomes difficult to determine whether the debate was conclusive or not. Otherwise put, this battle between the Jew and the Arab may be concluded, but not so the war.

This state of affairs is quite striking when compared with what happens in the second and last dialogue, between the philosopher and the Christian. Here, the fight is repeatedly asserted as over: "Let me speak the truth," says the philosopher to the Christian, "and say that now, for the first time, I find that you are certainly a philosopher. It would be unfitting and shameful to combat such evident reasoning" (109). The hostilities have come to a close. If a fight remains, it is now a common fight: "What does a thing's name matter, so long as the thing itself stays the same, and neither the happiness nor the aim in living justly differs between philosophers and Christians? We are an example. You and I set out to live just lives here of the sort for which we shall be glorified there, and we fight against the vices here" (113).

It is important to note that the end of hostilities between the Christian and the Arab philosopher, along with the promise of a new and common struggle, is granted on the basis of reason, which is to say not on a religious or theological basis. It thus remains consistent with the figuration of the enemy that, by the thirteenth century, would become fully sedimented in Christendom. The Jew is the theological (and internal) enemy, whereas the Muslim is the political (and external) enemy. Hence, when we return to Aquinas, we find that from the beginning of the *Summa contra Gentiles*, Aquinas distinguishes and separates the Jew from the Arab, the Jew from the Muslim, by affirming that a theological struggle, a religious disputation, is possible only on the basis of a prior agreement, a consensus and common ground, a common text. Such theological common ground is available only with the Jews, not with the Muslims. "The Mohammedans and the pagans do not agree with us in accepting the authority of any scripture. . . . Thus, against the Jews we are able to argue by means of the Old Testament, while against heretics we are able to argue by means of the New Testament. But the Mohammedans and the pagans accept neither the one nor the other."[146]

Aquinas then pursues this dissociative logic by proceeding to negate any theological or religious basis for Islam and to its prophet, likening him to political criminals. Muhammad himself would have admitted that Islam, the enemy that is Islam, is a political and military enemy. Mohammed himself would thus have claimed "that he was sent in the power of his arms—

which are signs not lacking even to robbers and tyrants (1.6).[147] Hence, even the faith of his followers had nothing to do with divine matters. "Those who believed in him were brutal men and desert wanderers, utterly ignorant of all divine teaching, through whose numbers Mohammed forced others to become his followers by the violence of his arms" (1.6).

In full agreement with Abelard, Aquinas offers reason as the last resort, indeed, as the last weapon that will enable communication with this enemy, that will force and enforce a consensus: "We must therefore have recourse to natural reason to which all men must give their assent" (1.2). But the realm of reason, much like the political realm, is where *jus divinum* does not apply, where the divine meets its limit. "It is true that in divine matters, it [natural reason] has its failings" (ibid.). Or, as a later author will put it, "it is much that the Moor should be more than reason."

2

Derrida, the Jew, the Arab

"And what could be more important than speaking of the Jew and the Arab today, here and now?"[1] What, indeed, could be more important, more urgent, than the Jew and the Arab? "The Jew, the Arab," that is to say also, between the Jew and the Arab the passage or the impossibility of a passage from the Jew to the Arab, the possibility or impossibility of the Arab, the Jew, and the Arab Jew.

"The Jew, the Arab," is a citation that I extract from a footnote in Jacques Derrida's "How to Avoid Speaking," a text that addresses the apophatic language of negative theology, where the phrase "the Jew, the Arab" suggests the articulation of a promise, the promise "to speak of the thing itself."[2] Two words or two names, the syntactic order of which appears contingent, which situate what is called, what Derrida calls, the Abrahamic. "The Jew, the Arab," and what is between them—nothing perhaps, but that is already much—here a comma, elsewhere a hyphen, between the Jew and the Arab and what one can await from them.[3] In this chapter, I would like to linger on this naming and on the questions that it raises in order to show that "the Jew, the Arab" is, perhaps primarily, the name of the Abrahamic in Derrida. "The Jew, the Arab" is the name of Abraham and Ibrahim, of the Abrahamic or, as Derrida also calls it, the Ibrahimic and even the Abra-Ibrahimic. More than a name, therefore, and more than one name.

The Abrahamic, between the Jew and the Arab—and between them also the Christian who finds himself at the margin, no more, perhaps, than a punctuation sign, here a comma in the phrase: "the Jew, the Arab." But this marginality of what is between the Arab and the Jew, if "marginality" is indeed the proper word to describe what is at stake here, is a troubled one in this phrase, for there is more to read in its punctuation and more than punctuation in it. To read "the Jew, the Arab," and therefore also the Christian, to read the names of the Abrahamic, if that is possible, as Derrida inscribes them in his recent and less recent texts, is what I propose to begin to do here, and with this reading to attempt to determine what kind of question it is that is raised with this naming. Is it a philosophical, rhetorical, political, religious, or autobiographical question? A literary one? In other words, is "the Jew, the Arab" an empirical or a transcendental question?

Maurice Blanchot noted that the question of the empirico-transcendental was, from the beginnings of phenomenology, an "explosive" one.[4] Other commentators have observed that such an explosion, or more precisely, a certain explosiveness, is pursued and furthered by Derrida (and one would indeed have to chart the bombs, volcanoes, and earthquakes, the explosions, the *ça éclate* and the *ça saute* that are disseminated throughout Derrida's texts).[5] It is in the neighborhood of such explosiveness, associated with the troubles that affect the empirico-transcendental distinction, that the Abrahamic occurs in Derrida's texts. With the names of the Abrahamic, and even within its silences, the "Abrahamic phrase," almost a formula, "Judaism, Christianity, Islam," recurs in proximity to names that recall so-called empirical regions and religions. Thus, it is also of history, of autobiography, of literature, religion, and of politics that the Abrahamic speaks—and these last two, religion and politics, will occupy a privileged place, for essential reasons we are continuing to explore. But with the Abrahamic, with the phrase and the names of the Abrahamic, what is to be read is the *condition* of a certain religion, of a certain politics, the condition of the theologico-political and of a history, not to say of history "as such," of autobiography, and of literature. Insofar as it transcends each of those "fields," the Abrahamic as condition reveals itself as exceeding legibility. It is, in other words, difficult to read. More than a historical moment (be it a general historical moment or a so-called "personal" or autobiographical moment in Jacques Derrida's history), the Abrahamic instead constitutes the occasion for an interrogation of the empirico-transcendental distinction, opening onto "what constitutes our history and what produced transcendentality itself."[6] And the Abrahamic naming, "the Jew, the Arab," can no longer simply be empirical, identitarian, or historicist.

"The Jew, the Arab," then. And if it could be read, toward which history, toward which dimension of "our history" would we find ourselves directed? What is given to read here? Names, I have said, and for the sake of brevity, I will simply list some of them as they appear in Derrida's texts: Abraham, Maimonides, Algeria, Levinas, Massignon, Genet, Jerusalem, Sultana Esther Georgette, Shatila, and, not surprisingly, Derrida. For the Abrahamic is also Derrida's name. But there are others, and since I will be unable to read all of them, let me focus on three names, the asymmetry of which is of course not irrelevant: Derrida, Schmitt, Abraham.

Pursuits of Derrida

To associate Derrida's name with "the Jew, the Arab," might already appear to promise an autobiographical reading, a highly localized historical reading. It may already be the promise of an empirical reading and a reading of the empirical. In turning toward the first of the three names that will occupy me in this chapter—"Derrida"—I hope to show that such is not simply the case. Yet is it not possible to determine the identity of Jacques Derrida? Is such an identity not available to determination?[7] Can one not simply consider that Derrida, Derrida himself, has finally spoken and finally told the story, given the last word, regarding his "identity"? Alternatively, should we reinscribe Freud's *Moses*, the place of a certain Egypt, as the end of identity in the empirical sense and affirm, with Geoffrey Bennington, that "Derrida is neither Jew nor Greek, but 'Egyptian,'"— that is, "North-African, analogically 'Egyptian,'" as Bennington writes earlier—but "in a non-biographical sense to be explored"?[8] To the extent that the biographical sets as its goal—but also fails—to situate the subject *chez lui*, "at home," what of biography, what of life, what one calls "life" *chez* Derrida?

These are the questions that are raised by the Abrahamic, but following them "*chez* Derrida" implies that we note that "*chez*" here means the impossibility of inhabiting and remaining at home, the impossibility of *demeure*, and therefore the impossibility of an appropriate use of the word *chez*.[9] Like a secret that "doesn't belong, [that] can never be said to be at home or in its place [*chez soi*]," the question of "life" here extends "beyond an axiomatic of the self or the *chez soi* as ego cogito. . . . The question of the self: "who am I?" not in the sense of "who am I" but "who is this 'I' that can say 'who'? What is the 'I,' and what becomes of responsibility once the identity of the 'I' trembles *in secret*?"[10] Here, as in many North African homes, the *chez* in the expression "Viens mon petit, viens chez ta mère" must mean "near" (*près de*) and not "in the abode of" (*dans la demeure de*).[11]

Some "autobiographical" affirmations by Derrida have no doubt enabled the stabilization of his name in an uncontested empiricity. One example among many others has been noted by Chantal Zabus.[12] It is a sentence that Derrida uttered on the occasion of an international colloquium that gathered African philosophers. Derrida was speaking there of "movements of deconstruction" and of "decolonization." At this particular moment, Derrida says that he speaks "without demagogic facility or conventional deference toward my hosts"; rather, he speaks as a sort of uprooted African, *comme cette sorte d'African déraciné que je suis,* "born in Algiers in a environment about which it will always be difficult to say whether it was colonizing or colonized."[13] One could affirm, therefore, and with good reason, that Derrida's "primary identity," the "Judeo-Algerian," was inscribed and delivered to us by Derrida himself. Derrida would have inscribed his "I" in identity, as well as in postcoloniality, since he would have "described himself as an 'uprooted African . . . born in Algiers.'"[14]

At the other pole of such a project of identification, one finds the resolutely "nonbiographical" reading proposed by Geoffrey Bennington, which appears to situate the question of the autobiographical outside of all empiricity. Between this nonbiographical sense and an empirical identification, what nonetheless "insists"—this is Bennington's word—is the question of identity, or, more precisely, the question of the name, of Derrida's name and the legibility of the "I" as it inscribes itself in the texts. This insistent question, the concern that expresses itself here regarding the legibility of the "I" in the reading of the Derridian text, is meant neither to erase nor to reinstate a naïve or even distinct empiricity in the so-called "autobiographical" text. What is at stake, rather, is to continue to interrogate the empirical, to continue to interrogate the empirico-transcendental distinction. It is this interrogation, as it articulates itself around identity, around a certain empiricism, that orients the pursuit of the Abrahamic that occupies me here.[15]

Let us therefore return to the passage quoted by Zabus, one that could legitimately be thought of as a rare explicit autobiographical moment, at least prior to "Circumfession." What Derrida writes there is that he speaks, that he says what he says and writes ("and I say it in a word," *et je le dis d'un mot*) "comme cette sorte d'Africain," "*like* [a] *sort of* . . .

African." Yet the double precaution (*"comme"* and *"cette sorte"*) is important. When Derrida invokes a phrase such as "in a word," *d'un mot*, it
hides metonymically an elaborate web of meanings. The irony of Derrida
saying anything "in a word" requires therefore no further comment. Derrida's word, if it is one, will therefore be complicated, as it is here, complicated by figuration (*comme*) and by the lack, precisely, of a precise identity
(*cette sorte*). Derrida will not assert, he will not assert (himself), or identify
(himself), not simply, (*comme*, as) "I" nor (as) "African." Derrida—if the
"I" in these texts can simply or ever be read as "Derrida"—Derrida, then,
and the "I" in the text, will perhaps speak *comme* (like, as) an "African,"
but because of the undecidability of the word *comme*, we will be unable to
say of which kind, by way of which figuration, this "African" will be, what
kind and what uprooting he will be (*sera*) or what he will follow (*suivra*).[16]

It should therefore be concluded that when Derrida says *"comme"* an
African, the operative gesture is one that speaks the African as Other,
rather than as a measure of identity. One ought not to lose sight of the
rhetoricity of the "comme," which also separates at the moment it appears
to join. But why speak of "will be," *sera* or "follow," *suivra*? It is by now almost banal to point it out, because Derrida himself, as well as his commentators, have lingered on this issue. When Derrida says that he writes
"like" an African, he writes "comme cette sorte d'Africain déraciné que je
suis." This is a phrase written in a language that one could call "suspended"
regarding its meaning. *Je suis* can be translated as both "I am" and "I follow," so the phrase complicates the possibility of deciding conclusively
whether or not Derrida *is* "this African" (*je suis, il est*) or whether he follows
him (*je suis, il suit*) and yet others, following (by) the trace of a number of
so-called identities (African, Algerian, Arab Jew, Hispano-Moor, and more
recently, Franco-Maghrebian, and later "animal" in "l'animal que je suis").
In the final analysis, the *je suis* of Derrida is more destabilizing than his use
of the word "like," *comme*. In other words, to say "I am African" or
"l'Africain que je suis," for Derrida, is ever more distant from the assertion
of identity that would appear to take place in "like an African."[17]

During a discussion that circled around the question of the "so-called
life of the author," that is to say, around the tendency to confuse such a life
with "the corpus of empirical accidents making up the life of an empirically
real person,"[18] Derrida said the following: "If one pursues," *si l'on poursuit*,
"carefully the questions that have been opened up here, then the very value
of empiricity, the very contours of an empirical text or any empirical entity,

can perhaps no longer be determined. I can no longer say what an empirical text is, or the empirical given of a text."[19] In other words, the "I" here can no longer say, and the "I" no longer knows itself as an empirical moment. It is not that the "I" abandons speech or knowledge. It does not even abandon itself. Rather, the "I" fails and falls to empiricity itself, to "accidents" that are said to be empirical and that abandon the "I," abandon it outside of its determinations and foundations, determinations and foundations that can no longer be maintained. In this abandonment, the autobiographical genre—if such exists—is unsettled and revealed as a problem. If the "I" no longer knows what this empiricity might be, what remains of the so-called "life" is what, no longer determinable, cannot be read.

Still, why would it be impossible to identify the "I" spoken here, the "I" that speaks and asserts, in *Monolingualism of the Other*, for example, that it is as, *comme*, the "most" or the "only" (among a group of two)? Isn't Derrida, Derrida himself, affirming a new identity after all, and, with the Abrahamic, affirming a new hyphen to be added to the already long list of hyphenated identities? Derrida seems to insist and lean in this direction: He speaks, and says that he speaks, of a hyphen, one that would signify identity. It seems necessary therefore to return to the issue of following and pursuing, *"je suis,"* as an alternative to being, *"je suis,"* as an otherwise than identity. Indeed, the "I" that I am trying to follow, I have said, is not *méconnaissable*—it is never a matter of saying that "I" is not—but remains difficult to arrest and to contain to the extent that "I" follows and pursues an identity and prior to it an ipseity: "What is identity" asks Derrida, "this concept of which the transparent identity to itself is always dogmatically presupposed by so many debates . . . and before the identity of the subject, what is ipseity? The latter is not reducible to an abstract capacity to say 'I,' which it will always have preceded."[20] Identity is therefore not denied, but affirmed insofar as it remains a question ("Our question is still identity") and to the extent that it is secondary and derivative because it is preceded—to the extent that it therefore follows—by an ability to say "I" to which it is not reducible. Derrida therefore speaks of the manner in which "it is always *imagined* that the one who writes should know how to say *I*."[21] This ability and this knowledge follow in their turn a power, the *-pse* of *ipse*, and it is a power, Derrida continues, that "troubles identity": "To be a Franco-Maghrebian, one 'like myself,' is not, not particularly, and particularly not, a surfeit of richness of identity . . . in the first place, it would rather betray a *disorder of identity," un trouble de l'identité.*[22] It is this "trouble" that I follow and that the *je suis* of Derrida operates.

With this trouble, or rather with these *troubles* (in French, one will often hear of *troubles* rather than of *révoltes,* uprisings or intifadas), the question of the Abrahamic, its explosive dimension, returns. In *Monolingualism of the Other,* "the Jew, the Arab" makes a hyphen out of a comma and surrounds itself with bombs. More precisely, Derrida writes, the silence of the hyphen "does not pacify or appease anything, not a single torment, not a single torture . . . A hyphen is never enough to conceal protests, cries of anger or suffering, the noise of weapons, airplanes, and bombs."[23] This ineffectual silence demands that we follow and pursue a logic that does not quite appear, but that nonetheless constitutes an apparition, a shadow or a specter, which Derrida conjures and invokes when inscribing an "I" that one could still call, though differently, "autobiographical." This phantomization stages the Abrahamic, a certain *outre-tombe,* even an *outre-bombe,* that Derrida calls and recalls, calls himself again, and indicates something that Derrida is not, not simply, even if he follows it, even if the "I" of his text follows. As such, the apparition therefore does not appear, in "Circumfession" and elsewhere, but intervenes at the moment where there emerges "a little black and very Arab Jew," enigmatic site of his "life," of "religion," and of the Abrahamic.[24] It concerns what Derrida calls the closest, the *chez,* the most proximate, which also remains infinitely distant, separated by no more but also no less than punctuation, there a hyphen, here a comma: "what my birth, as one says, should have made closest to me: the Jew, the Arab."

With "the Jew, the Arab," with the Abrahamic, we are confronted, on the one hand, with a Derrida preoccupied with ethical concerns and with what one could call an "ethics of memory." On the other hand, there is here a Derrida who has painfully inscribed incineration, suffering, and who exhorts us to an exposure to a reading field that is also a minefield. This is a field that Derrida describes "at the two sources of religion" at the sources of the theologico-political: "a non-identified field . . . like a desert about which one isn't sure if it is sterile or not, or like a field of ruins and of mines," *champ de mines,* "and of wells and of caves and of cenotaphs and scattered seedings; but a non-identified field, not even like a world."[25] With the Abrahamic and with its names, with "the Jew, the Arab," the "I" and the name of Derrida become double, at least. They explode over this minefield which, far from offering a placid topology, resists all localization.

With these names, it is no longer a matter of a mere latency, or, as we saw, of any kind of empiricity. The name occurs rather in the proximity of an explosion that maintains its unreadability. It is an event that, in troubling simultaneity, exposes and explodes the name of Derrida, the names of the Abrahamic, while founding them.

Political Theology I

Along with his seminar on the theologico-political and the publications that came out of it, one can witness in *Politics of Friendship* a defining moment in Derrida's elaborations of the Abrahamic. This moment comes about most strikingly around the name of the German legal theorist Carl Schmitt, whom Derrida discusses at length in *Politics of Friendship* and whose writings on the concept of the political and on the theologico-political distinction continue to bear relevance.

When he comes to defining "the enemy in the political sense,"[26] Carl Schmitt makes a surprising gesture, a gesture in which, as Derrida notes in another context, Schmitt appears "to defend himself from being a theologian."[27] Here, the fundamental distinction, the cut, between theology and politics that Schmitt's entire oeuvre was engaged in questioning, would thus be affirmed and reproduced. One of Schmitt's essential contributions, which informs everything that follows here, is to have underscored the intensity of the continuity between theology and politics.[28] The moment where that continuity comes undone and where it is actively denied in Schmitt's text is what will occupy us here.

Starting from the "often quoted" passage he finds at the source of Western theology—"Love your enemies"—Schmitt moves on and away from it and reaches for a political example. Yet he paradoxically arrives at this example without passage, without transition. More precisely, Schmitt denies the possibility of a passage and a transition between theology and politics, between the theological teaching of the Gospels and the political example that follows. No less clearly, however, Schmitt's text also syntactically makes the passage from one to the other, from the nonpolitical Gospels to the political example. In other words, even though the one follows the other in the text of the *Concept of the Political*, Schmitt nevertheless distinguished the theological teaching of the Gospels and the example of the political, the example of the political enemy.

Note that this is not just any example. It is the example of the political enemy par excellence, an example about which Derrida says that one "could say a great deal."[29] It is the example of Islam, and it intervenes in what Schmitt calls "the thousand-year struggle between Christians and Moslems."[30] Guided by Derrida's reading of Schmitt, I want to suggest that Derrida already has had much to say about this example, more than perhaps appears, and that what is at stake in what he has to say is the Abrahamic.

Having started from the theological teaching of the Gospels,[31] Schmitt arrives at the political enemy, Islam. He does so while announcing that the first does not mention, does not speak of the second. In "the often quoted 'Love your enemies,'" writes Schmitt, "no mention is made of the political enemy."[32] Derrida lingers on this moment and remarks that "Christ's teaching would thus be moral or psychological, even metaphysical, but not political."[33] From the Gospels, in other words, according to Schmitt, from their teaching, one would learn nothing about the political. One could not go from one to the other, there could be no transition between the biblical text and the political fact, since, in this case, one does not "touch" the other: "The Bible quotation touches," *berührt*, "the political antithesis even less than it intends to dissolve, for example, the antithesis of good and evil or beautiful and ugly."[34]

Schmitt arrives at the political as the historical event of a struggle and of a war. Derrida explains that for Schmitt, it is "war waged against a determinate enemy (*hostis*) . . . [that] would be the condition of possibility of politics."[35] It is this war, this determinate struggle, that, over the course of the last millennium, was at the source of Europe's political existence, a Europe that thinks itself Christian, that grants itself its Christianity and its Christendom, its "Christian politics," insofar as it is engaged in this struggle. "Never in the thousand-year struggle between Christians and Moslems did it occur to a Christian to surrender rather than defend Europe out of love toward the Saracens or Turks."[36] Clearly, what defines itself here is first of all the "being-political" of Europe, and only secondarily, though without derivation from the Christian sources, the being-Christian of Europe.

We thus find ourselves at the site where the thinker of the theologico-political interrupts the transition and the continuity between the theological and the political. Islam marks this interruption insofar as its appearance enables its abstraction, its being cut off from its status as a religious community, much in the same way as the being-political of Europe is no longer derived from its theological source, much as it is no longer deduced from the Gospels, now construed as "nonpolitical." The being-Christian of

Europe as being-political derives from the political struggle in which Europe has been engaged for a thousand years.

By now, it should be easier to understand what Derrida means when he explains that without an enemy, Europe would be a subject that "would lose its being-political," a subject that "would purely and simply depoliticize itself."[37] It should also be easier to understand the logic of the opposite movement as described by Schmitt regarding "a religious community, a church," that would become political only as "an organized power in this world." It is only then that such religious community "assumes a political dimension. Its holy wars and crusades are actions which presuppose an enemy decision."[38] Finally, it will be possible to deduce that without this enemy par excellence that is Islam, Europe, Christian Europe, would not or would no longer exist. Europe, and with it, the political, "nothing more and nothing less than the political as such . . . would no longer exist without the figure of the enemy," without *this* figure of the enemy that is Islam.[39] If such is, indeed, the case, it would demonstrate, were it still needed, that Islam is not only at the source of "our history," but also that it is one of the "conditions" of the history I am trying to read throughout this book.

This, then, is what is said about Islam as example, an example that is neither learned nor derived and that articulates itself in a transition without transition, in a discussion where the Gospels serve as a point of departure, a point of departure from which no goal is reached, from which no goal should be reached, a point of departure from which the political, and with it Islam, is always already distant. Islam, as it appears in the *Concept of the Political*, as the exemplary figure of the enemy, the figure of the exemplary enemy, of the political enemy, is an Islam that would have nothing to do with the theological. Yet although it is without theological derivation, Islam is not fully political. It is not political through and through. As a condition of the political, Islam, the struggle against Islam, is also a figure of a beyond, beyond the political. "Beyond" because, as Derrida explains, the war with Islam is "more than a political war."[40] It is "a struggle with the political at stake, a struggle for politics" where the political itself is therefore put under question from a certain outside. As paradoxical as it seems, Islam remains the exemplary political enemy, but it is also an enemy that "would no longer even be a political enemy but an enemy of *the* political."[41] The site of Islam—its interiority and exteriority vis-à-vis Europe and vis-à-vis the political—is therefore troubled and unsettled insofar as this site, Islam, is both political and nonpolitical.

The political and nonpolitical enemy of which Islam is the example moreover finds itself in proximity with another site—one could say that it undergoes a transition toward it—a site that also remains nonpolitical, but perhaps otherwise nonpolitical. In the dynamic of the Schmittian text, what occurs is yet another passage and another transition toward a nonpolitical other, another nonpolitical other. In this transition, the political enemy continues its passage in and toward the proximity of an enemy which would not be one, not really, but an enemy that would nonetheless remain an enemy—this time strictly nonpolitical. Whereas earlier we witnessed a transition from the nonpolitical to the political, the movement we will now follow would lead us toward the site of a nonpolitical enemy which is not one, in a passage of and from the political toward and beyond the political.

What would such an enemy be? What could the site, the place of such an enemy be? This is the question that Derrida asks in a different, but relevant context: "without an enemy, and therefore without friends, without being able to count one's enemies nor one's friends, where then does one find oneself?"[42] What would be the site and the identity of what is, strictly speaking, neither friend nor enemy, but that, beyond the political, becomes or perhaps *remains* an enemy of the political? What kind of an enemy would this be? And what would such an enemy look like? However different it would or could be from Islam, could the site or nonsite of such a being, such a subject or enemy, be rigorously and absolutely distinguished from any other enemy who is beyond the political, of any other enemy of the political—for example, Islam? What would this enemy be, an enemy that is neither enemy nor friend, neither in the political sense nor in the personal sense, who would nonetheless remain a "public enemy, because everything that has a relationship to such a collectivity of men, particularly to a whole nation, becomes public by virtue of such a relationship"—public, therefore, but not yet, or no longer, no longer sufficiently, political, and thus beyond or "beneath" the political, *au-delà ou en deçà du politique?*[43]

According to Schmitt, such a group or people would in fact not *remain*, it would not maintain itself, *sich zu halten*—it *should* not maintain itself—and, deserving no political existence, such a group or people would, perhaps, not deserve existence at all. The end or disappearance of such a people would appear to be of no significance. Its end would be no more than just that, *its* end. And that end would by no means be *the* end of the world, not the end of any world, nor would it be the end of the political: "If a people no longer possesses the energy or the will to maintain itself in the sphere of politics, the latter will not thereby vanish from the world. Only a weak people will disappear."[44]

In spite of possible echoes, and although in this text Schmitt never alters the linguistic definition of the political entity par excellence, namely, the state, as "the political status of an organized people in an enclosed territorial unit,"[45] nothing would authorize the recognition with any certainty of any determined people, of any example of such nonpolitical enemy, any example of such people without land and without state, under the features of this "weak people"—features that nonetheless recall the Jewish people. As a matter of fact, any interpretation that would see in what is almost a call for the disappearance of a weak people hints of a *deshumanization* to come, a prefiguration of what was going to happen to entire communities, religious and nonreligious, of European Jews, would still have to contend with everything Schmitt has to say about the humanist rhetoric that is deployed in the political sphere. As is well known, Schmitt was violently opposed to the humanist gesture that isolated the nonhuman in order to dismiss it, an opposition upon which Derrida comments at length.[46]

Schmitt's text thus progresses in a series of steps that both promise and interrupt a number of passages and transitions between the political and the nonpolitical, between the political and the nonpolitical we have just encountered under the figure of the "weak people." We have also seen that Schmitt attributes to Islam (and to Christianity and Christendom, if not to the Gospels) an exemplary political status. Then, after he gives us the means to identify or to imagine a sphere that, although a condition of the political, would also be beyond the political, Schmitt moves on without establishing any transition, Schmitt *passes*, and passes on, in other words, to another nonpolitical—the "weak people"—while leaving the passage itself, in this passage, indeterminate. Having taken as his point of departure the theological discourse of the Gospels, Schmitt was already denying or at least interrupting the passage and the transition from the theological to the political that his text nonetheless effectuates. By considering Islam as political enemy—political and not theological—and by ignoring the theological, by ignoring, at least here and explicitly, that under the features of the weak people one *could* recognize a people whose theological status occupies a most important place in this context—that is, the Jewish people—Schmitt renews and reproduces a gesture that interrupts once again the passage from the theological to the political and from the political to the theological. Schmitt does so here by keeping an apparently total silence on the nonpolitical, indeed theological status of the Jewish people.[47] Doing so, the thinker of "political theology" seems, here again, "to defend himself from being a theologian."[48]

Schmitt thus joins a long tradition that separates the political from the theological, the very tradition he is engaged in interrogating and criticizing. According to this tradition—which goes back at least to Augustine and continued to be reinscribed until and even after Franz Rosenzweig, as we will see—whether or not the Jewish people is a "weak people," as Schmitt has it, it would nonetheless remain absent from history and from the political sphere. In Rosenzweig's own words, words to which we will return and that carry an unmistakable Schmittian tone, "the Jewish people stands outside of history, "outside of the world . . . [and] outside of a warring temporality."[49] In this tradition, the existence of the Jewish people would remain purely theological. In Schmitt's text, then, whether or not such nonpolitical existence ever could be purely secular, purely theological, or simply unjustified, remains perhaps less interesting than its absence from Schmitt's analysis. This absence marks the interruption of a passage between politics and theology and the persistence of a distinction that is no less ancient and no less determining, a distinction in which the theologico-political finds its source, or, more precisely, its condition.

Islam *remains* a privileged example of this condition before a Europe that continues to think itself Christian, to presume that Islam, the Jewish people, or any other "being radically alien to the political as such" remains so and, as Derrida phrases it, that "in its purported purity," such a being "is not Europeanized and shares nothing of the tradition of the juridical and the political called European."[50] By the logic of its location in Schmitt's argument, Islam remains profoundly linked to the Jewish people, to a religious community the political status of which remains—without maintaining itself—suspended. The Jewish people, even less than the weak people, does not maintain itself, does not remain in Schmitt's text, not even as nonpolitical, not even where, with Spinoza, it finds itself at the source of Schmitt's analysis. Schmitt persists therefore while inscribing and denying at once the passage and the absence of passage between theological and political, between Islam and the Jewish people. Doing so, Schmitt appears to direct us toward a complex, not simply historical source of the theologico-political. This source is constituted by the movement of a distinction that produces—and operates in—Schmitt's text, a distinction that establishes an association, a common ground, and a passage, simultaneously distancing and separating the theological from the political, simultaneously distancing and separating, for the rest of history, Judaism from Islam, the Jew from the Arab.

Suspending the complicated hiatus constituted by the invention of the so-called "Semites" of Orientalistic fame, there is, as I have said, a long tradition.[51] It is a tradition with which we have begun to familiarize ourselves in the last chapter, one that coheres with itself only to the extent that it anxiously maintains the distance between Arab and Jew, to the extent that it shares a lack of reflection on the links and on the ruptures that are at work between Judaism and Islam. It is a tradition that virtually ignores these links and ruptures as they operate *within* what continues to call itself "Christian Europe." Were it to do otherwise, it would engage neither of these two famous headings in their isolation: "Islam and the West" and "Europe and the Jews." Were it to do otherwise, Europe would have to engage something that would come from another edge, indeed, from an other heading, as Derrida elaborates it.

Reading the Abrahamic from this other heading would involve a recognition of what we have begun to read in the previous chapter, what, in a different perspective, a historian recently spelled out, that "Muslims and Jews living in Christian lands are rarely treated in comparative perspective."[52] That such a comparative perspective would begin to place a heavy interrogating burden on the appellation "Christian lands" is still far away from us, whether as ancient history or as a history of the present. Studies that attend to the image of Islam in the West are, if not numerous, at least well known, and those attending to the history of the Jews in Europe can already fill libraries. One still awaits, however, a study that would engage *together*, and in a comparative perspective, the image of Jews and Muslims *in* Europe, as the history, therefore, *of* Europe. The fact that no such study exists, the fact of such massive silence begins to become clearer when considering that it reproduces the silence we have encountered in Schmitt, a silence that reinforces the dividing lines of the theologico-political and that finds its source in medieval Christian theology.

There is therefore a double source, a double root that separates the theological from the political, that cuts between theology and politics. This root is constituted by a discriminating gesture that follows a peculiar logic that operates and separates within a medium that was never homogeneous in the first place. This is what *Politics of Friendship* demonstrates. Within this medium, at the plural source of the theologico-political in its duality, in the proximity and distance that are put in motion with it, one sees "the fraternal figure of the friend return. As a brother enemy. This conflicting and conflicted figure, this divided brother," Derrida continues, belongs to "an immense tradition," the weight of which still bears on us here today, most particularly in the vicinity of the Abrahamic, that is to say, "the Jew, the Arab."[53]

At the plural source of the theologico-political, then, there is fraternity in the figure of the brother enemy, of the brother as cause for war and as "the possibility of a *fraternization*."[54] There is always more than one brother—"Hear O Ishmael" as Derrida often quotes. Yet until now (current newsworthy events included), the being-together of these brothers is always already "untenable," as Fethi Benslama explains. These remain "belligerent brothers, Jews, Christians, Muslims," who "do not even know what their unconscious gives them."[55] This untenable being-together, illegible in that it never appears as such, still operates as the condition of the theologico-political, and it constitutes a first step, a passage without passage, toward a genealogy of the Abrahamic, a genealogy that the Abrahamic—"the Jew, the Arab"—broaches.

Abrahamic Siblings

> A brother is always exemplary, and this is why there is war.
> —Jacques Derrida, *Politics of Friendship*

In the story of Abraham, as it is found in Genesis, there is a passage that, although strange, seems to have remained marginal to the concerns of the canonical Jewish commentators. It is a passage that is so dissonant with the general image of Abraham that the eminent biblical critic Claus Westermann writes that it "has nothing more in common with the patriarchal stories than the names Abraham and Lot."[56] It is important to take note of this dissonance, not only because of what it signals regarding all perceptions of Abraham, but also because in spite of the violence that surrounds him, Abraham is mostly known for his passivity. Competing with Isaac, Abraham is marked—he is the very image of passivity. And indeed, instances of an active role taking on Abraham's part are rare and would therefore seem to be worthy of attention.

The passage that will occupy us here, Genesis 14, is unique in that only here does one find Abram—it is still his name at the moment—engaged in a situation of pursuit, engaged in a military operation. Were one to follow Erich Auerbach, reading the binding of Isaac as the Hebrew equivalent of the *Odyssey*, one could then read Genesis 14, which Susan Niditch describes as "the first war text of the Hebrew Scriptures," as the Hebrew equivalent of the *Iliad*.[57] Genesis 14 has everything to do with war, even with holy war, according to some, and it also has everything to do with names, as Westermann's assertion makes clear. More precisely, it has everything to do with the names of Lot and Abraham. It would thus direct us toward a reading of the names of Abraham, toward a reading of what Fethi Benslama calls "the Abrahamic origins," which could or should become accessible to deconstruction.

It is indeed time to make one more step by turning again toward the Abrahamic, toward yet another Abrahamic sibling, a brother, who has been read, but whom we will have to read anew. One would perhaps have to begin here, and to begin again to elaborate upon the Abrahamic toward which Derrida engages his own readings, where dissociation is rethought out of hostility and friendship. The importance of the brother, the figure of the brother who sustains the entire edifice of Western politics, as Derrida demonstrates—even in, and perhaps beginning with, hostility—demands something else than a genealogy, an approach and a reading that, perhaps impossible, would nonetheless interrogate the ways in which the Abrahamic constitutes the "ground" of these politics. Such an elaboration, such a reading of the Abrahamic, would have to be done by way of another brother, another Abrahamic brother and another cause for war. Derrida asks,

Where, then, is the question? Here it is: I have never stopped asking myself, I request that it be asked, what it means when one says "brother", when someone is called "brother". . . . I have wondered, and I ask, what one wants to say whereas one *does not want* to say, one knows that one should not say, because one knows, through so much obscurity, whence it comes and where this profoundly obscure language has led in the past. *Up until now.* I am wondering, that's all, and request that it be asked, what the implicit politics of this language is. For always, and today more than ever [*depuis toujours et aujourd'hui plus que jamais*]. What is the political impact and range of this chosen word, among other possible words, even—and especially—if the choice is not deliberate?[58]

Did Abraham, that little-known brother, have a politics? Was he and did he have a brother? A brother that he called, that was called, "brother"? Let us pursue these questions and try to engage the way they are traversed by the Abrahamic, by a reading of the Abrahamic as it takes place, as it occurs in the biblical text, and most particularly, in a strange passage that articulates itself around the interrogation raised by Derrida, putting on stage an Abraham who could perhaps be called other.

On to the first war, then. It is a remarkable war, not to say that it is *the* war, the true mother of all wars, the first war of the world, of the biblical world, at least, and thus the First World War. As I have said, it is not only the first war narrated by the Bible (where already "the entire state is under arms and is torn from its domestic life at home to fight abroad," where "the war of defense turns into a war of conquest," Hegel, *Philosophy of Right*, 211), it is also the first occasion for Abraham's "conquest of the land" ("Abram conquiert la terre" is the title that the French translator, André Chouraqui, gives to this section). The first war is thus also a war for land, the war of Abraham for the land. It is the first holy war, the first Abrahamic explosion.

The biblical narrative reports that numerous kings, including the kings of Sodom and Gomorrah, who are apparently on the losing side, "made war," *ᶜasu milḥama* (14:1). Here, in an all too familiar situation today, it is already the case that the winner takes all, the winner took all:

And they took all the goods of Sodom and Gomorrah, and all their victuals, and went their way. And they took Lot, Abram's brother's son, *ben aḥi abram*, who dwelt in Sodom, and his goods, and departed. And there came one who had escaped, and told Abram the Hebrew—now he dwelt by the terebinths of Mamre the Amorite, brother of Eshcol, and brother of Aner; and these were confederate with Abram. And when Abram heard that his brother was captive, *vayishmaᶜ abram ki nishbah aḥiv*, "he led forth his trained men, born in his house, three hundred and eighteen, and pursued as far as Dan. (14:11–14)

In what follows, Abram is victorious: "he brought back all the goods, and also brought back his brother Lot," *ve-gam et lot aḥiv* (16). The first Abrahamic war is thus clearly a family matter. It is, more precisely, a matter of brothers.

As I have said, Genesis 14 drew little attention on the part of the great Jewish commentators. Given the problems it has occasioned for modern biblical scholarship, this is in itself noteworthy. Yet it is all the more strange because the second-century Aramaic translation by Onkelos does seem to signal that there is something troubling with this text, more precisely, something troubling with the brothers in this text. Onkelos is famous for his "corrections" of the biblical text, and it is indicative, indeed, symptomatic of his troubles that he offers such a correction here. When

Abram hears the rumor that brings him to war, Onkelos translates in a straightforward way: "Abram heard that his brother was taken captive," *ushmaᶜ abram ishtevei aḥuhi.* Two verses later, however, at "he brought back his brother Lot," Onkelos "corrects," if one can say so, and translates, "he brought back Lot, the *son* of his brother," *lot* bar *aḥuhi.* As long as it was a rumor ("Abram heard"), the semantic slide between "son of his brother" and "his brother" was not significant to Onkelos. So what if what he heard was that his brother, rather than the son of his brother was taken captive? Yet rather than see the second instance of the phrase "Lot, his brother," as a performative effect, as the production of Lot *as* brother insofar as he is cared for and saved as a brother, insofar as he is the cause of Abraham's war—rather than see in the phrase the biblical affirmation and approval of Lot's fraternal character—Onkelos chooses to correct the biblical text by restoring the "proper" kinship relations.

What is important here is the cause and reason that the biblical text offers regarding Abraham's involvement in a war that did not concern him. War, here the war of conquest, begins for what is after all a simple reason. Abraham, says the text, went to war, went in pursuit of his enemies, because of—but precisely, because of whom? For his nephew? For the son of his brother, as the text calls him at first? Or does he go to war for his brother, as the text also calls him? The rumor—for it is a rumor that reaches Abraham's ears—informs him that his brother has been captured. And it is because of this rumor, of what it tells him about his brother, that Abraham sets out in pursuit, sets out to make war, a war that will turn out to be a war of conquest.

But let us return to the word "brother"—in Hebrew, *aḥ.* One must take into account the semantic field of that word, which enables the descriptions we have read so far and which does not therefore necessitate correction. *Aḥ* is the brother, but it is also the family member, kin or relative, neighbor, and *prochain. Aḥ* is, finally, even the friend. And yet within the space of two very proximate verses, the biblical text itself introduces the distinction between "son of his brother" and "his brother," thus demanding interpretation. It is after all not the first time that we encounter Lot, and we already know that he is the son of Abraham's brother. Aside from the apparent uselessness of the text's recalling again this kinship relation, it is the way in which the text does so, speaking two verses later only of the brother, that may evoke surprise. It has long been a commonplace of biblical interpretation that any additional or repetitive information in the case of a text that is otherwise so sparse and concise must itself signify, mini-mally, that it requires some consideration. All the more reason to be sur-prised at the lack of interest that seems to have been felt by the major Jew-ish commentators. Onkelos's manifest anxiety could have set off an exegetical conversation. It did not.

There is one exception, as far as I could find, and it is an important one for what it reveals about the term "brother" and because it provides for an alternative space of intelligibility. In the eighteen-century commen-tary called *Or ha-Ḥayyim*, the Moroccan Kabbalist Ḥayyim Ibn ʿAttar writes the following: "'that his brother was captive' : this indicates that someone was taken captive and that [the captors] knew that he was Abra-ham's brother. With this word, it is revealed that they were the enemies of Abraham," *u-beze gilu ki oyieve Avraham hem.* "And that is the reason for his pursuing them." What the Bible indicates by using the word "brother," Ibn ʿAttar explains, is the declaration, by the captors and by the biblical text, that they are enemies.[59] The use of that specific word thus conveys crucial information about the reasons for the war: Because the word "brother" indicates that they are enemies, it provides the reason for Abra-ham's going to war. Abraham went to war for his brother because through the brother, through the word "brother," his enemies were revealed as en-emies. The text, therefore, did call for some attention. That it was given as late as the eighteenth century in the commentary of an Arab Jewish inter-preter does not diminish the originary tension, indeed, the explosiveness of an act of war.

The cause of this act of war is, therefore, the brother. More precisely, what the text effectuates within the space of two verses, between the two descriptions of Lot, is the production, the becoming-brother, of Lot inso-far as he is the cause of the Abrahamic war. With this becoming, the brother also becomes an effect of the war, a consequence of the Abrahamic war. The pursuit of Abraham, his entering the war, is both condition and effect of this becoming. But this becoming is also the becoming of the Abrahamic, a term of war and term at war, an explosive term if there is one, which, since its illegible or at least unread beginnings, since the First World War, engaged divided brothers, brothers separated by and in a war, by and in the Abrahamic.

From its double theologico-political source, as a doubled and redou-bled source, the Abrahamic did demand another reading, another reading of the name of Abraham and Ibrahim. With the Abrahamic, it is in the pursuit of this name and of this war, toward and in the sole Abrahamic pursuit documented by the biblical text, that Derrida's texts carry us. The pursuit of Abraham is the pursuit of a name that works the texts and that raises while renewing it the question of the rapport of religion and politics, the question of the theologico-political. This question is the Abrahamic, which worries and unsettles the hyphen of the Judeo-Christian in its positive and negative incarnations, which worries and unsettles, at least since the biblical Abraham, the being-Christian and the being-political of Europe, as well as the meaning of the words "Judaism," "Christianity," "Islam." Among the names that are deployed by the Abrahamic, "the Jew, the Arab" situates the insistence and the importance of a reading of the three religions, a reading that would not gather them in an illusory unity. To the contrary, such reading demands that history—our history—be rethought, a history that is all too sedimented in the manifest progression of the Abrahamic as the history of "Western" religions, in order of appearance, from Judaism to Christianity, from Christianity to Islam. The Abrahamic is also what desediments that history.

I began this chapter with the "explosiveness" of the empirico-transcendental in deconstruction. The bomb to which the Abrahamic exposes us "like a disarming explosion" may have already disabled a reading—any reading—of religion, in Derrida and elsewhere, any reading of "Jewish deconstruction."[60] But the Abrahamic, "older than Abraham," does more.[61] It does more than conjure a distant biblical past to which "Judaism" can be and has often been referred (this is the anti-Semitic and philo-Semitic *topos* of the Jew as biblical or prophetic, prefigurative and ante-Christian). The Abrahamic does more than harangue us toward a prophetic and messianic future that, more often than not, comforts because it presents, destroys, or steals no more than the images of the other. The Abrahamic breaks and tears as it utters words that break from their context, finding again a speech that cuts and unbinds. The Abrahamic also affirms a certain silence. It surrounds and articulates an insufficient comma ("the Jew, the Arab"), sometimes a hyphen. It is a hyphen that does not bridge anything, the silence of which, we have seen, "does not pacify or appease anything, not a single torment, not a single torture. It will never silence their memory. It could even worsen the terror, the lesions, and the wounds. A hyphen is never enough to conceal protests, cries of anger or suffering, the noise of weapons, airplanes, and bombs."[62]

The names of the Abrahamic are numerous—perhaps as numerous

as legion (French, foreign, or other). The explosiveness to which they expose us in Derrida's writings is compounded in the oscillation whose momentum may have started over with the two sons of Abraham, the two biblical brothers, Ishmael and Isaac, and before them with yet other brothers, as we just saw. The figurations of biblical fraternity open the distance within and between the "Christian roots of the motif of fraternity," within and between any notion of "fraternity."[63] As I have mentioned, Fethi Benslama writes that the being-together of these brothers, of Ishmael and Isaac, but also of Lot and Abraham, may in fact constitute the unbearable itself, the illegible itself. Two brothers—and between them war, the political and the theologico-political—two brothers thus provide the poles of an oscillation that never quite gathers as "the Jew, the Arab," the Arab Jew. The reading field to which the Abrahamic transports us in Derrida remains therefore that of an impossibility, a nonfigure that, in its invisibility and unreadability, reproduces and exceeds the so-called "Jewish-Muslim symbiosis," at once ancient and new, more ancient and newer than could, strictly speaking, ever appear or become manifest. The Abrahamic exposes us to the nonfigure that was long ago inscribed and erased in "the fold of this Abrahamic or Ibrahimic moment, folded over and again by the Gospels between the two other 'religions of the Book.'"[64] It was inscribed and erased by "Christian typologists [who] also used Esau, Pharaoh, and Herod to couple the Jew and the Muslim as carnal children of Abraham facing each other across the world-historic break effected by the Incarnation."[65] Figured and failing to figure as the promise and the threat of an alliance—the cut of circumcision—of the Arab and the Jew, the Arab Jew (Muslim and Jew, Moor and Jew, Arab and Jew), the Abrahamic articulates the nonfigure of the first as already the last, of the last and of the end, an explosive specter of uncertain and troubling existence. ("Judaism and Islam would thus be perhaps the last two monotheisms to revolt against everything.")[66] The Arab Jew, whose silent hyphen will prove both more and less than that of "Judeo-Christianity," fails to fuse and violently opens the field and the minefield of the Abrahamic that Derrida gives us to read. The Arab Jew, then, "and what could be more important than speaking of the Jew and the Arab today, here and now?"

3

De Inimicitia

The question of essence, the question of being ("What is?") has yet to become the question of the enemy, even (and perhaps precisely) where the enemy's ontological status has already collided with the weight of the real.[1] There is no support (air or ground support) for the claim that the enemy ever came to be, nor has the evidence for the enemy's being been secured. As we will see in what follows, at the point of contact or impact, and far from it as well, the enemy has no integrity—not even linguistic integrity—disrupting any sense of security, any certainty as to the difference between being and nonbeing,[2] the real and the imagined, war and peace. The enemy's attributes may be as negative as God's, but there is, as of yet, no *via negationis*, no negative polemiology, or study of war. God's biblical proclamations as to His own being-enemy may still constitute the promise of a negative theo-polemiology. Can one even speak of an enemy, then, and of a becoming enemy?

Such difficult theologico-political questions begin to indicate why scientific and nonscientific interests have yet to take the form of a history of the enemy. To engage this issue further, a certain philosophical formalism would be necessary. Unbound by any preexisting discursive or epistemological sphere, it would have to claim an enemy of its own—but is there any other kind, the enemies of my enemies being who they are? Within these (fictional) enemy lines—on the model perhaps of the "amity lines" described by Carl Schmitt—there could emerge the following questions: What is an enemy? Does the term "enemy" gather (or disseminate) a multiplicity of enemies (for the senses of "enemy" are just as many as its figures, as Aristotle would perhaps say)? Must there be more than one enemy? More than—and at least—two? If so, what are the kinds or types of enemies? Is the enemy a cause or an effect? (Is the enemy the cause of conflict or its effect or product? First or last? Aristotle, for one, suggests that enemies are "made," *poein*.)[3] Finally, what modes of relation (human or not, psychological or social, being with and/or being against, and so forth), what networks of meaning, sustain the enemy?

As Hent de Vries explains, it is one of Derrida's significant contributions to have pointed out that hostility "should be understood against the backdrop of an institutional development in the West." Hostility, that is, "the very postulation of an enemy," is "contingent upon the historical emergence of a public sphere that defines, constitutes, and orients the political, together with the primary distinction between friend and foe."[4] Yet as de Vries underscores, what Derrida also argues is that the enemy, "the principal enemy, the 'structuring' enemy, seems nowhere to be found." The enemy thus "ceases to be identifiable and thus reliable," and what is produced instead, and perhaps from the beginning, is "a mobile multiplicity of potential, interchangeable, metonymic enemies in secret alliance with one another."[5] Under the mode of a permanent hypothesis first suggested by Nietzsche and formulated by Carl Schmitt, the enemy thus disappears: "he seems nowhere to be found." This disappearance is constitutive— again, from the beginning—of the enemy.

"Following this hypothesis," one that would have remained unsubstantiated as (the impossibility of) a history of the enemy, "losing the enemy would not necessarily be progress, reconciliation, or the opening of an era of peace and human fraternity. It would be worse: an unheard-of violence, the evil of malice knowing neither measure nor ground, an unleashing incommensurable in its unprecedented—therefore monstrous— forms."[6] Such a history, which is not a history, constitutes the institutional development of a public sphere in Europe. It is a history without progress, during which the enemy has both become identifiable ("an identifiable enemy—that is, one who is *reliable* to the point of treachery, and thereby familiar"), during which the enemy has continued to be thought of as the neighbor ("One's fellow man, in sum, who could almost be loved as oneself: he is acknowledged and recognized against the backdrop of a common history"), and in which he would have remained a neighbor ("This adversary would remain a neighbor, even if he were an evil neighbor against whom war would have to be waged"). Such a history, in which the enemy has always already drawn away and vanished ("the principal enemy, the 'structuring' enemy, seems nowhere to be found"), is what this chapter seeks to engage in perhaps more direct a manner.[7]

Naming the Enemy

Even the dead will not be safe from the enemy if he wins. And this enemy has not ceased to be victorious.
—Walter Benjamin, "Theses on the Philosophy of History"
The Enemy has been here in the Night of our natural Ignorance.
—Thomas Hobbes, *Leviathan*

If death is "the last enemy"—and for Thomas Hobbes, death is indeed the "most terrible enemy of nature"—the first enemy remains Satan.[8] It is his work that Hobbes conjures in the letter of dedication to *Leviathan* to justify his use of the Holy Scriptures.

Writing from Paris to his "most honor'd friend, Mr Francis Godolphin" (brother of Hobbes's deceased friend, Sydney Godolphin, who had provided him "with real testimonies of his good opinion"), Hobbes admits that his own constructions, his "discourse of Common-wealth," may very well offend a number of people. Having expressed his uncertainty ("I know not how the world will receive it, nor how it may reflect on those that shall seem to favour it"), Hobbes does not seem to hesitate in implicating his addressee and "friend" in his perilous endeavor, going so far as to provide him with practical advice on how to handle and deflect the heat of criticism ("you may be pleased to excuse your selfe, and say I am a man that love my own opinions"). Either way, says Hobbes, it's nothing personal, "for I speak not of the men, but (in the Abstract) of the Seat of Power." Hobbes goes on to locate the potential nexus of harm, arguably the most offensive part of his discourse, in his treatment—his use and abuse—of the Bible, certain texts of which, he says matter-of-factly, "are the Outworks of the Enemy": "That which perhaps may most offend, are certain Texts of Holy Scripture, alledged by me to other purpose than ordinarily they used to be by others. But I have done it with due submission, and also (in order to my Subject) necessarily; for they are the Outworks of the Enemy, from whence they impugne the Civill Power."[9]

The first enemy, then, is Satan, and the Scriptures are his defensive apparatus. More precisely, as Hobbes later explains, "Enemy" is one of the names given to tormenters, of which Satan may be the primary example. There are other names, of course, names like "the Accuser," "Diabolus," "the Destroyer," or "Abaddon" and "Devil." Such are the names of "the Enemy"—the enemy first and foremost, and although they do not correspond to "any Individuall person, as proper names use to doe; but onely an office, or quality" (ch. 38, 314), they appear to take second place to the name "Enemy." As Carl Schmitt remarks, however, Hobbes would soon "make the concrete enemy evident."[10] He would soon reconsider this abstraction of "office, or quality" and bring the enemy closer to earth ("the Enemy and his kingdome must be on Earth also," ch. 38, 314), closer to an "Individuall person." Ultimately, Hobbes makes of every such individual (or at least of every human being) an enemy. In the well-known war of all against all, the most insistent name of "the Enemy" is, precisely, that of enemies. "That in a condition of Warre, wherein every man to every man, for want of a common Power to keep them all in awe, is an Enemy, there is no man can hope by his own strength, or wit, to defend himselfe from destruction (ch. 15, 102). But let us proceed slowly, for in spite of the apparent dominance of his name, the enemy withdraws. And we will have to consider that this withdrawal was already at work with the name "enemy," in Hobbes's text, a name that has all but escaped attention, eclipsed by and as a figure of the past, a "state of nature" or a Latin phrase, *homo hominis lupus.*[11]

A few pages into *Leviathan*, Hobbes first acknowledges that the enemy—or "the Enemy"—may well be a figment of one's imagination, the result of dream production. "And that as Anger causeth heat in some parts of the Body, when we are awake; so when we sleep, the over heating of the same parts causeth Anger, and raiseth up in the brain the Imagination of an Enemy" (ch. 2, 17). Hobbes is already indicating that the question of status, the ontological or fictional "state of nature"—and thus the very existence of the enemy—may be less relevant than expected here, insofar as the enemy—every man as enemy, the enemy in every man—is the result of passions or "appetites" that are supposed to be tamed by reason and, ultimately, left behind. The enemy withdraws, or so he should, and Hobbes clearly states that the end of men is, in fact, to seek peace, and to escape the "condition of war." "The finall Cause, End, or Designe of men . . . [is] getting themselves out from that miserable condition of Warre" (ch. 17, 117), no longer to be enemies to each other. Yet invoking "the Outworks of the Enemy" in the first pages of *Leviathan*, Hobbes seems to consider that there is a persistence, indeed, a permanence of the enemy, which, in the form of "certain Texts of Holy Scripture," threatens civil society, or, more precisely, "Civill Power."

Whatever its ontological status (and contingent on the ontological status of the state of nature, a matter, again, of enormous debate in Hobbes scholarship), the enemy is clearly more than a function, more than a "quality." The enemy can become an individual: He can be personified. As Hobbes explains later on, still speaking of the first enemy, "by Satan is meant any Earthly Enemy of the Church" (ch. 38, 314). Based on the letter of dedication and its claim about "the Outworks of the Enemy" in and as the Holy Scriptures, we may infer that this enemy can also take the shape of words, which can be as damaging, as harsh as, and perhaps even harsher than weapons.

Similar to the view Hobbes adopted in *The Elements of Law,* according to which "rhetoric is the greatest and most insidious enemy with which reason has to contend," what Hobbes describes in *Leviathan* is the aspect of language that is constitutive of language, but is also an abuse of language, and that, like the enemy, must be escaped and left behind.[12] Beginning with the invention of printing "for continuing the memory of time past," and going on to describe language itself, "whereby men register their thoughts; recall them when they are past" (ch. 4, 24), Hobbes insists on "the past" throughout his discussion of language in Chapter 4 of *Leviathan.* The general use of language includes "the Registring of the Consequences of our Thoughts; which being apt to slip out of our memory, and put us to new labour, may again be recalled, by such words as they were marked by. So that the first use of names, is to serve for *Markes,* or *Notes* of remembrance" (ch. 4, 25). Language thus preserves the past, and it is as such that it is properly used. Following his discussion of the abuses of language ("to these Uses, there are also foure correspondent Abuses"), Hobbes recalls that "the manner how Speech serveth to the remembrance of causes and effects, consists in the imposing of *Names* and the *Connexion* of them" (ch. 4, 26). It is as if the proper use of speech contained and tamed the past, as it contains and tames the abuse of language, a language "without which, there had been amongst men, neither Common-wealth, nor Society, nor Contract, nor Peace, no more than amongst Lyons, Bears and Wolves" (ch. 4, 24).

Language, then, escapes or perhaps only tames the wolf in man, revealing the way in which "political order for Hobbes is intimately dependent upon linguistic order."[13] At the same time, language also preserves the state of nature, and even—man is a wolf—the enemy.[14] It is at this point that Hobbes makes clear that, concerning words, it is a matter of usage, the use to which Hobbes puts Scripture and the use and abuse of speech. Thus, although nature has given "living creatures" the means to hurt each other, there is a kind of abuse—even, and explicitly, abuse of the enemy—

that is specific to words, which Hobbes condemns in no uncertain terms. "For seeing nature hath armed living creatures, some with teeth, some with horns, and some with hands, to grieve an enemy, it is but an abuse of Speech, to grieve him with the tongue" (ch. 4, 26).

Language then, can escape the state of nature but, constituted as a remembrance of things past, can also deploy man's enmity to man. This is not simply to be regretted, however, and there might be grounds to make justifiable use of the abuse, even the necessity to do so. This necessity is, in fact, essentially linked with the political and resonates with Hobbes's views on crime and punishment—a matter of great consequence to the enemy. Here, Hobbes will say only that to "grieve an enemy" with one's words is, indeed, an abuse of speech "unlesse," he continues, "it be one [enemy] whom we are obliged to govern; and then it is not to grieve, but to correct and amend" (ch. 4, 26).[15]

We will return to the link made between language and the enemy, between language and what appears as the taming and containing of the enemy. But before doing so, it might be important to consider further the matter of Holy Scripture, that is to say, the matter of Christianity as it emerges from the beginning of *Leviathan*, from the letter of dedication Hobbes writes for the book. This, too, is a vexed matter among scholars, but I am less interested in the relation between the two parts of *Leviathan* here than in remarking the strange way in which Hobbes, who spends so much time discussing "the Christian Common-wealth," generally abstains from referring to Christian love—or to any love at all, except as a general heading for "appetites."[16]

In *Leviathan*, moreover, Hobbes never refers to the commandment to love one's enemies. This is strange because Hobbes does offer a striking "summary" of the laws of nature, describing them as laws that, "dictating Peace," are meant to take men out of the "condition of war" in which they now, having become enemies, find themselves. Here is Hobbes's summary. "To leave all men unexcusable," he writes, the laws of nature "have been contracted into one easie sum, intelligible, even to the meanest capacity; and that is, *Do not do to another, which thou wouldest not have done to thy selfe*" (ch. 15, 109). The Judeo-Christian origins of this precept are, of course, hardly exclusive, yet echoing Matthew as they do ("In everything do to others as you would have them do to you," *Matthew* 7:12) one cannot but wonder about the disappearance of Christian love—and enemy love—from *Leviathan*. This disappearance cannot be accounted for here, though it does appear that Hobbes is aware of it when he writes that "they . . . that believe there is a God that governeth the world, and hath given Praecepts, and propounded Rewards and Punishments to mankind, are Gods Subjects; all the rest are to be understood as Enemies" (ch. 31, 246). Religion, Hobbes suggests, produces—or rather maintains—the distinction between friend and enemy, that is to say, it maintains the "condition of war" that makes man an enemy to man. And Christian love would be no different.

But the disappearance of Christian love from Hobbes's text should be juxtaposed to another absence, which brings us back to the question of language, namely, the absence of a definition of the enemy. Hobbes affirmed the necessity of definitions ("Seeing then, that truth consisteth in the right ordering of names in our affirmations, a man that seeketh precise *truth*, had need to remember what every name he uses stand for; and to place it accordingly; or else he will find himselfe entangled in words, as a bird in lime-twigs; the more he struggles, the more belimed," ch. 4, 28). Hobbes, no doubt, struggled with the enemy. There are, in *Leviathan*, as we began to see, Satanic and earthly enemies (of civil power, of the church). There are personal or private enemies toward whom honor regulates behavior: "To imitate is to Honour; for it is vehemently to approve. To imitate ones Enemy, is to dishonour. To honour those another honours, is to Honour him; as a signe of approbation of his judgement. To honour his Enemies, is to Dishonour him" (ch. 10, 65). There are "common enemies" (ch. 17, 118; ch. 18, 126; ch. 21, 150)—"And Law was brought into the world for nothing else, but to limit the naturall liberty of particular men, in such manner, as they might not hurt, but assist one another, and joyn together against a common Enemy" (ch. 26, 185)—and there are those whom, though they be "commanded as a Souldier to fight against the enemy," may "neverthelesse in many cases refuse [to fight], without Injustice" (ch. 21, 151). One should be taught to "resist the publique enemy" (ch. 23, 167) and there are cases when "a forraign Enemy" unites the population (ch. 25, 182). Enemies are not subjects ("all men that are not subjects are either Enemies, or else they have ceased from being so, by some precedent covenants," ch. 28, 219), and "a banished man" is "a lawful enemy of the Common-wealth that banished him" (ch. 28, 218). Living under the protection of a government implies submission to its authority. Later on, Hobbes explains that if a man "secretly" enjoys governmental protection, however, "he is liable to any thing that may bee done to a Spie, and Enemy of the State" (485). Not because "he does any Injustice," says Hobbes, "but that he may be justly put to death" (486).

Hobbes undoubtedly makes the most striking argument for a "generalized enemy." The opposition to (or affirmation of) his view of "human nature" may have obscured that this generalization silently reproduces a Christian gesture, one that, we have seen earlier, consists in transforming the neighbor into the enemy. Having located "appetite, or desire; the later being the generall name," at the root of human motions and emotions, Hobbes divides them into two basic headings: "That which men Desire, they are sayd to LOVE: and to HATE those things, for which they have aversion" (ch. 6, 38). This division is at the basis of Hobbes's conception of the war of all against all, his conception of the enemy. This is a dynamic conception, however, which speaks less to a "state" than to a becoming ("Though we perceive no great unquietnesse, in one, or two men; yet we may be well assured that their singular Passions, are parts of the Seditious roaring of a troubled Nation," ch. 8, 55). Indeed, anterior to or distinct from the "state of war" (which is not, Hobbes makes clear, a permanent state of battle, and may even include peace),[17] Hobbes describes a history—a history of the enemy—the becoming-enemy of man. In the narrative of this history, it is their equal capacities, the equality of all men that, along with their appetites, transform them into enemies. "From this equality of ability, ariseth equality of hope in the attaining of our Ends. And therefore if any two men desire the same thing, which neverthelesse they cannot both enjoy, they *become* enemies; and in the way to their End, (which is principally their owne conservation, and sometimes their delectation only,) endeavor to destroy, or subdue one another" (ch. 13, 87; emphasis added).

Although the state of nature is a logical necessity, if not a historical reality, it is here affected by contingency. It is only "if any two men desire the same thing," that they become enemies. In a manner akin to Jesus, Hobbes offers his own account, his own translation of the neighbor—that is, every human being—into the enemy (although, again, Jesus' commandment to love the enemy remains absent from *Leviathan*). Hobbes's account is not prescriptive, but descriptive, yet such a translation joins Jesus' in a gesture that can only be described as a generalization of the enemy. This enemy which is not one—and Hobbes, like Jesus, acknowledges that the enemy may also be the friend, explicitly dividing the enemy within— is, however, not simply many.[18] Insofar as the enemy is not one, he is incalculable (he is "not determined by any certain number"). Yet the enemy is also symmetrical, comparable,[19] and the number of enemies varies, therefore, according to "the Enemy we feare."

Nor is it the joining together of a finall number of men, that gives them this security; because in small numbers, small additions on the one side or the other, make the advantage of strength so great, as is sufficient to carry the Victory; and therefore gives encouragement to an Invasion. The Multitude sufficient to confide in for our Security, is not determined by any certain number, but by comparison with the Enemy we feare; and is then sufficient, when the odds of the Enemy is not of so visible and conspicuous moment, to determine the event of Warre, as to move him to attempt. (ch. 17, 118)

As Hobbes goes on to make clear, nothing is less certain, less permanent, than such a victory. The enemy—that is also to say, the name of the enemy—withdraws.[20] His odds are "not of so visible and conspicuous moment," and war may not erupt into a battle. On the other hand, as we have begun to see, the enemy's name is not a name that settles into a state, or one that can be defined in a permanent way. Considering Hobbes's assertions about language, this may make more sense than it seems, for "the names of such things as affect us, that is, which please, and displease us, because all men be not alike affected with the same thing, nor the same man at all times, are in the common discourses of men, of *inconstant* signification. (ch. 4, 31). This inconstant signification grounds and ungrounds the imperative to know the enemy.

But the enemy—everyman, the neighbor—is not simply unknown. He affects and is affected insofar as all men are affected, all men have appetites, if not always for "the same thing." The enemy is not the same thing for every man, even if every man is the enemy. This, in Hobbes, is the state of nature as the state of war of all against all, where "each individual *knows* that every other individual is willing to fight him."[21] In the midst of this inconstant signification, the enemy withdraws—he has been here—but the movement of his withdrawal parallels our own escape from another natural state: ignorance. "The Enemy has been here in the Night of our naturall Ignorance," writes Hobbes in a different, but relevant context (ch. 44, 418). In his having been here, the enemy has also made himself known—known, precisely, as the enemy.

If alterity has here been fulfilled (if not abolished) by the translation of every man into the enemy, the translation of the neighbor into the enemy, if alterity begins where knowledge encounters its limit—the enemy is not the other—then every man must know that every man is the enemy.[22]

In the space of his emergence from the night of our natural ignorance, in his withdrawal from conceptualization into the hypothetical and confused past of the state of nature, the enemy persists as having been here. This persistence, at once founds and abolishes a history, establishing and canceling the question of the enemy as requiring an answer, as demanding a response and responsibility. Having been here, the enemy is already constituted as an object of knowledge, agent or object of a violence that may or may not have become actualized, much less determined as war or battle, as psychological or social. Yet what can only be indicated here is that, as he draws away, the enemy also remains, and he remains to be read.

Losing the Enemy

> This would be, perhaps, as if someone had lost the enemy, keeping him only in memory, the shadow of an ageless ghost, but still without having found friendship, or the friend. Or a name for either.
> —Jacques Derrida, *Politics of Friendship*

From the moment the enemy appears—the enemy vanishes. The enemy is determined by distance, and distance, like the desert, grows. "If only I could sometimes sit far away," writes Nietzsche, "if not as far as my enemy."[23] The enemy withdraws, goes into hiding, and evades interrogation, surrendering at most to a confused multiplication of labels.[24] The enemy, which, akin but not identical to the figure of war "produces itself in a world where this symbol seems to have been all but effaced," draws away.[25] Of course, "the possible returns of this figure had to be perceptible, if only in a furtive (indeed fleeting) way."[26] Yet the question "Who is the enemy?" already functions as and within the deceptive modes of the enemy's disclosure. Question and answer will enable the enemy's naming, one in which the name performs its deictic function, ratting on the enemy in exchange for the uneasy comfort that accompanies the discovery of the enemy's location—the interrogation: service and disservice of intelligence.[27]

"Well," asks Socrates, "isn't it better to be a ridiculous friend than a clever enemy, *echthros*?[28] But where are the enemies? And where does the enemy begin? Who was the enemy first and the first enemy? And is there, can there truly be, a "last enemy"? Where, precisely, does one move from the enemy to the other, from the other to the enemy, and from one enemy to the next (that is, the neighbor, *Nächste*), from adversary to opponent, and from rival to enemy? "Your enemy," *echthros*, is everywhere, suggests Plutarch, for "through every friend and servant and acquaintance as well, so far as possible, [he] plays the detective on your actions and digs his way into your plans and searches them through and through."[29] One can therefore easily find or lose oneself in enemy territory, in the comfort of one's own home, and have one's body called upon to deploy sophisticated and remote-uncontrolled defense systems. The enemy may have to be confronted and can even be faced ("the enemy with a thousand faces") and faced down.[30] One could even be sleeping with the enemy.

Yet it is hardly the case that the enemy can simply be approached, the distance abolished, when the enemy is at once distant and proximate (hence the imperative to keep your enemies close, closer even than your friends—assuming, of course, that you can tell the difference), at once establishing and eluding spatial determinations, borders and boundaries, invading and occupying, exceeding the confines of body and soul, public and private, physical and spiritual, human and divine. Each time, the enemy multiplies divisions, or the enemy is accompanied by this multiplication of divisions, "for when there are a number of persons without political honours and in poverty," writes Aristotle, for example, "the city then is bound to be full of enemies," *polemion*.[31] Doing so (but what kind of a doing would this be? And is it a *doing* at all, an activity or an agency on the enemy's part? Is the enemy active or passive? Real or imagined?), even when failing to become an enemy agent, the enemy has already exercised the capacity or weakness to withdraw from categorization, yet never having even secured a breach in the protective walls of other languages, languages of the other or other language spheres, beginning perhaps with a resistance to grammatical reductions, a resistance to *singularity*.

The enemy—is there one?

Presenting all appearances of a substantial threat even when vulnerable, weak, or nonviolent, the inevitable outcome of a kind of essentialism, the enemy's being enemy, the enemy's essence, has managed to assert itself ("who *is* the enemy?") while paradoxically eluding the ontological apparatuses of scientific discourses of the most varied forms—What, after all, is an enemy? Could one argue—but on what secure basis?—for the semantic specificity (but in what language?) of "enemy" over against "opponent," "adversary," "rival," or "antagonist"? Does the enemy differ—and if so, how?—from other figures of hostility? From war and enmity? From war to war? Different kinds of wars and different attitudes toward war may imply a different—an essentially different—kind of enemy. War would thus translate into the enemy, into a change of enemy, and a change in the treatment of the enemy, even as it does not seem to lead to progress or to a different conception of the enemy. The enemy thus exceeds the parameters of war and remains a persistent and, it seems, constant site of multiple imperatives—and perhaps first among them the imperative to know ("Know thy enemy!"—the promise or threat of the failure of Enlightenment, the constitutive failure of knowing and understanding as the sure path of peace)—all the while disrupting as well as establishing the legality of such urgent and essential cognitive tasks.

> **Hostis**. In ancient language (Twelve Tables) this was syn. with *peregrinus* = a stranger. Later *hostis* = the enemy with whom Rome was at war. "*Hostes* are those against whom we (the Roman people) have publicly declared war or those who have done so against us." The earlier term for an enemy was *perduellis*. *Hostis* was also used of an individual, citizen or stranger, who was declared to be an enemy of the state by a statute or by the senate. He might be killed on Roman territory by any citizen with full impunity.
> —*Encyclopedic Dictionary of Roman Law*

Although the conceptualization of the following fact has only recently come under scrutiny toward an interrogation of the political, it is well known that, in ancient Greece, "public space was taken up by friendships and enmities," and "political life was conceived primarily in terms of friendship and enmity."[32] Aristotle suggests that faction is enmity, that is to say, it is what lawgivers "are most anxious to banish." On the other hand, Aristotle writes, "friendship," *philia*, "appears to be the bond of the state; and lawgivers seem to set more store by it than they do by justice, for to promote concord," *homonoia*, "which seems akin to friendship, is their chief aim, while faction," *stasis*, "which is enmity," *echthra*, "is what they are most anxious to banish. And if men are friends, there is no need of justice between them."[33]

Enmity and friendship, conceived along the lines of a certain equality, a symmetry, provided strict criteria for evaluating political regimes. According to Herodotus, for example, oligarchy "oftimes engenders bitter enmity; . . . violent enmity is the outcome, enmity brings faction [*stasis*] and faction brings bloodshed."[34] The older Stoics held that "only friendship can provide the basis of true political community." Thus, they opposed the "alienation and enmity among the fools whose alienation from themselves and from each other is due to their lack of virtue."[35] During the Roman Republic, friendship and enmity remained at the center of political concerns. Cicero "became a victim of the politics of friendship" (134), the result of Marc Anthony's enmity toward him. But more generally, "the fierceness of party struggles in the closing days of the Republic and the high stakes involved in such struggles . . . made commitment to one's friends more dangerous and less enduring" (136). At such point, *amicitia* was less "a sentiment based on like mindedness" and more "a weapon of politics." Establishing an order of things that opposed etymological signals, the Roman Republic put the enemy first. "*Amicitia* always presupposed *inimicitia.*" Or at least the enemy was on a par with the friend. "Enmities were just as important in the life of a Roman politician as were friendships. The stature of a Roman could be measured by the quality and quantity of his friends. Both enmity and friendship, either inherited or acquired, equally served as motives for political action" (144). Whether one had enemies or was an enemy, in other words, would always be found out.

Always vulnerable to some degree or other, even if not actually confronted with these probing questions, no enemy has successfully resisted or countered the force of intelligence-gathering and other knowledge-bound devices.[36] This does not mean that the enemy has not been victorious. On the contrary. It is meant to indicate that the enemy could and has, in fact, been known—historically prior to the unknown soldier, the unknown (as opposed to hidden) enemy has increased in numbers since the invention of partisan warfare, but such enemy is nothing more than one type of enemy, perhaps one constitutive moment of any enemy, if not a privileged one.[37] The enemy is knowable. The enemy constitutes a certain culmination of the knowledge drive and must come to be known as enemy. This has remained true even where—and perhaps because—the enemy has escaped the precise detection of philosophical questioning. "The entire philosophical approach to war culminates in its conceptualization,"[38] but not in a conceptualization of the enemy, unless access to concepts is predicated on their own mode of withdrawal, an essential getting it wrong that ensures their going, along with the enemy, into hiding.

—But let us change our ground, for it looks as if we were wrong in the notion we took up about the friend and the enemy.
—What notion, Polemarchus?
—That the man who seems to us good is the friend.

—And to what shall we change it now? Said I.
—That the man who both seems and is good is the friend, but that he who seems but is not really so seems but is not really the friend. And there will be the same assumption about the enemy.[39]

Unlike war (which, until recently, was logically contingent on the enemy without being a necessary condition of the enemy) or conflict (a life-and-death struggle can take place without enemies ever having been identified, much less defined), the enemy never quite achieved the secured status of a philosophical concept. Nor has the enemy been an object (and even less a subject) of political reflection as such. Describing a "city-state consisting not of free people but of slaves and masters, the one group full of envy and the other full of arrogance," Aristotle suggests about the enemy that "nothing is further removed from a friendship and a community that is political." Aristotle thus casts doubt as to whether the enemy could ever be a political entity or unit, indeed, a community, "since community involves friendship" and "enemies," *echthroi*, "do not wish to share even a journey in common."[40]

Is the enemy, then, an individual (human or not), a tribe, a city or a state, a people, or a race? (Just prior to President Roosevelt's 1942 Executive Order 9066 to intern Japanese-Americans in detention camps, the officer in charge of the U.S. Western Defense Command, Lieutenant General John L. De Witt, successfully defended the devastating argument that the Japanese were not only "alien enemies," but an "enemy race.") Is the enemy akin to these, a mirror reflection of the far side of the political unit? Is the enemy an object whose very existence, Jacques Lacan suggests by returning us to Freud, would always be vocally hostile and who "signals itself at the level of consciousness only to the extent that pain provokes a scream in the subject"? "The existence of the *feindliche Objekt* as such," continues Lacan, "is the scream of the subject."[41] Or does the enemy belong—if the enemy could ever safely be located within a relation of belonging—to the discourses of medicine ("And disease is an enemy," *echthros*),[42] physiology ("And [the body] a foe to sickness")[43] or psychology?[44] Is the enemy ethical ("On this view it appears the friend will be the good man and the bad the enemy")[45] or economic (in the eleventh century, Pope Urban II promised crusaders that, through their war effort, they would gain enemy property; American law, for its part, still maintains an effective definition of the enemy that was formulated in the 1917 Trading with the Enemy Act)?[46] Is the enemy a legal or theological entity signifying the possibility of a breach in the constitution of the body, in the constitution of the body politic? Is the enemy needed? Some people need enemies, Nietzsche pointed out, at least open enemies, *offene Feinde*, "if they are to rise to the level of their own virtue, virility, and cheerfulness."[47]

At the other end of a tradition that constitutes anything but a history of the enemy, Martin Heidegger, who, Derrida shows, raised the specter of a kind of "originary enmity," *ursprüngliche Feindschaft*, "never names the enemy."[48] Hannah Arendt, for her part, speaks of those for whom "a new type of criminal" appeared with Nazism, whose function in the law "is similar to the old crime of piracy."[49] Eichmann may be the ultimate enemy: He is "in fact, *hostis humani generis*," Arendt counters, but the enemy is not a pirate, not a criminal in that sense of the term.[50] Where, then, is the enemy? Is the enemy—within and without—all (or none) of the above? And could I be your enemy?

> It is *redundant*, however, to speak of an "unjust enemy" in a state of nature; for a state of nature is itself a condition of injustice. A just enemy would be one that I would be doing wrong by resisting; but then he would also not be my enemy.
> —Immanuel Kant, *Metaphysics of Morals*

Sporadic, partial, and provisional answers have nonetheless emerged to what has remained an inchoate, almost accidental question: the question of the enemy. One may thus recall these few—always few—pages dedicated to the enemy by, among others, Plato, Aristotle, Plutarch, Augustine, Aquinas, Hobbes, Kant, Hegel, Nietzsche, and, of course, Schmitt, whose decisionism was itself "a theory of the enemy."[51] Yet no discipline, no discursive or even legal instance has claimed or arraigned the enemy as its object, an enemy of its own and as its own. The enemy thus remains a permanent attribute (consider, however, that among the enemy's most significant attributes, there is one that hardly applies to the enemy: the "mortal enemy" does not comment on the enemy's "own" mortality), which is to say that the enemy remains an accident, a contingency of a no less indeterminate object or subject that always seems to deserve more attention. Indeterminate and disappearing, the enemy thus always emerges as new. "We have watched the war machine grow stronger and stronger," write Deleuze and Guattari, "we have seen it set its sights on a new type of enemy, no longer another State, or even another regime, but the 'unspecified or whichever Enemy,'" *l'Ennemi quelconque.*[52]

"Whichever enemy" would thus be an essential feature of the enemy. Whether philosophical or theological, legal or martial, psychological or social, open or secret, the enemy remains contingent on various discussions of friendship or of war, and perhaps even more of "peace," of slavery and punishment, the city and the family, without ever coming to "belong"— always no longer belonging—to any of them. The effect of a declaration or of an oath (the enemy is always the sworn enemy), the enemy has been here and the enemy has been named.[53] The enemy thus participates in a double agency: Beyond the enemy's own, however uncertain, another agency inquires, suggesting that the question of the enemy may command or be commanded by the question of performance, the question of naming and doing: what to do *with*—and, more often, what to do *to*—the enemy. So Plato: "But now what of the conduct of war? What should be the attitude of the soldiers to one another and the enemy," *polemios?*[54] Yet because of the enemy's constancy, one might say, the enemy's resilience, even, some have claimed to know the enemy, others to have seen the face of their enemy. Most have claimed ownership of the enemy. Whatever or whoever the enemy may be, the enemy matters mostly to the extent that the enemy is mine.[55] Nietzsche's "noble man" even goes so far as to *desire* his enemy: "he desires his enemy for himself, as his mark of distinction."[56] And Genet only sought, wanted to discover, never to uncover, the declared enemy.[57]

Still, it's nothing personal. The enemy is nothing personal, and reiterating that fact, Hegel himself may have been following a long tradition, one that registered in Rousseau who, in turn, opposed Hobbes's conception of the state of nature.[58] Rousseau declares the enemy a nonperson, beginning with the guilty criminal as "public enemy," an enemy, and therefore not a citizen ("and when the guilty party is put to death, it is less as a citizen than as an enemy"),[59] but more importantly not a moral person ("for such an enemy is not a moral person, but a man; and in this situation the right of war is to kill the vanquished").[60]

Fighting his own personal demons, if not his own enemies, Hegel is also engaged in redefining the personal, as well as the "human" in "humane," suggesting that in modern war—and Hegel seems to be interested in the enemy only insofar as there is war—personal hatred, along with the personal enemy, is vanishing. In his own manner, Hegel thus seems to renew the distinction made by Rousseau between person and man or human.[61] "Modern wars," Hegel writes, "are therefore humanely waged, and person is not set over against person in hatred. At most, personal enmities appear in the vanguard, but in the main body of the army hostility is something vague and gives place to each side's respect for the duty of the other."[62] Here, the enemy is human, and though he may not be a moral person, the enemy is due respect. Yet there remains some obscurity as to what this respect entails if the enemy is not personal. Hegel, who just a few lines earlier had reminded us that "states are not private persons,"[63] offered only a political definition of the enemy, and it is one that, Carl Schmitt says, "has been evaded by modern philosophers."[64] What, then, is the enemy?

Constitutive of the community, the enemy is not the other. Carl von Clausewitz suggested as much when, though once again limiting the question of the enemy to the thinking of war, he wrote that "war is not waged against an abstract enemy, but against a real one."[65] Indeed, for Clausewitz war engages a known enemy and seeks to constitute the enemy as an extension of one's will. The first definition Clausewitz offers of war is therefore "an act of force to compel our enemy to do our will."[66]

In an early and striking formulation that achieved the status of definition only in Carl Schmitt's work, Hegel suggests that the enemy is difference. The enemy is an ethical difference, a difference of ethical life with itself posited by itself as something "to be negated," *ein zu Negierendes.* Hegel writes:

In its movement ethical life enters difference and cancels it; [its] appearance [is] the transition from subjective to objective and the cancellation of its antithesis.

This activity of production does not look to a product but shatters it directly and makes the emptiness of specific things emerge. The above-mentioned difference in its appearance is specific determinacy and this is posited as something to be negated. But this, which is to be negated, must itself be a living totality. What is ethical must itself intuit its vitality in its difference, and it must do so here in such a way that the essence of the life standing over against it is posited as alien and to be negated. . . . A difference of this sort is the *enemy,* and this difference, posited in its [ethical] bearing, exists at the same time as its counterpart, the opposite of the being of its antithesis, i.e., as the nullity of the enemy, and this nullity, commensurate on both sides, is the peril of the battle.[67]

The enemy, then, is not the other. And, as Schmitt puts it, "the enemy is not merely any competitor or just any partner of a conflict in general. He is also not the private adversary whom one hates."[68] Rather, the enemy is ethical life as another life, another "living totality" that ethical life must subsequently posit "as alien and to be negated." The enemy is not a product, but the result, nonetheless, of an "activity of production": that seeks to "shatter," *zerschlägt*, its own difference, the difference that it enters and sublates. Together with ethical life, and as ethical life, the enemy is, in this movement, *aufgehoben*. Its nullity, its "to-be-negated," the movement of ethical life as it goes through difference, through the enemy, is fully commensurate to both sides. Hegel earlier writes that "in war the difference of the relation of subsuming has vanished, and equality is what rules. Both parties are identical," *Indifferenzen*. "Their difference is what is external and formal in the battle [i.e., they are on different sides], not what is internal, but something absolutely restless continually swaying to and fro (Mars flits from side to side)."[69] This oscillating movement is the movement of ethical life before the outcome of the battle is decided in such a fashion as to terminate relations in peace, that is to say, in the restoration of difference: "both parties put themselves into the previous position of difference from one another, difference without connection or relation."[70]

But if the enemy is not personal, what, then, are the parties involved? Maintaining the strict symmetry he already posited, Hegel is unequivocal: "For ethical life this enemy can only be an enemy of the people and itself only a people."[71] Presumably, for Hegel, as for Plato, "everyone shall regard the friend or enemy of the State as his own personal friend or enemy."[72] Hegel goes on to add another sentence quoted by Schmitt. "This war is not one of families against families but of peoples against peoples, and therefore hatred itself is undifferentiated, free from all personalities."[73] With the enemy, Hegel reiterates, it is always war—in peace, there would be no enemies—but it's nothing personal. More precisely, perhaps, with the enemy, it is all about nothing, "the nothing of the enemy," *das Nichts des Feindes.*

Inter-diction 3: *Hostis Via Negationis*

The enemy is not the other. This goes both further than and falls short of Socrates' "extremely clever" friend who convincingly argued that "nothing is so hostile to like as like, not so hostile to the good as the good," which locates enmity outside of oppositionality.[74] Rather, to the extent that the enemy is called *hostis*, "he is neither the stranger nor the enemy," as Emile Benveniste says in *Indo-*

European Language and Society.[75] Often feminized—the war of the sexes would have to be rewritten, perhaps, from the perspective of a history of the enemy (as if it were possible)—the enemy is not a man, but a woman, and may be called *hostia*, in which case, the victim is "the victim which serves to appease," *compenser*, "the anger of the gods," an offering, in other words.

As *hostis*, the enemy is not simply a stranger, "not a stranger in general. In contrast to the *peregrinus*, who lived outside the boundaries of the territory, *hostis* is 'the stranger in so far as he is recognized as enjoying equal rights to those of the Roman citizens.'" This not only implies a kind of "reciprocity," it also tells us that the enemy is not natural. The enemy "supposes an agreement or contract," *une convention*. The enemy is not simply not Roman—note the double negative. ("Not all non-Romans are called *hostis*.") The enemy is not. Between the citizen and the enemy, a rapport of equality and reciprocity enables the passage from *hostis* (now designated as "he who stands in a compensatory relationship") to hospitality (77/F93).[76]

Ultimately, what could be only inside, the stranger within and the guest, could not remain. At the level of the signifier, the institution, which maintained the relations between citizen and *hostis*, loses its force. Relations between tribes, between human beings, are abolished. They are not. "All that persists is the distinction between what is inside and outside the *civitas*. By a development of which we do not know the exact conditions, the word *hostis* assumed a 'hostile' flavor," *une acception "hostile"*, "and henceforward it is only applied to the 'enemy'" (78/F95). This historical and contingent change, which inexplicably transformed the stranger into an enemy, sedimenting the distinction between inside and outside, by the end of the first volume of Benveniste's study is reinvested with a necessity that lacks explanation, as well. It offers itself, however, as explanation, as enabling comprehension. "This," Benveniste says without quite clarifying what the referent of such shifty shifter is, "this cannot be understood except by starting from the idea that the stranger is of necessity an enemy and correlatively that the enemy is necessarily a stranger. It is always because a man born elsewhere is *a priori* an enemy that a mutual bond is necessary to establish between him and the Ego relations of hospitality, which would be inconceivable within the community itself" (294/F361). The enemy is not within.

The enemy is not the other. The enemy is the brother.[77] Exploring the terms of kinship, Benveniste notes the possibility and impossibility of sibling rivalry, of the brother-enemy. Benveniste distinguishes the brother from the enemy, confining both to the distance of a doubling. The Sanskrit word for "nephew" (son of the brother) also bears the sense of "rival, enemy," something that is "well attested." This proved hard to take, so etymologists suggested that the word might instead mean "cousin" (son of the father's brother), "because it is difficult to imagine the 'nephew' acting as a 'rival', whereas among cousins rivalry is easier to understand. In Arab society, 'cousin' takes on the sense of 'rival', 'enemy'. But the truth is that this notion appears to be alien to the Indo-European world," where even cousins would have "an amicable relation" (209/F260). Besides, this sense of "rival, enemy" is "limited to Sanskrit" (210/F261). Strictly speaking, however, the term "ought to designate only 'the brother's brother', which is nonsense, at least in Indo-European, where all brothers have the same relationship to each other." It is within "the social conditions which seem to have been peculiar only to India, [that] the kinship of cousins was associated with the behavior of rivals" (213/F265). The enemy is not within.

The enemy is not the perpetrator, nor is the enemy always human. Nature often turns out on the list of usual enemies, yet the enemy is never simply natural. The enemy is not primary, but derivative of the infinity of appetites, derivative of the accidents that others are (Hobbes), that they can always be. The enemy is an outgrowth plagued by potentiality, even as the impossible possibility that is the last enemy. All of this makes the enemy quite inhuman—already inhuman, all too inhuman. Particularly mine. No enemy is worse than mine, but I have often been said to be my worst enemy (still, the enemy may bring out the best in us. It is thus often the case that "we feel more ashamed of our faults before our enemies than before our friends."[78] Perhaps this is what Adorno meant when he wrote of "the subject as the subject's foe."[79] Be that as it may, resisting topographical confinements, the enemy is in our walls. "What remains of idealism is that society, the objective determinant of the mind, is as much an epitome of subjects as it is their negation. In society the subjects are unknowable and incapacitated," they become enemies to themselves.[80]

There emerges, at last and at the very least, an enemy within. Hegel had described in detail the process here invoked by Adorno, writing of society, of the community as predicated upon the "interference" it must run. "The community," Hegel writes, "only gets its existence through its interference with the happiness of the family, and by dissolving self-consciousness into the universal."[81] What the community does, then, is to become an enemy, or, as Hegel puts it, to create or engender an internal enemy. Where Adorno sees the subject, though, Hegel sides with womankind.[82] The community, he writes, "creates," *erzeugt*, it produces and reproduces "for itself in what it suppresses and what is at the same time essential to it an internal enemy—womankind in general."[83] In Adorno's terms, womankind—the internal enemy—functions as both "a screen for society's objective functional context *and* a palliative for the subject's suffering under society."[84] At this juncture, then, Hegel blames the victim—he blames the enemy.

He also begins to account for the enemy's guerilla tactics. The enemy, here too, hides and draws away, stealing away into confined spheres and stealing public property, engaging in terrorist activities and sabotage work, bringing home the trophies of its looting. It is here that Hegel introduces an expression that, for essential reasons that are all part of a history of the enemy, has attracted much more critical attention.[85] "Womankind—the everlasting irony of the community—changes by intrigue the universal end of the government into a private end, transforms its universal activity into a work of some particular individual, and perverts the universal property of the state into a possession and ornament of the family."[86] The enemy—whose name is womankind—is a thief. But the community must continue to exist. It must produce and reproduce itself and, in a striking and proto-Foucauldian analysis of the productive aspects of power, of suppression as productive, Hegel writes that the community "can only maintain itself by suppressing this spirit of individualism, and, because it is an essential moment, all the same creates it and, moreover, creates it by its repressive attitude towards it as a hostile principle."[87] Unsurprisingly, perhaps, Hegel's syntax makes it difficult to distinguish fully between poles, positive or negative, between production and reproduction, between reproduction and self-production. The "hostile principle" that is the result of the reproductive powers of the community may thus be the community itself, as much as its enemy. For Hegel, then, the enemy reproduces (itself). Or, perhaps, the enemy is not.

The Enemy Objects

> But in our attempts at understanding this situation we must beware of interpretations which seek to translate it in a two-dimensional fashion as though it were an allegory, and which in so doing forgets its historical stratification. The two-fold presence of the father corresponds to the two chronological meanings of the scene.
> —Sigmund Freud, *Totem and Taboo*

> Being *able* to be an enemy, *being* an enemy—perhaps that presupposes a strong nature.
> —Friedrich Nietzsche, "Why I Am So Wise," *Ecce Homo*

"We are ignorant," Freud writes, "of what an affect is."[88] This ignorance does not disable, but rather displaces discussions of affect. It is, in fact, displacement that carries Freud's discussion of affect, in spite of repeated statements of ignorance, inconclusiveness, and ambivalence. But displacement onto what? Attending to anxiety as "something that is felt," indeed, as an affect, Freud insists that affects must be considered as dynamic configurations, sometimes inscrutable ones, knots of psychic operations that are so complex that they cannot be disentangled or even hierarchized ("Up till now we have arrived at nothing but contradictory views . . . none of which can, to the unprejudiced eye, be given preference over the others. I therefore propose to adopt a different procedure. I propose to assemble, quite impartially, all the facts that we know about anxiety without expecting to arrive at a fresh synthesis," 132). Yet addressing neuroses or phobias as privileged pathways toward an understanding of affects such as anxiety, Freud suggests that a necessary and even productive displacement turns the inquiry toward the object.

Earlier, Freud had identified "one thing alone" as responsible for turning an "emotional reaction" into a neurosis. Freud writes about "Little Hans" that his "emotional reaction," his fear of his father, could have been "entirely comprehensible." What, then, made Hans's emotional reaction into a less than comprehensible neurosis? Freud answers that it "was one thing alone: the replacement of his father by a horse" (103). It is the change of object, its substitution and "displacement," that is constitutive of the neurosis and that enables the (pathological) resolution of a conflict. Freud therefore calls attention to the object—to the enemy object, *feindliche Objekt*, as Lacan writes—which he proceeds to designate as "a substitutive object," as one of the privileged pathways toward an inquiry into the question of affect. Thus, when Lacan says that psychoanalysis has nothing to say about anger, one might consider that this is rigorously precise. Psychoanalysis attends less to anger than to its objects, its substitutive objects ("the totem may be the first form of father-surrogate"), and thereby raises the question of the enemy.[89]

The enemy is not the other. The enemy is the father. In *Totem and Taboo*, Freud breaks the familial, politico-military complex of hostility and associates the "treatment of enemies" (36/G328) with the "taboo upon rulers" (41/G333) and, finally, with the father. Freud revisits once again the argument he had made concerning Little Hans and explains that the enemy is not simply the object, result, or effect of affect, at least not only of a hostile one. Freud writes that "the impulses which [are] expressed towards an enemy are not solely hostile" (39/G330). Barely mentioning the word "enemy," but attending to countless instances of *Feindseligkeit*, hostility, Freud comes perhaps closest to writing a history of the enemy—a history that, Freud shows, is not reducible to a history of enmity or hostility.

At the beginning of this history, Freud locates that most difficult enemy object, the father. Freud seeks to bring to light a covert history, an unconscious "current of hostility," an "opposing current of intense hostility," one that even when manifested is "not admitted as such, but masquerades as a ceremonial" (49). He then goes on to suggest yet another association, one that will further contribute to an understanding of this hostility and to its role in the constitution of the enemy object. Freud offers "the model upon which paranoiacs base their delusions of persecution" as "the relation of the child to his father" (50). The chain of substitution established by the study of taboos thus links a series of objects that are consistently more than, but nonetheless also, enemy objects, objects that belong to distinct discursive spheres that we would recognize as family, politics, religion, and the military. Each of these objects constitutes a displacement as well as an analogy of and a substitution for the father. "When a paranoiac turns the figure of one of his associates into a 'persecutor', he is raising him to the rank of a father " (50/G341). In each of numerous cases of intense hostility,

Freud invokes "emotional ambivalence" and roots this ambivalence in the object, in the particular way in which the father is such a paradigmatic object and thus comes to constitute the first enemy.[90]

Revisiting in "Inhibitions, Symptoms and Anxiety" the "conflict due to ambivalence" of Little Hans, Freud goes on to maintain that the substitutive motion that affects the enemy object can find its origins equally in the child and in the father.[91] In other words, Freud suggests, it may have been the father's fault all along. "So long as the pressure exercised by the primal father could be felt, the hostile feelings toward him were justified, and remorse on their account would have to await a later day."[92] At the beginning, then, was a father who constituted a danger for the child, one who was, perhaps from the very start, an enemy. Yet the father does not—he cannot—remain an enemy for long. Indeed, it is equally the case that, in the beginning and from the beginning, there was substitution. And it is this substitution that not only constitutes neurosis, but that also produces the enemy object, the enemy as substitutive object. Even if it is the father's fault, even if the father constituted an actual clear and present danger, the child's anxiety must still be understood as pathological, and this pathology must still be accounted for ("In view of all that we know about the structure of the comparatively simple neuroses of everyday life, it would seem highly improbable that a neurosis could come into being merely because of the objective presence of danger, without any participation of the deeper level of the mental apparatus").[93] What Lacan would call the *Non du père*, "No of the Father," undoubtedly functions here as an initiation into danger.

Since "the unconscious seems to contain nothing that could give any content to our concept of the annihilation of life," the father intervenes as part of a mechanism that substitutes for that absence. The castration complex amounts to a faint substitution, a pedagogic introduction to the absolute danger that death is. In this introduction, the father, always already a substitute, is, of course, key. "I am therefore inclined to adhere to the view that the fear of death should be regarded as analogous to the fear of castration" (130/G272). Lacan's "No of the Father," a structure that has little to do with the presence of an empirical father, can be seen at work in the "first experience of anxiety which an individual goes through," birth, which is "objectively speaking" a "separation from the mother" that "could be compared to a castration of the mother" (130). Freud insists, however, that this clear and present—if substitutive—danger does not suffice to allow us to understand the pathological reaction of the child, his anxiety.

One must therefore turn to the substitutive chain of enemy objects as it constitutes itself in the mental apparatus of the child.

Such are precisely the terms in which Freud explains Little Hans's neurosis. Substitution, then, made Little Hans's "emotional reaction" into a neurosis. "What made it a neurosis was one thing alone: the replacement of his father by a horse" (103/G248). This replacement is also a "displacement," a kind of substitution that, strictly speaking does not substitute for anything. (Since substitution is here "the only thing" and considered independently from the "actual" figure of the father, a father that cannot be, therefore, the origin of the pathology.) It is a mechanism, *the* mechanism, whereby, once again, a "conflict due to ambivalence" can be if not resolved, then avoided, and the avoidance is what maintains the substitutive chain of enemy objects in motion from the beginning. The conflict, then, "is not dealt with in relation to one and the same person," is not dealt with, that is, in direct relation to the father. Rather, Freud continues, the conflict "is circumvented, as it were, by one of the pairs of conflicting impulses being directed to another person as a substitutive object" (103/G248). Freud then goes on to describe this object as a "father-substitute" (104/G248), one that, we just saw, was so from the very beginning.

The series of double or ambivalent impulses continues to operate "in" the object and to constitute the enemy object as always already double. Hence, if in the first stage of the neurosis the father is considered a (passive) enemy (an object of aggression), he later goes on to become what *Totem and Taboo* had described him as having already been: the (active) enemy (the subject of aggression). Hans's first "instinctual impulse" was, no doubt, "a hostile one against the father," yet that hostile impulse is repressed and attributed, by way of yet another substitution, to the father himself. "Instead of aggressiveness on the part of the subject towards his father, there appeared aggressiveness (in the shape of revenge) on the part of his father towards the subject."[94] Thus the father becomes what he already is: the enemy.[95]

Freud later reiterates that through "isolation" (which we have considered earlier), the substitutive object enables the avoidance of a conflict due to ambivalence. It is this avoidance of conflict that produces anxiety. "Symptoms," writes Freud, "are created so as to avoid a *danger-situation*" (129), and there is, as we have seen, danger. "For the anxiety belonging to a phobia is conditional; it only emerges when the object of it is perceived—*and rightly so since it is only then that the danger-situation is pres-*

ent" (125). The father is thus repeatedly acknowledged by Freud to be a dangerous enemy. This is why the protective mechanism of substitution becomes operative. Having produced a "father-substitute," the subject goes on to choose another enemy-object—no longer, and yet still, the father—which becomes *the* enemy. "There is no need to be afraid of being castrated by a father who is not there," Freud explains, repeating the claim he made in *Totem and Taboo*. The absent father is, of course, no less powerful, for "on the other hand, one cannot get rid of a father; he can appear whenever he chooses" (125–26). This is the well-known argument we have already rehearsed, one in which the totem constitutes yet another link in the chain of enemy-object substitutions. "If he [i.e., the father] is replaced by an animal, all one has to do is to avoid the sight of it—that is, its presence—in order to be free from danger and anxiety" (127). And thus the enemy draws away.[96]

The nosology that Freud ultimately develops always involves substitutions and topographical articulations and disappearing acts. Distinct defense mechanisms are put in place that constitute and deconstitute the enemy object in complex ways along shifting lines of interiority and exteriority, the enemy within and the enemy without. "In phobia of animals the danger seems to be still felt entirely as an external one, just as it has undergone an external displacement in the symptom. In obsessional neuroses the danger is much more internalized." (145). Freud designates these two spheres of enmity as "social" versus "moral." "That portion of anxiety in regard to the super-ego which constitutes *social* anxiety still represents an internal substitute for an external danger, while the other portion—*moral* anxiety—is already completely endo-psychic" (145–46). Based on the material we have been exploring, it might become possible to argue for a translation of Freud's terms ("social," "moral") into "political" and "theological." The rest of this book will continue to substantiate this argument.

Appendix 1. Rosenzweig's War

> Thus the Nay finds its opponent directly in front of itself here. But the metaphor of a pair of wrestlers is misleading. There is no pair. This is a wrestling match not of two parties but of one: the Nought negates itself. It is only in self-negation that the "other," the "opponent," bursts forth out of it.
> —Franz Rosenzweig, *The Star of Redemption*
>
> It is not by coincidence that revelation, once it started on its way into the world, took the road to the West, not to the East.
> —Franz Rosenzweig, *The Star of Redemption*

The Star of Redemption, writes Nahum Glazer, is "the most curious of 'war books.' A militant book it is, especially in its first parts, and confident of victory in its final passages. The enemy it attacks is the philosophy of German idealism, the home it defends is the individual."[1] Like love, which in the *Star* declares war on death ("ihm sagt die Liebe Kampf an"), Rosenzweig's war book is thus itself a declaration of war.[2] The link between the conditions in which the book was written (World War I, the Macedonia trenches) and its status as a declaration of war would thus already suffice to require that one attend to what Rosenzweig had to say about war. I am not speaking of his martial rhetoric—although, as Jacques Derrida suggests, the military may be constitutive of the entire body of knowledge upon which the *Star* rests ("Nothing that is military is foreign to knowledge, to the matheme and to mathematics").[3] Rather, the question concerns Rosenzweig's conception of war, and within it, more importantly, perhaps, the question of the enemy.

I say "more importantly" because consistently underlying Rosenzweig's discussion of war, one finds a preoccupation with the love of neighbor and thus—following Jesus' famous dictum—the love of the enemy. To the extent that one can read in the *Star* a theory of war—and Rosenzweig claimed precisely that—the question I want to ask here is a simple one: What is the theologico-political dimension within which war inscribes itself? Otherwise put, given the articulation of religion and history, theology and politics, such as they govern the *Star*, does a consideration of war affect a reading of the book, and if so, how? Does it add anything to an understanding—if understanding there can be—of the question of the enemy? What kind of a question is the enemy?

Clearly, the question of war touches on key moments of Rosenzweig's thought, as well as on crucial distinctions that are made and unmade throughout *The Star of Redemption*. To put it briefly for now, war—that is to say, history—and the love of neighbor are predicated on the same condition of possibility, the necessary distinction between self and other.[4] Yet to maintain this distinction—to abide by the commandment to love one's neighbor—undoes another crucial distinction, that between religion and politics. More precisely, for Rosenzweig, because they love their neighbors, Christians cannot distinguish between religious and political wars. On the other hand, because they in turn abolish the distinction between self and other, because they love the neighbor without mediation (*unmittelbar*), Jews stand outside of the "warring temporality" that is history. Jews, in other words, know nothing of war.

Yet there is another crucial moment to this theologico-political configuration within which war inscribes itself, one that is less contingent than the very limited conversation on it has, so far, allowed. I am referring to Rosenzweig's discussion of Islam.[5] Indeed, considered in the light of war, and as the first example in the *Star* of a holy war, *Glaubenskrieg*, we will see that Islam is situated at the opposite pole from Judaism—that ahistorical and apolitical marker. Failing in its religious dimension, failing as a religion, Islam is paradoxically an essential—if essentially negative and vanishing—moment in the political theology that is *The Star of Redemption*. Islam is war, "pure political" war.

Messianic Politics

The Jewish people, writes Franz Rosenzweig, knows no difference between self and other. It knows no distinction between inside and outside, between the love of self and the love of neighbor. In this matter, the Jewish people knows or feels, as the English translation has it, "no conflict": "the Jewish people feels no conflict between what is its very own and what is supreme; the love it has for itself inevitably becomes love for its neighbor" (329/G365). The Jewish people is thus situated beyond all distinctions (between self and other, nation and world, "home and faith, earth and heaven"). For it, for the Jews, between man and world (as well as between man and God) there is no medium or mediation. It is *unmittelbar*. Better yet, because none of these terms constitutes a means, *Mittel*, toward an end for them, the Jews live in the blissful ignorance of war. Eerily echoing a distorted representation of a vanishing history, Rosenzweig insists, therefore, that the Jewish people "knows nothing of war" (329/G366).

What Rosenzweig calls "messianic politics"—that is, a theory of war—would establish a link, possibly a causal link, between the love of neighbor and war, between the love of neighbor and the world.[6] The demonstration still awaits us for this equation of war with the world, but for now we may stay with the link that the neighbor—the love of neighbor—articulates between man and world. Rosenzweig states it in an earlier section called "the neighbor" (234/G261). "The bond of the consummate and redemptive bonding of man and the world is to begin with the neighbor and ever more only the neighbor, the well-nigh nighest" (235/G262). The relation to the world is thus first of all a relation to the neighbor—it is mediated through the neighbor. Hence, because the Jewish people makes no distinction between self and other, between love of self and love of neighbor, because it experiences or feels no conflict, no distance or mediation between these terms, it knows no war.

This way of the Jewish people in loving the neighbor thus abolishes a crucial distinction—between self and other—that Rosenzweig otherwise insists on reinscribing by emphasizing the "like" in "love thy neighbor like thyself" ("Man is to love his neighbor like himself. Like himself. Your neighbor is 'like thee,'" 239/G267). The neighbor may be another self, according to Rosenzweig, but the neighbor is not you. He is "'Like you' and thus not 'you'" (240/G267). Clearly asserting that the neighbor is like the self, but not identical with it, the commandment to love one's neighbor aims therefore to maintain the distinction between self and other. Through it, "precisely here in the commandment to love one's neighbor," the other's "self is definitely confirmed in its place" (239/G267).[7]

The imperative is therefore to preserve, in the rapport of man and world, the relation between self and neighbor, precisely that distinction (*Unterscheidung*) between the two that the Jewish people abolishes or experiences as having been abolished. To return to the passage with which we began: For the Jewish people, the rapport with the neighbor is immediate and unmediated (*unmittelbar*) and thus seems to follow a logic whereby oppositions (between nation and world, between home and faith, earth and heaven) have become irrelevant. The Jewish people is thus different from other peoples because it does not maintain the distinction they do, the difference between self and other. Yet whereas the Jews abolish the difference between self and other, the love of neighbor makes another distinction irrelevant. It demands the irrelevance of the distinction between one neighbor and the next: "every neighbor who occurs to [man] must be 'any' thing, the representative of any other, of all others. He may neither ask nor discriminate: it is its neighbor" (240/G267).[8]

> Such were the circumstances under which Jesus came to establish a spiritual kingdom on earth. In separating the theological system from the political system, this made the state to cease being united and caused internal divisions that never ceased to agitate Christian peoples.
> —Jean-Jacques Rousseau, *On the Social Contract*

Christianity is the embodiment of, is quite precisely true to, this lack of discrimination (*Unterscheidung*) between one neighbor and the next. For it, there are no boundaries, no limits, and there is neither Jew nor Greek, neither close nor far. This is why Christianity cannot maintain a basic distinction that the Jews used to make between distant peoples and those who are geographically closer. Biblical Judaism had upheld the distinction between "a very distant people" and the seven nations of Canaan, whereas "the peoples of the Christian Era can no longer maintain this distinction" (331/G367). This new state of affairs relates directly to war and makes explicit the rapport of the love of neighbor with war. Indeed, if the neighbor is the site of the self's relation to the world, then that rapport must affect as well the self's attitude toward war.

Leaving aside the nature of biblical Judaism in its rapport with war and with the neighbor, it remains important to consider that the lack of consideration between distant and close, the lack of discrimination between neighbors that is ordained by the love of neighbor, is at work in its truest form in Christianity. The Christian love of neighbor, Rosenzweig seems to say, abolishes the distinction between one neighbor and the next. By not discriminating between neighbors—as they must not—Christian peoples also abolish the distinction between holy war and political war:

In keeping with the spirit of Christianity, which admits of no boundaries, there are for it no "very distant" peoples. Holy war and political war, which in Jewish law were constitutionally distinguished, are here blended into one. Precisely because they are not really God's people, because they are still in process of so becoming, therefore they cannot draw this fine distinction; they simply cannot know how far a war is holy war, and how far merely a secular war. (331/G367)

While the Jewish people knows no war because, for the Jewish people, for God's people, the distinction between self and other has been abolished, and while Christendom maintains that distinction, what the Christian peoples cannot maintain, what they have abolished, is the distinction *between* others, the difference between one neighbor and the next, and therefore the difference between God and world. This is, of course, familiar territory which, Amos Funkenstein suggested, constitutes the *Urformell*, the originary formula of the *Star*: "zum Vater kommen—beim Vater sein"— one people is on its way to God, the other is with God.[9]

Unsurprisingly, this basic historical distinction affects everything, including war. Christianity cannot know whether a war is theological or political. The distinction, for it, is undecidable ("they cannot know at all"). For Judaism, on the other hand, all wars are political. "Whatever wars [the Jewish people] experiences are purely political wars" (331/G368). Being God's people, the Jewish people may experience war, yet it does not know war. Upon this peculiar *Fronterlebnis* hangs the value of Rosenzweig's empirical diagnostic of the Jewish people in its relation to war. But be that relation as it may, the argument is well known and unequivocal. The Jewish people remains "bound to be outside the world." Living in a state of eternal peace, radically undisturbed by its experience of wars that are only and always political, the Jewish people is "outside of time agitated by wars," *steht es außerhalb einer kriegerischen Zeitlichkeit* (332/G368). It stands outside of warring temporality.

In the wartime that is history, in warring temporality, where the Jewish people no longer stands, but where Christianity walks, discriminations between neighbors, between one neighbor and the next, are no longer operative, should no longer be so. As a result, one can no longer tell whether war is theological or political. One is caught within a temporality that is both theological and political. One is caught within the love of neighbor that makes no distinction between one neighbor and the next, that demands there be no difference between one neighbor and the next. One is caught within Christendom. This is the temporality that put an end to the pagan world. Christian love establishes a new bond between man and man, between man and neighbor. It asserts and affirms a politics of indifference. It is not that the church abolishes differences, therefore. Rather, it maintains them as irrelevant. It leaves "everyone as it finds him, man as man, woman as woman, the aged old, the youths young, the master as master, the slave as slave, the wealthy rich, the paupers poor, the sage wise and the fool foolish, the Roman a Roman and the barbarian a barbarian" (344/G382).[10] Just as the love of neighbor did not abolish distinctions, but made them irrelevant, the bond of the church "must not place anyone in the status of another" while bridging the chasm between them. This is the love of neighbor as brotherly love. Love makes everyone—everyone—into a brother, maintaining the "separating space" as it traverses it, affirming the differences as it abolishes their relevance. The Pauline echoes are unmistakable. "It is left for love only to traverse the separating space. And thus it traverses in its flight the hostility of nations as well as the cruelty of gender, the jealousy of class as well as the barrier of age. Thus it permits all the hostile, cruel, jealous, limited ones to catch sight of each other as brothers in one and the same central moment of time" (346/G384). This time, it is now clear, is wartime. Here, the temporality of Christian love becomes wartime. But how is it that by disregarding the prime directive to distinguish between self and other the Jewish people manages to pull out of the war of the worlds, whereas, true to the call for an indiscriminating love of neighbor, Christianity comes to lose itself in a constant theologico-political war, indeed, a war of the theologico-political? Rosenzweig may have alluded to an answer—or at least its rudiments—when referring to the "tyrants of the kingdom of heaven" who "would like to adduce to kingdom of heaven forcibly." Rosenzweig does grant that theirs is an "act of love," *die Liebestat*, yet it is one that is unwittingly transformed into a "purposive act," *Zwecktat* (271/G302). Here, then, rather than love of neighbor as love of the proximate, as love of every proximate, one wrongly seeks to extend love to the "next-but-one," that is to say, to the next next, the next and less proximate, the more (or less) than neighbor, *der Übernächste*. Violence ensues, and love breeds vengeance, paradoxically fostering and delaying the advance of another war front.

This is the unfortunate aspect of love for the next-but-one: although it effects an authentic act of love, it nevertheless comes to nought in the attained goal just like the purposive act. The violence of its claim wreaks revenge on it itself. The fanatic, the sectarian, in short all the tyrants of the kingdom of heaven, far from hastening the advent of the kingdom, only delay it. They leave their nighest unloved, and long for the next-but-one and thereby exclude themselves from the host of those who advance along a broad front, covering the face of the earth bit by bit, each of them conquering, occupying, inspiring his nighest. (271/G302)

Insofar as Rosenzweig never refers to love of the enemy, it may be equally difficult to affirm or to deny that an echo of the peculiar "hastening of the Kingdom," that is the love of the enemy operates here. Is not Christianity one of those sects that seek to bring the kingdom of God by extending love, the love of neighbor, to the less than neighbor? But more than to Christendom and its rapport with the neighbor and with the enemy, we will have to attend to this conversion of the act of love into a purposive act, the violent attempt to bring about God's kingdom upon the earth by extending the love of neighbor to the next neighbor, an act of love *manqué* that inevitably clashes with the conquest and occupation of the land, this "advance along a broad front" that covers "the face of the earth bit by bit," "conquering, occupying" (and yes, even inspiring the neighbor. But toward what?), that is the true and truly religious act of love.

In Rosenzweig's theological and historical configuration, "Jew and Christian assure us" of the divine origin of an act of love out of which "the soul is declared of age, departs the paternal home of divine love, and sets forth into the world." Under the joint assurance of Jew and Christian, the commandment to "love thy neighbor" is "the embodiment of all commandments" (205/G229). In this political theology, the Jewish people is marked as the theological pole, the theological goal of a Christian "way," marked by its undecidable oscillation. In the warring temporality that is Christendom's, between the theological and the political, which it cannot tell apart, war—war "itself," one could say, but more precisely, nonreligious, "purely political" war—seems to have disappeared. If it is true that "the Jewish people has left its holy war behind" (331/G368), and Christianity knows war as theologico-political (that is to say, as undecidably political or theological, political and theological), an account of messianic politics would still have to account for the persistence of an act of war that is no act of love, an act of love turned purposive act, an act of political war: "whatever war [the Jewish people] experiences are purely political."

"That Remarkable Case of Plagiarism"

> The Lord's saint must anticipate the judgment of God; he must recognize his enemies as the enemies of God.
> —Franz Rosenzweig, *The Star of Redemption*

If the essential link that Rosenzweig makes between war and the love of neighbor is consistent with his understanding of history as the history of war, it becomes only apparently surprising that "he tried to deny his war experience [had] any impact at all on his thinking."[11] Indeed, Rosenzweig is being quite consistent if arguing that the impact of war could not be felt on the Jewish people, who remained, we recall, outside of warring temporality. World War I could be experienced only as a political war, and it thus remained distant, outside of the theological realm within which the Jewish people stands. Such war could not be known, would not have to be known, and could thus not make any impact on a Jewish philosopher (assuming, for now, that Rosenzweig would have abided by such description).

So much for political war, then. But what of holy war? We know that nothing could be further from the experience of the Jewish people, who left holy war behind. Furthermore, the very distance between the Jewish people and holy war is structurally related to the lack of distance, the lack of mediation, that it experiences between self and other in its love of the neighbor. Similarly, though quite distinctively, the structural relation between war and love of the neighbor is at work for Christendom, which maintains the distance between self and neighbor. Hence, for Christendom, war is undecidably theological and/or political. Again, then, the question emerges: What of holy war?

It hardly seems accidental that the first mention of holy war, *Glaubenskrieg*, in *The Star of Redemption* is made in reference to an entity that receives comparatively little coverage in the book: "that remarkable case of plagiarism" that is Islam. Indeed, consistent with the structural links between war and love of neighbor I have been describing, it is in the context of distancing Islam from love that Rosenzweig introduces, for the first time, the notion of holy war. Rosenzweig does so, before moving on to discuss the neighbor, in a section called "Love in the World." Once again—for by now, Islam is already a recurring example—Rosenzweig invokes Islam as an example, or, more precisely, as a counterexample of the act of love, as instead an act of love that, once again, turns into a purposive act.[12]

If the act [of love] were the product of a given volitional orientation on the basis of which it were now, sure of its goal, to diffuse freely into the limitless material of reality; if, in short, it were to emerge as infinite affirmation, then it would not be an act of love, but a purposive act. It would no longer emerge, fresh as the moment, from the volitional orientation of character. Rather, its relationship to its origin in this orientation would be one of subservience, conclusive and concluded once and for all. In other words: it would be, not the act of love of belief, but—the way of Allah. (215/G240)

Here, Rosenzweig continues, is something that distinguishes Islam from love, for Islam is not on the way to, but rather in the way of love. Unable to achieve any more than a purposive act (which, we have seen, "comes to nought" and brings down with it "the fanatic, the sectarian, in short all the tyrants of the kingdom of heaven" who "leave their nighest unloved"), Islam is on a way of subservience, and this, "more than its content," predictably "distinguishes it from the love of neighbor" (216/G240). To walk in the way of Allah is thus not to love the neighbor—it is not to love at all. Rather, "walking in the way of Allah means, in the strictest sense, the spread of Islam by means of the holy war" (215/G240).

If Judaism knows nothing of war—loving the self and, unmediated, the neighbor, and thus experiencing only political war—Islam knows nothing of love, and thus spreads nothing but holy war. This, then, is Rosenzweig's political theology. At the theological pole, Judaism experiences only political war. At the political pole, Islam spreads only holy war. And in between lies Christendom, undecidably theologico-political. This is because Islam fails to secure any theological status. In what is much more than the expression of a contingent prejudice, Rosenzweig claims that Islam may be theologically oriented, but knows nothing of religion: "Islam has neither creation nor revelation, although it struts about, full of pomp and dignity with both of them as it found them" (117/G130). The power of its God is therefore "like that of an Oriental despot" (ibid.). In its world, in the world of Islam, "God's love was, after all, not actual love here either. . . . Thus Islam knows of a loving God as little as of a beloved soul" (172/G192–93). Because Islam knows nothing of religion, it knows nothing of faith: "This serenity of the soul, in a faithfulness born of the night of defiance, is the great secret of belief. And again Islam proves to be outward acceptance of these concepts without inner comprehension. Again it has made them entirely its own—but for the inner conversion. And again, therefore, it does not have them at all" (171/G191). To the extent that Islam does not know or understand faith, to the extent that it does not even have faith, Rosenzweig will oppose Islam to belief itself ("For belief, on the other hand . . .") and claim that Islam's confession (*Bekenntnis*) is thus no confession at all. It says nothing about faith (*Glaube*): "Islam's confession that 'God is God' is not a confession of belief but a confession of disbelief," *ein Unglaubensbekenntnis* (181/G202). Given this failure of the theological and this failure of love, on Islam's part, Islam's act of love cannot be anything but a purposive act, an act of war and an act of holy war (*Glaubenskrieg*) without faith (*Glaube*).

When he comes to take "one last comparative look at Islam" (225/G251), Rosenzweig thus goes on to distinguish Islam further from the other terms of his theologico-political configuration. He makes Islam incommensurable. Rosenzweig argues that Islam "simply cannot be compared" (226/G252). Islam itself perpetuates the incomparable, the isolation of each historical period. Islam is thus a figure for history itself, for the modern interest in history—in what is perhaps the worst sense of the word for Rosenzweig, who once cried out "Ich bin kein Historiker!"—"I am no historian!"[13] "Thus it is that the soil of Islam nourished the first real historical interest since antiquity, a really and truly scientific interest in the modern sense, without any ulterior 'philosophy of history'" (225/G251).

Most modern and most historical—most purely political—Islam returns only once in *The Star*, and it returns as the enemy of the church. "True," Rosenzweig writes, reviving the medieval equation of "Muslim" with "pagan," "the Church of Rome had been able to penetrate the physical world of the living peoples and to assert itself in successful counterattack against the aggressive paganism of the Crescent" (280/G311).[14] Here, Rosenzweig adds, the church "really created a new world of its own." In that world, we recall, Christendom is incapable of deciding whether the war it conducts is a religious war or a secular one. In the new world thus created, from the joint perspective of Judaism (which experiences only political wars) and Christendom (which cannot tell the difference), Islam is at war, Islam is war, pure political war. This is why Islam has nothing to do with love and with the love of neighbor. Not Islam, therefore, but only Judaism and Christianity assure us of the importance of the commandment to love the neighbor. The passage bears quoting again at greater length: "Love thy neighbor. This is, as Jew and Christian assure us, the embodiment of all commandments. With this commandment, the soul is declared of age, departs the paternal home of divine love, and sets forth into the world" (205/G229). In this narrative, it is not the Spirit of the World that marches on, whom Hegel famously encountered. Yet the soul of which Rosenzweig speaks does march on, "sie wandert hinaus in die Welt," and its figures, both figures of humanity, *Gestalt der Menschheit*, as Rosenzweig calls them, are the Jew and the Christian (395–96/G440–41). We know then that this double figure is a split soul, but it is a loving soul, a Judeo-Christian, theologico-political soul, that has, indeed, taken its last look, its last comparative look, at Islam. This, then, is Rosenzweig's political theology.

In Jewish man, man was one, and a living one at that, for all his contradictions, for all the ineradicable conflicts between his love by God and his love for God, between his Judaism and his humanism, between patriarch and messiah. But in Christianity, this man separates into two figures, not necessarily two mutually exclusive and antagonistic figures, but two figures going their separate ways, separate even when they meet in a single person as is always possible. And these separate ways again lead through all that broad country of humanity in whose districts form and freedom appear to be in perpetual conflict. (351/G389)

No one, perhaps, has gone as explicitly far as Rosenzweig in extirpating, ultimately eradicating, Islam from the figure of humanity, that is to say, from the theologico-political, from the religious and historical world configuration that is constituted by Judaism and Christianity ("Before God, then, Jew and Christian both labor at the same task. He cannot dispense with either. He has set enmity between the two for all times, and withal has most intimately bound each to each," 415/G462).

What I have sought to demonstrate is that the status of this exclusion, as it occurs in *The Star of Redemption*, is anything but contingent. Rather, it constitutes Rosenzweig's political theology, the theologico-political configuration that links three, rather than two entities commonly referred to as "religions." This term, "religion," means of course very little to Rosenzweig, who recasts each "element" (God, world, and man) as privileged in its relation to one of the three "religions." Judaism is with God, Christianity is man on its way to God, Islam is the war of the world. Judaism is theological, and it therefore experiences war as political. Christianity is the embodiment of the theologico-political, unable to know the difference when it comes to war. Islam, finally, is fully detheologized and can therefore spread nothing but holy war. Constituting history as a "warring temporality," as a war that is a political war—the history of nations at war, the history of nations as war—Rosenzweig casts Islam as at once the most obvious and the most hidden figure of the world as political. He casts Islam as the most extreme opposite, the most distant figure in its relation to Judaism, in relation to the theological space that Judaism occupies. Rosenzweig casts Islam as the political enemy.

It was the distinguished Orientalist and historian of philosophy Shlomo Pines who, uniquely attentive to Rosenzweig's treatment of Islam, claimed that the key to this treatment resided in Rosenzweig's disagreement with Hegel. "On this issue," that is, on the issue of Islam, Pines writes, "Rosenzweig was confronted with a problem: For Hegel, both Islam and Judaism belonged to the same kind of religions. Rosenzweig's task therefore, as he saw it according to many indications, was to separate the two by way of an essential distinction."[15] Hegel did, to an extent (and we will return to this), collapse the distinction between Judaism and Islam. More precisely, perhaps, Hegel made and unmade the distinction between Judaism and Islam, articulating it in terms of religion and politics, by confining them—as religions of the Sublime—to a realm that was fundamentally outside of politics. As Pines shows, Rosenzweig had no disagreement with Hegel on his characterization of Islam as such a religion, a "fanatic" religion, as Hegel had it. Yet Rosenzweig went even further than Hegel in isolating the specificity of Islam, and more importantly, in infinitely widening the gap that separates it from Judaism. For Rosenzweig, Islam is, strictly speaking, neither religion, as we have seen, nor politics. It is incapable of love, incapable of relating to the neighbor and to the world as Judaism and Christianity do: "the bond of the consummate and redemptive bonding of man and the world is to begin with the neighbor and ever more only with the neighbor, the well-nigh nighest" (234/G262).[16]

Islam, one could say, cannot relate to the world because it is the world. As Rosenzweig had put it in *Hegel und der Staat*, "a relation, as close and necessary as it may be, always rests on an external presupposition, namely, its very own terms."[17] Moreover, Islam's very existence—that is to say its theologico-political existence—may be as much in doubt as its "own" conception of being (Islam's concept of "Being is accordingly not being-there, not something universal, and yet only momentary and thus as a whole daily in need of renewal," 122/G135). It remains separated from what defines it, to which it is related—in this case, the faith of *Glaubenskrieg*. It was thus Rosenzweig's peculiar contribution to draw Islam out entirely, to reinscribe a long Christian history whereby the gap between religion and politics would be so explicitly widened, a Christian history whereby Judaism's most distant opposite would be Islam.[18] What Rosenzweig makes explicit is the structure of the theologico-political as constitutively Abrahamic. By enacting the exclusion of Islam, by making visible the becoming of the theologico-political as the Judeo-Christian, Rosenzweig made Islam into the invisible enemy. He also made Islam the political enemy. With the *Star*, with what can be seen as a certain culmination of its history, the enemy draws away, and with him, the Jew, the Arab.

PART II

4

The Enemy's Two Bodies (Political Theology Too)

> This *analogy* is the very site of the theologico-political, the hyphen or trans-
> lation between the theological and the political. It is also what underwrites
> political sovereignty, the Christian incarnation of the body of God (or
> Christ) in the king's body, the king's two bodies.
> —Jacques Derrida, "What is a Relevant Translation"

> Yesterday we dined with a Traveler—We were talking about [the actor Ed-
> mund] Kean—He said he had seen him at Glasgow "in Othello in the Jew,
> I mean er, er, er, the Jew in Shylock" He got bother'd completely in vague
> ideas of the Jew in Othello, Shylock in the Jew, Shylock in Othello, Othello
> in Shylock, the Jew in Othello, &c &c &c he left himself in a mess at last.
> —John Keats to Thomas Keats, July 1818, *The Letters of John Keats*

"The body is with the king, but the king is not with the body. The
king is a thing—"[1] Hamlet's cryptic statement, which has baffled centuries
of readers, began to make sense only in the light of medieval political theology.[2] At the center of this doctrine, famously brought to light by Ernst
Kantorowicz, there lies, therefore, a body. More precisely, two bodies lie
there, the king's two bodies, along with the possibility of their violent separation.[3] Political theology, the doctrine of a complex relationship—one
might say, the community—of sacred and social, divine and human, and
of religion and politics, comes together and falls apart under the figure of
those two bodies that are one, the two bodies in one king, the two bodies
as one thing: "The king is a thing."

The striking story of this coming together and falling apart is the
narrative, the tragic narrative, of *Richard II*, a narrative in which, Kantorowicz writes, Richard "'undoes his kingship' and releases his body politic

into thin air" (35). "Bit by bit," Kantorowicz continues, Richard "deprives his body politic of the symbols of its dignity and exposes his poor body natural to the eyes of the spectators" (36). Political theology, the theory of the king's two bodies, comes together insofar as the king's body politic, "god-like or angel-like," (27) remains attached to the king's body natural. Shakespeare's play, at the same time as it provides Kantorowicz with a priv-ileged example of political theology, a privileged example of the unity of the theologico-political, also constitutes a staging of the undoing of this unity, "that most unpleasant idea of a violent separation of the King's Two Bodies" (41).

"Political Shakespeare"[4] here, however, primarily refers to a notion of community where unity and association—the figure that Kantorowicz em-phasizes is the "symbol" (17)—provide the focal point of the narrative, a unity of the "body natural" with "the body politic," a unity of the sover-eign with the transcendent source of his authority, a unity of the commu-nity with its sovereign, and finally, a unity of the secular with the spiritual. In what follows, I want to pursue the work that has been done on political theology in Shakespeare and ask about the coming together and falling apart of another community, that of Arab and Jew. To be textually more precise, I want to ask about the community and "fellowship" (as Marlowe's Barabas suggests to Ithamore), of those two Venetian bodies who, not quite *of* the community, are nonetheless "situated in a potentially threat-ening position very near the 'inside' of authority and power." These two Venetian strangers and Venetian enemies are, then, the Moor and the Jew.[5]

> Why this is something! Make account of me
> As of thy fellow; we are villains both:
> Both circumcisèd, we hate Christians both.
> Be true and secret, thou shalt want no gold.[6]

There is to this day no comparative study, no extended association by way of literary analysis, of the two plays once best known as *The Merchant of Venice* and *The Moor of Venice*, an absence that has failed to be noticed even by the very few who do engage the comparison.[7] This state of affairs could hardly be considered arbitrary, for the divide between the two plays can be justified, affirmed, and confirmed by way of varied and convincing terms. Such terms extend from comedy versus tragedy, religion versus race, and theology versus politics all the way to law versus love, ancient versus modern, Jew versus Moor, and more.[8] In the context of political theology, moreover, it is striking that *The Merchant of Venice* presents us with multiple examples of successfully negotiated friendships and love affairs, whereas *The Moor of Venice* is filled with betrayal and the falling apart of social relations: "all the bonds that link humanity and make living together possible have been dissolved by Iago," writes Alan Bloom,[9] and the same may be said concerning audience response. As Stephen Greenblatt points out, the tragedy of *Othello* "heightens audience anxiety" and thus performs the painful state of dissociation, the harsh separation between the stage and an audience who is unable "to intervene and stop the murderous chain of lies and misunderstandings." In contrast, a "sardonic detachment" is impossible to maintain in the case of *The Merchant of Venice*, where "the audience's pleasure depends upon a sympathetic engagement with the characters' situation."[10] It should not be entirely surprising, therefore, that *The Moor of Venice* is predominantly considered a nonpolitical play.[11] Stanley Cavell, for example, claims that there is no longer "any argument . . . with the description [that], compared with the cases of Shakespeare's other tragedies, . . . this one [i.e., *Othello*] is not political but domestic."[12]

In a different perspective, one will find confirmation of the divide between the two plays in that *The Moor of Venice* is located within the sphere of politics, even if, as Tom Cohen points out in an illuminating essay, he has a negative connection to political power, even if "the Moor never represented a sovereign subject to begin with."[13] It is thus "more insistently time-bound, concerned with the here and now rather than with eternal verities," whereas *The Merchant of Venice* clearly stages a struggle over metaphysical truths.[14] Laurence Danson confirms this line of thought by arguing that a "concern with the idea of kingship" may be relevant for a number of Shakespeare's plays, "but it is virtually irrelevant to a consideration of *Othello*. And similarly with this matter of Christian doctrine: In *The Merchant of Venice* the relationship of justice to mercy, and the theological vocabulary the theme entails is strikingly prominent."[15]

It would thus be futile to argue that the division of the two plays, the absence of any extended comparative study, is "wrong." Indeed, what one could call the incomparability, even the incommensurability of the two plays is, to my mind, crucial. For if, as has been argued,[16] the association and dissociation of theology and politics is at work within each of the two plays, the narrative that is produced by their separation, its staging in two thoroughly distinct plays, becomes highly relevant. And if it is indeed the case that each play stages in its own fashion a certain political theology, then the distance between the two plays, each of which ostensibly sounds one of the two notions—politics and theology—as its "major" note, this distance, this separation of theology from politics, comes to the fore as worthy of being read.

Prefiguring the image of Hobbes's Leviathan and testifying to the development of a notion of corporation and incorporation, of the body as a model of community, the theory of the two bodies that articulates itself in *Richard II* found one of its sources in the transfer of Paul's theology to political thought. In Ephesians 5, (Pseudo-)Paul was thus thought to have already provided the ground for a political theology: "For the husband is the head of the wife just as Christ is the head of the Church, the body of which he is the savior" (5:23).

The hermeneutic transfer of this verse from the church to the state, to the political sphere "proper" in the hands of medieval jurists, produced a new definition of "the relations between Prince and state" on the basis of a powerful analogy that led, for example, to basing the staging of coronations on the model of marriage ceremonies. In this way, the classical spirit-body distinction was refigured, by way of the husband-wife analogy, into a theologico-political notion. Hence, if it was said that "the man is the head of the wife and the wife the body of the man," a jurist could infer that "after the same fashion, the Prince is the head of the realm, and the realm the body of the Prince."[17] Love and matrimony thus provide the analogical basis for thinking the body politic that is "at one and the same time a plural entity consisting of all . . . subjects and a single entity, the King."[18] This "bodily thought" considers that rather than instituting the opposition of body to spirit, the body politic is at once both the relationship between the sovereign and the community and the community itself.

Elaborating on Kantorowicz's research, Albert Rolls can therefore suggest that the relationship of Desdemona to Othello ("she shunned/The wealthy, curled darlings of our nations," *O*, 1.2.67–68) constitutes an important moment toward an understanding of Shakespeare's political theology.[19] Like other Moors in Shakespeare, such as Aaron and Morocco, Othello can no doubt claim a political and military status: "I fetch my life and being/From men of royal siege" (1.2.21–22), "My parts, my title, and my perfect soul/Shall manifest me rightly" (1.2.31–32), a status that, as Iago points out, the state itself is temporarily eager to approve ("the state . . . cannot with safety cast him," 1.1.145–47). This politico-military configuration explicitly includes Desdemona (even if perhaps inappropriately, or not seriously), whom both Othello and Iago figure as a "fair warrior" (2.1.180) or as "the general." (2.3.310).

A well-recognized storyteller and rhetorician, if also a troubled reader, Othello ultimately "writes" a story that proves to be a matter of state, worthy of being reported to the state ("and to the state/This heavy act with heavy heart relate," 5.2.368–69).[20] Othello is thus undoubtedly a statesman bound to the community and the city of Venice, and yet his statesmanship can be questioned if the foremost and exemplary member of this community is "abused, stolen from me and corrupted/By spells and medicines bought of mountebanks," as Brabantio charges (*O*, 1.3.61–62), rather than bound to him by love, as would fit the head and the body.[21] Othello himself associates Desdemona with Venice and may even be suggesting that he is married to the city itself when he tells Desdemona: "I took you for that cunning whore of Venice/That married with Othello" (4.2.91–92).[22] Arguing for the political meaning of the "character of the relationship between Desdemona and Othello,"[23] Allan Bloom pursues Brabantio's questioning and relates this strange unity, "the strange love that united Othello and Desdemona," to Othello's failed statesmanship (38). Bloom concludes by rhetorically performing the analogical gesture that transfers love to politics, and, more precisely, love to bad politics: "What was supposed to be love now turns into a tyranny" (56).[24]

> This is Venice: My house is not a grange.
> —*Othello* 1.1.103–4

At this moment in the history of the theologico-political, there is little doubt that association (or love) strikes the dominant and preferred if at times also tragic note. It constitutes the political imperative and normative ideal that governs the community, as well as the relation of theology to politics. To revisit the question of Shakespeare's political theology is therefore to pursue the bodies of two lovers, two bodies as—and in relation to—the body politic, insofar as they are linked. But it is also to pursue the relation—of love and enmity, of association and dissociation, of coming together and falling apart—that operates between them in Shakespeare's writing. It is to pursue a community in its making and unmaking.[25]

The term "political theology" is itself the site of a dissociation, one

in Kantorowicz's own book. There is no doubt that Kantorow-
\ware of the complex history of this notion, a history that goes
_ᴄ at least to Varro, whom Augustine quoted in *The City of God*.[26] Yet
Kantorowicz abstains from referring to this history and to the fact that the
phrase "political theology" was revived, in the 1920s, by the German legal
theorist Carl Schmitt. Like Kantorowicz, who by the 1950s had developed
a different, more discreet political agenda, Schmitt was engaged in questioning the descriptive and prescriptive value of the notion of secularization. He lamented, warned against, and questioned the attempt to con-
ceive of political existence detached from theology. Hence, Schmitt's
famous statement: "All significant concepts of the modern theory of the
state are secularized theological concepts not only because of their historical development—in which they were transferred from theology to the
theory of the state, whereby, for example, the omnipotent God became the
omnipotent lawgiver—but also because of their systematic structure, the
recognition of which is necessary for a sociological consideration of these
concepts."[27]

In Schmitt's reading, the political ("the modern theory of the state")
is constituted upon the separation of theology from politics ("secularization"), yet this separation is not a strict and hermetic rupture. Rather, the
separation itself becomes the site of a "transfer," of a structural translation
of theology into politics. The latter thus preserves theology (even if insufficiently, according to Schmitt) as a constitutive moment "within" it. Both
medieval *and* modern political doctrines must therefore be understood as
moments of the theologico-political. Both, in other words, could be described as "political theologies." In Kantorowicz's account, medieval political theology hinges on the king's two bodies, that is to say, on the relation
between the king and the body politic. Constitutive of this complex political relation is love, as we saw around the relationship of Othello and Desdemona. More importantly perhaps, and as Schmitt also emphasized, law
and jurisprudence provide the privileged space of political thought, the
privileged space for the transfer of theological concepts to political ones.
Law and love thus constitute a grid according to which one can engage a
reflection on the history of political theology, a grid in which these two
terms—law and love—appear as founding concepts. The more compelling
readings of *The Merchant of Venice* as a reflection on theologico-political issues put the two terms at the center of their argument.[28]

Yet to privilege law and love would run the risk of ignoring enmity, and more specifically the dissociative dimension with which we began. It would run the risk of ignoring the narrative of a "violent separation of the King's Two Bodies" as it occurs in *Richard II* and elsewhere. Schmitt's discreet followers (Kantorowicz, and Straussians such as Bloom) may have placed more emphasis on love and friendship, but in so doing, they occluded more than their relationship to Schmitt. They also ignored that Schmitt had underscored the importance of friendship, as well as that of enmity and hostility. Seeking, in fact, to determine what the "special distinction" is that "can serve as a simple criterion of the political and of what it consists," Schmitt offers a radical addition to the distinctions made "in the realm of morality" (good and evil) or in the aesthetic realm (beautiful and ugly). As to the political sphere, Schmitt writes, "the specific political distinction to which political actions and motives can be reduced is that between friend and enemy."[29] Schmitt goes on to emphasize that this distinction "denotes the utmost degree of intensity of a union *or* separation, of an association *or* dissociation."[30]

Another chapter in Shakespeare's political theology would therefore have to ask about the dissociation, about the "undoing" of the unity of the king's two bodies and "that most unpleasant idea of a violent separation" of theological from political under the figure of the enemy. It would have to ask about the place of the enemy in political theology.[31] Hence, whether or not Schmitt is correct in asserting that the political entity exists as such only insofar as the decision is made regarding the friend-enemy distinction, the perspective that he thereby offers for a history of political theology and of political history is undeniable, for it underscores the minor note of Shakespeare's political theology, the dissonant note of dissociation and enmity. Following Schmitt, therefore, and his claim that the failure to decide on the friend-and-enemy distinction is the destruction of the political entity, there remains the question of the theological history of that distinction, the theological history of the concept of enemy—a concept that Schmitt confines, as we saw, to the political and private spheres. It is this staging of political theology considered from the perspective of the friend-enemy distinction that is placed under renewed scrutiny by Shakespeare. It is a staging that demonstrates that the apparently marginal division, the perhaps only emerging dissociation of theology from politics, is located on a larger trajectory that hinges upon the concept of the enemy. Shakespeare maps out this theologico-political trajectory and the crucial moment in which it comes together and apart as the history of political theology.

Only an Arab could have understood or depicted a Jew so
"convincingly" as in *The Merchant of Venice.*
—Wole Soyinka

Let me restate the obvious, then. Shylock is a theological enemy. He
is "the Jew Shylock," the "mere enemy" (*MV*, 3.2.260), that is to say, the
absolute enemy, who hates and is hated on the explicit basis of his religion.
And if he does lend the money, as Antonio calls on him to do, it is not "as
to thy friends," but rather "as to thine enemy" (*MV*, 1.3.129–31). Othello,
on the other hand, "horribly stuffed with epithets of war" (*O*, 1.1.13), bears
all the mark of a political and military enemy. Othello, whom Iago—that
is, "I hate the Moor" Iago—and others call "the general" (2.3.310) is employed against the "general enemy Ottoman" (*O*, 1.3.49–50). Othello fights
the Turk, and as the final scene suggests, he himself may very well be the
"malignant" and "turbaned Turk" (5.2.351). As John Gillies writes, "his
symbolic association with the Turks is a critical commonplace."[32] Othello
is a Moor, and "the Moors were popularly considered barbarous, heathens
naturally at war with Christians and Europeans."[33] And though he himself
wonders "Are we turned Turks?" (*O*, 2.3.166), his conversion, and more
generally his religious status, remains mysterious. As Julia Lupton puts it,
"the play never decisively determines whether he was converted from a pagan religion or from Islam."[34]

Given the dimness of a "religion question" in the play, any claim that
it has anything to do with the theological must be prepared to do argu-
mentative battle. Indeed, were one to argue, as Julia Reinhard Lupton does,
that "in *Othello* religious difference is more powerfully felt than racial difference," one would still have to account for the apparent exhaustion of
that power in the history of Shakespearean criticism.[35] Similarly, were one
to emphasize that "ranking somatic, religious or national differences *vis-à-
vis* each other is to continue to think of them as discrete categories," and indeed that such a separation is mistaken, as James Shapiro and Ania Loomba
do, one would still have to account for the way the two plays—and they are
two very distinct plays that cannot be collapsed into each other—stage and
sediment that separation between the Jew and the Moor.[36]

If we return to the matter of the body, we will notice that in spite of
his concern with carnality and with flesh and "fair flesh," Shylock's own
flesh seems to have failed to inscribe itself onto his progeny. Shylock's flesh
"turned," and "there is," therefore "more difference"—the difference, one

might say, introduced by the word "more"—between Shylock's flesh and Jessica's, "more difference between thy flesh and hers than between jet and ivory" (*MV*, 3.1.36–37). Between Shylock's "jet" and "fair Jessica's" ivory, we witness the turns of Samuel Marochitanus, "a blackamoor turned white," a Jew turned Christian and therefore white.[37] In Shylock's case, at any rate, the body of the Jew who, making both "breed as fast," "cannot tell" whether "gold and silver" are as "ewes and rams" (*MV*, 1.3.92–93), fails to ensure its own carnality, the reproduction of its own flesh.[38] As such, Shylock could be said to constitute a peculiar body, one that is also devoid of body, devoid of flesh. In his famous monologue, Shylock needs in fact to insist that he does have a body, eyes, hands, organs, and more: "Hath not a Jew eyes? Hath not a Jew hands, organs, dimensions, senses, affections, passions . . . ?" (*MV*, 3.1.51–52).[39] Standing for the letter of the law, for a reading "according to the flesh," Shylock seems to lack a reliable and convincing body—"I never felt it till now" (*MV*, 3.1.81–82). He stands for the embodiment of the law and justice while lacking both. "Is that the law?" he finally asks. The theological enemy is also the failure to master the flesh. Shylock simply doesn't cut it.

In this, Shylock also fails to stand up to the comparison with Othello. Indeed, whereas Shylock consistently fails to exercise and even to understand the law—whereas he fails, as Martin Yaffe recently wrote, even to be a good Jew ("far from being a paragon representative of [Jewish law], he is knowingly inconsistent with regard to it"), and whereas Shylock even fails to bring down the power of "Jewish" revenge, Othello never fails.[40] "His problem," Stanley Cavell convincingly writes, "is over success, not failure."[41] Both the play as a whole and the character of Othello powerfully recall, as Alan Bloom recognizes, "the God of the Old Testament who commands love and promises revenge unto the third and fourth generation for those who are not obedient."[42] Othello, like the biblical God—"He's that he is" (*O*, 4.1.270), against Iago's "I am not what I am" (*O* 1.1.64)— is indeed jealous. He is "the jealous husband" who "acts out on the human scene a god's role; he is . . . a leader who can command and punish wherever he goes. He insists on honor and wreaks bloody vengeance on those who disobey."[43] Othello—"fire and brimstone!" (4.1.233) and "Justice to break her sword!" (5.2.17)—is thus not only "a judge,"[44] he is also "a decent general doing justice on the basis of acts done," and he rightfully regards himself as "the dispenser of justice":[45] "Good, good, the justice of it pleases; very good" (*O*, 4.1.206–7).

And yet with the staging of this "Semitic" justice (as Julia Lupton suggests), one can already notice that the incommensurability between Shylock and Othello is beginning to feel counterintuitive.[46] It is not as if Othello could, with any more certainty, be located on the site of the successful body or that of the powerful flesh.[47] It is not as if he could, with any more certainty, be located on the side of the political, rather than on the side of the theological. In spite of the absence of comparative studies of the two plays, in spite of this unremarked, if not unremarkable absence, it would be difficult to dismiss the obviousness of the link between them, a link that is at once so strong that it hardly merits lingering over, and so weak, so minor, as to go virtually unnoticed in its obviousness. Lupton summarizes this obviousness and writes that "*Othello*, one of Shakespeare's middle tragedies, has often[48] been read as a rewriting of *The Merchant of Venice*: both are set in the mercantile city-state of Venice, both employ clearly marked 'others,' and both use the theme of conspicuous exogamy to heighten the conventional comedic situation of young lovers blocked by an old father."[49] Alan Bloom concurs and asserts that "Othello and Shylock are the figures who are the most foreign to the context in which they move and to the audience for which they were intended."[50] Bloom strengthens the link between the plays when he states that "*Othello* is about a man who tried to assimilate and failed," whereas "in *The Merchant of Venice*, we see the soul of a man who refused to assimilate."[51] Finally, Leslie Fiedler humorously suggests that, in the writing of the two plays, it is "almost as if Shakespeare had said to himself: *Let's try that Venetian fable again, but this time let's turn everything upside down.*"[52]

In the light of the recent claim that, regarding discussions of the Jew Shylock, "the distinction between theology and race" has now been "eliminated," it remains therefore striking that most discussions of either one of the two plays rarely even mention the other.[53] It is as if the author of *The Merchant of Venice* had never even written *The Moor of Venice*, and vice versa. Even in the works I have mentioned, the divide between the two plays remains so consistent as to become invisible in its peculiarity. Indeed, if, as James Shapiro argues on the basis of Shylock's distinct hue ("jet") and his association with Tubal and Chus (*MV*, 3.2.285), "*The Merchant of Venice* provides another instance of the identification of Jews with blackness,"[54] and if, as Shapiro also has it, "the conventional critical view that what sets Shylock apart is his religion has deflected attention away from the more complex ways in which Shakespeare situates Jews within a larger, confused network of national and racial otherness," then the very persist-ence of the divide between the two plays along the lines of "religious" ver-sus "national and racial otherness," along the lines of the theological versus the political—in Shapiro's own work as well as in others—should become conspicuous.[55] It has not.

I cannot conclude without pointing out that as Shakespeare writes and as the separation between the two Venetian enemies is reinscribed and sedimented, what comes undone with it is the unity of the theologico-political. What was previously considered a complex (if difficult) unity, the coming apart of which represented catastrophe or senselessness itself ("the body is with the king, but the king is not with the body. The king is a thing—"), this unity of theology and politics has come apart in such a way as to become invisible even to those who argue against it. But this coming apart occurs in a particular staging, the staging of a separation that logi-cally, historically, and rhetorically precedes the separation of theology from politics.

Beginning with the title, Shakespeare marked the distance between the two dimensions of the body politic, the two dimensions of the polis of Venice, and he did so under the figure of two enemies: the theological en-emy and the political enemy, the merchant of Venice and the Moor of Venice.[56] The arbitrariness of the decision that separates between Moor and Jew, and historically between Muslim and Jew, between Arab and Jew, however, could not have failed to appear in Shakespeare's own text. Indeed, it is striking that having "convinced" generations upon generations of read-ers that the two plays, indeed, the two bodies, had nothing in common—though we all know that "nothing" in Shakespeare hardly amounts to nothing (and in fact when Hamlet says "The king is a thing—," Guilden-stern interrupts with "A thing, my lord? And Hamlet replies "Of noth-ing")—it is Shakespeare himself who made manifest that much as the community is constituted by the unity of theology and politics, so there is a community, unimaginable and dissociative as it is, of two bodies, the Jew's and the Moor's, or, as Othello himself suggests in a famous variant, the Moor's and the Judean's (*O*, 5.2.345), which invisibly sustains the link between two plays that ostensibly address two distinct kinds of "erring" and "extravagant" strangers, two distinct kinds of enemies.

"This passage has not been explained":[57] A jealous husband comes on the stage, catches his wife in a compromising position with a man he knows to have long been a friend. At this point in *The Merchant of Venice*,

Lorenzo ("I shall grow jealous of you shortly, Lancelot, if you thus get my wife into corners," 3.4.26–27) walks in on Lancelot and Jessica. Then, upon Jessica's report, he hears Lancelot's criticisms regarding his engagement to "the Jew's daughter." Noting that there are two distinct moments to Lancelot's diatribe, "Fair Jessica" reports to Lorenzo with great accuracy what Lancelot told her first: "He tells me flatly there's no mercy for me in heaven because I am a Jew's daughter." She then goes on to the second point made by Lancelot: "and he says you are no good member of the commonwealth, for in converting Jews to Christians, you raise the price of pork" (3.5.29–33). To this accusation, Lorenzo responds by telling Lancelot that he, Lancelot, does, in fact, the "same." Doing so, Lorenzo illustrates ever so fleetingly the comparability of Jew with Moor, of Shylock with Othello: "I shall answer that better to the commonwealth than you can the getting up of the Negro's belly. The Moor is with child by you, Lancelot!" (3.5.34–36).

Unreadable as it has remained, Lorenzo's associating Jew with Moor upon the figure of a pregnant body, which may or may not be saved according to the spirit (revisiting what results when "mercy seasons justice," Shakespeare would have provided, this time, Othello's answer: "I that am cruel am yet merciful" 5.2.86), thus appears to produce and to dismiss at the same time the unimaginable community of Jew and Arab, of theological and political enemy. The dual body of the enemy occurs at the moment when its salvation, as enemy body, will make it disappear. The two bodies are therefore associated at the very moment when their dissociation—the dissociation of theological from political—is asserted and denied. This is political theology at its best, but it is also political theology at its end. With it, Shakespeare traces the history of the concept of enemy. More importantly, perhaps, Shakespeare announces the modern separation of theology from politics at the same time that he demonstrates that at the historical root of the theologico-political, one does find two bodies, the body of the Jew and the body of the Moor, the Jew and the Arab. If the history of reading *The Merchant of Venice* and *The Moor of Venice* is any indication, the association and dissociation of these two bodies hardly stands to reason, but then again, it is "much that the Moor should be more than reason."

5

Muslims (Hegel, Freud, Auschwitz)

And (which is even worse than all great movements of destiny and by itself impossible) the life of a world would expire in some particular instance.
—Friedrich Hölderlin, "The Ground for 'Empedocles'"

Insofar as it implies the substitution of a literal expression with an attenuated or altered expression for something that one does not want to hear mentioned, the formation of a euphemism always involves ambiguities. In this case, however, the ambiguity is intolerable.
—Giorgio Agamben, *Remnants of Auschwitz*

Mais ça il ne faut pas le dire.
—Hélène Cixous, *Benjamin à Montaigne*

Writing in the first issue of *Yad Vashem Studies* (Jerusalem, 1957), Nahman Blumenthal attends to the words of the Holocaust. He attends to the Holocaust as a linguistic event and argues that an inquiry into the "language of the Nazis" is "far from being a matter unto itself, nor is it a question of linguistic inquiry."[1] Rather, Blumenthal continues, "a historical understanding of the period is contingent upon an understanding of the language of the Nazis." Blumenthal suggests, therefore, that this "inquiry into language" is not simply a matter of linguistics, not simply a matter of a narrow academic discipline.[2] Instead, insofar as understanding is "contingent" upon such an inquiry into language, it takes place, must take place, *prior* to any historical work and as a condition of this work: "an inquiry into language must serve as a preamble to historical inquiry" (55). This requirement, perhaps an impossible one, is only one of the many problems that such an inquiry might encounter. Indeed, Blumenthal describes another problem about which "there is doubt as to whether its place is within the inquiry into the language of the Nazi period," whether it can find its place there. This problem, Blumenthal continues, is

the matter of words which became part of the languages of the dominated peoples. The Jews, victims of the Nazis, used Nazi words to a great extent because their own language lacked these words—because they lacked the concepts adequate to the terrible tortures invented and practiced by the Germans. Among the saddest things, perhaps, is that the killers imposed even their language upon their victims. Another matter—continuous with what was said earlier—is the question of what, among these words, remains in linguistic usage to this day, as well as what is likely to remain in it in the future. Words have been partly tied to our present and to our memories of that period, and one cannot do without. These words have already settled in Hebrew and Yiddish literature and have become part of our cultural history. (54–55)

In this chapter, I want to shift, momentarily and quite painfully, the inquiry that governs this book—the Jew, the Arab—and turn toward language in order to consider one of the "words that have already settled in Hebrew and Yiddish literature and have become part of our cultural history." Here, I will first follow Blumenthal's lead, beginning with his understanding of "our cultural history," emphatically restricted to Israeli culture and literature. Yet because the "inquiry into language" Blumenthal calls for is "not a matter unto itself, nor is it a question of linguistic inquiry," a reading of the haunting or colonizing of language ("these words have already settled") cannot be certain of its place. There is a doubt, *safeq*, as to its place. I will start therefore with a founding moment of Israeli literature in order to ask about a single word that articulates, as well as constitutes, some of the apparently settled, if unsettling haunting of "our cultural history," in order to engage the question of this word's relation to the Holocaust (or, rather, to what may have settled in it of the Holocaust), in order then to move on, if slowly, to read Hegel, Freud, Auschwitz, in order to read what Jacques Derrida enjoins us to read with the Jew, the Arab, in order, finally, to read what Giorgio Agamben called a "perfect cipher," the (word) "Muslims."[3]

Tatters of Human Existence

"The Prisoner," *Ha-shavui*, the emblematic 1948 story by the Israeli author S. Yizhar, is a story about power and subjection.[4] More precisely, perhaps, it is a story about military power and absolute subjection. In this story, there are soldiers, Israeli soldiers (they are, in the text, only belatedly identifiable as Israelis) who decide, for lack of "action," to take prisoner a shepherd and his sheep (in the story, it will also belatedly turn out that he is an "Arab" shepherd). Written in wartime by "a writer who is, after all, an establishment figure" and published in Hebrew in a "literary organ of the Israeli establishment," the story is intended for an Israeli audience. Moreover, as Robert Alter describes it, the story certainly "speaks for the confused, wavering conscience of any average citizen in time of war."[5] "The Prisoner" therefore offers more than a staging of the first Arab-Israeli war in Israeli literature. It constitutes the Jew and the Arab, the Muslim and the Jew, as the haunting figure(s) of an encounter where nothing comes together but what I will call the "partaking" of roads taken and not taken, a *partage des voies*. In the existing English edition of Jean-Luc Nancy's *Le partage des voix, partage* is translated as "sharing," but it also could be translated as "division," a sense that is lost in English. Here, I want to appropriate the term "partaking" for this sense of *partage,* a sense beyond "sharing," and to appropriate it by taking it apart—as "part taking": both "parting and taking part," without the participatory, fusionary logic of "sharing."[6]

"The Prisoner" is first of all a story about soldiers, portraying "the imperiousness of the Jewish soldiers and the contempt with which many of them treated the conquered people."[7] It calls for and is meant to produce an identification with the soldiers—even if negatively charged. (The story ends by making this identification literal by turning to a soldier involved in holding the prisoner, presumably any soldier, and commanding—to what effect, the story never tells—the prisoner's release.) The story also appears to be told from the perspective of a soldier who, torn between his military duty and his humanist ethics ("Be a man!" 310/H108), ultimately carries out the momentous image of the Israeli military ethos, the ethos of soldiers who will later famously "shoot and weep," *yorim u-bokhim.* This perspective governs the story, even if the distance between the group of soldiers and the soldier-narrator is not quite stable and even if one cannot be assured of the latter's identity, which appears to change over the course of the story. As Alter argues, "the most plausible explanation for this [narrative] shift is that the anonymous soldier-narrator of the beginning of the story is the soldier in the back of the jeep at the end" (292).

Given the plausibility of this structure of identification, it might be useful to linger on a moment of the story in which the narrative flow is suspended and the individuality of the soldiers is explored. At this hinging moment, the focus shifts to a sphere of the soldiers' life that the story has ignored until now, their life outside the military situation in which they find themselves. In this other, civil sphere, soldiers are individuals who have conducted and will continue to conduct activities that bear only a distant or contingent relation to "the trenches, the troubles, the disorder" (298/H95). As the soldiers gather around the prisoner they have captured, the text presents a "whole scene," a panoramic vision as if in a series of "pictures," photographs presumably taken by the first soldier who is represented. Out of this vision, individuals emerge as individuals, even if only to retreat into the collective and to "reel back into the crowd." Each and every one of them is both a man and an individual, and, though nameless throughout, each appears in both his anonymity and his singularity. Each and every one of these men partakes of the action in a distinct way, ultimately merging into "a happy circle," *ma*ʿ*agal me*ʾ*ushar.* The narrative dynamic that brings each and every one into this circle (*eḥad,* "one," is a word that is rhythmically repeated) is worth quoting in full.

One man was taking pictures of the whole scene, and on his next leave he would develop them. And there was one who sneaked up behind the prisoner, waved his fist passionately in the air and then, shaking with laughter, reeled back into the crowd. And there was one who didn't know if it was proper or not, if it was the decent thing to do, and his eyes darted about seeking the support of an answer, whatever it might be. And there was one who, while talking, grabbed the water jug, raised it high over his head, and swilled the liquid with bared teeth, signaling to his audience with the forefinger of his left hand to wait until the last drop had been drained for the end of his slick story. And there was one wearing an undershirt who, astonished and curious, exposed his rotten teeth: many dentists, a skinny shrew of a wife, sleepless nights, narrow, stuffy room, unemployment, and working for "the party" had aggravated his eternal query of "*Nu,* what will be?"

And there were some who had steady jobs, some who were on their way up in the world, some who were hopeless cases to begin with, and some who rushed to the movies and all the theaters and read the weekend supplements of two newspapers. And there were some who knew long passages by heart of Horace and the Prophet Isaiah and from Haim Nahman Bialik and even from Shakespeare; some who loved their children and their wives and their slippers and the little garden at the side of their houses; some who hated all forms of favoritism, insisted that each man keep his proper place in line, and raised a hue and a cry at the slightest suspicion of discrimination; some whose inherent good-nature had been permanently soured by the thought of paying rent and taxes; some who were not at all what they seemed and some who were exactly what they seemed. There they all stood, in a happy circle around the blindfolded prisoner. (298–99/H96)

There is much in this description that deserves to be dwelled on, yet what is astonishing about it is that, in 1948, it was already invoking, indeed, quoting, all too recognizable images, photographic and "literary" images.[8] The passage is moreover haunted by a testimonial discourse that has pitted *Bildung* and *Kultur* against extreme violence. Yizhar is offering here his own version of *Wo wärst du Adam?* and doing so much before Heinrich Böll wrote his extended and exemplary story of an educated and cultivated German officer who nonetheless "followed orders" to their very end.[9] Clearly, the violence that is exercised here, "the familiar process by which power dehumanizes those who exercise it," as Alter describes it, is a violence, a process, and a power that have to be distinguished in their specificity. It is particularly important therefore to consider that Yizhar does not once indicate that the struggle in which the soldiers are involved was, for the Israelis, a "war of independence." Such ideological justification, so easy to invoke, appears thus excluded at the outset.

And yet this violence—"acts of excessive cruelty," as Hannan Hever has it—this power constitutes the ground upon which the narrator assaults the "you" who is supposed to stop it.[10] Indeed, it is precisely insofar as he ("you") will follow orders ("hiding behind a stinking what-can-I-do-it's-an-order," *ma la ʿasot—pquda* 309/H108) that the addressee is called upon. For "this time," *ʿatah* there is an alternative. This time—but what could have been the other time in the first war of the Zionist state?—"this time you have the choice. . . . It's the day when, at last, you have the choice in your hands" (ibid.). Clearly, Yizhar is invoking the fact that now, "at last," Jews (now Israelis) are powerful soldiers who do not have to be led like the flocks of sheep that set the stage for the story: These Jewish soldiers have the choice to resist and the choice to act. It would thus be difficult to ignore that, like so much of Israeli culture and literature, like so much of what Nahman Blumenthal calls "our cultural history," Yizhar's story is indeed about the "settling," *shvitah*, of a complex and difficult history. Clearly, "The Prisoner" is haunted by the memory of cultivated, sensitive, and overall "ordinary men," men who nonetheless engaged in horrifying acts of violence.[11] Yizhar's story is haunted by the Holocaust.[12] But there is yet more to this haunting.

As the soldiers earlier had walked back to their base of operation with their prisoner, the latter also had begun to appear as the figure of a singular subject, a subjected man who "seemed to shrink within himself, dazed and stupefied, his mind a ruin in which everything behind him was loss and all before him, despair" (297/H94). The prisoner is "enveloped by dumbness, the silence of an uprooted plant—his misery so palpable that it flapped about his head in a rhythm of terror, rising and falling with the blindfold (tied to his brow with a brute twist of disdain) so that he was pathetic but also ludicrous and repulsive" (ibid.).

This image of absolute subjection, this figure of terror, stupefaction, muteness, and despair, does not arrest the narration, and within the same sentence, with no more than a semicolon marking the separation of its parts, the narrator moves on from this description of the prisoner to a description of the landscape: "how the grain turned more golden in the splendor of the sun; how the sandy paths followed their course between hills and fields with the faithful resignation of beasts of burden." The shepherd, now a prisoner, had already been seen as part of the landscape in which flora, fauna, and human inhabitants all merge into one ("on the plains and in the valleys flocks of sheep were wandering; on the hilltops, dim, human forms, one here and one there, sheltered in the shade of olive trees," 294/H91). The narrator had expressed impatience with relating the ways of this peaceful world and the motions of the soldiers in it, the "how" of those who make up that landscape, punctuated, as I have said, only by the soft interruption of semicolons: "It's too long to tell in details how we made our way through . . . ; how our prisoner was enveloped by dumbness . . . ; how the grain turned more golden . . . ; how the sandy paths followed their course" (297/H94). The landscape, like the fatigued soldiers, like the prisoner, and like the hills and the paths, all share in what had earlier been described as "a kind of easy unconcern—the unconcern of good days when there was no evil in the world to forewarn of other evil things to come" (294/H91). Lacking signs and forewarning indicators, the landscape (and what is in it and of it) is unconcerned and, one could almost say, beyond good and evil. Like beasts of burden, the landscape (and what is in it and of it, quiet flocks and "dim, human forms") is thus marked by a "faithful resignation."

At first there were "quiet flocks . . . grazing, flocks from the days of Abraham, Isaac, and Jacob," markedly located "in the distance." Closer now, there begin to emerge "designs of a different sort," designs that "cast their diagonal shadow across the pastoral scene" (295/H91). Things are thus moving closer, or at least "we" are: "We were nearing our base of operations" (297/H94).

Signs of the base, an empty Arab village, became more frequent. Interrupted echoes. An abandoned anthill. The stench of desertion, the rot of humanity [the word "humanity" is not in the Hebrew original], infested, louse-ridden. The poverty and stupefaction of wretched villagers. Tatters of human existence. A sudden exposure of the limits of their home, their yards, and of all within. They were revealed in their nakedness, impoverished, shriveled, and stinking. Sudden emptiness. Death by apoplexy. Strangeness, hostility, bereavement. An air of mourning—or was it boredom?—hovered there in the heat of the day. Whichever it doesn't matter. (297–98/H94–95)

Between life and death, what insists through the complex multiplicity of voices is a peculiar "unconcern," then. "It doesn't matter" whether the air is of "mourning" or "boredom"; "it doesn't matter" whether "an empty Arab village" is still populated, whether it still shelters (an obscene word, in this context) "wretched villagers" whose state of stupor, *timtum*, hardly qualifies as "human existence."[13] A "faithful resignation," perhaps a theological stupidity, *timtum*, which recalls "the days of Abraham," is still haunting and haunted by "tatters of human existence." It has thus long settled with the human dust of "dim, human forms."

What are we to make of this encounter between these military and militaristic, yet human figures (here created and perfected in response to a history now perceived as a history of passivity and weakness) and these "tatters of human existence"? How are we to read those "wretched villagers . . . revealed in their nakedness, impoverished, shriveled, and stinking" represented by the Arab shepherd, this singular being—if it is one— "only a miserable nothing, a subdued shriveled creature, a mask wrapped in a cloth, someone shrunken and stooped like a worthless sack, frightened, dissolving into nothingness" (309/H107)? Who is this subjected and submitted and vanishing ghost of a religious persuasion, this barely organic remnant, this figure of absolute subjection and of "faithful resignation" to violence and a "death by apoplexy"—a death that seems to have escaped its victims' own knowledge? And who are these "dim, human forms"? Who are the Jews here? And who are the Muslims? In what follows, I will try to argue that the rudiments of an answer have long exhibited themselves as the history of a word, a genealogy of a figure of absolute subjection.

Hegel

Perhaps there is no sublimer passage in the Jewish law than the command, "Thou shalt not make to thyself any graven image, nor the likeness of anything which is in heaven or in the earth or under the earth," etc. This command alone can explain the enthusiasm that the Jewish people in their moral period felt for their religion, when they compared themselves with other peoples, or explain the pride which Mohammedanism inspires.

—Immanuel Kant, *The Critique of Judgment*

It has long been noted that Immanuel Kant's discussion of the sublime involves a movement and a motion ("the mind feels itself moved"), indeed, an emotion, wherein not agreement (as in the beautiful), but a certain disagreement occurs ("*accord-discordant*" writes Gilles Deleuze).[14] "The satisfaction in the sublime does not so much involve a positive pleasure as admiration or respect, which rather deserves to be called negative pleasure" (*Critique of Judgment*, section 23). This affective (affected and affecting) disagreement is itself carried within a general movement of dissymmetric distinctions and "divisions," as Kant calls them, beginning with the sublime itself, which is divided between "the mathematically and the dynamically sublime" (section 24). The division of the mind, its movement, says Kant, "may be compared to a vibration, i.e. to a quickly alternating attraction toward, and repulsion from, the same object" (section 27). Hence, in the sublime, the "subjective purposiveness of the mental powers" (imagination and reason) is generated "by means of their conflict." This conflict, which nonetheless produces a certain unity, if not a harmony, is also staged in the passage from *The Critique of Judgment* that I placed at the beginning of this section.

I want to argue here that Kant's "Analytic of the Sublime" articulates a disparate, emotional, and conflictual unity (an "accord discordant") that will eventually lead us to G. W. F. Hegel and beyond. This argument should also illuminate a series of conflicts (active or dormant) and comparisons that articulate themselves in the highly particular configurations that occupy me here between Judaism ("the Jewish people") and Islam ("Mohammedanism"), religion and politics, as they relate to yet another series, this time of affects and emotions. Here, the Kantian sublime, and most particularly "enthusiasm" and "pride," will point toward political and religious feelings (the "absence of affection," *Affektlosigkeit*, among them) which may or may not bear a necessary relation to sublimity.[15] The account that I seek to provide here is *not*, however, of the sublime, but of "faithful resignation," indeed, of subjection and submission (to the law, to power) in its relation to Jews. And to Muslims.

> It is curious that Kant puts the most crucial issues of judgment—politics and religion (. . .) in such a structurally indeterminate place.
> —Gayatri Spivak, *Critique of Postcolonial Reason*

> All resistance would be altogether vain.
> —Immanuel Kant, *Critique of Judgment*

It would be extreme to suggest that, with the sublime, Kant developed a theory of subjection, or even a general political theory. As Hannah Arendt famously argued, Kant "never wrote a political philosophy," nor do his political writings truly manage to "constitute a 'Fourth Critique.'"[16] Yet the "Analytic of the Sublime" does deploy a political lexicon. Part of the treatment of the aesthetic, the "Analytic" is, "epistemological as well as political through and through," as Paul de Man puts it.[17] Beginning with "enthusiasm," Kant's political lexicon, as it deploys itself "with" (and the status of this "with" is of course what is in question here) the sublime, has been read in productive ways, and in it one may therefore recognize the rudiments of a theory of subjection, a vocabulary of power, violence, and resistance, of freedom and submission. Nowhere is this clearer, perhaps, than in the recurring descriptions of the *Gewalt* (force, violence, and dominion) exercised by reason over imagination and sensibility.[18] The feeling of the sublime, Kant writes, is "a feeling that the imagination is deprived and robed of its freedom," accompanied, among other things, by a feeling of "the cause to which it is subjected" (section 29).

Nature ("Of Nature Regarded as Might," section 28) is one of the prominent sites in the context of which Kant speaks at length of violence and dominion (*Gewalt*), of might and power (*Macht*), and, indeed, of submission—or the lack thereof—under the figure of resistance (*Widerstand*).[19] The sense of the word "political" here could be clarified further, if space permitted, yet impoverished as that sense would become as a result, it could nonetheless be confined to recognizable boundaries of "governance."[20] In section 29, for example (and one knows the importance of examples in the *Critique of Judgment*), Kant proceeds by deduction from the sublime to popular feelings—via the "rights of men"—and to "governments" and their policies vis-à-vis religion and religious feelings ("Thus governments have willingly allowed religion to be abundantly provided . . . and seeking thereby to relieve their subjects, they have also sought to deprive them"). As we shall see, it will therefore be more precise to speak of a theologico-political dimension, a theologico-political vocabulary, invoked by Kant on the sublime. That being said, it does not cancel the necessity of proceeding with care and attending to the ways in which distinctions are multiplied throughout the "Analytic." If the sublime is to be distinguished from itself, if it is not quite comparable with itself, then nothing standing at the site, *Stelle*, of the sublime (whether itself sublime or not) will remain, in fact, standing as standing-with. A consistent and dissymmetric incommensurability, a space of incomparability, will have to settle between and within each term *raised*, one could say, with and by the sublime.

Henceforth, the "satisfaction in terror" in the face of nature's might, *Macht*, is not to be confused with courage in the face of war (which "makes the disposition of the people who carry it on . . . the more sublime") or with "respect" for "a general" (when compared, for example, with respect for "a statesman"), or with the admiration of "the savage" and the "civilized" alike for "the soldier." Yet this admiration for the soldier is linked to a certain subjection—as an absence thereof—when it is described as a "peculiar veneration" for the fact that the soldier's "mind is unsubdued by danger."[21] Whether or not subjection and submission *accord* themselves with the sublime is a question that may be difficult to resolve, but it undoubtedly belongs to the intricacies of the "Analytic."[22] It is a question that Kant goes on to explore by linking sublimity to nature (and its power) and to religion. The feeling of the sublime may thus be distinguished from "subjection, abasement and a feeling of complete powerlessness," but this distinction testifies to the way in which Kant's exploration of such phenomena is in fact linked—even if not "*necessarily* linked"—with the question of political and religious power (*Macht* or *Gewalt*) (section 28; emphasis added).

The religious and political connotations evoked throughout, as well as the conflicts and divisions, the conflicting motions and emotions that emerge in relation to sublimity, involve in complicated manners fear, admiration, enthusiasm, but also "(which seems strange)," adds Kant parenthetically, "the absence of affection (*apatheia, phlegma in significatu bono*)" (section 29). Kant goes on to include "despair," *Verzweiflung*, and "affections of the *languid* kind (which make the very effort of resistance an object of pain—*animum languidum*)," and more. Each of these emotions or affects—and the lack thereof—is divided and distinguished from itself, by Kant.[23] I do not, therefore, recall them here in order to collapse the essential distinctions, the internal conflicts of forces, that are operative between and within each of them, but because they appear in the context of Kant's discussion of political and religious power (Kant has just mentioned "Eastern voluptuaries" and their massage practices, section 29) and because they precede, perhaps even announce, one of the most important and well-known moments of Kant's analysis.[24]

This is the textual moment with which we began this discussion, a moment when politics and religion, something like a theologico-political difference, at any rate distinct and incommensurable motions of the sublime, nonetheless occur together in a community "by means of conflict" and incomparability, a relation, perhaps, "without relation." "Perhaps," Kant says, "there is no sublimer passage," *Stelle*, "in the Jewish law than the command, 'Thou shalt not make to thyself any graven image,'" *Bildnis*, "'nor the likeness,'" *Gleichnis*, "'of anything which is in heaven or in the earth or under the earth,' etc. This command alone can explain the enthusiasm that the Jewish people in their moral period felt for their religion, when they compared," *verglich*, "themselves with other peoples, or explain the pride," *Stolz*, "which Mohammedanism inspires" (section 29).

The command, the law, *Gebot* and *Gesetz*, thus occasion not one, but two distinct feelings in two distinct constituencies (and even this at distinct periods, *Epoche* or *Periode*). The law that forbids any image or likeness, parable, or simile (*Gleichnis*) has to be distinguished from itself and seen as incomparable insofar as two distinct feelings emerge at its place, which is no longer one by virtue of the sublime.[25] (It is the place, *Stelle*, that is the "sublimer," and the law takes place at this place.) These feelings articulate themselves as sites of dissymmetric comparisons (between the Jews and other peoples; between Islam and that above which it rises, feels itself raised and inspired, and finally between Judaism and Islam).

Does the sublime, then, bear comparison, *Vergleich*? And a thought of relation? Or will Kant, here too, have "introduced comparison where he says it should have no place" at the very site, *lieu*, *Stelle*, where likeness and comparison are impossible?[26] At the very site where comparison—and sublimity—locates and position (*stellt*) the impossibility of comparison as com-parison, the impossibility of being on a par together? What, then, are the operative distinctions that must be remarked here? What, for example (and Kant's discourse is entirely about examples, of course), is the status of a "people" as opposed to a "religion"? Of a people who, because of a feeling ("the Jewish people . . . felt") for its religion, compares, *verglich*, itself to other peoples? What is the difference between a people, who is the subject of its feelings, and a religion, which inspires strictly speaking no one, or at least no people, no determinate subject (itself? an other?)? And what kind of feelings, in turns, are "enthusiasm" and "pride"? Are they worthy of sublimity? How do these religious feelings connect with the "civil relations" (of Judaism and Islam) as Kant describes them in *Religion within the Limits of Reason Alone?*[27] How do religion, enthusiasm, Judaism, pride, politics, apathy, and Islam relate to each other? Do they, in fact, relate? And if so, under what logic of distinction, by means of what conflict?

My lack of competence, among other reasons, prevents me from answering these questions in any satisfying manner. Moreover, I have been unable to find assistance in any discussion of this famous and frequently discussed passage of Kant on the *Bilderverbot*, any discussion that would account for the juxtaposition, indeed, the comparison of Islam and Judaism in it.[28] The obviousness of the stringent enforcement, the well-known Abrahamic (if notably *not* Christian) iconoclasm of both Judaism and Islam, hardly strikes one as sufficient in order to account for the nature of the bond at the heart of an analysis that seems to suffer only a multiplication of distinctions and differences. Could the two religions, in this context, ever amount to the same? Could a harmonious unity around the divine command be produced at the very moment that the "most sublime" example (but is it an example, merely an example?) is presented? The multiplication of figures of "the Orient" among Kant's examples ("pyramids," of Egypt and of ice, in section 26; "Eastern voluptuaries" and "Mohammedanism," in section 29), the strange lack of a definite subject of the "pride" linked to Islam, testify to an exegetical need. Who, after all, is "inspired" by Islam? Islam, the religion, has no subject, political or other, no subject feeling for it, for Islam, and yet Islam is said to be a cause nonetheless: There is inspiration because of Islam. The theologico-political distinction between Islam, on the one hand, and the Jewish *Volk* and the religion for which it feels, on the other, twice announces and locates within *and* without the distinction between "Jews" and "Islam," between politics and religion.

By the time he deploys his theologico-political vocabulary, and although "unfortunately he does not always appear to use his terms consistently,"[29] Kant is already participating in a discourse that, in the eighteenth century, was in the process of violently emerging: the invention of political despotism. Through it, the incomparability of religion and politics, of Judaism and Islam, most particularly under the figure of subjection, would not become quite stable.[30] Yet, and most significantly, perhaps, what would become most visible of the configuration produced by the Kantian sublime in connection to subjection was precisely what has dropped out of view of the Kantian text: Islam. In the discourse on despotism, on the other hand, and in the pages that follow it, it "seems strange" that Judaism (which had already been absented from the *Observations on the Feeling of the Beautiful and Sublime*), this time, and again, drops out of view.

> But in the despotic world, absolute power is exercised usually
> by means of the graphic signifier.
> — Alain Grosrichard, *Sultan's Court*

The Western invention of "despotism" as a *political* category has been exquisitely documented by Alain Grosrichard in *The Sultan's Court: European Fantasies of the East* (1979).[31] It is a discourse that, with and without Kant, invokes power and might, religion and politics, and a number of emotions and affects, most prominently fear and terror, enthusiasm, apathy, and despair. The invention of despotism (prior to Montesquieu, it was the political philosopher Jean Bodin who, in the sixteenth century "introduced the noun 'despotism' to designate a specific form of government") involves the translation of a domestic term into a political one—the *despotes* was the head of the household, *not* a political figure.[32] Yet this inventive gesture was structurally linked to another no less potent, if perhaps less visible invention: the "apathy" and the "faithful resignation" of the despot's *subjects*.[33] What emerged at this momentous historical point in the writings of Montesquieu and others was also the invention of absolute subjection, its rapid and unceasing translation, "a quickly alternating attraction toward, and repulsion from, the same object" (as Kant describes the sublime), religion and politics as the conflictual union of incomparables. This strange translation occurs through the identification of an entire people—not yet a race—said to be "naturally cowardly," in whose state of stupor and of stupidity, a state in which there appears in the soul "a new kind of terror . . . [that] virtually stupefies it," *un nouveau genre de terreur qui la rend comme stupide.*[34] How did an entire people become the privileged example of a "natural" and absolute submission? Not entirely naturally, as it turns out, since this state is induced by the Muslims: "The flood tide of Mahommedans brought despotism with it," and despotic government "is most agreeable" to the Mahommedan religion.[35]

Montesquieu opens *The Spirit of the Laws*—a book that explicitly tends toward an articulation of "political virtue"—with a kind of "grand enfermement" of his own, the exclusion of subjection, of blind subjection to fate, from the realm of reason into absurdity. "They who assert that a blind fatality produced the various effects we behold in this world talk very absurdly; for can any thing be more unreasonable than to pretend that a blind fatality could be productive of intelligent beings? There is then, a prime reason; and laws are the relations subsisting between it and different beings, and the relations of these to one another" (1.1). Laws, therefore, do not provide an escape from the realm of subjection constituted by blind fatality, for out of such a realm, reasonable beings who are ruled by reasonable laws could not emerge. Rather, reason, a prime reason, *une raison primitive*, is the condition of emergence of laws. Laws exist only insofar as they are in relation to this reason ("Law in general is human reason, 1.3), insofar as they institute and constitute reasonable relations. Laws have nothing to do with subjection to fate and are not even opposed to the absurdity of blind fate. The absolute subjection to fate that is blind fatalism therefore bears no relation to the spirit of the laws.

And yet such absolute subjection as a theologico-political notion is precisely what Montesquieu goes on to articulate under the figure of despotism, a figure that is central to his political project (it emerges quite early on, at the opening of book 2).[36] I do not wish here to engage Montesquieu's monumental book here—nor could I do justice to it. I do not want to revisit the careful analyses made by Grosrichard on which I am relying here, either. My purpose is to recall the manner in which, in the writings of Montesquieu and others, during the eighteenth century, absolute subjection, "faithful resignation" ("one glories in the contempt of life," 3.8) became attached to Muslims. Indeed, if the privileged, if not exclusive example of despotism was the Ottoman sultan, its structurally opposed pole, the privileged example of the submitted, became, therefore, the Muslims: "they cast behind them everything which has any concern with this world. . . . Add to this that indifference for all things which is inspired by the doctrine of unalterable fate" (24.11).

Subjection is predicated upon one principle, "the principle of despotic government," fear, *crainte*. It is "the spring of this government," a government that demands "the most passive obedience." "Man's portion here, like that of beasts, is instinct, compliance, and punishment" (3.9–10). Such subjection, like blind fatalism, excludes reason and excludes one from reason: "Excessive obedience supposes ignorance in the person that obeys: the same it supposes in him that commands, for he has no occasion to deliberate, to doubt, to reason" (4.3). What thus joins subject and sovereign is "natural stupidity" (5.14). There is no greater absurdity, and indeed, "the concept of despotism, as it is understood by Montesquieu, is merely the container for an absurdity."[37]

Montesquieu offers many examples of the absurd political regime that is despotism ("despotism," explains Grosrichard, "calls into question the essence and the existence of *the political as such*").[38] Chronologically first among these examples is already a religious one: the pope. And yet before mentioning the pope as an example, Montesquieu formulates a "fundamental law" of despotic government, "the creation of a *vizier*" (2.5). The example of the pope should therefore clarify Grosrichard's claim that Montesquieu's main purpose was not at all to target distant regimes. And yet the rhetorical and temporal structure of the argument on despotism does locate despotism squarely in the East. More precisely, it locates the paradigm of absolute subjection in Islam.[39]

In those states religion has more influence than anywhere else; it is fear added to fear. In Mahommedan countries, it is partly from their religion that the people derive the surprising veneration they have for their prince. . . . [It is] especially in Mahommedan countries, where religion considers victory or success as a divine decision in their favor; so that they have no such thing as a monarch *de jure*, but only *de facto*. (5.14)

Having demonstrated the "religious," nonpolitical character of "faithful resignation" as the nature of the Muslims' existence ("we are here politicians and not theologians," 25.9), Montesquieu compares them to the Jews—who are said later to be "blind" (25.13), and he does so in a part of the book that is devoted to the rapport between law and religion ("Of Laws in Relation to the Establishment of Religion and Its External Polity," 25). The comparison, too, remains confined to religion, with no explicit rapport made with "political virtue" (see e.g. 25.2–4). What, then, of the theologico-political context of subjection, then? What of the Jew *and* the Arab?

> For this consciousness has been fearful, not of this or that particular thing or just at odd moments, but its whole being has been seized with dread; for it has experienced the fear of death, the absolute Lord. In that experience it has been quite unmanned, has trembled in every fiber of its being, and everything solid and stable has been shaken to its foundations. But this pure universal movement, the absolute melting-away of everything stable, is the simple, essential nature of self-consciousness, absolute negativity, *pure being-for-self,* which consequently is *implicit* in this consciousness. This moment of pure being-for-self is also explicit for the bondsman, for in the lord it exists for him as his *object.* Furthermore, his consciousness is not this dissolution of everything stable merely in principle; in his service he *actually* brings this about. Through his service he rids himself of his attachment to natural existence in every single detail and gets rid of it by working on it.
> —Hegel, *The Phenomenology of Spirit*

Comparing the incomparable, as well, but bringing the three monotheistic religions together with the question of subjection and "faithful resignation," was Montesquieu's great admirer, the "Christian," as opposed to "Kant the Jew," Georg Wilhelm Friedrich Hegel.[40] Hegelian comparisons, and those in particular, are, of course, numerous and complex (moreover, they obviously do not exhaust what Hegel has to say on religion and on other religions). To the extent that he does compare Islam and Judaism in the context of a thought of "faithful resignation," however, Hegel, like both Kant and Montesquieu, renews the question of subjection *and* of the Jew, the Arab.

From the earliest writings, Hegel associates the Jews with the "thoroughgoing passivity" of worship, the "testimony of their servitude."[41] He also recalls Kant's notion of the Jews' "misanthropy" as a form of subjection to necessity. Almost incidentally writing a chapter of a history of the enemy, Hegel speaks here of the Jews', through necessity, becoming "enemies": "their necessities made them the enemies of others," *Feinden.*[42] (This state of *Feindseligkeit,* Hegel also names "the demon of hatred," and hatred is of course one of the recurring marks of Judaism for Hegel.)[43] This condition also appears to be explained by Moses' "seal" that Moses imprints upon his legislation, one that brings us closer to the Orient and to the still-unnamed Arab or Muslim, thus producing—indeed, commanding by law—a form of apathy, one could say a kind of *Affektlosigkeit*, or at least the loss of all pleasure and happiness: "Moses sealed his legislation with an orientally beautiful threat of the loss of all pleasure and all fortune."

What Moses sought was to present the servile spirit with its own representation, that of terror: "He brought before the slavish spirit the image of itself, namely, the terror of physical force."[44] The English translator explains that with the use of the word "orientally," the image evoked by Hegel "was not a kindly one, like those of Greece, but a nonnatural one, a threat of terror, like those to which people under oriental despotisms were accustomed."[45] The French editor concurs and writes that "one finds here the prefiguration of the 'Lordship and Bondage' dialectic."[46] Writing in the same years, Hegel further provides an explanation of the "Oriental threat" alluded to in "The Spirit of Christianity." What requires an explanation is that "two determinations" are "apparently contradictory," but nonetheless "intimately linked" in the "Oriental character," "the thirst for absolute domination" and "the willing subjection to any enslavement." In the Orient, then, "domination, power and violence, is the essence of social relations." Hegel continues: "Such a fixed, determined character does not tolerate anything outside itself but what it dominates and what dominates it." Hence, it is always the case that "one dominates, and the other is dominated." What accounts or more precisely enables this state of affairs is, of course, "the law which dominates all."[47]

In this particular passage, the Jews are the only "Orientals" named explicitly (at times even the only ones to be distinguished from others). Yet there are more instances where Hegel explicitly compares, opposes, or simply juxtaposes Jews and Arabs, Judaism and Islam.[48] The logic of the link thus established (or undone) may, however, very well be like the association between an Arab and a stranger, *ein Fremd*, over "a cup of coffee." What is established with the partaking "is not what is called a symbol. The connection between symbol and symbolized is not itself spiritual, is not life, but an objective bond; symbol and symbolized are strangers to one another," *sind einander fremd*, "and their connection lies outside them" (248/G364). There may very well be a unity, yet what is lacking in it—this is, of course, well known—is recognition. Even then, however, it is not clear whether the word "unity," or indeed "identity," *Identität*—especially

in its political sense—applies. Religion gets in the way, and under the theologico-political weight of a discordance, the (one) people and the (one)
state, the "people as state," crumbles. "The question arises how far a no-
madic people, for instance, or any people on a low level of civilization, can
be regarded as a state. As once was the case with the Jews and the Mo-
hammedan people, religious views may entail an opposition at a higher
level between one people and its neighbors and so preclude the general
identity which is requisite for recognition."⁴⁹

It is in the later, even posthumous writings, that Hegel brings
together—if togetherness were still a possible term—the thought-un-
thought of "faithful resignation" and "the Jew, the Arab" in the most striking way. As should have become clear, it is through a crisis in and of the
theologico-political that this thought articulates itself. It does so in no simple manner. Hence, whereas the *Philosophy of Right* had surprisingly
brought "the Jewish people" into "the Germanic realm," *das Germanische
Reich*, under the "extreme" of "absolute negativity" (222/G511), the *Lectures
on the Philosophy of History*, no less surprisingly, bring Islam into "the German World," *die germanische Welt*. But who are the Jews? And who are the
Muslims?

> For Arabs and Jews have only to be noticed in an external and
> historic way.
> —Hegel, *Lectures on the History of Philosophy*

The crisis of the theologico-political that takes place at this point is a
sundering and a separation between politics and religion: "while the West
began to shelter itself in a political edifice . . . the very opposite direction
necessarily made its appearance in the world."⁵⁰ But the movement of a
dissociation is yet more complex and can be said to take place as well
within what Hegel calls "the East." Hence if "only among the Jews have we
observed the principle of pure unity elevated to a thought," it is nonetheless the case that Islam partakes of that singular exclusivity. The difference,
as we will see, is not essential, and it has to do only with universality. For
now, though, it is important to note the motion of affect, the emotions, associated, in Hegel's language, with the Muslims.

The Muslims, Hegel explains, are "dominated by abstraction," yet
this does not mean that they are devoid of emotions or passion. In fact, in

their struggle to accomplish the movement of this domination of abstraction, they have struggled "with the greatest enthusiasm" (358/G431). Forgetting—or disagreeing—with Kant's insistence that the two are not to be confused, Hegel gives this enthusiasm the name of "fanaticism."[51] It makes the individual into "one passion and that alone." The individual *is*, he becomes, in fact, one passion. There is, therefore, only one principle in Islam, one principle that is not one, but double: "La religion et la terreur," says Hegel in French, religion and terror. Such would be the French name of Muslim enthusiasm, then, and it may therefore be compared not only to the Terror of Robespierre, but to love, in which "an equal *abandon*," a total recklessness, and a lack of consideration and concern takes precedence and, indeed, dominates. One is simply *rücksichtlos*, inconsiderate and unconcerned (359/G432). This lack of concern does not preclude action, for "never has enthusiasm, as such, performed greater deeds," and yet, through its comparisons, this particular enthusiasm becomes incomparable. It becomes or remains wholly singular, since it is "restrained by nothing, finding its limits nowhere," since it is an enthusiasm that is "absolutely indifferent to all beside" (ibid.).

By the time of the *Lectures on the Philosophy of Religion*, the main affect associated with Islam has thus expectedly become fear. "In the Islamic doctrine there is merely the fear of God."[52] This translation of affect from "fanaticism" to "fear" does not imply the cancellation of the prior term, nor does it erase the relevance of the sublime. It is in fact in a section on "the religion of sublimity" that Hegel brings those affects, Judaism, and Islam, into the peculiar togetherness we have been following. The "servitude," common to both Islam and Judaism, servitude to the one God, institutes incomparability and continues to diminish the distance or the proximity between them—the sublime is, of course, about the proper distance from the object.[53] It is very much a matter of negotiating space between or within, and Hegel explains later that "the formalism of constancy which we find in the Jewish spirit in reference to its religion" can be observed "in the same way as in Islam we find the formalism of expansion" (742/G628).

The question of spatio-political expansion and dissemination, *Verbreitung*, brings us back to what differentiates Judaism from Islam, the question of universality, which Judaism is said to lack entirely. Here, too, it is a theologico-political matter that relates to subjection. It is on the question of "world dominion" that Islam is distinguished from Judaism and said to be closer to Christianity as "The Religion of Expediency (Roman Religion)" (the latter also bearing comparison with the religion of sublimity) (*Lectures* 2: 498–512). Under this figure, Hegel explains, Christianity's purpose is "a universal condition of the world, world dominion, universal monarchy." So, too, in Islam, "world dominion is the purpose," even if this dominion is of an "abstract," "spiritual nature" (500/G398–99). Hegel does note that this abstraction, the ground of Islam's "fanaticism," is "at the present stage" not so abstract: "the purpose is still an external, empirical purpose, an all-encompassing purpose but on the plane of empirical reality—i.e., the purpose is a *world dominion*" (ibid.). Here again, the problem is one of association, of unity and unification. Objects remain as if strangers to each other, because the kind of "absolute unification of universal power" implied is, "so to speak, a raw unification, one that is devoid of spirit." Having been shown to be too universal, if not too spiritual, too crude, in its politics of world dominion, Islam can then be brought back to, incompared with, Judaism.[54] It can be faulted for lacking particularity, for having "no defining characteristic like the Jewish sense of national value," no "concrete historical content."[55]

This final comparison of Islam with Judaism does not achieve any more unification—at least not a spiritual one. Yet I hope it will have shown that Hegel has much more to say about Islam and the Muslims than commentators have allowed in this context.[56] Hegel did have quite a bit to say about the Jews. And about the Muslims. Moreover, it should be clear that an understanding of "thoroughgoing passivity" and of absolute subjection gains much by being juxtaposed—as Hegel often does—with "the Jew, the Arab," the Jews and the Muslims. It is in this context that Hegel deploys a vocabulary and a conceptual apparatus that, after Kant and Montesquieu, would continue to determine much of the history I am trying to trace here. Hegel himself situates Judaism and Islam within a theologico-political history of subjection, although he does so predominantly in terms of "antithesis" and "by contrast," thus recalling, distinctively, Kant's sublime: Judaism and Islam, religion and politics, hate and love, universality and particularity, spirituality and lack thereof, and absolute surrender. This, then, is the religion of the Jews. And the Muslims.

This religion "is a spiritual religion, like the Jewish," but in it "no particularity is retained."[57] In it, "human beings have value only to the extent that they take as their truth the knowledge that [God] is the one," which is to say that they have little value. Indeed, "the surrender of the natural will," the "negation" of the "natural self," generates a religion that "hates and proscribes everything concrete" and a God "in relation to whom human beings retain for themselves no purpose, no private domain, nothing peculiar to themselves." Their very existence is thus called into question: "Inasmuch as they exist," Hegel writes, "humans do in any case create a private domain for themselves," but this is of little significance "because they lack reflection." In addition, coupled with this, one also finds the complete opposite, the "tendency to let everything take its own course, indifference with respect to every purpose, absolute fatalism, indifference to life; no practical purpose has any essential value."[58] If Kant invented Jewish law as sublime, and if Montesquieu invented despotism, theirs was undoubtedly a paving and a partaking of the ways. After them, though, it is no less undoubtedly Hegel who invented the Muslims.

Freud

> I was eight or nine, a fair in El-Biar. I could no longer find my parents and blinded by tears I had been guided toward my father's car, up behind the church, by the creatures of the night, guardian spirits. Spirits, why are spirits always called upon in letter writing? . . . something like speculating with spirits, denuding oneself before them; he wrote only (on) letters that one, one of the last along with Freud finally. This is Europe, *centrale*, the center of Europe.
> —Jacques Derrida, *The Post Card*

We are getting closer to the center of Europe, to Central Europe, where Freud is searching out Europe's other, fixing in his turn an alterity defined by a range of sightings and repressive forgettings—what we might call "oversights." At this time, Freud—concerned in his work with the effect of phantom oversights and mental deliberations—is on the verge of an exposure to "the Jew, the Arab," the Jews, "faithful resignation," and the Muslims, whose ghostly aura he marks out. "Driving away the phantoms that were at that time supposedly haunting [Wilhelm] Fliess," Avital Ronell writes, Freud "was 'seriously' working on specters."[59] By way of a double gesture that both conjures and excludes, from the opening of *The Psychopathology of Everyday Life*, a peculiar shape "is made to remind the reader of something that cannot be altogether forgotten, something that spooks or haunts" the text about to be broached: "Nun ist die Luft von solchem Spuk so voll." Freud is here calling upon Goethe's text, which names the ghostly stakeout. But, literary as this *West-östliche* gesture may be, it hardly amounts to a matter of figuration, as Ronell has shown. The haunting shape is not a figure, nor, in the not quite logic of spectrality, does it ever achieve ontological stability. The shape is a thing, a "something," that can hardly be identified—and if at all, it could be ascertained only by way of its effects. The stock of Freud's ghostly conjuring engenders a whole field of geopolitical speculation whose borders he probes in the *Psychopathology.*

What takes shape under this heading and, subsequently, under the name of Signorelli has been altogether overlooked to the extent that it articulates, in Freud's text, an early instance of a haunting of and by religion. By bringing together uncertain shapes of Judaism, Christianity, and Islam—suspending for now the status of such "togetherness"—Freud's example does not break down, but it breaks out by unexpectedly providing protocols of reading "religion" and its attendant hyphens. Overlooked, and thus reproducing the (failed) forgetting that constitutes it in Freud's account in the "first" place, the no less spectral and unreadable shape of the *Psychopathology* pivots on the Abrahamic.

Although it appears as a shape, the articulated "something" fails to gather into a secured or unified figure. The story of its vanishing appearances—the inscription of a no less failing forgetting—could be said to begin, after the Goethe citation in Freud's text, in the opening pages of the *Psychopathology.*[60] Freud takes us on a car trip in which talking ensues, but he does not describe this occurrence as a "talking cure." He becomes involved in the story of a "conversation with a stranger" and a "melancholy event."[61] It is a sad occasion, in part no doubt because here, even Freud's own "talking out" failed to happen. Freud remains mostly silent, but this is a silence that provides the occasion for a greater clarity in the order of figuration—the revelatory occasion, at any rate, of a famous event, which came to be known as the "Signorelli example."

Freud had notoriously forgotten the name of the artist "who painted the magnificent frescoes of the 'Four Last Things'[Death, Judgment, Hell, and Heaven] in the Orvieto cathedral" (2/G13). This serves as more than an "example." Freud calls it an "event" or *Ereignis.* In connection with this event, Freud tells his readers that he has a lot on his mind about which he cannot talk—Freud says this much: He must remain silent. He was constrained to be silent, he says ("what is there to be said?" 5), at least on the topic ("I did not want to allude to the topic," 3) and therefore had to interrupt himself: "It was a motive which caused me to interrupt myself while recounting what was in my mind" (4). Freud had names on his mind. In the Signorelli example, a number of names testify to the strange shape and to what Freud understands as "a sort of compromise." By way of this compromise, the names, remembered and forgotten, remind Freud "just as much of what I wanted to forget as of what I wanted to remember." The names, he continues, also "show me that my intention to forget something was neither a complete success nor a complete failure" (4/G15).

Freud furtively begins to assemble a Shakespearean cartography. In the twin spaces of "not complete success" and "not complete failure," what inscribes itself are the impossibly shared destinies of the Arab and the Jew that had been etched by Shakespeare. Freud's unforgettably forgotten moment is occupied by Othello's near success and by Shylock's incomplete failure. At the center of Europe, Freud is about to meet the "sick man"— perhaps even the "dying man" of Europe.[62] Enter the stranger(s). Freud tells us that he was "driving in the company of a stranger, a foreigner," *mit einem Fremden,* "from Ragusa in Dalmatia to a place in Herzegovina." Driving east, Freud continues to map Europe's violent "ethnic" conflicts, yet he also turns and veers back, closing in on Italy. Freud's mind is approaching Venice, which is why the "conversation had turned to the subject of travel in Italy" (2/G14). At some point, Freud had turned to his "traveling companion" and asked him about Orvieto, inquiring about the magnificent frescoes of the "Four Last Things" in the cathedral.

Freud was changing the subject. He and this by no means extravagant "stranger" "had been talking about the customs of the Turks living in *Bosnia* and *Herzegovina*" (3/G14; emphasis original). "Those people," Freud had reported, "are accustomed to show great confidence in their doctor and great resignation to fate" (ibid.). Freud realized that he had neglected to pursue the lines of thought that brought him to the Turks and their resignation toward death, and he had therefore refrained from telling—though he wanted to do so—"a second anecdote which lay close to the first in my memory."

Although Freud had suppressed the anecdote when conversing with the stranger, he proceeds to divulge it to his readers. In this anecdote, the main characters are not "turning Turk" so much as they could be said to be "turning ghost." "These Turks place a higher value on sexual enjoyment than on anything else, and in the event of sexual disorders they are plunged in a despair which contrasts strangely with their resignation towards the threat of death" (3/G14–15). This is the "topic" to which Freud did and did not allude when he interrupted his conversation about the cathedral at Orvieto, a strange contrast that he did and did not relate in his conversation with a stranger. Freud did say that he was talking about the Turks, about their sexuality and their "resignation towards the threat of death." Yet it is not entirely clear—certainly not to Freud, and would not be for another twenty years—whether or how the topic of this anecdote is in fact distinct from "the topic of 'death and sexuality,'" which Freud tells his readers in the next sentence he wished to leave unspoken. The confusion here may derive from the fact that the later "topic" is figured as an addition, a supplement: "I did *more* [than suppress the account of the Turks]: I also diverted my attention from pursuing thoughts which might have arisen in my mind from the topic of 'death and sexuality'" (3/G15; emphasis added). Freud allows that his views "have from the very first been *dualistic*," and insists on a certain unbridgeable doubling (of death and sexuality, of Italy and Bosnia, of forgetting and remembering, success and failure, of Christian and Muslim, etc.).[63] He also begins to alert us to the phantomatic shape of a *trait d'union*, a shape where the difference between terms is not simply one of either unity or opposition, but of dualistic disjunction.

In Freud's telling, the rumored phantomatic shape of "those people" ("I had told him what I had heard from a colleague practicing among those people") occurs as the partial veiling of the (author of the) Christian figuration of Death, Judgment, Hell, and Heaven. This phantomatic shape, in turn, comes to constitute a larger shape that may hardly be said to gather anything. (Note, again, that Freud writes about a "strange contrast," not about a gathering. Freud does so even if being plunged into despair over sexual enjoyment does not necessarily appear—later will perhaps no longer appear—as particularly contrasting with a "resignation toward death.") If this shape indeed gathers in the mode of contrast, it is therefore only covertly, perhaps forgetfully, as "a sort of compromise" that never loses its strangeness. Moreover, what may have become noticeable is the way in which, in Freud's telling, this shape is further haunted by another strange contrast. I have said earlier that the "Signorelli example" constitutes a haunting by religion, indeed, a religion and shape where the forgetting of unforgettable terms is as necessary as it is to both succeed and fail: the spectral shape of the Abrahamic. The Jew (Freud interrupting his telling, (n)either telling (n)or forgetting) the Christian (Signorelli) (about) the

Muslim. "Signior," Freud would have said, prayed, or conjured—had he remembered the unpronounceable name of Il Signior—"it is the Moor."

In this shape, the haunting of forgetting (with and by remembering) affects yet another strange contrast that Freud would revisit when, displacing Abraham and the Abrahamic onto another "figure," he associated "in one figure, the father, the founding father and the stranger,"[64] the Jew and the Egyptian, Moses, and inevitably—following insistent fantasmatic projections and complex modes of denegations that were not lost on Freud and on the basis of which Egypt is to this day associated with and dissociated from the "East" and from the "Arab world"—the Jew and the Arab.[65] What associations, what semantic and emotional investments could there be between and within these terms, between what links and dissociates them? Freud, the Arab, the Christian, the Jew. What "mental geography" brings and fails to bring these together in the mode of contrast?

> Why on the sudden is your colour changed?
> —Christopher Marlowe, *The Jew of Malta*

Freud's mind follows turns and conversions that, at the center of Europe, also remain fixed in an Italian vicinity, never too far from Venice. He brings together, under the heading of a strange contrast, shapes of the Abrahamic. Discreetly signaling toward both Othello and Shylock, Freud does *more*. He does more than merely confirm that a Turk could turn ghost, that a "blessed Jew" could turn Moor, and that such a "Blackmoor" could, in turn, turn "white." Minimally, however, Freud *entame*, he broaches and breaches, as Derrida says, he provides an introductory reading of the phantomatic if unreadable and not entirely forgettable shape of the Abrahamic at the center of Europe.

Freud thus directs our reading of the Abrahamic toward a shape of forgetting as it is occurring, a movement of vanishing where what "turns Turk" also continues to "turn ghost." When it appears or reappears in the texts of survivors of Nazi extermination camps—though the term "appearance" has already proven inadequate—it remains as unreadable as Kafka's Abrahams,[66] open only to the repeated and uninterpreted inscription of its being forgotten, the movement of a disappearance that is itself beginning to vanish. Doing so, the spectral shape of the Abrahamic maintains the complex movement of memory's successes and failures described by Freud and the conflicted, emotional incomparisons we have tried to read. And it does so, as Primo Levi remembers the forgotten and unforgotten forgettable, "without leaving a trace in anyone's memory."[67]

Auschwitz

Vive la mort!

The despotic city, however populous it is, is itself a silent, dismal desert, haunted by a flock of dispirited victims.
—Alain Grosrichard, *Sultan's Court*

LTI, *Lingua Tertii Imperii*, as Victor Klemperer has called it, is the "artificial" language that made up an essential part of the Nazi machinery. It functioned not so much by avoiding words as by using words, "improper" words, to describe and deny, to reveal and conceal at the same time. "The key to the entire operation," Raul Hillberg has said, "was never to utter the words that would be appropriate to the action. Say nothing; do these things; do not describe them."[68] The language of the camps is one well-known instance, though one perhaps less studied. Including words such as *Häftlinge* for "prisoners," *Kapos* for "Police Comrade," *Kameradenpolizei, fressen* (German for "animal eating") for "eating," and *Figuren,* "figure," "shape," or "figurine," for "corpses,"[69] this instance of LTI often continues to be used by survivors, yet often requires translation even for German speakers. Holocaust literature often includes, therefore, glossaries. Recognizable proper names such as "Canada" and "Mexico" are among the words that still call for an explanation, often a kind of "cultural" translation, and thus make it into these glossaries.[70]

The possibility of such translations—the history of absolute subjection, as I have tried to trace it here—as well as the early usage of these words, their integration into LTI, make it debatable to what extent Primo Levi's later assertion can be accepted unproblematically regarding the essential difference, the radical absence of any partaking between LTI and other languages, between LTI and other times and other places: "the Lager's German was a language apart: to say it precisely in German,[71] it was *Orts- und Zeitgebunden,* 'tied to place and time.'"[72]

The question here may be formulated in terms of success and failure. It is a question of the success (or failure) of the Nazi regime to operate, among other atrocities, a "semanticide" (what has been called "the death of the German language")[73] and to decontextualize words *fully*. Can such an attempt be compared to the attempt to establish an elusive and ultimately psychotic "purity"? Interestingly enough, an early testimony both to this "cleansing" attempt (and perhaps to its failure, as well) was voiced quite early on by a Catholic theologian, Pius XI, in his famous 1937 encyclical entitled *Mit brennender Sorge* (With burning concern). The pope expressed his opposition to the "secularization" of Christian terms such as "revelation," *Offenbarung*, "faith," *Glaube*, "immortality," *Unsterblichkeit*, and "grace," *Gnade*. Such distortion, he complained, "can only be intended to confuse or worse to do evil." If Hitler "doesn't want to be a Christian," Pius wrote, "he should at least refrain from enriching the language of his heresy with the Christian lexicon."[74] What I would tentatively call a linguistic failure here is no more than the continued recognizability of LTI as a *Christian* language, in Pius XI's sense, the way in which it invokes, builds upon, and "draws on" what, in a slightly different context, Inge Clendinnen has called "existing capital."[75]

Another, more oblique site to raise the question of linguistic success or failure may be found in the constancy of LTI, the way it is still part of "our cultural history," as Blumenthal put it, as well as the ways in which it quickly turned into names those words that, spared their intended ambiguity or secrecy, no longer need translation.[76] Nazism's best known "euphemism," may be the most significant example. The "final solution" is a phrase that has come to name quite precisely what it was meant to conceal.

But the language of the *Lager*, as an instance of LTI, also articulates another "gray zone," the area of camp life—that peculiar "life in death" that camp life was—in which both oppressor and victim were partaking. Indeed, one of the troubling and peculiar aspects of camp life has to do with this partaking—not a sharing, but a cooperation that incomparably implicated, although obviously not entirely, the victims in their oppression and extermination. This "gray zone" has left traces in the complex phenomena that have maintained the psychic investment that still binds Nazi and Jew together in many cultural and political sites, rendering the question of comparison particularly thorny, as well as less pertinent. But to return to the language of the *Lager* and the cooperation it sustained: There were words—there is at least one—in this language that mark the disturbing porosity, the contamination, between victim and perpetrator, between Nazi and Jew, but also between camp life and "normal" life. ("When this name appeared," says one witness, "I do not know, nor can I say who created it, the camp-prisoners or the SS.")[77] One might want to speak here of an exception—an extreme case—that ruled or governed an entire discourse long before World War II and continued to do so during and most disturbingly, perhaps, *after*, and to this very day. That single word—but there are others—is the one word I have been trying to follow here by tracing something like a theologico-political history of absolute subjection. It is a word that, in English, remains insistently, if inconsistently untranslated and instead transliterated.[78] That word is *Muselmann*—in the plural, *Muselmänner*, Muslims.[79]

Many of those assaulted relinquished the struggle and became *Muselmänner*, 'Muslims', men and women reduced to staring, listless creatures, no longer responding even to beatings, who for a few days or weeks existed, barely—and who then collapsed and were sent to the gas. We can guess [sic] that the term *Muselmänner* refers to the docile acceptance of one's destiny popularly ascribed to Islam and "the East". The term, like the condition, was current in many camps among prisoners and guards: a small linguistic indicator of the coherence of the *univers concentrationnaire*.[80]

Seeing them from afar, one had the impression of looking at Arabs praying. This image was the origin of the term used at Auschwitz for people dying of malnutrition: Muslims.[81]

The "Musselmänner"—those resigned, extinguished souls who had suffered so much evil as to drift to a waking death. Turning their backs on life and the living, they felt no further terror or pain. They were dead but didn't know it.[82]

All the *Muselmänner* who finished in the gas chambers have the same story, or more exactly, have no story; they followed the slope down to the bottom, like streams that run down to the sea. On their entry into the camp, through basic incapacity, or by misfortune, or through some banal incident, they are overcome before they can adapt themselves; they are beaten by time, they do not begin to learn German, to disentangle the infernal knot of laws and prohibitions until their body is already in decay, and nothing can save them from selections or from death by exhaustion. Their life is short, but their number is endless; they, the *Muselmänner*, the drowned, form the backbone of the camp, an anonymous mass, continually renewed and always identical, of non-men, who march and labor in silence, the divine spark dead in them, already too empty to really suffer. One hesitates to call them living: one hesitates to call their death death, in the face of which they have no fear, as they are too tired to understand.

They crowd my memory with their faceless presence, and if I could enclose all the evil of our time in one image, I would choose this image which is familiar to me: an emaciated man, with head dropped and shoulders curved, on whose face and in whose eyes not a trace of thought is to be seen.[83]

The Muslims are everywhere. At the center and at the margins of Europe and its literature, visible and invisible, they figure a disappearing non-act where passivity and subjection endure. Indeed, "Muslims," this most visible and invisible of words, has been a manifest site, a site of manifestation, an "image," as Primo Levi says, for absolute subjection, and a figure of recognition—and at bottom, if there were one, the only question I would have is this: *How did this "recognition" become and remain possible* since the earliest days? In 1946, David Rousset already spoke of "les 'musulmans', les faibles," in his *L'univers concentrationnaire*.[84] Eugen Kogon described them in some details his *Der SS-Staat* in 1946,[85] and in 1947, Primo Levi wrote his own major account of them. In 1958, Elie Wiesel added his haunting descriptions of "a weak one, a 'Muslim' as we used to say."[86] Published and translated in numerous languages, Tadeusz Borowski, Bruno Bettelheim, Terrence Des Pres, Wieslaw Kielar, Hermann Langbein, Robert Jay Lifton, and Filip Müller, and more recently Yehuda Bauer, Wolfgang Sofsky, Jorge Semprun, Alain David, and Inge Clendinnen mention them in a variety of details.[87] Emil Fackenheim thought it wise to add to their unbearable name yet another name, another calling. The Muslims, he chillingly writes, "may be called the most truly original contribution of the Third Reich to civilization."[88] "Philosophers," he added, perhaps referring to himself, "are faced with a new *aporia*. It arises from the necessity to listen to the silence of the *Muselmann*."[89]

Lately, otherwise than silence and with Giorgio Agamben's *Remnants of Auschwitz*, it seems that "perhaps only now, almost fifty years later, is the *Muselmann* becoming visible, perhaps only now may we draw the consequences of this visibility."[90] Perhaps. Undoubtedly, "there is little agreement on the origin of the term *Muselmann*."[91] Yet some questions remain as to "the most likely explanation of the term,"[92] questions that I have tried to address here, even if only obliquely: How did this translation occur? How did it sediment and settle? How did this "image," this incomparable "figure" that bore many names in different camps, come to be called, still and predominantly called, "Muslim"? How did the Jews, but not only the Jews, perhaps not even mostly the Jews, and yet still the Jews, come to be (called) Muslims? And what of the invisibility, silence, and unreadability of this name? What is clear is that no one familiar with Holocaust literature and scholarship since the end of World War II could have failed to read this name—but we will have to interrogate that word "reading," as well, could have failed to see on the countless pages of this literature the word "Muslims."

C-a-f-f-e-e
C-a-f-f-e-e,
trink nicht so viel Caffee!
Nicht für Kinder ist der Türkentrank,
schwächt die Nerven, macht dich blaß und krank.
Sei doch kein Muselmann,
der ihn nicht lassen kann!

C-o-f-f-e-e
C-o-f-f-e-e,
don't drink so much coffee!
The Turk's drink is not for children;
it weakens the nerves and makes you pale and sick.
Don't be a Muslim
who can't help it![93]
—Popular German Song

Its particular status, invisible yet everywhere, may already make the word "Muslim" itself serve as a "cipher" for the exception, the limit case that governs where the spheres it "ties" over come together and fail to come together. It is "here," in this nonsite, that "a kind of ferocious irony" is articulated: "the Jews knew that they would not die at Auschwitz as Jews."[94] It is "here" (and we have been "with," if not "at," this impossible "here" since the beginning of this chapter) that the cooperation, the parting and part taking of life and death, of Jew and Muslim, of theology and politics, inscribes itself and erases itself. I do not know where, ultimately bound to the weight of words that may or may not speak the unspeakable, the greatest enigma lies, whether it is in the persistent invisibility of that word (an invisibility that is all the more remarkable given its dissemination), or whether it is in the fact that it may now become more readable, as I am at least trying to argue.[95]

"Those people," then, who "still live, but do not know it"[96] are vanishing ghosts and, much farther from Venice, they still bring together—and this togetherness is more than ever suspended—disparate theatrical genres (comedy and tragedy, Shylock and Othello, the *Merchant* and the

Moor of Venice). They are named "Muslims," as Hélène Cixous recalled. They are "the deported, for example, as what were called 'Muslims.'" They are named, then, even if they do not quite figure, although Cixous subtly remarks that "everyone there has a sort of role, everyone is dressed up, travestied."[97] In the context of recalling the Muslims, Cixous reminds us that we are also reading (and not reading) Shakespeare. Cixous thus reiterates and gives to be read the *trait d'union* whose haunting shape provides the "strange contrast" of a nongathering in Freud, reminding us that "one never dares think of Hell as a comedy." "After" the theological and the political, hell and comedy take the haunting shape of a strange contrast, that of Jews and Muslims, Arabs and Jews. The Abrahamic, if that is what this is, remains. It remains a haunting shape that is "made to remind the reader of something that cannot be altogether forgotten, something that spooks or haunts the text about to be opened, and in ways from which no one knows how best he may escape."[98]

"One knows that they are only here on a visit, that in a few weeks nothing will remain of them but a handful of ashes in some near-by field and a crossed-out number on a register."[99] According to other witnesses, they are the prisoners "who had been destroyed physically and spiritually, and who had neither the strength nor the will to go on living."[100] Lacking in that they provide no reason to invest in them, those whom Levi described as having turned Muslims provide little hope of "later . . . perhaps" deriving "some benefit."[101] Insistently marked for their failure to submit to a logic of value and capital, the Muslims are "the men in decay [with whom] it is not even worth speaking." They are the "weak, the inept, those doomed to selection," those who stopped fighting, living dead or walking corpses who were no longer able to fold their legs. Unlike Freud's "Turks," who are "plunged in a despair that contrasts strangely with their resignation towards the threat of death," the Muslims were mostly Jews ("most frequently, one saw Muslims among the Jews"),[102] but not only (and perhaps no longer) Jews, and they are turning ghosts.

Various testimonies about the "Muslims" were compellingly reproduced and discussed in Agamben's *Remnants of Auschwitz*, which draws on the research of two Polish sociologists, Zdislaw Ryn and Stanislaw Klodzinski. Vivid as they are, the testimonies gathered appear to inscribe hardly more than the Muslims' disappearance. Yet, although forgotten and forgettable, leaving no trace in anyone's memory, as Levi puts it, on the far side of the human, they remain sites of memory. As problematic as their existence as memory traces seems to have been, they were already memory effects, referential extrapolations that recalled (still recall) the "faithful resignation" that has been accompanying us throughout this chapter. To witness the Muslims was to witness a "state of resignation,"[103] the look of "Arabs praying,"[104] as if one already had the impression that this was "a Muslim procession, a kind of common prayer of Muslims,"[105] as if one saw in them "the eternal Muslim."[106]

Grammar fails to accompany the Muslims as bereft of agency, as having lost all will to live. Kafka's words could perhaps articulate this failure of grammar along with the vanishing of those

> of whom it is recounted that they have no other longing than to die, or rather, they no longer have even that longing, but death has a longing for them, and they abandon themselves to it, or rather, they do not even abandon themselves, but fall into the sand of the shore and never get up again. . . . Anyone who might collapse without cause and remain lying on the ground is dreaded as though he were the Devil, it is because of the example, it is because of the stench of truth that would emanate from him. Granted nothing would happen; one, ten, a whole nation might very well remain lying on the ground and nothing would happen.[107]

This nonevent ("nothing would happen") constitutes and undoes the being of the Muslims in their lack of, precisely, being. They hardly constitute anything, but out of this "them" which is not one issues of naming are multiplied: "one hesitates to call them living: one hesitates to call their death death in the face of which they have no fear"[108] Their name, although it is only one in a long, often forgotten, disseminated chain, is spared the uncertainty of naming, even if it produces added layers of forgotten perplexities (indeed, "to a reader unfamiliar with the KZ-literature," concentration-camp literature, "the word Muslim must appear strange and un-understandable").[109] They are "Muslims, that is to say, people of absolute fatalism. Their submission was not an act of will, but to the contrary, evidence that their will was broken."[110]

As figures of "faithful resignations," the Muslims thus appear as quasi-theological figures. Yet this, too, testifies to the vanishing logic that marks them, for the theological, too, registers only in its disappearance:

> An explicit political meaning has also been attributed to the extreme threshold between life and death, the human and the inhuman, that the *Muselmann* inhabits. . . . At times a medical figure or an ethical category, at times a political limit or an anthropological concept, the *Muselmann* is an indefinite being in whom not only humanity and non-humanity, but also vegetative existence and relation, phys-

iology and ethics, medicine and politics, and life and death continuously pass through each other.[111]

What is missing from this otherwise compelling account is therefore precisely a theological threshold. The Muslims testify to the theological in that they are lacking in divinity, in that they mark the death of a divine (non)humanity. They are "non-men who march and labor in silence, the divine spark dead within them."[112] This death, this lack of living divinity, echoes many a theodicy that accounts for the Holocaust by including and expelling God from Auschwitz. If the Muslims are possible, so the logic would go, there cannot be a God. Or: God cannot be present at the site of the Muslims. Over against the Jews, whose racialization was always a detheologization, Muslims (or Arabs) would thus testify to a theological absence rather than to the absence of theology. And although they do not appear to have registered much on the Nazi radars, when and if they did, it was mostly as theological, indeed, religious citations.[113]

But the paradoxical threshold also inscribes itself onto political meaning. As figures of absolute subjection, the Muslims can no doubt represent a degree zero of power, the sheer absence of a political displaced by a (negative) theology. Muslims, Wolfgang Sofsky writes, "document the total triumph of power over the human being" as well as "the destruction of social relations . . . a simultaneous destruction of the social sphere, the *vita activa* and *vita mentalis*."[114] They are also said to have "died a death that was social" (202). Yet it is not clear whether this constitutes a contradiction with the "mute animal togetherness" that characterized them, as well: "most of the time, they squatted side by side in silence, seeking a physical nearness that supplanted language" (203). Such a possible contradiction is compounded by a translation of weakness into power, as reflected in the equivocal cases in which what occurs is a suspension of the ability to recognize power and/or the lack thereof: "their lethargy was frequently mistaken for laziness, or a form of passive resistance against the orders of the supervisors and prisoner functionaries" (ibid.). "The passivity of the *Muselmann* was an insult to power" (204). What remains clear is that they were "the camps pariahs," standing "below the lowest rung of the system of social classes" (203). The prisoners wrote them off (204).

Among the many unbearable difficulties that thus emerge, one has to do with the impossibility of following the absent webs of theological and political memory traces that philologically and otherwise link "Europe and the Jews," "Islam and the West," and Freud's Turks with the camps' Muslims. What is indisputable, however, is that memory and its failure constitute and unravel, expose and explode such links. These unbearable links can, even if with great difficulties, be named and recalled as "the Jew, the Arab." It is the unreadable link of the theologico-political at its end, between life and death, of life and death, a link that has failed—that cannot but fail—to present itself to this day as the elusive shapes of the Abrahamic, along with its unreadability and the impossibility of its theologico-political history.

"We write you, motherland"

> But in his eyes, the death announcement is already inscribed.
> —Zdzislaw Ryn and Stanislaw Klodzinski

With the "faithful resignation" of the Muslims, we are also brought back to (and beyond) the problems raised by Nathan Blumenthal regarding Israel, Palestine, and Israeli literature and culture.[115] To what extent has the word "Muslim" become "part of our cultural history"? What of "the Jew, the Arab," then, what of Muslims in Israeli literature? By now, it should be clear that the question I have wished to raise can no longer maintain itself as the slightly more explored one of "The Arab in Israeli literature."[116] The enemy draws away, and indeed, the question raised by the Muslims has a pervasive, if vanishing aspect, since the "ferocious irony" of which Agamben speaks has made it impossible to know whether the Muslim is an Arab, a Jew, a Christian, and even a man or a woman.[117] I opened this lengthy discussion with the Israeli writer S. Yizhar. I want to conclude—if a conclusion there could be—with Dov Shilansky and Ka-Tzetnik.

> That Israeli youth learned about sex and perversity, and derived sexual gratification, from books describing the manner in which Nazis tortured Jews, is all the more disturbing, considering that we are speaking about a society whose population consisted of a large proportion of Holocaust survivors and their offspring.
> —Omer Bartov, *Mirrors of Destruction*

Dov Shilansky—a major figure of the Israeli establishment, ex-speaker of the Israeli Knesset, and one of the early and active leaders[118] of Menahem Begin's Herut and later Likud Parties—provides only a title here, and it is possible that the invisibility of which I have tried to write has reproduced itself in my attempt to read his book, published in 1961 and translated into English, in Israel, in 1962, called *Musulman* (Hebrew: *Muzelman*).[119] Although the book—the narration of which takes place in Tel-Aviv and "in the immigrant *ma ʿabara* at Abu-Kabir" after the 1948 war (86)—contains descriptions under which one may recognize familiar figures, the word "Muslim" (that is, "Musulman") does not appear in the body of the text. It thus remains mainly in an untranslated title and in an afterword by "the Author": "The Muslims were debilitated human creatures, too enfeebled to work and so doomed to die—of suffocation, of starvation, in the burning-pit or in the crematorium—because they were no longer of any use to the Germans." Shilansky continues: "Everything I have narrated in this book and the many descriptions of Muslims and their fate are not the product of my imagination" (256/H248).

The subjection of the Jew turned Muslim, his submission to the absolute will of the kapo ("der Kapo zeigte mit dem Finger auf ihn"),[120] received perhaps its most potent descriptions in the Hebrew writings of Yehiel Feiner, a.k.a. Yehiel De-Nur, still better known under the name which he took for himself, that is, for the others, Ka-Tzetnik 135633. It is not by accident that Tom Segev opens his book *The Seventh Million* with a powerful evocation of Ka-tzetnik. *The Seventh Million* documents what is perhaps one of the most disturbing psychic continuities linking the Nazi period to "our cultural history," that is, as Yizhar's "The Prisoner" shows, the history of Israel, as well as the history of Palestine, indeed, the Jew, the Arab. Segev describes how he himself belongs "to a generation of Israelis whose image of the Holocaust was formed by what they read as teenagers in Ka-Tzetnik's books" (5). Ka-tzetnik, the "author," became famous later than his books—among the first Holocaust books in Hebrew—at least later than the first ones. This personal fame came with the Eichmann trial, where he began to testify, only to collapse at what Segev describes as "the most dramatic moment of the trial, one of the most dramatic moments in the country's history" (4). His books have been translated into scores of languages, beginning in the late 1940s.[121]

They are disturbing books. Tom Segev writes that he read the book from which I will quote here when he was but a young boy: "I have never since read anything about the Holocaust that so disturbed me" (5). As an explanation for such effect, Segev volunteers "no small measure of kitsch and pornography" (ibid.). They are also gripping books, says Omer Bartov, perhaps for a similar reason, "their obsession with violence and perversity."[122] Bartov also testifies to "the common view in Israel of Ka-Tzetnik as an icon of Hebrew-language representation of the Holocaust" (202). What is more important, perhaps, and without concerning ourselves with the accuracy of Bartov's statement, is that Ka-Tzetnik "writes from the point of view of the drowned, the mussulman" (195). Bartov also engages in a naming of his own and renames him, "God's Mussulman (193).

What does this mean? Along with the fact of Ka-Tzetnik's popularity, it simply means that the Muslims are, again, everywhere in Ka-Tzetnik's work, that is to say, everywhere in the Hebrew imagination of the Holocaust. By this I do not mean to claim that they are "present," but rather that the word "Muslim," however translated and transliterated, however readable and unreadable, is a word that has "settled" in Israeli culture and literature. I want to conclude with this settlement of the Muslims—and this only. I am quoting from *Kar'u lo piepel* (They Called Him Piepel), a novel translated as *Piepel*, but also as *Moni: A Novel of Auschwitz*, and even as *Atrocity*. The English editions include a "map" entitled "The Hierarchy at Auschwitz" that runs from the S.S. Camp Commandant, Rudolf Hess all the way down to "camplings" and to "Mussulmen."[123] This hierarchy is also a sexual one, as the text makes very clear.

"He also knew that Franzl was not satisfied with him. *I'm not having any Muslim in Bed!* Block Chiefs like a good fleshy Piepel to make love to after a spell of hustling Muslims, [*shladei-muzelmanim*, skeletons of Muslims] to the crematorium. What would happen to him when Franzl was through with him?" (26/H18–19). Moni, the boy whose perspective is followed in third-person narration, figures a challenge of language: He must fit the image of the Piepel, the sexual slave of "Prominents," block chiefs and kapos. He also figures a challenge to the reader, who must read words such as "life" and "love" and translate them into "Auschwitz life" and "Auschwitz love." Bread, in Auschwitz, is "Auschwitz bread," and sky is "Auschwitz sky," and the days and the nights mark "Auschwitz weeks" while one breathes, perhaps, "Auschwitz air." Yet this constant and necessary translation is predicated on a reinscription of a familiar meaning, to the point of a rupture that must, however, fail, reinscribing therefore an understanding that is as unavoidable as it is unbearable.

"Hundreds of human shadows drag by Moni, this way and that. Their blank stares collide with him as they seek something not remembering what. . . . With contraband it is best to go amidst Muslims. No one pays attention. It is for them that Auschwitz was created" (53/H43). But walking with the Muslims, Moni quickly comes to question whether he is becoming one of them and berates himself: "Just look at yourself! Look at your pants, your jackets, rotting and wrinkled like a Muslim's! You want to be a Piepel looking like that? . . . You're going to burn in the crematorium, I tell you, and I won't feel one bit sorry for you, you stinking Muslim!" (54–55).[124]

Muslims are everywhere, around and even "in" Moni. Yet although they bear comparison with sense perception ("the Muslim sentries sniff them with a special Muslim sense" 92/H79), they do not register on the senses: "Moni no longer saw the bones of the Muslim pile beneath Berele [*hayu . . . ke-lo-hayu*, they were as if they were not]. They were now a part of the Auschwitz commonplace which the eye no longer notices for its everydayness" (60/H49).[125] The Muslim—but is it the Jew or the Arab?—withdraws, and with its vanishing, what emerges again, and painfully so, is the question of reading: "A crush. A surge. Muslims. Skeletons. Skeletons. You do not see them. Just as you do not see the paper but the words written on it. They are merely the Auschwitz backdrop against which you see only Prominents."[126]

Appendix 2. Corpse of Law: The Messiah and the Muslim

> This figure probably constitutes the true sense of the division of the single
> Messiah (like the single Law) into two distinct figures, one of which is con-
> sumed in the consummation of history and the other of which happens, so
> to speak, only the day after his arrival.
> —Giorgio Agamben, "The Messiah and the Sovereign"

> The rest we must not call subjects, but enemies of God.
> —Thomas Hobbes, *De cive*

"The very existence of philosophy," writes Giorgio Agamben, "is always already constitutively related to the law, and every philosophical work
is always, quite literally, a *decision* on this relationship."[1] This assertion opens
a "zone of indistinguishability" between law and philosophy.[2] Reading and
attending to such zones is not only Agamben's politico-philosophical imperative, it constitutes his texts as works that situate themselves in this zone, between philosophy and law, between philosophy and politics. But this
politico-philosophical imperative still has to ask about the decision that has
produced the disappearance of a "zone of indistinguishability" between two
other, if not necessarily different bodies, theology and politics. It is to this
zone as it articulates itself in Agamben's reading of the messianic ("the figure
through which religion confronts the problem of the Law") in Walter Benjamin and Franz Kafka that I want to attend in what follows.[3]

Going back to "the difficult relationship between philosophy and
law," one has to consider that what Agamben here means by "law" is "the
entire codified text of tradition," that is to say, the text of *religious* tradition, which he describes as "Islamic *shari'a*, Jewish Halakhah, or Christian
dogma."[4] Law is thus theological law, and, as the word "sacred" in *homo
sacer* further suggests, there is little distinction between law and theology,
the juridical and the theological.[5] The decision of philosophy regarding its
"difficult relationship" with law would always be theological as well. To
read law as theological, that is to say, to read the law *and* the theological,
opens what may be the same (or perhaps another) zone of indistinguisha-

bility. But to speak of indistinguishability between law and theology, law and religion, as it emerges from Agamben's work on the messianic and its relation to *homo sacer* does not, or should not, simply conflate the two, nor, were it to produce such a conflation, could it be taken as the last word. This last word, at any rate, would not be without remainder or remnant, the remnant of a body of law, a body in the law. It is not surprising that Agamben would turn to Kafka (and to Benjamin) in order to engage the question of the remnant, for to read law as theological is also to interrogate the life that maintains itself in relation to it, and it is to ask whether the theological body of and in the law is still living. Most of all, to read this body of and in the law is to call for "an attentive and unprejudiced delimitation of the respective fields of the political and the religious," to "make it possible to understand the history of their intersection and complex relations."[6] Such delimitation will attend to the possibility or impossibility of reading the remnant as theologico-political.

Residua Desiderantur

> The remnant is a theologico-messianic concept.
> —Giorgio Agamben, *Remnants of Auschwitz*

Formulated in what could be read as the *Urzelle* or "germ cell" of *Homo Sacer*, the 1992 Jerusalem lecture entitled "The Messiah and the Sovereign" suggests a theological genealogy for Agamben's account of "sovereign power and bare life."[7] Instead of Greek or Roman law, one finds Jewish law at its beginning. More specifically, the messianic, the "essential character" of which "may well be precisely its particular relation to the law," stands at the door leading into it.[8] In this section, I will follow the reading protocols set by Agamben in his text on the Messiah, a text in which Kafka (and Benjamin on Kafka) occupies a crucial position, for reasons that will become clear. Inscribed within a complicated network of readings (Agamben calls upon Kafka's most attentive readers: Walter Benjamin, Gershom Scholem, and Jacques Derrida), Kafka's parables open the question of the messianic as an interpretive problem, and with it, the rapport of theology with law and of law with politics comes to the fore. The parables take us "right into the milieu of Kafka's world," tracing and, indeed, staging the messianic. They figure a world in which "the distortions which it will be the Messiah's mission to set right someday" affect more than our sense of space: "surely they are distortions of our time as well."[9] Yet we will be led to consider that this staging of the messianic may not be about just any Messiah. Rather, it is one of "the most antinomical messianic communities, such as that of Sabbatai Zevi, who stated that 'the violation of the Torah is its fulfillment,'" that constitutes a privileged example and perhaps an alternate and hidden beginning for a genealogy of modern politics, for a genealogy of *homo sacer*.[10] Much like messianic time, which clarifies "the structural analogy that ties law in its original state to the state of exception," it is that "most radical" of "messianic movements," that of Sabbatai Zevi, that clarifies and announces, in turn, the historico-political culminating point of Agamben's genealogy of *homo sacer*.[11] Finally, the messianic may begin to clarify the apparent passage or relation from a "force of law" (Scholem's "being in force without significance") to a "form of law" (Kant's "simple form of law") and, finally, to a corpse of law.

> Und er läßt es gehen
> Alles, wie es will,
> Dreht, und seine Leier
> Steht ihm nimmer still.
>
> And he lets it all go
> Everything, as it will,
> He turns, and his organ
> Never stays silent.
> —Wilhem Müller, "Der Leiermann"[12]

Kafka's parable, entitled "Die Wilden, The Savages,"[13] speaks most hauntingly to the "true sense of the division of the single Messiah (like the single Law) into two distinct figures."[14] In it, "messianic music" (of which Jacob Taubes spoke) appears as the anguished music of life, "life in all its might."[15] "This barrel organ," Kafka writes, "can play only one tune," and it is being played by eternity, "eternity in person," which "turns the handle" of the organ. If, as Agamben argues, it was Kafka's intuition that "the messianic is at once both the abolition and the fulfillment of the 'as if'" and that "he who stands within the messianic vocation no longer knows the *as if*, no longer disposes of similitude,"[16] then to suggest that life is being "played" by eternity, *die Ewigkeit*—if not by the eternal, *das Ewige*—is to deploy a messianic logic. It is to establish by way of analogy a fragile structure of transcendence whereby the player either is absent from the world of the instrument, which has, after all, no might, no force of its own, or, belonging to "another world" and to "another time," the player—eternity in person—has nonetheless made itself "present in this world and time."[17] I quote Kafka's parable in its entirety.

Those savages of whom it is recounted that they have no other longing than to die, or rather, they no longer have even that longing, but death has a longing for them, and they abandon themselves to it, or rather, they do not even abandon themselves, but fall into the sand on the shore and never get up again—those savages I much resemble, and indeed I have fellow clansmen round about, but the confusion in these territories is so great, the tumult is like waves rising and falling by day and by night, and the brothers let themselves be borne upon it. That is what, in this country, is called "giving someone a leg up"; everyone here is always ready with such help. Anyone who might collapse and remain lying without ground [or: without cause] is dreaded as though he were the Devil, it is because of the example, it is because of the stench of truth that would emanate from him. Granted, nothing would happen; one, ten, a whole nation might very well remain lying and nothing would happen; life in all its might would go on just the same; the attics are still chockablock with flags that were never unfurled; this barrel organ can play only one tune, but it is eternity in person that turns the handle. And yet the fear! How people do always carry their own enemy, however powerless he is, within themselves[18]

The powerlessness that inscribes itself throughout this text would certainly participate in stripping the musical instrument, life, of any force of its own, thus maintaining the need for an outside player, an outside and even divine force or power.[19] Yet it remains questionable whether Kafka's syntax enables a secure determination of the musical instrument as a figure for life. Rather, it may very well be that only insofar as life, mighty and powerful life, would go on could one then find in the attics unfurled flags and single-tune organs. In this reading, then, eternity would not be external to life. "An ancestor of those holders of power in Kafka's works who live in the attics,"[20] eternity would be what turns the handle of stowed-away organs when life, "life in all its might," goes on. A force of life that rules life from outside of life, or a force of life in life, eternity finds itself at the same time outside and inside the "musical" order.[21]

The interpretation of the parable thus pivots on the possibility of distinguishing between inside and outside, or more precisely, of distinguishing whether inside and outside are relevant categories of interpretation.

Whereas one reading locates eternity on the outskirts of life, the second includes this figure of exteriority (the player vis-à-vis the instrument) in a space of interiority within which there is no exteriority—the attic. This no doubt would confirm that "another world and another time" have made "themselves present in this world and time."[22] Life, as and "in daily life," would indeed be "the only life we have," as Kafka puts it in "On Parables."[23]

The debate over the conception of law in Kafka's work between Gershom Scholem and Walter Benjamin raises precisely the question of such a life, "the only life we have," exploring the relation of (the force of) law to life, as Agamben demonstrates. The debate thus has everything to do with "the specific problem that messianism must muster."[24] This is not to suggest that Kafka has not in fact systematically undone messianism and theology, along with literature and interpretation.[25] Yet the hermeneutic alternative in the parable reinforces its messianic dimension (law and life), since whether to locate eternity "in" the attic or "out," on the outskirts of life, would "amount to the same thing," as Benjamin will say.[26] In either case, the parable itself insists, "nothing would happen." To maintain that there is a player, a person and a transcendent subject, eternity, would thus be to maintain oneself in the "as if" (*as if* life were a musical instrument, *as if* eternity were a person). It is to consider eternity, the subject, or the law *as* a "being in force without significance," as Scholem put it.[27] This is why what we have been hearing is "messianic music." Such is, for Kafka, the question of the messianic, which "is at the same time the abolition and the fulfillment of the *as if,* and the subject who wants to maintain himself infinitely in similitude (in the *as if*) while contemplating his own ruin simply loses the game."[28]

Kafka's parable is about messianism because it opens a "zone of indistinguishability" between life and its figure, between life and what rules and governs it, activates and "turns [its] handle," between life and eternity, between life and law. Much like the students of the law who occupied Benjamin, Scholem, Derrida, and now Agamben, we remain with the question of whether we have lost eternity (as a figure of transcendence) or simply cannot decipher it. And as Benjamin sensed, either way "amounts to the same" insofar as the force of eternity (the force of the law as lost or undecipherable, the terms of the debate in the Benjamin-Scholem correspondence) continues to be upheld by the students.[29] Akin to the "small displacement that seems to leave everything intact,"[30] Kafka's messianism ("nothing would happen") attends to the indistinguishability of a rapport with a law that is no longer a law.[31]

Such, at least, is what Agamben offers as a Benjaminian reading of this messianism ("I will seek indirectly to present Benjamin's conception of the messianic task in the form of an interpretation of one of Kafka's allegories," writes Agamben).[32] In Agamben's account, whereas Scholem insists that the relation with the law is one in which law "does not signify," yet "still affirms itself by the fact that it is in force," Benjamin objects to "Scholem's notion of a being in force without significance."[33] Benjamin argues that "a law that has lost its content ceases to exist and becomes indistinguishable from life." Benjamin reads Kafka as announcing "law's fulfillment," its "becoming indistinguishable from the life over which it ought to rule."[34] With Kafka, Benjamin would thus let "no form of law remain in force beyond its own content."[35] Life, daily life, life in all its might, would also be the musical instrument that, no longer accompanying anything with its only score, remains lying in overfilled attics.

Was Scholem correct, then, or did he misunderstand Benjamin (and Kafka) when he launched the accusation that his "exclusion of theology" went too far?[36] Regarding Kafka's work, the question still remains undecidable, yet Benjamin does provide a few clues as to where his reading falls when he entitles a section of his Kafka essay "The Little Hunchback"[37] and staunchly defends himself by stating that "not only do I unhesitatingly recognize the theological possibility as such . . . but also maintain that my essay has its own broad—though admittedly shrouded—theological side."[38] For both Scholem and Benjamin, then, Kafka's parables maintain, rather than abolish theology. They are structured by an exigency that is theologico-political, that is, the messianic as "a sort of theology passed on by whispers, dealing with matters discredited and obsolete."[39] But what remains, what remains lying on the ground without ground, also remains to be read as remnant, as theologico-political remnant. We have begun to read the messianic as it inscribes itself in "The Savages." We must still attend to those who have remained, and remained abandoned, those savages.[40]

No doubt "The Savages" is a parable in which absolute loss lets nothing, no eternity or law, maintain its transcendence. The impossibility of distinguishing whether eternity is a figure for the player of life or whether it is stowed away in a crowded attic among unused flags and abandoned instruments—or both—indicates that what remains is life itself, "life in all its might," which is the only life we have. This loss of eternity, its indistinguishability as law or life, indeed constitutes an experience of abandonment—if such words ("constitute," "experience") still make any sense here. To invoke again Benjamin's words on Kafka's attics, here "are the places of discarded, forgotten objects."[41] The parable pushes "the experience of abandonment to the extreme" and demonstrates that "only where the experience of abandonment is freed from every idea of law and destiny (including the Kantian form of law and law's being in force without significance) is abandonment truly experienced as such."[42] What emerges is a new idea—one might even say a new "messianic idea"—one in which "the relation of abandonment is not a relation" and where "being together . . . *does not have the form of relation.*" In describing this remnant, this remaining without relation, Kafka's parable implies nothing less "than an attempt to think the politico-social *factum* no longer in the form of a relation."[43]

Following Kafka, what Agamben calls for is a thinking in which relation is thus no longer the governing term and in which difference is considered "beyond every form of a connection."[44] Before returning to the terrible "messianic music" that continues to play in the background, I want to consider the way in which Kafka's text, beginning with its syntax and its punctuation, partakes of these considerations by voiding the textual elements of relation—as narration and as relation, causal or other—a relation that the text nonetheless maintains ("those savages of whom it is recounted," narrated, *erzählt*). Like the "band of brothers" that has already dissolved with the rhythm of the waves, the text itself breaks down into unrelated clauses juxtaposed by implausible commas and self-multiplying repetitions.[45] Such multiplication, the repetition of *mehr* in *oder vielmehr* ("or rather") which wanes into a *nicht einmal mehr* ("no longer even") and a *niemals mehr* ("never again"), echoes the rhythmic repetition of another parable in which the phrase "another Abraham" had punctuated the narrative. (Kafka's savages actualize, in more ways than one, the promise made to Abraham that his descendants will be "as numerous as the stars of heaven and the sands on the seashore.")[46] Or rather, it highlights and announces yet another repetition, this time of an *es ist wegen* ("it is because") "without cause" that culminates where the "example," *Beispiel*, is as much to blame, as impossible and as unbearable a cause, as the "stench of truth."[47] Beings who do not even long to be—that is, strictly speaking, beings who, void of *conatus*, no longer *are*—the savages are not even endowed with the attribute of abandon, but they fall and are instead abandoned, fulfilling and abolishing at the same time the Abrahamic promise in which the multiplication (*mehr*) in and as the sand of the shore has already dissolved into the waves of the sea. To the extent that one could speak of *their* death (as in "their *own* enemy"), they are carried by it, without ground, and without cause (*Grund*), no matter how many unreadable causes (*wegen, seinetwegen*) remain. The savages, the brothers, let themselves be carried, and they carry their enemy. Yet carrying (*tragen*) "itself" is hardly maintained by a subject, be it waves or people, and it seems as powerless as the enemy within.

The juxtaposition of brothers and enemies—the politics of friendship—articulates another layer of dissociations, one where no relation remains but the form of relation.[48] The parable presents itself as a *récit* told, *erzählt*, in which "nothing would happen," not even relation, "and a whole nation might very well remain lying and nothing would happen." The form of relation is maintained by a figure that carries the parable further as it abolishes its temporal, narrative extension. This figure, a resemblance, *Gleichnis*, carries over the "I" from the fraternity of the savages to the fraternity of the brothers to whom it is bound-unbound in a relation-nonrelation of having and belonging ("those savages I much *resemble*," *gleiche*, "and indeed I have fellow clansmen," *Stammesbrüder*, "round about"). Much as people carry "their own enemy" and the brothers are carried by the waves, we encounter the "I" as "rising and falling by day and by night," if not by night and fog, another of "these holders of power in constant, slow movement, rising or falling."[49] He is carried over, meta-phorized and para-boled, com-pared, itself a parable (*Gleichnis*) of the savages, playing on the side of the savages, an illustration and an example of their abandon.

The "I" thus becomes one of "these curious carriers of the word" that "make it somewhat difficult indeed to speak convincingly of a poetic utterance."[50] In his "own" belonging-in-abandon, the "I" finds itself neither inside nor outside, both inside and outside, "merely pushed back and forth within a peripheral pocket that somehow touches upon" the band of brothers "without properly getting in touch with it."[51] The "I" becomes anyone, "anyone who might collapse without cause and remain lying on the ground," "dreaded as though he were the Devil," he could be one or double, ten or a whole nation, as powerful, *mächtig*, as life, and as powerless, *ohnmächtig*, as the enemy within.[52] The "I" is a figure of uncertainty that "probably constitutes the true sense of the division of the single Messiah . . . into two distinct figures, one of which is consumed in the consummation of history, and the other of which happens, so to speak, only the day after his arrival."[53]

Muslims

Perhaps the necessity to appear before a court of justice gives rise to a feeling similar to that with which one approaches trunks in the attic which have been locked
up for years.
    —Walter Benjamin, "Franz Kafka"

Relation to the law remains interrupted, without relation.
    —Jacques Derrida, "Before the Law"

There is a strange moment in *Homo Sacer* that engages the question
of belonging and abandonment, of belonging-in-abandon, while throwing
something like a dark light unto the remnant constituted and deconsti-
tuted by "The Savages." Having defined *homo sacer* as "a person who is
simply set outside human jurisdiction without being brought into the
realm of divine law," Giorgio Agamben goes on to describe the particular
mode of exception under which "*homo sacer* belongs to God in the form of
unsacrificeability."[54] One may understand this not falling under divine law
while nonetheless belonging to God as the structure of the exception as included exclusion as Agamben describes it.[55] And yet the question of how
to describe a belonging that would not be within the law remains. The
question is made all the more urgent when Agamben argues that the task
of political theory is to find a space that would be void of relation, and
most particularly of relation to law, even in the mode of the exception,
even in the ban that banishes the subject *from* law: "Only if it is possible to
think the Being of abandonment beyond every idea of law (even that of
the empty form of law's 'being in force without significance') will we have
moved out of the paradox of sovereignty toward a politics freed from every
ban."[56] I cannot presume to answer to this daunting imperative, but I do
want to suggest that what could be called its theological dimension remains to be read. My question, then, is how does *homo sacer* "belong" to
God? And is this belonging still a relation?

"Belonging," *appartenanza*, is precisely what Agamben argues has
been called into question by his inquiry. It is not only that "every attempt
to ground political communities in something like a 'belonging'" can no
longer be pursued or indeed legitimated, but that such a relation has never
been the ground of politics: "the original political relation is the ban (the
state of exception as zone of indistinguishability between outside and in-

side, exclusion and inclusion)."[57] But the abandonment of belonging is also the situation of that "most extreme figure" of "a being from whom humiliation, horror, and fear had so taken away all consciousness and all personality as to make him absolutely apathetic."[58] The *Muselmänner* or Muslims are—if they are—those beings "of whom it is recounted that they have no other longing than to die, or rather they do not even have that longing, but death has a longing for them, and they abandon themselves to it."[59] They are exposed and abandoned to an abandonment—their own powerless enemy—that they always carry within themselves. Abandoned, yet paradoxically situated within companionship, the Muslim belongs without legality: "he was not only, like his companions, excluded from the political and social context to which he once belonged," he "no longer belongs to the world of men in any way, he does not even belong to the threatened and precarious world of camp inhabitants who have forgotten him from the beginning." The Muslim thus "moves in an absolute indistinction of fact and law, of life and juridical rule, and of nature and politics."[60] Recalling the very precise terms with which Agamben described Benjamin's understanding of Kafka ("a law that has lost its content ceases to exist and becomes indistinguishable from life),[61] the Muslim testifies to a situation where the exception has become the rule and where "a law that seeks to transform itself entirely into life" also "finds itself confronted with a life that is absolutely indistinguishable from law."[62]

Primo Levi writes that the law to which the Muslim testifies "is recognized by all."[63] Yet one would have to take the measure of the haunting difficulties involved in such recognition, in recognizing the abandon of the savages as a figure for the Muslim (and, perhaps primarily, in the Muslim a figure for concentration camp inmates). But in attempting to read Kafka's text, one must nonetheless try to attend to the questions it raises, to the imperative to which it abandons its readers. Kafka's "prophetic" descriptions notwithstanding, his parable enjoins us to return to the question of the theologico-political, to the question of a belonging without legality, the "companionship" and the "belonging to God" of *homo sacer* and of the Muslim. It is therefore to Primo Levi that Agamben turns when pursuing, in *Remnants of Auschwitz*, the series of inquiries he began in *Homo Sacer*.

"Where man is alone and where the struggle for life is reduced to its primordial mechanism, this unjust law is openly in force, is recognized by all. . . . With the Muslims, the men in decay, it is not even worth speaking . . . even less worthwhile is it to make friends with them."[64] "Although engulfed and swept along without rest by the innumerable crowd of those similar to them, they suffer and drag themselves along in an opaque intimate solitude, and in solitude they die or disappear."[65] "They followed the slope down to the bottom," and like Kafka's savages, who "fall into the sand on the shore," they are "like streams that run down to the sea."[66] "They, the *Muselmänner*, the drowned, form the backbone of the camp, an anonymous mass, continually renewed and always identical, of non-men who march and labor in silence. . . . One hesitates to call them living: one hesitates to call their death death, in the face of which they have no fear, as they are too tired to understand."[67]

"After" the messianic, then, the Muslims "are" the remnant. But how could the remnant be "theologico-political"? How could they—they, the Muslims—"belong to God"? If Kafka did attend to the messianic in "The Savages," if he did attend to the theologico-political, he has done so by way of an absence or a disappearance. The question of what happens—what kind of event occurs—when law ex-tinguishes itself "into" or dis-tinguishes itself from life, "life in all its might," pivots around the issue of a life without law, of a belonging without legality, which in turn is figured, in Agamben's text, as a "belonging to God." Primo Levi offers something like a reading of these issues and the rudiments of an answer that has until now escaped attention. Levi's answer takes us straight to the dispute over messianism and to the heart of Scholem's contribution to our understanding of messianism. Levi confirms Agamben's gesture whereby the Messiah constitutes a necessary step, perhaps an alternative beginning, in the genealogy of *homo sacer* that leads to the Muslims. Levi points toward the messianic origin of the Muslim's abandonment. Within the Muslims, Levi writes, "the divine spark is dead."[68]

It is Gershom Scholem who has explained in the most laborious and detailed manner the significance of the "divine spark," the "forces of holiness, sparks of divine light,"[69] "sparks of the holy which are scattered among all people" and "must be brought home."[70] With these divine sparks, Scholem accounted for the "tragic dialectic" whereby it became "contingent upon the Messiah himself . . . to fulfill a mystical mission: to liberate and 'elevate' the sparks of holiness and the holy souls."[71] What Scholem refers to as a "Jewish variation of the ancient conception of the *descensus ad inferos*"[72] is the catastrophic event whereby the Jew becomes Muslim, whereby "the Messiah must live with 'the Turk,' for as the exile draws to a close the Messiah himself must be exiled."[73] This event oscillates between tragedy and a "ferocious irony" (Agamben) and reinscribes the unaccountable (and unaccounted for) catastrophe: that the Jew became a Muslim. The "divine spark," which, Levi asserts, the Muslim has lost in his descent to the inferno of Auschwitz, corresponds with horrifying precision to what is "consumed in the consummation of history," to the descent into Islam of the exemplary figure of the messiah "who attained a higher level of fame and influence than had any Jewish messiah since Jesus."[74]

> Or are we obligated to descend with him into this world of
> the abyss, that is, Islam?
> —Jacob Taubes, *Politische Theologie*

This "totally unanticipated catastrophe" remains as difficult and obscure today as the question of the theological in Kafka.[75] And it is no accident that the consistent evacuation of the significance of the theological ("a force without significance," in Scholem's own phrase) repeats the evacuation of the Muslim from the Jew in the double figure of the Messiah—the Messiah and the Muslim, the Messiah and the *Muselmann*—and that it remains, indeed, in force. Rather than attending to the significance of Islam (that is to say, perhaps, also to the significance of the singular *name* of the *Muselmann*), scholars have continued to ignore key theological moments (such as Levi's "divine spark"), together with the enigma of Auschwitz, which turned the Jew into a Muslim.[76] Islam (by now, that most "theological" of names) has remained an unreadable cipher, or a sign for—Christianity. Or, simply, for religion. In Kabbala studies, for example, Moshe Idel recently explained that new explanations concerning Sabbatai Zevi's conversion to Islam are to be framed within "echoes of Christian Kabbalah," studied "within the context of the two rival religions, Islam and Christianity," and that, ultimately, the "important case" of Sabbatai Zevi testifies to a "direct influence of christology on Tzevi himself."[77] As another scholar summarizes it, Zevi's "conversion to Islam was interpreted as if it echoed the conversions of Jews of Iberia to Catholicism."[78]

Consistent with the erasure of a "zone of indistinguishability" between the Jew and the Muslim, and between the theological and the political, the leading scholar of Sabbateanism, Yehuda Liebes, continues to maintain that "messianism is constituted by two contrasting tendencies: a political and worldly one, and a spiritual and supernatural one."[79] Liebes writes that "the Sabbatean messianic movement was mainly a movement of religious rather than political redemption."[80] In so doing, Liebes operates a double gesture whereby he addresses, quite exceptionally, the importance of Islam in Sabbateanism (an importance that one would have found hard to refute, given Zevi's letter to his own *Stammesbrüder*: "My brothers, know . . . that the True One, which only I have known for many generations and for which I have toiled, wanted me to enter Islam with all my heart."[81] Sabbatai also signed his letters "Muhammad").[82] Yet Liebes reinscribes the division as that of theology from politics.

The theological explanations whereby "the Messiah has not really become a Turk; rather he is now ever a Jew"[83] thus correspond precisely to the evacuation of significance of Islam in the case of the Messiah and in the case of the Muslim, the *Muselmann*—the Jew, the Arab. More importantly, it corresponds to the evacuation of the theological dimension, "the divine spark" to which Primo Levi testified. That this testimony articulated the *absence* of the divine can in no way be translated into an absolute, as if it, too, had disappeared "without leaving a trace in anyone's memory."[84] If the law, that is to say also the theological, has become "absolutely indistinguishable" from life, the meaning of this indistinguishability remains to come. It is an event that occurs—if it occurs—in a zone of indistinguishability and that "arrives *at* not arriving . . . manages not to happen."[85] It may also and *at the same time* be the story of "how something has really happened in seeming not to happen."[86] Between the Jew and the Arab, between politics and theology, no more than the messianic remains, no more than a "small displacement that seems to leave everything intact."[87] *Es würde nichts geschehn.* No more and, therefore, no longer, *nicht einmal mehr, niemals mehr*, perhaps never again. "It is as if nothing had come to pass."[88]

Notes

INTRODUCTION

I have benefited from (and altered) the translation of Sargon Boulos published in Darwish, *The Adam of Two Edens*, 51–53. I am most grateful to Joseph Massad for his help in improving my translation. Throughout this book, I have used existing translations wherever possible, emending only if such emendation was called for, based on my use of the texts. If no translation existed, I have provided my own. When quoting non-English works, an unmarked number will generally refer to the English text, "F" for French, "G" for German, "H" for Hebrew, and "I" for Italian. Indications are made only when necessary.

1. Hesitations and waverings as to the "proper" designations that would describe the past and current situation in Israel/Palestine are well known and they say much about the agenda served by each alternative, consciously or not. Who, after all, are the adversaries? Israelis and Palestinians? Jews and Muslims? Jews and Arabs? Political realists and religious extremists? "Jew" and "Arab" remain dominant, if only because they are the terms that determine the daily life of millions, having been inscribed on Israeli ID cards. There, Jew or Arab come before the law and under the heading "nationality," a category distinguished from "citizenship," that is, "Israeli." (Note that, in one register, "Jew" is here detheologized, whereas "Arab" continues to be distinct from any religious content, an ethnic, political marker.) In a proximate context, Bernard Lewis documents the Eastern European genealogy of the distinction between nationality (i.e., ethnic nationality) and citizenship. Lewis also points out that the institutionalization of this distinction involved the transformation of religion into ethnicity (in our case, "Jew") and a confinement, even a kind of eradication of religion as an identity category (here, "Arab," which stands for and erases "Muslim" or "Christian"). The significance of this "secular" institution that leaves religion behind is traced by Lewis to the Soviet Union. The pragmatic, if not historical reasons are made clear in Lewis's comment that "ethnic nationality, unlike religion, cannot be changed by an act of conversion" (Lewis, *Semites and Anti-Semites*, 34). Whether one speaks of "Israelis and Palestinians" (with nationalism as the primary factor), "Jews and Muslims" (with

religion as the primary factor) or "Jews and Arabs" (with poised, so-called "democratic" *politics* on one side and "fanatical" *religion* on the other), one therefore is never simply mistaken, but maintains instead a state of affairs that, institutionalized by the state of Israel, reinscribes invisible or uninterrogated distinctions between and within religion and politics and between and within "Jew" and "Arab."

I should here point out that, except for short asides, Israel and Palestine will not occupy, in any direct manner, a prominent place in this book which, to my mind, may nonetheless constitute a modest companion volume to the inquiries led, most importantly, by Amnon Raz-Krakotzkin, inquiries to which I am more than greatly indebted. In the particular context out of which I write here, Raz-Krakotzkin has suggested an original recasting of the concept of binationalism (borrowed in part from Hannah Arendt) in order to avoid what currently constitutes a dominant object of consensus that was already at the center of the Oslo accords: *separation.* Separation, as Raz-Krakotzkin explains it, is another name for "a kind of autonomy whose function is to separate the Palestinians from the Jews" (Raz-Krakotzkin, "A Peace without Arabs," 66). It also preserves (and aims to solidify) the history I will try to describe here.

Phrased another way, and more urgently, separation is what was already at work when "Tel-Aviv became the only city in the West to which the entrance of Arabs was forbidden. In many ways, then, we can regard the attitude behind the peace process as close to the radical right in Europe: the steps taken before and after the Oslo Accord are exactly those demanded by Le Pen and his followers in France" (67). What is missing from a debate with such shared parameters is "any considerable political position which could combine the discussion on Israeli-Jewish identity with the discussion on Palestinian rights" (75). What is missing is an examination of historical consciousness and of the question of historical interpretation (68–69), which Raz-Krakotzkin calls a "bi-national approach, namely one which does not separate the discussion on Israeli society from the Jewish-Palestinian conflict" (75). As Raz-Krakotzkin puts it elsewhere, binationalism "implies the realization that Palestinian history and Palestinian national identity are part of the discussion of Zionist history, essential parts of the context of responsibility. The definition of Palestinian rights and the definition of Jewish rights are one and the same. This is the context of responsibility that Zionism has created. . . . A binational perspective leads to . . . the definition of a common Jewish-Arab space" (Raz-Krakotzkin, "A National Colonial Theology," 321; see also his "Binationalism and Jewish Identity: Hannah Arendt and the Question of Palestine").

2. Mamdani, *When Victims Become Killers,* 24. Further references will be made parenthetically in the text. For a related discussion of the role of law as producing "the juridical subjects over whom its power is distributed" in colonial and postcolonial contexts, see Massad, *Colonial Effects.* Massad takes on the crucial task of tracing what he calls a "prehistory of juridical postcoloniality" (22).

3. Massad, *Colonial Effects,* 4.

4. Mamdani, *When Victims Become Killers*, 25. On this too, see Massad's *Colonial Effects* and its description of a similar process of distinction between civil law and tribal law in Jordan, a process that, between 1921 and 1976, established that "all Bedouins are ostensibly equal in the civil code but are constituted as different through the application of tribal law" (50). As a result of British pressure, the Bedouins were to be "governed by a new set of laws as early as October 1924, when the Mandatory-Hashemite state enacted the Law of Tribal Courts" (52, and see 56–66). Massad goes on to explore the links between this division and the distinction of the traditional versus the modern. He discusses the territorial confinement of the Bedouins and their role in historical fantasy, tourism, and law enforcement (the military and the police).

5. André Chouraqui explains that already with the Act of Capitulation of July 5, 1830 which established French rule, a fundamental change had occurred within the Algerian population. The act "implied the abolition of the traditional relationships between Moslems and Jews. Nevertheless, a distinction was maintained between the two based not on religion, but on the concept of nationality" (Chouraqui, *Between East and West*, 143). Chouraqui does not elaborate on the new juridico-political division here established between nationality and citizenship, but he does describe how religion continued to define the legal situation of the Jews—until 1870, that is. "The rabbinical courts," he writes, "were entrusted with the administration of justice" (144). By 1834, those rabbinical courts were deemed "unsatisfactory" by the French, and with the Crémieux decree, "the Jews indigenous to the departments of Algeria are declared citizens of France. In consequence their civil status and their personal status will be regulated according to French law" (Decree of October 24, 1870, quoted in Chouraqui, 150). For more on the history of Algerian Jews and the role of the Alliance Israélite Universelle in the French "civilizing mission," see Halevi, *A History of the Jews*; Rodrigue, *Images of Sephardi and Eastern Jewries*; and Derrida, *Monolingualism*. It is one of the ironies of history that Algerian Jews are often considered to be descendants of French *colons*, indeed *pieds-noirs*, rather than as what they historically were in their majority, namely, indigenous Jews of Algeria. A number of European Jews, coming for the most part from Alsace-Lorraine, did begin to arrive after the 1870 Franco-Prussian war. Yet even the local French authorities disregarded this immigration and continued to relate to Jews as indigenous, reminding the Jews of that fact, for example, on census forms. Hence, until 1931, the official census forms still asked whether one had gained citizenship via the Crémieux decree or was a descendant of someone who had so benefited ("Etes-vous israélite naturalisé par le décret de 1870 ou issu d'un israélite naturalisé par ce décret?" Quoted in Allouche-Benayoun and Bensimon, *Juifs d'Algérie*).

6. It may not be entirely trivial to consider that the term "enemy" is not indexed in Mamdani's book. Nor, for that matter is "Israel." This is hardly an accident—indeed, it is probably overdetermined in both cases, but it remains quite re-

grettable, because what Mamdani has to say about both "terms" is an essential part of his argument and a crucial contribution to the issues these terms entail.

7. For a parallel argument that seeks to link, along different lines than those explored here, racism and anti-Semitism as coconstitutive of Europe, on the "verso" side of its concepts and, perhaps, nonconcepts, see Alain David, *Racisme et antisémitisme*. David also finds his inspiration in Derrida's work and underscores the importance of a vanishing, making the "troubling *constat* of an erasure of racism and anti-Semitism from the order of concepts" (50), the absence or withdrawal, one could perhaps translate, of a concept of the enemy (and see 96 n. III and 112–13).

8. Nancy, "The Deconstruction of Christianity," 115. Further references will be made parenthetically in the text.

9. In "Above All, No Journalists!" Derrida offers an accented reading of Nancy, one that I try to follow here, suggesting that there is, in the proximity of Christianity, a temptation that relates to war and, as I will argue in the next chapter, to the enemy. Can one reflect on and event admit to the specific Christian history of war and of the enemy? By asserting that "one is tempted to admit that all Christianization is at war with its contrary," Derrida alerts us, together with Nancy, to a distance that is also a temptation ("one is tempted") between "us, Europeans"— see below—and Christianity at war, Christianity as war (Derrida, "Above All, No Journalists!" 79).

10. Derrida, *The Other Heading*, 7/F14. Further references will be made parenthetically in the text.

11. I quote here from Gasché's illuminating discussion of Husserl, Heidegger, and Derrida in "The Debt of Europe," 124.

12. Ibid., 126.

13. Ibid.

14. Ibid.

15. Derrida, *The Other Heading*, 10–11/F16–17.

16. Guénoun, *Hypothèses sur l'Europe*, 58 n. 87. Further references will be made parenthetically in the text.

17. Regarding this second aspect, the constitution of the political out of religious difference, Guénoun only asserts the necessity of a task to come. Such reflection, he argues, exceeds the limits of his book.

18. Among the important and exemplary studies that consider Islam and the West as well as *in* the West are: Daniel, *Islam and the West*; Waardenburg, *L'islam dans le mirroir de l'occident*; Djaït, *Europe and Islam*; Said, *Orientalism*; Grosrichard, *Sultan's Court*; Rodinson, *La fascination de l'islam*; Corn, *L'Europe et l'Orient*; and Cardini, *Europe and Islam*. See the next chapters for some more discussion of treatments of "Islam and Europe" in the Middle Ages and after.

19. Important exceptions, such as Galiston, "The Ontology of the Enemy,"

Buck-Morss, *Dreamworld*, and prior to both, even Arendt, *Origins* and Genet, *L'ennemi*, unwittingly occlude this disappearance.

20. Foucault, "Il faut défendre la société," and see also Foucault's transcribed course, *"Il faut défendre la société."* In his published work, to my knowledge, Foucault did not engage the question of the enemy. Compare, concerning World War I, the historian George Mosse, who describes in striking terms "the advent of a new kind of war," a change he situates in the emergence of nationalism and, with it, of the citizen-soldier. Mosse documents a series of changes, including the history of the cemetery, military and civil, as well as a generalization of the "war experience." Yet for lack of any comparable (or comparative) discussion of the enemy in Mosse's book or elsewhere, there is room to remain skeptical about the significance of similar, if fleeting assertions concerning the enemy ("Politics," writes Mosse without mentioning Carl Schmitt, "were increasingly viewed as a battle which must end in the enemy's unconditional surrender." Mosse, *Fallen Soldiers*, 161; see also 163–64 and 172–81).

21. The link between war and the enemy constitutes a central and difficult moment of Carl Schmitt's reflections. (Schmitt after all both affirms and suspends that link, asserting that no "actual" fighting need take place between enemies who challenge each others' very existence.) Elaborating on the history of European law, Schmitt came closest to write a history of the enemy in *Der Nomos der Erde*—most notably, perhaps, in his argument that "Roman law was able to distinguish the enemy, the *hostis*, from the robber and the criminal" (Schmitt, *Nomos*, 22), his tracing of the emergence of the *justus hostis* and, between the eighteenth and nineteenth centuries, of the enemy as *inhuman*, the enemy as *"Unmensch"* (72); his descriptions of the criminalization of the enemy, tantamount to a "destruction of the concept of enemy" (93); and finally his famous claim to a joint depoliticization announced by the "sublation" of the concept of *justus hostis* from theological and philosophical discourse ("der Begriff eines *justus hostis*, kann also . . . aufgehoben werden," 143) and finally to the disappeance of the friend/enemy distinction described in Schmitt's *Concept of the Political.*

If there is a concept of the enemy, it is no doubt in law that one could find its most consistent formulation. In this context, the legal work of Richard Zouch (b. 1590) stands out as a unique example singled out by Schmitt of a systematic and sustained classification regarding the concept of enemy. In his *Elementa jurisprudentiae* (ca. 1629), Zouch articulates crucial legal distinctions regarding different kinds of enemies: *Inimici* between whom no bond, especially no legal bond, exists; *adversarii*, who are bound in a legal community, a community that war may end up dissolving; *hostes*, the "proper" enemies, among which one should distinguish *justi hostes* or, if the reason for war is unjust, the *injustus hostis* (see Schmitt, *Nomos der Erde*). Still, as was briefly considered by Foucault in his 1976 course at the Collège de France ("Il faut défendre la société," 1976, see previous note), the question of the enemy exceeds the matter of war: "Can and must all phenomena such as antagonism, rivalry, confrontation, of struggle between individuals, or between groups or classes, be gathered in the general mechanism, the general form that war is?" (Foucault, *"Il faut défendre la société,"* 40). Distinct adversaries, at times even enemies ("ennemi de classe" and "ennemi de race," 72; "sauvage" or "barbare," 173–75, political versus "biological" enemies, 228), are at the center of Foucault's teaching in this course (see, for example, 44, 49, 53, 67, 85, 159). Foucault also raises the possibility, already known from medieval political thought, that the sovereign may be an enemy (51). Yet there is no history of the enemy, no discursive account of the mechanism whereby the enemy in its specificity is described, produced, or rendered operative. For significant, if narrowly specific exceptions that attend to chapters of s history of the enemy, see Buck-Morss, *Dreamworld* (on the Cold War) and Galison, "The Ontology" (on World War II).

22. "Enemy" might therefore constitute an instance of what Catherine Malabou calls "a conceptual symptom," the growing demand to "become a concept," to reach, in other words, "the status of condition of intelligibility" (Malabou, "Ouverture," 7). To a large extent, I have been guided throughout by Malabou's incisive—and, indeed, "explosive"—elaborations of a formative, plastic history of such becoming concept. (For the relation between history and plasticity and for further developments on concept formation, see also Malabou, *L'avenir de Hegel.*)

23. Triki, *Les philosophes et la guerre,* 84.

24. A recent and prominent example may be considered here. In Michael Hardt's and Antonio Negri's *Empire,* the enemy is both central and marginal, an insistent, if not consistent operative term that is invoked and called upon for further conceptualization. ("One element we can put our finger on at the most basic and elemental level is *the will to be against,*" 210.) What remains unclear, however, is whether *Empire* constitutes or deconstitutes such a conceptualization. To that extent, one may say, with *Empire,* that, in "Empire," the enemy is all but disappearing, its effectivity being the occasion of an invisibility, the lack of clarity that occurs in the enduring process of a vanishing that is also a demand for identification, a process that *Empire* itself describes early on as an ambiguous banalization. "Today the enemy, just like the war itself, comes to be at once banalized (reduced to an object of routine police repression) and absolutized (as the Enemy, an absolute threat to the ethical order)" 13). There are still enemies, but the enemy is less and less a martial one. Hence, "the enemies that Empire opposes today may present more of an ideological threat than a military challenge" (35). According to *Empire,* the (martial) enemy draws away, and war is over (if you want it): "The history of imperialist, interimperialist, and anti-imperialist war is over. The end of that history has ushered in the reign of peace. Or really, we have entered the era of minor and internal conflicts. Every imperial war is a civil war, a police action" (189). And yet the enemy remains, and even nongovernmental organizations (NGOs) have enemies, although these, too, are less than martial. Indeed, and somewhat surprisingly, they have theological enemies. Like their religious predecessors, "like the Dominicans in the late medieval period and the Jesuits at the dawn of modernity," hu-

manitarian NGOs are groups that, "through their language and their action . . .
first define the enemy as privation . . . and then recognize the enemy as sin" (36).

Hardt and Negri also lament the lack of conceptual clarity—and the discursive
misplacement of the enemy—when it comes to "the current enemy of Empire."
This enemy, however, is legion, and the rhetoric of *Empire*—the rhetoric of "Empire"—that describes the problem oscillates uncontrollably between singular and
plural. (Under U.S. dictation, what is set in motion is "a process of armed con-
tainment and/or repression of the current enemy of Empire. These enemies are
most often called terrorist, a crude conceptual and terminological reduction that
is rooted in a police mentality," 37.) Some mistake and even mask the enemy.
("The strategy of local resistance," for example, 45), and this needs to be corrected.
Joining a vague and ambivalent fight against "postmodernists," Hardt and Negri
lament the fact that "postmodernists are still waging battle against the shadows of
old enemies": "We suspect that postmodernist and postcolonialist theories . . . fail
to recognize adequately the contemporary object of critique, that is, they mistake
today's real enemy" (142, 137). There is a "new enemy" that is not only "resistant to
the old weapons but actually thrives on them, and thus joins its would-be antago-
nists in applying them to the fullest" (138). Calling for the end of the mistaken
regime, "we should be careful to recognize the form of the dominating power that
serves as the enemy" (145). We should first recognize the true enemy. "The first
question of political philosophy today is not if or even why there will be resistance
and rebellion, but rather how to determine the enemy against which to rebel. Indeed, often the inability to identify the enemy is what leads the will to resistance
around in such paradoxical circles. The identification of the enemy, however, is no
small task."

It is a difficult task because "we suffer exploitation, alienation, and command
as enemies, but we do not know where to locate the production of oppression"
(211). The true or real enemy, write the authors of *Empire*, is "a specific regime of
global relations that we call Empire" (46). The enemy is here, but the enemy is also
new and coming. The enemy is still ahead, and the task of confronting the (right)
enemy is thus affirmed, a necessary step that remains ahead. "Recognizing a common enemy and inventing a common language of struggles are certainly important tasks and we will advance them as far as we can in this book" (57). Throughout *Empire*, the enemy is thus both lamented (we no longer know the enemy, we
have mistaken the enemy) and identified, even called and wished for. The enemy
is both underconceptualized and overconceptualized. It is as if we had already
thought enough about the enemy. There is an enemy—or there will and must be
one—and the pressing question is thus: What are we to do with it—or more precisely, *to* it? "The problem we have to confront now is how concrete instances of
class struggle can actually arise, and moreover how they can form a coherent pro-
gram of struggle, a constituent power adequate to the destruction of the enemy
and the construction of a new society" (404). As we will see in the next chapter, it
is perhaps no coincidence that this task—the task of destroying the enemy—takes

Christian love as its model. By the end of *Empire*, it is thus the Christian "militancy" of Saint Francis of Assisi that "makes resistance into counterpower and makes rebellion into a project of love" (413).

25. Like the Hegelian God strikingly described by Malabou, the enemy may only be visible for and as a moment—moments of the theologico-political. "Dieu," writes Malabou in one powerful sentence, "se voit un moment," God sees himself a moment. Borrowing Malabou's phrasing and variations on and for the moment, one could advance the following: First, the enemy would see and show itself for a moment, in a unique and unrepeated instant and instance (*exemple*). Or, the enemy would see and show itself for a certain duration, even an epoch, but at any rate, for a (more or less limited) time, thus engaging itself in time. In a third sense, the enemy would see and show itself *as* a moment: to the extent that the enemy sees itself, it sees its reflection as moment. "Moment" thus becomes an attribute of the enemy, which sees itself qua moment. Finally, in the logical sense, the becoming-visible of the enemy is its becoming, a moment of its essence as it becomes, its becoming as becoming-moment (Malabou, *L'avenir de Hegel*, 166).

26. Interestingly, in his *Nomos der Erde*, Schmitt would ultimately document the operations of something like a concept of the enemy in the sphere of law. Yet such a confinement of the enemy to the realm of law seems only to have buttressed a general lack of philosophical and political reflections on the enemy. I will later engage the absence of an "ontological question" concerning the enemy, as Derrida pointed it out. For now, it will be enough to signal that this is precisely the question that vacillates and withdraws in Schmitt's own text, appearing and vanishing depending on how one reads the "they" in Schmitt's misquotation of *The Education of Henry Adams* at the very end of *Der Nomos der Erde*: "if the foe is not what they say he is, what are they?" (Schmitt, *Nomos der Erde*, 299).

As should already be clear, Derrida's entire discussion in *Politics of Friendship* is crucial for what I am trying to address throughout this book. I will underscore here the particular importance of the following: "What is said of the enemy is not symmetrical and cannot be said of the friend, even under the heading of structural or shared conditions of possibility" (Derrida, *Politics of Friendship*, 122/F144). William Desmond has commented that very little has been written on enemies or enmity. "Some thinkers," he states at the beginning of his inquiry, "have written on war, some on the need of an enemy, such as Friedrich Nietzsche and Carl Schmitt. But on the nature of an enemy in a manner analogous to the nature of love itself? Not many have written, to my knowledge" (Desmond, "Enemies," 127). Like Schmitt, Desmond places the stakes quite high ("And if we do not know what an enemy is, do we really know what a friend is?"), and yet, by suggesting at the outset the symmetry of enmity and friendship, even of enmity and love (the former being the "reverse negative" of the latter), Desmond posits limits that have to be interrogated. As Kant put it in *Lectures on Ethics*, "Enmity is more than a lack of friendship." Desmond also leaves the political enemy entirely out of his purview and has nothing to say about war. As I will argue, the question of the

enemy is not reducible to the question of war, even if it is hardly independent
from it, something that would be only partly addressed, if at a different level of
analysis, by what Vilho Harle describes as "the current interests of peace researchers in culture, language and their relationship to the questions of peace and
war." And yet, based on the content of the special issue of *History of European
Ideas* he edited, it is not entirely clear what Harle means when he writes that these
same "peace researchers have invested considerable energy in the problems of the
'enemy'" (333), or indeed what "concepts" of the enemy, aside from Schmitt's, are
being considered by the scholars Harle gathered. The articles discuss figures such
as Eliade, Arendt, and Schmitt, the "psychology of enmity," and "the image of Europe in Russian literature and culture." Aside from Schmitt's own writing, these
otherwise engaging studies do not constitute, to my mind, convincing evidence of
elaborate "concepts" of the enemy. (See also Harle, *The Enemy* and Buck-Morss,
Dreamworld.)

   27. See Derrida, *Acts of Religion*, and see below, Chapter 2, "Derrida, the Jew,
the Arab."

   28. Quite informative and representative of a field that remains otherwise marginal, Steven Wasserstrom (who has since moved far away from this particular
sphere of expertise) has well covered the state of scholarship on "the Jews of Islam"
and the so-called "Judeo-Muslim symbiosis" (Wasserstrom, *Between Muslim and
Jew*). Wasserstrom describes the problems associated with the study of this "symbiosis" as a practical and methodological issue (3–14). Rightly tracing the currency
of the term to the works of Shlomo D. Goiten and Bernard Lewis, however,
Wasserstrom does not interrogate the sphere of "religion" within which he locates
his subject, nor does he offer reasons for such a confining location and earlier failures to produce them. (Wasserstrom squarely states that his inquiry is a matter of
"comparative religion" and "interreligious relations," rightly taking to task the no
doubt insufficient work done there: "the study of religion has barely begun to in-
tegrate the extraordinary phenomenon of Jewish-Muslim symbiosis, much less re-
think the paradigm itself," 7.) More pointedly, perhaps, Wasserstrom fails to question the *distance* that is already presupposed, established, and sedimented by
words, foremost among them words such as the word "between." More widely
put, Wasserstrom fails to consider the importance of language (his own, as well as
that of his "subjects") and its role in rethinking what he calls "the problem" (the
subtitle of his book is *The Problem of Symbiosis under Early Islam*). This is more
than a terminological issue over the use of the term "symbiosis," and is instead the
question of a *relation* of Arab (or Arabic) and Muslim (what finally, of "the Arab,
the Muslim," and what, finally, of the word "and"?), and of Arab *and* Jew. In fact,
Wasserstrom barely addresses the issue of a shared language of "Jew" and "Muslim," Arabic. (Hence, it is more than halfway through the book that Wasserstrom
finally notes that, in the Middle Ages, "in fact, Jewish and Muslim theologies [and
almost all other discursive fields, for that matter—GA], both written in Arabic, of
course, had dovetailed to a remarkable extent," 145.) As well, Wasserstrom never

engages the lexical shift that leads from Goiten's *Jews and Arabs* to Lewis's *Jews of Islam*. Between Muslim and Jew, the distance is never closed. And the Arab withdraws.

1. Levinas, *Totality and Infinity*, 21/Fix.
2. Ibid.
3. Schmitt, *Concept of the Political*, 32. And compare, of course, Hobbes, who writes that "a state of war consists not in actual fighting, but in the disposition thereunto." (Hobbes, *Leviathan* 1.62.) I return to Hobbes in Chapter 3, "De Inimicitia." In the textual configuration that will emerge in that chapter, in the light of the enemy, there is perhaps room to interrogate Foucault's claim as to the novelty of a perception of war as "une sorte d'état permanent," "une généralisation de la guerre," in the seventeenth century (Foucault, *"Il faut défendre la société,"* 144).
4. Levinas, *Totality*, 21/Fix. As Derrida notes, "Levinas never speaks of Schmitt" (Derrida, *Adieu*, 147 n. 95). Schmitt is thus "situated at the opposite extreme from Levinas," evoking an "absolute opposition" and embodying "the absolute adversary." The discourse of the enemy, Derrida continues, in Schmitt at least is "the discourse of totality." There are, therefore, "paradoxes and reversals" in that Levinas seems to grant Schmitt the political—rather than ethical—dimension of the enemy, thus affirming the nonalterity of the enemy. It is perhaps in the suggestive context here offered by Derrida that one could read Levinas's terrible answer in 1982, following the massacres at Sabra and Chatila, to the following question: "For the Israeli, isn't the 'other' above all the Palestinian?" Levinas does not quite explain why, but he recoils from the question and rejects it: "My definition of the other is completely different." Where there is war ("if your neighbor attacks"), Levinas seems to say, the other is not the other, but the enemy—alterity, but "with another character." Thus it would be only "in alterity" that "we can find an enemy." Levinas says: "The other is the neighbor, who is not necessarily kin, but who can be. And in that sense, if you're for the other, you're for the neighbor. But if your neighbor attacks another neighbor or treats him unjustly, what can you do? Then alterity takes on another character, in alterity we can find an enemy, or at least then we are faced with the problem of knowing who is right and who is wrong, who is just and who is unjust. There are people who are wrong" (Levinas, "Ethics and Politics," 294).
5. Levinas, *Totality*, 21/Fix.
6. Ibid., 24/Fxii.
7. Hence, as Edith Wyschogrod explains, Levinas does not simply "identify war with the order of the same." Rather, "war is at its most primordial level the law of being" (Wyschogrod, "Derrida, Levinas, and Violence," 190).
8. Levinas, *Totality*, 21/Fix.

9. Ibid., 24/Fxii. And compare Schmitt: "It is not war as such that shatters order . . . the essence of the European *jus gentium* was to circumscribe war. The essence of these wars was meant to measure forces in an orderly fashion, in front of witnesses and in a circumscribed space. Such wars are the very opposite of disorder. They include the highest form of order of which human efforts are capable" (Schmitt, *Nomos der Erde*, 157–59).

10. Nancy writes that war is the "execution or putting to work of sovereignty itself" (Nancy, *Being Singular Plural*, 102). But in making a decision over the enemy, the sovereign seeks to strip another sovereign of his sovereignty, to subject him, even destroy him. What is thus confronted is not other, but an alter ego. "The right to wage war is the most sovereign of all rights because it allows a sovereign to decide that another sovereign is its enemy and to try to subjugate it. . . . It is the sovereign's right to confront his *alter ego*" (106). If Nancy is right that sovereignty remains to be thought ("No possibility anywhere for thinking sovereignty *hic et nunc* or for thinking beyond it," 109), I would want to add that this failure of thought is all the more striking regarding the enemy, at the opposite side—apparently—of sovereignty.

11. All references to Paul's Letter to the Romans (henceforth Rom.) and all other biblical references are to the New Revised Standard Version (New York: Oxford University Press, 1989). The citation here is from Rom. 3:31.

12. Taubes, *Politische Theologie*, 27.

13. Proverbs, 25:21–22.

14. Taubes, *Ad Carl Schmitt*, 23.

15. Levinas, *Totality*, 222. Wyschogrod points out that "although it is a central motif in his thought, nowhere does Levinas provide a sustained discussion of war" (Wyschogrod, "Derrida, Levinas, and Violence," 190). In the section I just quoted, Levinas reconsiders the equation between war and totality and argues that war does testify to exteriority, "it is a relation between beings exterior to totality" (Levinas, *Totality*, 223; see also Levinas, *Otherwise*, 119/F152, where a provisional definition of the ego is offered as "a free subject, to whom every other would be only a limitation that invites war"). Yet, this relation of war is finally not a relation of alterity, but is derivative of it: "Violence can aim only at a face" (*Totality*, 225). Prior to war, one finds a "relation that subtends war, an asymmetrical relation with the other, who, as infinity, opens time, transcends and dominates the subjectivity." This relation "can take on the aspect of a symmetrical relation" (ibid.). It is notable that Levinas uses the word "adversary," *adversaire*, rather than "enemy" throughout. One notable exception operates a momentous substitution, a reading of which guides this entire book: "The enemy or the God over whom I can have no power and who does not form a *part* of my world remains yet in relation with me" (*Totality*, 236/F212).

16. Schmitt, *Concept of the Political*, 28–29. I return to this issue regarding Schmitt's rapport to the New Testament in the next chapter.

17. Taubes, *Politische Theologie*, 72. It is worth noting that the importance of

the friend-enemy distinction does not explicitly figure in Schmitt's own *Political Theology*. Schmitt concludes his main critique of liberalism with the charge that liberalism "wants to dissolve metaphysical truth in a discussion." With such discussions and with endless negotiations, Schmitt continues, liberalism defers "the decisive bloody battle" and, more gravely, "permit[s] the decision to be suspended" (*Political Theology*, 63). The decision is postponed along with the "decisive" bloody battle, but with it, the question of enmity begins to emerge within *Political Theology* itself. Having stressed in this early book the importance of theology for an understanding of the political, it took a few more years for Schmitt to place the enemy at the center of his political theory in *The Concept of the Political*. Schmitt ended up never making explicit the connection between political theology and the concept of the enemy. Moreover, he maintained that the only relevant opposition within this concept was that of the private versus the public or political enemy.

18. It is important to note that in the "oldest surviving commentary on Romans, written by the most important Christian theologian between St. Paul and St. Augustine," Origen of Alexandria, the "last enemy" is already (or still) God's enemy (introduction to Origen, *Commentary on the Epistle to the Romans*, 1–2). It is "he who sinned beyond all others" who "is recorded by Paul as the last enemy to be destroyed" (299).

19. Commenting on Romans 9, Lloyd Gaston emphasizes that, exegetical history aside, the Jews are not always mentioned as the targeted adversary (Gaston, "Israel's Enemies in Pauline Theology," 411). More specifically, regarding 1:18–3:20, Richard Longenecker notes that "problems begin to take form when one attempts to identify exactly who is being talked about or addressed in the passage. Is it Gentiles in 1:18–32, Jews in 2:1–5, Gentiles in 2:6–16, then Jews again in 2:17–3:19, with a conclusion in 3:20? Or is it Gentiles in 1:18–32 and Jews in 2:1–3:19 with a conclusion pertaining to both in 3:20? Or is it humanity generally in 1:18–2:16 and Jews (or a particular type of Jew) in 2:17–3:19, with a conclusion in 3:20? Earlier interpreters such as Origen, Jerome, Augustine and Erasmus wrestled with this issue, and it continues to plague commentators today" (Longenecker, "The Focus of Romans," 51). Exegesis as the permanent possibility of war.

20. An alternate reading has "god-hated," thus announcing the debate over the passive versus active reading of enmity in 11:28, to which I return below.

21. The very same verb, *paradidomi*, appears where God is said to have "given up," *paredoken*, his own son: "He who did not withhold his own Son, but gave him up for all of us." (8:32). This very common verb is found in the New Testament with a variety of meanings that recall earlier usage elsewhere in ancient Greek texts, "to hand over, give back, become ripe, commend (oneself), transmit, deliver, betray" (*Theological Lexicon of the New Testament*, vol. 3, 13). Though common in its usage, the term has been the object of exegetical questioning (see for example, Joseph A. Fitzmyer, *Romans: A New Translation*, 272, 274, 284. Fitzmyer later notes the parallel use of the term for Jesus being "given up" in 8:32, 532). Furthermore, the New Testament, and Paul first of all, made it a "technical term for

Jesus' passion" (21). It is to be "taken first in its legal and judicial sense, but it conveys moreover a moral or psychological nuance and a theological value." The editor of the *Theological Lexicon of the New Testament*, Ceslas Spicq, concludes by mentioning that that same term was also used to describe the actions of Judas Iscariot—treason (*paradosis, prodosia*). On other uses of similar language to describe Jesus and the Jews, see Jennifer Glancy, "Israel vs. Israel," 192–93; see also Richard B. Hays, *Echoes of Scriptures*.

22. As Glancy writes, Israel's deferred inclusion in the narrative of salvation "entails life from the dead" ("For if their rejection is the reconciliation of the world, what will their acceptance be but life from the dead!" 11:15), (Glancy, "Israel vs. Israel," 197).

23. See C. K. Barrett, *A Commentary on the Epistle to the Romans*, 150; see also Emile Benveniste, *Indo-European Language and Society*, 289–90/F356.

24. On the divine warrior and the call to divine warfare, see Thomas R. Yoder Neufeld, *'Put on the Armour of God'*. Although Neufeld focuses on Ephesians, rather than on Romans, he points out some important parallels (in military imagery, for example) between the two letters (see esp. 76 and 85–86).

25. Scholars have long commented on "the metaphor of warfare" upon which Paul calls. James D. G. Dunn also notes that the motif of slavery and captivity is "consistent" with the images of war, "since defeat in battle usually resulted in the prisoners of war being sold as slaves" (Dunn, *Word Biblical Commentary 38A [Romans 1–8]*, 395).

26. Theodor Zahn, *Der Brief des Paulus an die Römer*, 360.

27. Ernst Käsemann, *Commentary on Romans*, 205

28. The word "God" in "enemies of God" does not appear in Greek or in Latin, although it appears to be implied from the context. Some commentators (and many modern translations) fill it in, while others extrapolate the enemies of God from elsewhere in the text. Thomas Aquinas, for example, does not spend much time on the enemies of 11:28, but reads 5:10 as the occasion to consider the ways in which man is said to be *inimicus Deo* (Aquinas, *Opera omnia, In Epistolam ad Romanos*, 449).

29. Christopher Bryan, *A Preface to Romans*, 183.

30. In the restricted context of 1:30, Bryan may be right in stating that "there seems to be no particular reason that an active sense, 'hating God', should seem preferable" (Bryan, *A Preface to Romans*, 80 n. 37). Yet the larger context regarding activity and passivity is clearly troubled, as Bryan himself recognizes (see esp. 73).

31. The debate rages on here, too, and one could probably trace a number of theologico-grammatical parallels as a kind of history of its interpretations. From Paul himself to Origen ("each person becomes as bad and as detestable an enemy of God as much as he multiplies deeds which merit enmity," Origen, *Commentary on the Epistle to the Romans*, 299), Pelagius ("sinners are enemies because they show contempt," *Pelagius's Commentary on St Paul's Epistle to the Romans*, 91) who emphasize the active participation of the enemies (Pelagius reads the enemies of 11:28

as Paul's enemies: "they are my enemies because I preach Christ to you," 130), to Martin Luther, who states unequivocally: "This term *enemies* in this passage is taken in the passive sense, that is, they are worthy of being hated and God hates them, and for this reason so do the apostle and all who are of God" (Luther, *Lectures on Romans*, 431–32/G397). Not surprisingly, Aquinas is no less categorical in the opposite direction: "it is impossible that He should hate anything" (Aquinas, *Summa contra Gentiles*, vol. 1, ch. 96, 292). And yet, a third solution suggests itself: "In this case there is no reason it [i.e., the word *echthroi*] should not be understood as mutual hostility between God and sinners" (Fitzmeyer, *Romans: A New Translation*, 401). The difficult relationship between agent and object of love—and hate—is explored by Plato in *Lysis* ("And so, not the object of hatred is the enemy, but the hater," 213a, in Plato, *Collected Dialogues*, 156). See also, in a different context, Peter Galison's discussion of the active versus passive enemy in "The Ontology," 231–32.

32. Here emerges, perhaps, what can be called, after Malabou, the "plasticity" of the enemy as the "originary unity of agency and passivity, of spontaneity and of receptivity" (Malabou, *L'avenir de Hegel*, 249). The enemy, one could say, is "plastic"—that is to say also, explosive. It would demand therefore what Malabou refers to as an "explosive reading." The necessity of a distinction between activity and passivity is, of course, a political question. Kant, for example considers it to be constitutive of the *political* concept of citizen. Finding its point of departure in the "quality" of free will, Kant writes that this quality "requires a distinction between *active* and *passive* citizens" (Kant, *Metaphysics of Morals*, §46, §92).

33. "The background is not so much one of 'trespassers' (2 Cor. 5:19; Col. 1:21) and 'estranged persons' in an alien universe (Col. 1:21), as 'enemies of God' who stand in need of being delivered from their exposure to 'the wrath of God.' And human impotence to secure deliverance is accepted here, since men and women are both 'powerless' and 'ungodly.'" (Ralph Martin, "Reconciliation: Romans 5:1–11," 44). John Piper comments on Rom. 5:10 that "'enemies' is also rendered 'helpless'. . . . The Christians are being called upon to let their enemies experience what they experienced while they were still God's enemies" (Piper, *'Love Your Enemies,'* 104).

34. *Theological Dictionary of the New Testament*, vol. 2, 814. Ralph Martin compares with exaggerated confidence the different states of affairs (states of war) regarding the interpretation of various verses on hostility. Martin writes about Rom. 5:10 that "interpreters are hopelessly divided over the question: does 'being enemies' mean 'while were hating God' (active) as in *Romans* 1.30; 8:7, or 'while God was opposed to us' (passive)?" and concludes that in this case "two arguments tip the scales on the side of the latter" (Martin, "Reconciliation: Romans 5:1–11," 38). Martin later asserts that "God's hostility to sinners is the essential background of Paul's doctrine" (42).

35. Käsemann, *Commentary on Romans*, 315.

36. Levinas, *Totality*, 21.

37. Commenting on Levinas's "state of war," Derrida shows that the structure of the exception is at work regarding God, as well. God "is implicated in war" and his name is "a function within the system of war." Yet, Derrida continues, "war supposes and excludes God." War—the permanent possibility of a state of exception—is the condition of possibility and impossibility of our relation to God: "We can have a relation to God only within such a system" (Derrida, *Writing and Difference*, 107).

38. In the state of war—that is to say, in the permanent possibility of war—law is "reduced to the zero point of its significance, which is nevertheless in force as such" (Agamben, *Homo Sacer*, 51).

39. Derrida, "Before the Law," 203–4.

40. Ibid., 204.

41. Ibid., 173.

42. Ibid., 174. I return to this difficult dimension of the messianic in more details in Appendix 2, "Corpse of Law."

43. Agamben, *Il tempo che resta*, 45.

44. Ibid., 54.

45. See also Alain Badiou on *la division du sujet*. Arguing that the subject is the "weaving," *tressage*, "of two subjective ways that Paul calls the flesh (*sarx*) and the spirit (*pneuma*)" and that "the opposition of the spirit and the flesh has nothing to do with that of the soul and body" (Badiou, *Saint Paul*, 59), Badiou nonetheless insists on reinscribing a rapport of absolute distinction between genealogy (*filiation*) and enslavement. Badiou admits that Jesus is "Lord, *kurios*," and Paul a "slave, *doulos*," but the new subjective path constituted by the "Christ-event . . . must not be confused with slavery." On the contrary, it is "absolutely different" (67).

46. See Schmitt's famous distinction between personal and political enemies, to which I return in the next chapter, but see also *Theological Dictionary of the New Testament* (s.v. *echthros*, *echthra*), which considers only "personal and national enemies" even when discussing "enemies of God." As far as I could find, the expression "theological enemy" rarely appears, if at all, in the literature on these issues.

47. On "subject and subject," see Étienne Balibar, who argues that "the whole history of the philosophical category of the 'subject' in Western thought is governed by an *objective* 'play on words', rooted in the very history of language and institutions. . . . Simply the fact that we translate as *subject* the neutral, impersonal notion of a *subjectum*, i.e. an individual substance or a material substratum for properties, but we *also* translate as *subject* the personal notion of a *subjectus*: a political and juridical term, which refers to *subjection* or *submission*, i.e. the fact that a (generally) human person (man, woman or child) is *subjected to* the more or less absolute, more or less legitimate authority of a superior power, e.g. a 'sovereign'. This sovereign being may be another human or supra-human, or an 'inner' sovereign or master, or even simply a transcendent (impersonal) *law*" (Balibar, "Subjection and Subjectivation," 8). A more extensive consideration of the enemy (and of Paul's enemy) would both reinforce and extend the history traced by Balibar.

48. In Plato's *Republic*, a central moment of the discussion on the enemy is "What should be the attitude of the soldiers to one another and the enemy?" (Plato, *Republic*, 468a). The first matter brought up in the answer to this question is "the matter of making slaves of the defeated" (469b). I return to the question of subjection in Chapter 5.

49. I quote from Peter Abelard's commentary on Romans in Abelard, *Expositio in Epistolam ad Romanos*, vol. 2, 494.

50. Butler, *The Psychic Life of Power*, 2. Further references will be made parenthetically in the text.

51. Ronell, *Stupidity*, 5.

52. Ibid., 56.

53. See Agamben, *Il tempo che resta*, 19–20.

54. Boyarin, *A Radical Jew*, 7.

55. "In the beginning, there is ruin" (Derrida, *Memoirs of the Blind*, 68/F72; see also 116–17/F119).

56. Nancy, "The Deconstruction of Christianity."

57. Lyotard and Gruber, *The Hyphen*, 1/F3. Further references will be made parenthetically in the text.

58. Ronell, "True Lyotard."

59. Agamben, *Il tempo che resta*, 19.

60. Badiou, *Saint Paul*, 5. Further references will be made parenthetically in the text.

61. Freud, *The Future of an Illusion*, *The Standard Edition*, 21:6.

62. Freud, *Civilization and its Discontents*, *The Standard Edition*, 21:112.

63. Ibid., 109.

64. Ibid., 114.

65. Ibid., 110.

66. Ibid., 110.

67. Aquinas, *Summa theologiae* 2a2ae, 25.8, vol. 34, 105.

68. Freud, *Civilization*, 109.

69. Ibid., 110.

70. Ibid., 111. When he returns at the end of the book to the commandment to love the neighbor, Freud no longer invokes or mentions the love of enemies (cf. 143; see also Freud's "Why War," where love of the neighbor, but not love of the enemy, is mentioned again as "more easily said than done").

71. Ibid., 110 n. 1.

72. Ibid., 111.

73. Matthew 5:43–44.

74. Freud, *Civilization*, 109.

75. Klassen, "'Love Your Enemies': Some Reflections on the Current Status of Research," 1. It is notable that the *Gebot der Feindesliebe*, though foundational (but of what?) and widely known, did not occasion a larger number of scholarly studies. Commenting on this poor state of critical studies on the commandment as of

1979, John Piper expressed his own surprise at the fact that "(to my knowledge) no monograph exists which treats in a thorough way the history of this commandment in the various level of the New Testament tradition" (Piper, *'Love Your Enemies,'* 1). Looking, more modestly, for an interpretation of the commandment in the twentieth century, Wolfgang Huber writes of "an alarming vacuum" (Huber, "Feindschaft und Feindesliebe," 129). If one turns to the Middle Ages, however, what becomes striking is never the absence of the commandment. To mention but a few major examples, "Love your enemies" is discussed at length by Augustine in *De doctrina Christiana* and by Aquinas in the *Summa theologiae* and the *Summa contra Gentiles*. It is "perhaps the most frequently cited Scriptural reference in Francis [of Assisi]'s *Opuscula*" (Mastnak, *Crusading Peace*, 193). What remains either implicit or simply unthought in this case is not that there are enemies and that they should be loved—even if this is something that might reveal itself impossible—but the meaning of the word "enemy." It is as if the "concrete" question of who the enemy is cannot be addressed in properly theological (one might say, theoretical and abstract) discussions.

76. Klassen, "Love Your Enemies," 8.

77. Augustine, *City of God*, 10, 3. Augustine elsewhere explains that "the will of God, in the principle of loving God and neighbor, is concisely introduced to all believers, since from these two precepts hang the whole law and all the prophets (cf. Matthew 22:37–40)—that is, the love of our neighbor which the Lord himself commends to us even to the point of loving our enemies " (*Augustine on Romans*, 79).

78. Derrida, *Politics of Friendship*, translation slightly altered, 32–33/F51.

79. Ibid., 64/F82.

80. Ibid., 285/F317.

81. For an indispensable account of such generalization, see Derrida on "generalized writing" in *Of Grammatology*, e.g. 55/F81.

82. I quote here from Samuel Weber's "Wartime," a reading of Freud's 1915 "Thoughts for the Times on War and Death" (Weber, "Wartime," 98).

83. Freud, "Thoughts for the Times on War and Death," *The Standard Edition*, 14:293.

84. Weber, "Wartime," 100.

85. Ibid., 101.

86. Nietzsche knew it, of course, when he wrote that "the Christian . . . makes no distinction between foreigner and native, between Jew and non-Jew" (Nietzsche, *The Anti-Christ*, no. 33); and so did William James, who suggested that, although Jesus' statement might constitute "mere Oriental hyperbole," it promises "a level of emotion so unifying, so obliterative of differences between man and man, that even enmity may come to be an irrelevant circumstance" (James, *Varieties of Religious Experience*, 311). In a similar spirit, Klassen writes that the commandment "transcends all human divisions which are in fact brought into unity in Christ" (Klassen, "Love Your Enemies," 2). John Piper concurs and evokes the

Pauline *adiaphora*: "because it seemed in general to devaluate the distinction between Jew and gentile—a distinction grounded in the Torah, Jesus' command to
love the enemy as well as the friend contained the seed for the dissolution of the
Jewish distinctive" (Piper, *'Love your Enemies,'* 92). In her dissertation on Augustine, Hannah Arendt in turn argued that in this case, "the neighbor loses the
meaning of his concrete worldly existence, for example, as a friend or enemy"
(Arendt, *Love and Saint Augustine*, 94; see also 101–12).

87. "All people should be loved equally," writes Augustine while discussing
love of God, of neighbor, and of enemy (Augustine, *On Christian Teaching*, 21). I
return to this statement below.

88. Wolfgang Huber is therefore right when he asserts that the commandment's radicality resides in its new definition of the enemy as the to-be-loved, "als
der zu Liebende" (Huber, "Feindschaft und Feindesliebe," 139). Yet no less importantly, the commandment redefines the neighbor as not to be distinguished
from the enemy.

89. Freud, "Inhibitions, Symptoms and Anxiety," *The Standard Edition*,
20:120.

90. Augustine, *The City of God*, 1, preface. Further references will be made in
the text.

91. Keeping in mind the importance of the distinction between *hostis* and *inimicus* advocated most vocally by Carl Schmitt, two things should already be obvious here. First, that the use of the terms is not as consistent as Schmitt would
have it. Augustine refers, for example, to the "public enemy," *publicus inimicus*, as
well as to the (collective) enemies of Christianity using the term *inimicus*, which
must therefore transcend the sphere of the private (which in turn is not quite the
domestic). And Cicero refers to "the two cities that were the deadliest foes," *ever-
sis inimicissimis*, "of our empire" (Cicero, *On Friendship*, 119). Second, the notion
of "enemies of God" is neither simply public nor simply private, neither simply
political nor simply nonpolitical, thus disrupting the distinctions between private
and public, domestic and political. As Walter Bauer puts it: "In the concept 'enemy' there lies an obscurity from the beginning. One must love the enemy. Good.
But when the enemy himself is at the same time the enemy of God, what then?"
(Bauer, "Das Gebot der Feindesliebe und die alten Christen," 48). This zone of indistinguishability, this realm of indifference, may also account for the general,
more extended use of *inimicus* over against a restricted, more directly martial use
of *hostis*. Throughout the Middle Ages (toward which we shall soon turn) the "enemies of the Church, *inimici ecclesiae*," were also referred to as *hostes*—see, for example, Guibert of Nogent's "autobiography," in which he writes of *Dei hostes* (an
expression also found in the Latin works of Hobbes) in reference to Jews and Muslims (Guibert de Nogent, *Autobiographie*, 246). In the twelfth century, Peter of
Poitiers referred to Peter the Venerable as dedicated to the struggle against "the
three greatest enemies of holy Christianity," *tres maximos sanctae Christianitatis
hostes*, "Jews, heretics and Muslims" (quoted in James Kritzeck, *Peter the Venerable*

and Islam, 216). Finally, and as we will see, Thomas Aquinas argued that in time of war, deceiving the enemy is not tantamount to lying. In making this case, he will refer to the enemy (clearly not the personal enemy, as Aquinas is talking about war) as *inimicus.*

92. See Russell, *The Just War in the Middle Ages,* the first chapter of which is devoted to Augustine.

93. *Augustine on Romans,* 79.

94. Augustine, *De doctrina Christiana.* Further citations will be made in the text.

95. Robbins, *Prodigal Son/Elder Brother,* 140; see also Derrida, *Politics of Friendship,* 186–88.

96. Although my inquiry remains, for the most part, focused on the question of the theologico-political and on the enemy as a theologico-political issue, it should be clear that the logic of enmity is, at this point at least, as social as it is theologico-social, as private or domestic as it is theologico-domestic, and so forth.

97. Compare with Aristotle, for whom "friendship is irreducible and heterogeneous to the tool (*órganon*), to instrumentalization or—if one can widen or modernize things in this way—to all technical dimensions" (Derrida, *Politics of Friendship,* 197).

98. Bud Bynack alerts me to Pogo's famous troping in the Walt Kelly comic of Commodore Perry's claim from the War of 1812. In the words of the cartoon 'possum in the 1971 Earth Day strip, "We have met the enemy and he is us" (http://members.bellatlantic.net/~vze3y3t2/whmte.htm).

99. Klassen has somewhat hyperbolically argued that the commandment to "love your enemies" hardly has a history: "From as early as the second century . . . to modern times the idea has been either relegated to the personal realm or more frequently totally confined to a select group of Christians in religious communities" (Klassen, "'Love Your Enemies': Some Reflections on the Current Status of Research," 8). As I am hoping to show, the "personal" here may be, if not "political" (in a restricted sense, at least), then quite theological, and therefore not so "relegated" to a limited sphere. As Klassen himself shows, some have argued that "the religious, the political, and the personal enemy are all meant" in Jesus' commandment (H.-W. Kuhn, quoted in Klassen, 11). In his discussion in *The Just War in the Middle Ages,* Russell refers only once to the commandment to love one's enemies. He does so in the context of explaining how "certain [biblical] passages appeared to prohibit Christian participation in war. In His Sermon on the Mount Christ counseled His followers not to resist evil but to turn the other cheek to blows. Christians should love their enemies and not judge one another" (Russell, *The Just War in the Middle Ages,* 10). Yet in this rare instance, the consequences of the commandment seem to have been exclusively confined to the question of conducting warfare, as if the enemy necessarily belonged to a martial sphere. Hence, "early churchmen tended to condemn warfare in general" and "concluded that wars violated Christian charity." At that time (prior to Constantine's conversion), "many

Christians rejected worldly military service in favor of the *militia Christi*, a pacific expression of their struggle against evil" (11). Aside from Gratian's *Decretum*, Russell fails to bring any example of the continuation of this attitude on the basis of exegetical engagement with Jesus' "Love your enemies" or with Paul's Romans 12–13 (11 n.). Generally speaking, the "absence" of the enemy from discussions of war is more pervasive than any discussion confined to the Middle Ages could reveal. The question of the enemy is, of course, not reducible to war as a political and military enterprise. It is as if the enemy not only exceeded the thinking of war, but had altogether transcended it, disappeared from it. Otherwise put, once there is war, law and philosophy are silent, and the enemy need no longer be thought or accounted for: No account of his becoming enemy would be necessary. "Once there is war"—but is there any other time than the time of war?

100. Aquinas, *Summa theologiae*, 2a2ae, 25, art. 8.

101. It is to this second interpretation that Aquinas dedicates his discussion of the love of neighbor in the *Summa contra Gentiles* ("That We Are Ordered by Divine Law to the Love of Neighbor," 3: 117 "How Man Is Ordered by the Law of God in Regard to His Neighbor," 3: 128, "That Sanctifying Grace Causes the Love of God in Us," 3: 151, "That Divine Grace Causes Hope in Us," 3: 153). It should be noticed, however, that there is no mention whatsoever of loving the enemy in any of these passages. Aquinas goes so far as to quote Matthew as the proof text for the commandment to "love thy neighbor," but stops short of referring to "love your enemies" (3: 117). As far as God is concerned, Aquinas is unequivocal: "God hates nothing" (1: 96). If God is said to hate, it is only by similitude," *similitudinarie* (ibid.; see also 1: 91).

102. Aquinas, *Summa theologiae*, 2a2ae, 40: "On War, *De bello.*"

103. And compare with the following gloss on Julianus Pomerius's advocating that "we should love our neighbors because they share with us the same nature": "the Jews and Saracens are our neighbors and ought to be loved by us as we love ourselves; nevertheless, all works of love ought to be employed according to each man's condition" (quoted in Kedar, *Crusade and Mission*, 102 & 102 n. 17).

104. Every text anthologized by Cary Nederman and Kate Langdon Forhan acknowledges in one way or another the (negative) importance of enemies. Typical (and atypical, for its explicit and urgent phrasing) of this acknowledgment, the "Treatise on the Laws and Customs of the Kingdom of England Commonly Called Glanville" opens with the following words: "It is not merely necessary that royal power be adorned with weapons against rebels and nations rising up against the kingdom and its ruler, but it is also appropriate that it be equipped with laws for the sake of peacefully ruling subjects and peoples, so that in both times, namely, of peace and war, our glorious king may perform [his duties] so fruitfully that, by the destruction with the strong right hand of the pride of the unbridled and the untamed and by the moderation of justice for the humble and the meek by the staff of equity, he will always be victorious in subduing his enemies" (*Medieval Political Theory*, 62).

105. Funkenstein, *Perceptions*, 170.

106. See Contamine, *La guerre au moyen âge*.

107. Moore, *The Formation of a Persecuting Society*, 5. At this point, it might be relevant to consider that Moore never mentions Arabs or Muslims as targets of "the persecuting society." In her glowing review of Moore's book, Miri Rubin reiterates that "heretics, lepers, Jews, homosexuals, and prostitutes were increasingly labeled as enemies of and dangerous to the Christian body politic. . . . A language of religion was emerging" (in *Speculum* 65 [1990]: 1025). Rubin regrets that "the question of gender is little considered" (1026), but has not a word about Muslims, either men or women, who populated Europe between 950 and 1250 and after. In a related, if different context, one may also consider Hans Mayer's wonderful *Outsiders*, a book that focuses on "women who are exceptional because they ignore the rules; men who are outsiders on account of sexual inclination; the Jewish outsider within bourgeois society" (Mayer, *Outsiders*, xviii). Although he makes passing references to "Moors," it is clear that Mayer, too, fails to consider Islam or Arabs as constitutive of "Europe," or even as "outsiders."

108. Cohen, *Living Letters*, 5.

109. Mastnak, *Crusading Peace*, 6; see also the work of Kedar, *Crusade and Mission*, and Bartlett, *Making of Europe*.

110. Mastnak, *Crusading Peace*, 23; and further: "The type of war now coming into existence was new. First it was a peace war. The peace movement's *militiae* were not just armies fighting for peace, as armies had often done; they were peace armies, the force of peace. . . . [And] war was ordered by the Church itself" (27).

111. Mastnak, *Crusading Peace*, 96.

112. Funkenstein, *Perceptions*, 178.

113. "Instead of the sole active, readily visible non-Christians in Christian experience, the Jews now became a subset of a larger class of unbelievers, and this eventually upset their position in Christian thought," Cohen, *Living Letters*, 156. The "classical" account of the demonization of the Jews is Joshua Trachtenberg, *The Devil and the Jews*. This is not the whole story, of course. Clearly, there are many others levels of interaction, each divided against itself, in the West at this time, none of which could be entirely reducible to enmity.

114. In his careful choice of words, Jeremy Cohen both accounts for and performs the continuing success, to this day, of the separation between Arab and Jew: Neither "officially present in Christendom" nor a "religious minority," Muslims and the changes in perceptions and attitudes toward them would continue to prove irrelevant, at least as a theological or religious issue. Cohen, *Living Letters*, 150. This is not an accident, nor the result of ignorance, since Cohen's book proves quite knowledgeable about the situation of the Muslims in Europe and quite atypical in its attention to the Christian association of Jew with Muslim.

115. Ibid. Cohen also notes that "the Jews invariably presented Christendom with a paradigm for the evaluation and classification of the Muslim 'other,' a springboard for formulating a deliberate response to him and his faith. As a result,

there arose in Christendom an array of multidimensional associations between the two faiths and their followers" (161).

116. In "On War against the Turk," Martin Luther deploys his criticism of the church's war policy as ignoring Jesus' teaching: "They undertook to fight against the Turk, in the name of Christ, and taught and incited men to do this, as though our people were an army of Christians against the Turks, who were enemies of Christ. This is absolutely contrary to Christ's doctrine and name" (*Luther's Works* 6:165). Interestingly enough, however, the doctrine to which Luther refers stops short of Matthew 5:44. It stops short of the love of enemies. "It is against this doctrine because he says that Christians shall not resist evil, fight, or quarrel, nor take revenge or insist on rights [Matthew 5:39]" (ibid.). Although he does make an argument against war, Luther makes no suggestion that one should love the "enemy of Christ": "I will tell my dear Christians a few things, so far as I know the real truth, so that they may the better be moved and stirred to pray earnestly against the enemy of Christ our Lord" (176). For more on Luther and the "enemies of the Church," see Tarald Rasmussen, *Inimici Ecclesiae*.

117. Wolfgang Huber explains how the difficulties as to the legal status of the commandment to love one's enemies were resolved in law by invoking the difference between *praecepta* and *consilia evangelica*. The division between these two levels of prescription resonated (*sich im Einklang befinden*) with the distinction between *jus naturale* and *jus divinum*. The commandment to love one's enemies never acquired force of law: "One cannot compel man to love his enemy by way of law, since law—as an enforcing institution—is itself made up of 'hostility,' upon which the rational order itself is dependent" (Huber, "Feindschaft und Feindesliebe," 145).

118. Peter the Venerable, letter 130, in Cohen, *Living Letters*, 247.

119. "Alexandri II epistola ad omnes episcopos Hispaniae [al., Galliae]," *Patrologia Latina* 146:1387.

120. An endless number of legal, theological, polemical and other sources testify to an association (be it thematic, conceptual, or simply affective) of Jew and Arab in the Middle Ages. That wealth of sources is matched by the almost complete scarcity of scholarly studies that attend to both Jews and Arabs in their relation to, indeed, as constitutive of the history of medieval Christendom. The association is thus "acknowledged" in the mode of a denegation and of a dissociation. Aside from restricted mentions, the enemy's two bodies have given rise to two distinct bodies of work. Largest among these two is, of course, "Europe and the Jews," whereas "Islam and the West" is still growing fast. There are exceptions, of course, most of which are highly localized (as the following notes should make clear) and, although they may indeed attend to *both* Jews and Arabs, to both Judaism and Islam, they rarely amount to more than occasional oases in a massive scholarly desert.

See, for example, Kruger, "Medieval Christian (Dis)identifications: Muslims and Jews in Guibert of Nogent," and Dominique Iogna-Prat, *Ordonner et exclure.*

It is here, where the "comparison" between Jew and Arab would seem to be mos̩ necessary, that it is most missing—to the point of caricature. Robert Chazan can thus dedicate an entire book to Friar Raymon Martin's *Pugio Fidei adversus Mauros et Iudaeos* and barely ever mention Islam (Chazan, *Daggers of Faith*; see also, with the same general disregard for Islam's relevance, Dahan, *La polémique chrétienne*). More recently, two impeccably researched books summarize the work of a long and venerable tradition of historians for whom the persistence of a distinction, the confinement of a specialization, have remained unquestioned. The "success" of a theologico-political configuration the mechanism of which was put in motion in the Middle Ages is perhaps one of the most vivid testimonies to an already doubtful process of secularization. These two books—Mastnak's *Crusading Peace* and Cohen's *Living Letters*—contain enough historical knowledge to explode the fundamentally erroneous, but widely held notion that Muslims were "the enemy outside Western Europe" and Jews "the enemy within Europe itself" and to begin anew (Heng, "The Romance of England: *Richard Coer de Lyon*, Saracens, Jews, and the Politics of Race and Nation," 142; see also Harle, *The Enemy*, esp. ch. 3). Were the object of the present chapter confined to a historical question (in the narrow sense of the term), there would be little to add to the work of Cohen and Mastnak and little with which to disagree. Of exemplary probity, both Cohen and Mastnak refer numerous times to "the other other" of Europe, an other to which their book remains, however, explicitly and strangely opaque. Each proclaims and maintains an exclusive interest in only one of them, Islam or Judaism, the Jew or the Arab, but as Heng puts it, it is instead "as if the two infidel nations were halves of a single body of aliens" (hence, as an example, the Fourth Lateran Council assigned a distinction in clothing to mark off both Jews and Muslims, 145). Much like "the modern mind"—if there is such a thing—"the medieval ideological mind" was indeed well "able to confuse Jews with Muslims" (Heng, "The Romance of England," 145), even and perhaps especially when it remained highly invested in distinguishing between them.

121. A long tradition that goes back to Eusebius sees in the Arabs the descendants of Hagar, Abraham's slave-wife, hence the name "Agarenes." Beginning with Paul's figurative reading, however, the Jews were said to be Hagar's descendants, as well. Richard Southern documents some of this conflicted tradition in his *Western Views of Islam*, 16–17, 16 n. 9 and n. 10. For an essential and most illuminating discussion of the place of Hagar in its relation to question of genealogy in the Abrahamic context, see Benslama, "La répudiation originaire."

122. Southern, *Western Views*, 5.

123. See also Romans 4, where Paul elaborates on Abraham as the nongenealogical ancestor of the faithful.

124. Agobard, "On the Superstitions of the Jews," quoted in Blumenkranz, *Les auteurs chrétiens*, 166.

125. Griffith, "Jews and Muslims in Christian Syriac and Arabic Texts of the Ninth Century," 65. Griffith cites the Nestorian patriarch Timothy I (723–823)

who, defending the Christian faith at the Abbasid court in Baghdad, writes of "the new Jews among us," opposing them to "the old Jews" of the days of Herod. Griffith meticulously documents the attempt by Christian apologists "to make a doctrinal correlation of Islam with Judaism" and, Griffith continues, "to appeal to an anti-Jewish animus that was current among Christians and Muslims" (82). Griffith later shows the development of what he calls "the 'New Jews' theme'" (84–87).

126. Moore, *Persecuting Society*, 37; see also Prudence of Troyes, who narrates the 852 conquest of Barcelona by the Muslims as being the result of Jewish treason (quoted in Blumenkranz, *Auteurs chrétiens*, 183).

127. Quoted in Blumenkranz, *Auteurs chrétiens*, 152.

128. Quoted in Blumenkranz, *Auteurs chrétiens*, 251 n. 4. In another text, Ademar (ca. 988–1034) describes the Jews as a fifth column who, along with the Muslims of the Iberian peninsula, had written to Jerusalem to accuse the Christians there and to warn of the arrival of the Christian armies from Europe. In yet another text, Ademar writes of God's punishing and avenging wrath against both Jews and Muslims, bringing the plague to hundreds of thousands of them (252). For more on Ademar (and on Muslims and, although incidentally, Jews), see Frassetto, "The Image of the Saracen as Heretic in the Sermons of Ademar of Chabannes."

129. *La chanson de Roland*, v. 3662.

130. Camille, *The Gothic Idol*, 138. On Christian perceptions of the Crusades as revenge for the killing of Christ and for the Muslims as "reenacting the passion, retorturing Christ," see Tolan, "Muslims as Pagan Idolaters in Chronicles of the First Crusade."

131. "The Play of the Sacrament" in Davis, ed., *Non-Cycle Plays and Fragments*, 62.

132. Powell, "The Papacy and the Muslim Frontier," 189; see also the extensive documentation provided by García y García in his "Jews and Muslims in the Canon Law of the Iberian Peninsula in the Late Medieval and Early Modern Period'" see also Carpenter, "Minorities in Medieval Spain: The Legal Status of Jews and Muslims in the *Siete Partidas*." Lomax also discusses the relation of the papacy to Muslims and Jews in his "Frederick II, His Saracens, and the Papacy," 181 and 191 n. 6.

133. Cohen, *Living Letters*, 162.

134. Carlo Ginzburg described in some details the association of Jews with Muslims (and lepers) who, beginning in the fourteenth century, were accused of poisoning wells (Ginzburg, *Ecstasies*, 41–42). Trachtenberg traces the continuity of this motif all the way to the sixteenth century, citing Martin Luther's own allusions to these "tales of collusion" (Trachtenberg, *The Devil and the Jews*, 184–85). For more on Luther on Jews and Muslims, see Wallmann, "Luther on Jews and Islam." Malcom Barber also attends to this motif of collusion in "Lepers, Jews and Moslems: The Plot to Overthrow Christendom in 1321," but as Barber shows, this particular idea had already begun to emerge in Matthew Paris's chronicle in the thirteenth century (17).

135. Cohen, *Living Letters*, 158. Cohen continues and insists that "the former from without, the latter from within."

136. There is therefore much of interest in the Cutlers' book *The Jew as Ally of the Muslim* and much to be affirmed in it. Yet because of their explicit dedication to "the struggle to achieve the Massignonian vision," that is, to bring about a quasi-eschatological unification of the "three branches of the *same* religion, the religion of Abraham," they disregard and even dismiss the dissociative forces (and more importantly, the reasons for these dissociations) at work in "Christian Europe" (Cutler and Cutler, *Jew as Ally*, 1). Although the Cutlers hardly make a claim for scholarly status (insisting throughout that their endeavor is not only derivative, but also guided by explicit religious—that is, Christian—motives), it is quite instructive to consider the responses to the book by some of today's major Jewish medieval historians (Jeremy Cohen, Gilbert Dahan, Bernard Septimus, Reuven Firestone, Steven Bowman).

The response is massive and overall unanimous. The Cutlers should be commended for their endeavor, but they are simply wrong: "From a considerable corpus of medieval writing on Jews and Judaism," writes Bernard Septimus, "the authors adduce not a single source that explicitly alleges an ongoing Judeo-Islamic axis and only a few that allege isolated instances of collaboration" (Septimus in *American Historical Review* 92 [1987]: 1188). Septimus continues: "This book is obviously the result of much labor and devotion, and to have to reject its conclusions so roundly is painful . . . but the problem posed by the book still awaits an open-ended examination of the evidence and a more sober mode of historical analysis" (1189).

Jeremy Cohen, who, in *Living Letters*, invokes much of the same evidence used by the Cutlers, writes in his 1988 review of the Cutlers' book that "it should now be clear that despite the length of its text, its two hundred pages of notes and bibliography, and its noble calls for extensive international scholarly collaboration, this book fails to prove its thesis" (Cohen in *Judaism* 37 [1988]: 242). Hence, one can speak only of "the alleged Christian tendency to view the Jews as the hostile agents of Islam" (240).

Gilbert Dahan, for his part, "cannot understand how the Cutlers can see . . . an 'equation' between Jews and Muslims" and finds that the book is "too questionable from a scholarly point of view as well as from an ethical one" (in *The Jewish Quarterly Review* 79, no. 4 [April 1989]: 375). Dahan importantly points out that numerous Christian writers do write about Muslims and Jews, but "most of the texts, theological, legal, and literary make a distinction between Jew and Muslim" (376). Dahan quickly abandons any argumentation regarding Islam and proudly, if puzzlingly concludes that "today the arguments of J.-P. Sartre's *Reflexions sur la question juive* are outmoded. In the field of culture, of ethics and of history (and of course in the field of religion) Judaism has a positive definition" (377).

Finally, Steven Bowman concludes that "with respect to various theses of the authors, this reviewer must defer that the jury is still in session and will remain so until real evidence is supplied. At the same time this reviewer commends the Cutlers' efforts to broaden the methodology of the study of anti-Semitism" (Bowman in *Speculum* 63 [1988]: 388). The jury is still out, but do not the scholars protest too much?

137. Cohen, *Living Letters*, 160.

138. Bernard of Clairvaux, quoted in Cohen, *Living Letters*, 221.

139. Cohen, *Living Letters*, 275.

140. In his commentary on Romans ("I refuse to be a philosopher if I would be unfaithful to Saint Paul," quoted in Graboïs, "Un chapitre de tolérance intellectuelle," 648), Abelard considers the Jews' faulty understanding of the love of neighbor as love of friends. The true meaning of the commandment, he therefore finds in the love of enemies and doing good to them (Abelard, *Expositio in Epistolam ad Romanos*, 3: 492. Earlier, when discussing the love of neighbor, Abelard does not mention the enemy, 1:219).

141. Abelard, *Collationes*. This is a critical edition of the Latin text with an English translation.

142. On the controversy as to whether Abelard's "philosopher" is or not a Muslim, see the discussion by the editors of the *Collationes* (esp. l-li); see also Cohen, *Living Letters*, 285 and 285 n. 51, and Julia Gauss, "Die Auseinandersetzung mit Judentum und Islam bei Anselm," 106–7.

143. It may be interesting to note that, having provided ample documentation to that effect ("Muslims, whom many European [sic] Christians commonly called pagans" (Cohen, *Living Letters*, 174 and 174 n. 18; see also the remark on this "age in which pagan usually meant Muslim," 179), Cohen becomes much more uncertain when dealing with this particular pagan, Abelard's philosopher. At this point, and without explanation, pagans are only "presumably Muslims" (278). This is a bit awkward. In his *De fide catholica*, Alain de Lille called the section against Islam, "contra paganos." For an extended discussion of the "lack of distinction between the terms 'Saracen' and 'pagan,'" see Gloria Allaire, "Noble Saracen or Muslim Enemy? The Changing Image of the Saracen in Late Medieval Italian Literature," 175–77.

144. Much later in the dialogue, the philosopher will continue to affirm his nonscriptural allegiance: "I am very surprised that, amongst the reasonings with which you are trying to argue against me, you also put in remarks based on the authority of your scriptures, which you well know will not be at all compelling to me" (Abelard, *Collationes*, 179).

145. Ibid., 107. The military metaphors—if metaphors they are—are not too numerous in the text, but they are quite telling. They also testify to the fragility of the distinctions, theologico-political distinctions, as they are made in Abelard's text, in its rhetoric and in the staging of the scene of encounter and conflict. Hence, for example, the Jew refers to the Christian as "this brother of mine who professes himself a Christian . . . is armed, as it were, with two horns—the two testaments—and so he will be able to resist and combat the enemy more strongly"

(13). And compare, of course, with the statement of Peter the Venerable, who "accused the Muslims of resorting to violence because they did not have reason on their side: Muhammad relied not on reason but on arms, and instead of giving an answer to those who asked him questions, he turned to stones, sticks, and swords" (Peter the Venerable, *Liber contra sectam*, quoted in Mastnak, *Crusading Peace*, 175). Between the two Peters, between the two friends, there is a notable difference in the matter of reason.

146. Aquinas, *Summa contra Gentiles*, 1.2.

147. Writing a century earlier, John of Salisbury had defined tyranny as one of the forms of high treason, a crime "executed against the body of justice itself." Tyranny, he continued, is "not only a public crime, but if this [crime against justice] can happen, it is more than public." Hence, John deemed "the tyrant a public enemy," *publicus hostis*, and "whoever does not prosecute him transgresses against himself and against the whole body of the earthly republic" (*Policraticus*, 3.15). As in the structure of the messianic as we saw it earlier, Schmitt links the becoming enemy of the tyrant as articulated by John of Salisbury to that of the pirate, both as kinds of enemies of humanity (Schmitt, *Nomos der Erde*, 34–35, and see below, Appendix 2, "Corpse of Law").

CHAPTER 2

1. Taylor, *Nots*, 54.

2. Derrida, "How to Avoid Speaking," 135 n. 13.

3. In *The Hyphen*, Lyotard and Gruber have contributed greatly to the reflections that surround the hyphen. The privileging of the hyphen that links the Jew to the Christian in the phrase "Judeo-Christian" ("It is distinct from all the other hyphens that associate and dissociate the name of the Jew from those of the nations where Jews are dispersed and exiled," 15), however, is placed under interrogation when Lyotard writes that, for Paul, "the Israel of the flesh . . . was born in the Sinai (in Arabia, [Paul] specifies) . . . Are we to conclude that Jews, *like* Arabs, are slaves of the flesh, and so are disinherited?" (21). I will return to the association and the dissociation pointed out here, as well as on the importance of the word "like."

4. Blanchot, "L'athéisme et l'écriture" in *L'entretien infini*, 375. Paola Marrati-Guénoun describes the "contamination of the transcendental and the empirical" in Derrida's work, focusing mainly on the question of time (Marrati-Guénoun, *La genèse et la trace*, 17). In a more general perspective, Marian Hobson demonstrates the importance of Derrida's questioning of the empirico-transcendental distinction (Hobson, *Jacques Derrida*, esp. ch. 1).

5. See Krell, *The Purest of Bastards*.

6. Derrida, *Of Grammatology*, 23/38F, quoted in Hobson, *Jacques Derrida*, 20.

7. The suspension of the word "identity" in quotation marks is, as we will see, Derrida's. (See *Monolingualism*, 13.)

8. Bennington, "Mosaic Fragment: If Derrida Were an Egyptian . . ." in Bennington, *Legislations*, 209.

9. See the discussion of *chez* in, for example, Derrida, *Other Heading* and *Politics of Friendship*; see also Weber, "Reading and Writing *chez* Derrida," in Weber's *Institution and Interpretation*.

10. Derrida, *Gift of Death*, 92.

11. This is Weber's example, drawing from Belgian usage (*Institution*, 88). The North African version, of course, would more likely be "*Va* chez ta mère."

12. Zabus, "Encre blanche et Afrique originelle: Derrida et la postcolonialité."

13. Derrida, "The Crisis in the Teaching of Philosophy," in *Who's Afraid of Philosophy?: Right to Philosophy I*, 103/F160, translation modified.

14. Zabus, "Encre blanche et Afrique originelle," 262.

15. For a notable exception to the general cursoriness regarding Derrida and autobiography, and for an important corrective to persistent readings of Derrida's "Jewishness," see Jill Robbins's compelling review of "Circumfession": "Circumcising Confession"; see also Hent de Vries' important comments on Derrida's "quasi-autobiography" in de Vries, *Philosophy and the Turn to Religion*, esp. 344–48.

16. Derrida has invoked this duality often, of course, and it has been noted by his readers as well. See, for example, Krell, *The Purest of Bastards*, 193.

17. Another way of pursuing what Derrida wants to say in what could be called his autobiographical thought was suggested by Robert Smith. Smith leaves aside what Zabus considers "autobiographical" and produces instead an elaborate and impressive Derridean "contribution" to a *theory* of autobiography. Smith does so while spending surprisingly little time reading the manner in which Derrida inserts the "I" in his texts, the manner in which the appearance of empiricity takes place in the texts (Smith, *Derrida and Autobiography*). To express wariness over the forgetting of the "I" in the reading of the Derridean text by Smith and others is not to criticize them as if from the opposed vantage point, however. It does not warrant the restitution of a naïvely empirical "I" in the so-called "autobiographical" text. In Smith's wording, "appeals to biological knowledge" should not be "reduced immediately to empirical data concerning the biological" (91). Not "immediately," but then what is still required is to address what could be called, after Derrida, "empirical effects."

18. Rodolphe Gasché, in Derrida, *Ear of the Other*, 41/F59.

19. Derrida, *Ear of the Other*, 44/F62–63.

20. Derrida, *Monolingualism*, 14/F31–32.

21. Ibid., 28/F53.

22. Ibid., 14/F32.

23. Ibid., 11/F27.

24. Derrida, "Circumfession," 58/F57.

25. Derrida, "Faith and Knowledge," 76.

26. Schmitt, *Concept of the Political*, 29/G29.

27. Derrida, *Politics of Friendship*, 162, translation altered.

28. Recall the famous opening sentence of Schmitt's *Political Theology:* "All significant concepts of the modern theory of the state are secularized theological concepts . . ." (Schmitt, *Political Theology*, 36). Underlying my discussion is the implicit question of whether Schmitt's notion of the enemy is also a "theological" and "secularized" concept.

29. Derrida, *Politics of Friendship*, 89.

30. Schmitt, *Concept of the Political*, 29.

31. After the discussion that followed the delivery of this chapter in an earlier lecture version, Derrida noted that there remains room to ask what status the Gospels had for Schmitt. Is it the same theological status that Schmitt attributed, for example, to dogma, theological concepts, and religious anthropology? Are the Gospels a part of Christianity as a juridical theory? As attentive as he is to the "sociology of concepts" and to the conflictual history of language, of tradition, and of texts, one could have expected Schmitt to clarify his views on the place and role of the Gospels. What sustains the question is perhaps the "equivocal character" of the expression "theologico-political," as noted by Jean-François Courtine, as well as the possibility of reading the theologico-political as including in a general manner "the mutual implications of the sacred and the social," the possibility of reading Schmitt as opposing any conception that would make of religion a private matter (Courtine, "A propos du 'problème théologico-politique,'" esp. 110–12). Consider also Schmitt's *Roman Catholicism and Political Form*, where Schmitt insists on the political character of Catholicism, its "being eminently political" (16).

32. Schmitt, *Concept of the Political*, 29.

33. Derrida, *Gift of Death*, 103.

34. Schmitt, *Concept of the Political*, 29.

35. Derrida, *Gift of Death*, 103.

36. Schmitt, *Concept of the Political*, 29.

37. Derrida, *Politics of Friendship*, 77.

38. Schmitt, *Concept of the Political*, 48/G48.

39. Derrida, *Politics of Friendship*, 84.

40. Ibid., 89.

41. Ibid., 89.

42. Ibid., 77.

43. The quote is from Schmitt, *Concept of the Political*, 28.

44. Ibid., 53.

45. Ibid., 19.

46. Derrida, *Politics of Friendship*, 84–85.

47. This is all the more surprising because, as Christoph Schmidt points out, Schmitt had quite a lot to say about the Jewish people and about its role in the "massacre of the Leviathan" and in "secularization." (Schmidt, "The Political Theology of Gershom Scholem," 152). According to Jacob Taubes, "the Jewish problem pursued Schmitt all his life" (Taubes, *Ad Carl Schmitt*, 25).

48. Derrida, *Politics of Friendship*, 162, translation altered.

49. Franz Rosenzweig, *The Star of Redemption*, 332/G368, translation altered. On these aspects of Rosenzweig's thought and its Christian sources, see Funkenstein, *Perceptions*, 291–95. (I return to these issues in Appendix 1, "Rosenzweig's War.") In *Galut*, Yitzhak F. Baer clearly reinscribes the Jewish people in a nonhistorical history that finds its clearest formulations in Christian theological conceptions of the *civitas dei*. On Baer and on the role of Zionist historiography in the preservation and development of these conceptions, see Raz-Krakotzkin, "'Without Accounting for Others.'" Recent sedimentations of a tradition that inscribes the Jewish people as nonpolitical and nonhistorical are particular in that they affirm the end of this history outside of history, the end of an existence without political status. Yosef Hayim Yerushalmi recently wrote that "as a result of emancipation in the diaspora and national sovereignty in Israel Jews have fully re-entered the mainstream of history" (Yerushalmi, *Zakhor*, 99). As he repeats and affirms Yerushalmi's view, Benjamin Harshav writes that, thanks to these same changes, "Jews exist now, and exist in the center of consciousness of general society" (Harshav, *Language in Time of Revolution*, 9). For an extensive discussion of the "return to history," see Raz-Krakotzkin, "The Zionist Return to the History of Redemption."

50. Derrida, *Politics of Friendship*, 89.

51. Most admirably among scholars, Edward Said (and, to some extent, Maurice Olender) have attended to Orientalism as the invention of, among other things, the "Semites," a unique and somewhat changing if perhaps also ephemeral figure whereby the Jew and the Arab merge into one as a fundamentally "religious" entity. Continuing a practice launched most forcefully perhaps by Hegel (as we will see in Chapter 5, "Muslims"), Orientalists all but equate Jew and Arab and credit them, the "Semites," with nothing but the most abstract invention of *religion*. A people devoid of political history, their cultural sterility akin to a monotheistic desert, the Semites constitute the clearest site of a distinction produced by the only century that genuinely believed itself "secularized." When religion is thoroughly distanced from politics, the Jew and the Arab can finally merge, one people at last (valued positive, as in Disraeli, or negative, as in Renan). Rereading a history of the enemy from Hegel to Rosenzweig, one could witness this Orientalist invention, first the disappeance—the enemy draws away ("The Orient was almost a European invention . . . now it was disappearing," Said, *Orientalism*, 1)—then the renewed separation of Arab from Jew, and finally the transformation of the Arab into the Jew's "creeping, mysteriously fearsome shadow" (Said, *Orientalism*, 286).

As the rest of this book should make clear, theologico-political fault lines remain determining in spite of this hiatus (and see Olender, *Les langues du paradis*), as they remained determining of what has been called "Jewish Orientalism" as it emerged from German-Jewish culture, in particular. Beginning with Abraham Geiger, a different, if parallel kind of proximity between Arab and Jew was affirmed by Jewish scholars, one in which "Judaism"—that most Orientalist of inventions, as Susannah Heschel makes clear—could be proud "for producing Islam" (Heschel, "Revolt of the Colonized," 71). Enters the Semite in the work of Geiger himself, continuing an always already moribund career all the way to Bernard Lewis and Steven Wasserstrom, Shlomo Deshen or Norman Stillman, via Ignatz Goldziher, Morris Steinschneider, Joseph Horovitz, Shlomo D. Goiten, David H. Baneth, Eliyahu Ashtor, Hartwig Hirschfeld, Erwin I. J. Rosenthal, and other well-known European (that is, also, American and Israeli) Jewish Orientalists interested, more or less mournfully, more or less negatively, in this "Judeo-Muslim symbiosis." Yet there emerged a major rebellion against Geiger's scholarly and political (and, at that time, non-Zionist) endeavor, a rebellion that was led most prominently by Gershom Scholem on the scholarly front (and there are successors), and more generally by so-called Political Zionism on the cultural and political fronts. Heschel explains that "the Zionist revolt against the alleged marginalization of Jews in history that had resulted from Diaspora experience turned out to be a revolt against Judaism, not a revolt against the West" (69).

Siding with the West, Zionism and its scholars—and perhaps most salient among them, Kabbalah studies—revolt, seeking to reintegrate "history" and to liberate themselves from "the East," seeking to liberate themselves, first, from Judaism itself (the new invention that, aside from scientific subtleties, took pride—among other contributions to world civilization—in its Islamic offshoot), from a Judaism that potentially signified a "binational" Arab Jewish existence, then from Islam, and, finally, internally and externally, from the Arabs (see Shohat, "Sephardim;" Alcalay, *After Jews and Arabs*; Anidjar, "Jewish Mysticism;" Raz-Krakotzkin, "A Few Comments on Orientalism;" and Raz-Krakotzkin, "Between 'Brit-Shalom' and the Temple").

This, then, is the anti-Semitism of Zionism, which, seeking the end of exile, *shlilat ha-galut*, strives to bring to an end the alleged ahistorical (non)existence of the "sick" and "exilic" Jew, be he the Oriental, *mizrahi*, Jew, or the no less Oriental Eastern Jew, *Ostjude*, both equally Diasporic Jews, and no more than unhealthy obstacles to the "new Jew" (see Raz Krakotzkin, "Exile Within Sovereignty," Boyarin, *Unheroic Conduct*, Almog, *Sabra*, and Hart, *Social Science*). (In a not unrelated manner, for the past forty years or so, Jewish studies in the United States has been seeking, more or less successfully, to break away from its "Middle Eastern" or "Semitic" home departments, finding itself more comfortably housed in history or religious studies departments). No less Orientalistic than its elders in its conceptions of the East, Zionism more pointedly reinscribes what was already at work in the early invention of the Semites: the European wedge that, now called "secularization," would turn away from religion, distance itself from the only invention of its Semitic, monotheistic, and desert origins ("Les Juifs dehors!"—Herzl heard, and abided), and separate religion from (modern) politics, separate, finally, the Jew from the Arab. Political Zionism, then, is another name for the beginning and end of the "Semite," its paradoxically double internalization and exteriorization. The enemy within, the enemy without: the Arab, out of the Jew, and the Jew, out of Europe, exported, deported.

52. Nirenberg, *Communities of Violence*, 10 n. 23.

53. On the "immense tradition," see Derrida, *Politics of Friendship*, 148.

54. Derrida, *Politics of Friendship*, viii.

55. Derrida "Lettres sur un aveugle: *Punctum caecum*," 99.

56. Westermann, *The Promises to the Fathers*, 74.

57. Niditch, *War in the Hebrew Bible*, 11.

58. Derrida, *Politics of Friendship*, 305/F339.

59. Ibn ᶜAttar could be said to follow the lines drawn by the Zohar. In its commentary on Genesis 14, the Zohar locates the episode under the sign of enmity, as an intertext to Psalms 83 ("See how your enemies are stirring, see how those who hate you rear their heads," 83:2) and to Exodus 15 ("Your right hand, Yahweh, shatters the enemy," 15:6). The Zohar insists that none other than Abraham was the real target of the attack, accounting for the value of Lot based on his resemblance to Abraham: "Lot closely resembled Abram, so that thinking they had Abram, they went off." For the Zohar, Abram is the cause of enmity, the cause of the first war: "The reason of their war to Abram was Abram himself, for this whole war was because of him" (Zohar, trans. H. Sperling and M. Simon. [London: Soncino Press, 1984]), 1: 86b, 289).

60. The quote on the explosion is from Derrida, *Post Card*, 188.

61. Derrida, "Circumfession," 309.

62. Derrida, *Monolingualism*, 11.

63. Derrida, *Politics of Friendship*, 268 n. 10.

64. Derrida, *Donner la mort*, 149. This passage was not included in the David Wills translation of Derrida's *Gift of Death*

65. Lupton, "*Othello* Circumcised," 78–79.

66. Derrida, "Faith and Knowledge," 51.

CHAPTER 3

1. Derrida remarks that even for Schmitt, reflecting while in prison after World War II on the question of the enemy, "the question that resounds in this cell is not the converse of the question in *Lysis* (Who is the friend?), or even the general or ontological question (*What is* the enemy? *What is* hostility or the *being-hostile* of the enemy?)" (Derrida, *Politics of Friendship*, 161). In an early version of *Politics of Friendship*, Derrida suggests an explanation for the absence of the ontological question concerning the enemy: "the question 'what is?' (*ti estin*)' the question of essence or truth, has *already* unfolded itself, as the question of philosophy, *starting from* a certain experience of *philein* and *philia*" (Derrida, "Politics of Friendship," 369). It would thus be the uninterrogated parallel—indeed, the association—between friend and enemy that has stood in the way of philosophy's re-

flections, or lack thereof, on the enemy. Derrida undoes that association in *Politics of Friendship*, an undoing I am trying to follow throughout this book.

2. In what constitutes the most extended reflections on the enemy, Derrida insists on the suspension of "the thesis of existence wherever, between a concept and an event, the law of an aporia, an undecidability, a double bind occurs in interposition, and must in truth impose itself to be endured there" (Derrida, *Politics of Friendship*, 39/F59)

3. "It is evident, then . . . that it is possible to prove that men are enemies or friends, or to make them such if they are not; to refute those who pretend that they are, and when they oppose us through anger or enmity, to bring them over to whichever side may be preferred" (Aristotle, *Rhetoric*, 1382a).

4. De Vries, *Religion and Violence*, 356.

5. Derrida, *Politics of Friendship*, 84, quoted in ibid., 357.

6. Derrida, *Politics of Friendship*, 83/F101.

7. All quotations are from Derrida, *Politics of Friendship*, 83–84.

8. Hobbes, *Elements of Law*, quoted in Johnston, *Rhetoric*, 34.

9. Hobbes, *Leviathan*, 3. Further references will be made parenthetically in the text. I will indicate chapter numbers first, followed by page numbers. Referring to later sections of *Leviathan*, Johnston explains that, for Hobbes, "The Scriptures have been deliberately corrupted to prevent our seeing their full light" (Johnston, *Rhetoric*, 136).

10. Schmitt, *Leviathan in the State Theory*, 94.

11. Schmitt remarks that "numerous characterizations by Hobbes have become winged words, as, for example, *bellum omnium contra omnes* [the war of all against all] or *homo homini lupus* [man is a wolf to man]" (ibid., 94).

12. Johnston, *Rhetoric*, 56.

13. Ibid., 58. As Johnston explains later on, "What causes men's reason to fail is the misuse of language. . . . To restore men to their natural reason requires nothing other than the elimination of this distortion" (64).

14. If the enemy is the site of a preservation of the state of nature, a certain structural necessity begins to take shape between the enemy and the sovereign, in whom, Agamben describes, "the state of nature survives." Hobbes's sovereign may thus be "the only one to preserve its natural *ius contra omnes* [law against all]" and sovereignty therefore would be "an incorporation of the state of nature in society." Yet the enemy would nonetheless constitute another, if hidden instance of "a state of indistinction between nature and culture, between violence and law." As Agamben argues, "exteriority—the law of nature and the principle of the preservation of one's own life," that is to say, the enemy in everyman, "is truly the innermost center of the political system" (Agamben, *Homo Sacer*, 35–36). See also, in a different context, Buck-Morss, *Dreamworld*, 8–15.

15. Hobbes writes that "Harme inflicted upon one that is a declared enemy, fals not under the name of Punishment. . . . For the punishments set down in the

law, are to Subjects, not to Enemies; such as are they, that having been by their own act Subjects, deliberately revolting, deny the Soveraign Power" (ch. 28, 216).

16. Bud Bynack reminds me that "in terms of seventeenth-century Protestant theology, it's not strange at all that Hobbes would not discuss love of an enemy under the rubric of natural law. The distinction between, on one side, the laws of nature (and the Golden Rule or the universalization of self-love), and, on the other, the law of grace, which included the injunction to love one's enemies, was a common topos. The distinction conforms, temporally, to the original institutions of Creation, followed by the state of humanity after the Fall, and then to the state promised by Christian redemption. Among other things, the commonplace was one way of explaining the distinction between Jews, on the one side, who were said to operate under the first set of laws, and Christians, on the other, who were said to be held to the second, as well.

"From the Puritan point of view, John Winthrop deployed this topos to remind his listeners of their civil obligations in his famous lay sermon on the *Arbella* in 1630, on the way to Massachusetts Bay and the 'citty upon a hill': 'There is likewise a double Lawe by which wee are regulated in our conversacion one towardes another . . . the lawe of nature and the lawe of grace. . . . By the first of these lawes man as he was enabled soe withall [is] commaunded to loue his neighbor as himselfe. . . . The Lawe of Grace or the Gospell hath some difference from the former as in these respectes first the lawe of nature was giuen to man in an estate of innocency; this of the gospell in an estate of regeneracy; 2ly, the former propounds one man to another, as the same fleshe and Image of god, this as a brother in Christ alsoe, and in the Communion of the same spirit and soe teaches vs to put a difference between Christians and others. . . . 3ly the Lawe of nature could not giue rules for dealing with enemies for all are to be considered friends in the estate of innocency, but the Gospell commaunds loue to an enemy. proofe [:] if thine Enemie hunger feede hime; Loue your enemies doe good to them that hate you Math: 5.44' (John Winthrop, "A Modell of Christian Charity," in *The Puritans: A Sourcebook of their Writings*, vol, 1, ed. Perry Miller and Thomas H. Johnson [1938; New York: Harper Torchbooks, 1963], 196–97)."

17. "For WARRE, consisteth not in Battell onely, or the act of fighting. . . . So the nature of War, consisteth not in actuall fighting; but in the known disposition thereto, during all the time there is no assurance to the contrary. All other time is PEACE" (ch. 13, 89). Time, for Hobbes, is therefore mostly wartime ("and therefore the notion of *Time*, is to be considered in the nature of Warre," ibid.).

18. Participating in a long tradition from Plato to Heidegger that maintains the coconstitution, even the symmetry, of friend and enemy, Hobbes asserts that the enemy can be the friend, and vice versa, and so can even the foreign enemy. Similarly, the external enemy can become the internal enemy, and war becomes civil war, "for though [men] obtain a Victory by their unanimous endeavor against a forraign enemy; yet afterwards, when either they have no common enemy, or he

that by one part is held for an enemy, is by another part held for a friend, they must need by the difference of their interests dissolve, and fall again into a Warre amongst themselves" (ch. 17, 119). Kant, on the other hand, may have been engaged in the most systematic—if brief—undoing of the link, symmetry, and reciprocity between friend and enemy, and even between enemy and enmity. "Enmity," *Feindschaft*, wrote Kant, "is more than lack of friendship," *Freundschaft*, and "a friendless man is not necessarily a general enemy." "One can have an enemy without enmity," Kant continued, placing the onus on unilateral declarations. "Enmity is an express disposition to do harm to another" (Kant, *Lectures on Ethics*, 209–10/G265–66). Incidentally, but for a notable exception, in his argument against Hobbes, Kant does not engage in any explicit way the question of the enemy (see Kant's "On the Common Saying: 'This May be True in Theory, But It Does Not Apply in Practice,'" where the section "On the Relationship of Theory to Practice in Political Right" is written "Against Hobbes," in *Kant: Political Writings*, 73–87). The exception is, of course, the discussion of the "unjust enemy" in *The Metaphysics of Morals*, esp. section 2 on "International Right" (§§53–61; the "unjust enemy" appears in §60). Schmitt discusses Kant's peculiar contribution to changing conceptions of the enemy in *Nomos der Erde*.

19. Aside from the well-known argument on human equality, as Gregory Kavka points out, Hobbes assumes that "every party *knows* that every other has good reason to attack him" (Kavka, *Hobbesian Moral and Political Theory*, 101).

20. The term "enemy"—so essential, one would think, to a reading of Hobbes—never made it into the index of the edition I am using, or into any other index I was able to consult. Schmitt himself hardly invokes the term when attending to Hobbes. Indeed, having asserted that some of Hobbes's conceptions "are effective because of their political force" and "make the concrete enemy evident," Schmitt goes on to write, on the same page, that "in contrast to the later *Behemoth*," *Leviathan* "does not depict an enemy." Rather, "it shows a god that assures peace and security. Nor is it a political friend-myth." Schmitt seems to suggest that this is not the most political moment (in the Schmittian sense) of Hobbes's thought: "The use of the leviathan to represent Hobbes' theory of state is nothing other than a half-ironic literary idea born out of a fine sense of English humor" (Schmitt, *Leviathan in the State Theory*, 94).

21. Kavka, *Hobbesian Moral and Political Theory*, 92.

22. As Derrida puts it in a different, but relevant context commenting on Schmitt, the question of the enemy "is no longer a theoretical question, a question of knowledge or of recognition, but first of all, like recognition in Hegel, a calling into question, an act of war. The question is posed, it is posed to someone; someone puts it to himself like an attack, a complaint, the premeditation of a crime, a calling into question of the one who questions or interrogates. It is posed to oneself in terms of a break into the other, or its breaching. One cannot question oneself on the enemy without recognizing him —that is, without recognizing that he is already lodged in the question" (Derrida, *Politics of Friendship*, 162–63/F187–88)

23. Nietzsche, "Joke, Cunning, and Revenge: Prelude in German Rhymes," no. 25 in *The Gay Science*, 51.

24. In a rare discussion of the Greek terms for "enemy" in Plato, Leon Harold Craig notes the inverse disproportion of space dedicated to war and peace in the *Republic* (war largely dominates), versus the "hundreds of references to the several species of love, and the scant dozens to any kind of hate." Craig also remarks that, "of the available range of everyday terms for hating and loathing, the philosopher declines to use several (e.g., *stygein, apoptiein, echthairein*) and restricts himself to two families of words." This lexical singularity should already displace the question of affect and its relation to enmity. Craig goes on to write that "one term for hatred, *echthra*, appears most frequently as a kind of enemy (*echthros*). In fact, there are more references to *echthroi* (thirty-eight) than to *polemioi* (the term for 'enemies' derived from the word for 'war', *polemos*, and employed twenty-three times)" (Craig, *The War Lover*, 55).

25. Nancy, *Being Singular Plural*, 101.

26. Ibid., 105.

27. As I have already indicated, the question of the enemy must be addressed as distinct from the question of war. That, however, is of course not to say that the latter is irrelevant for an understanding of the former. In this context, it may therefore be important to note that commenting on Clausewitz, André Glucksmann describes war as a "work of intelligence" (Glucksmann, *Discours de la guerre*, 29).

28. Plato, *Phaedrus*, 260c in *Collected Dialogues*, 505.

29. Plutarch, "How to Profit by One's Enemies," 87c. Plutarch mostly uses the term *echthros* throughout the treatise.

30. See Galison, "The Ontology," and Buck-Morss, *Dreamworld*. See also Harle, *The Enemy with a Thousand Faces*. Collapsing the enemy and "the Other," Harle nonetheless writes an informative book that, unaware of the novelty or rarity of its topic, attends to what could amount to a "tradition" linking all the faces of the enemy. Harle attends mainly to constituted identities ("the history of humankind is the history of identity politics," 4) that have been cast as parts of an eternal, if tragically misunderstood, struggle between good and evil. "It is clear that ethnic conflicts, genocides, and other expressions of the absolute hate against the Other represent an extreme and therefore highly important case of identity politics. This extremity reflects the distinction between the Friend and the Enemy, that is, the struggle between good and evil" (4). In his translation of Carl Schmitt (invoked here in a bibliographical footnote), however, Harle abolishes the history of the tradition he claims to write ("The tradition of the struggle between good and evil has a long and wide history."). The struggle between good and evil, much like the constitution of enemies resulted from that struggle, has always been so, he writes. "Therefore, there was nothing new and unexpected in the Bosnian genocide or in the later, but related, genocide in Kosovo." At times, Harle does allow for a distinction between "Other" and enemy ("The Zeitgeist . . . was and is based

on enmity against Others defined as the Enemy," 5), but does not account for the change from one into the other.

31. Aristotle, *Politics*, 1281b.

32. Hutter, *Politics as Friendship*, 25. Further references will be made parenthetically in the text.

33. Aristotle, *Nichomachean Ethics*, 1155a. Kostas Kalimtzis comments that "Aristotle, and all writers in the fourth century, considered *echthra* or 'enmity' to be the signature trait of *stasis*" (Kalimtzis, *Aristotle on Political Enmity*, 121). *Stasis*, "which is enmity," was constitutive of the *polis*, according to Aristotle, who, however, emphasized the centrality of friendship and dedicated much more space to it than to enmity or even war. Annick Charles-Saget points out that, although the affirmation should be nuanced, it remains the case that "during the classical era, the Greeks engage in war but do not think it." (Charles-Saget, "Guerre et Nature," 93). Scholarly literature follows closely and, focusing on friendship, massively ignores the not so parallel questions of enmity and the enemy—see for example, the wonderful studies of André-Jean Voelke, *Les rapports avec autrui* (which mentions *echthra*, "enmity" or "hatred," only in passing); Jean-Claude Fraisse, *Philia: La notion d'amitié dans la philosophie antique*; Paul Schollmeier, *Other Selves*; Suzanne Stern-Gillet, *Aristotle's Philosophy of Friendship*; and see more references below. Agamben recently commented on the constitutive dimension of *stasis* by recalling the extraordinary law attributed to Solon that required "all citizens, on penalty of being stripped of their citizenship, to take side in times of *stasis*," to become enemies (I quote here from Kalimtzis's summary of Aristotle on *stasis*. Agamben delivered his lecture on *stasis* at NYU's Casa Italiana, October 25, 2001); see also Loraux, upon whom Agamben relied (Loraux, *The Divided City*, 102–8).

34. Herodotus, *Histories*, 3.82, quoted in Hutter, *Politics as Friendship*, 126.

35. Hutter, *Politics as Friendship*, 126.

36. Although knowing and understanding are often considered paths to peaceful coexistence, it is easy enough to recognize that they are also conditions of enmity, confrontation, and war. "To know the Other," writes Guy Brossollet, is the "indispensable method toward the ability to confront him . . . the inquiry is immense. . . . To know the Other, of course, but also to know others, neighbors, allies, friends and neutrals, the decisions and attitudes of whom interfere with ours, and diminish, in the very midst of alliances, our freedom of action" (Brossollet, *Essai sur la non-bataille*, 13).

37. Whereas the unknown or faceless enemy is an ancient topos, the unknown soldier is, of course, very recent, a part of "the cult of the fallen soldier," as George Mosse describes it (Mosse, *Fallen Soldiers*, 95–98).

38. Triki, *Les philosophes et la guerre*, 115.

39. Plato, *Republic*, 334e–335a.

40. Aristotle, *Politics*, 1295b. I follow here the translation of C. D. C. Reeve (Indianapolis: Hackett Publishing, 1998) 119. In the *Rhetoric*, Aristotle considers

"enmity and hatred" and suggest that they address a collective. Aristotle counterposes hatred (*misein*)—if not enmity, which is no longer mentioned—and anger, which "has always an individual as its object, for instance Callias or Socrates, whereas hatred applies to classes; for instance, everyone hates a thief or informer" (Aristotle, *Rhetoric*, 1382a).

41. Lacan, *Le séminaire VII: L'éthique de la psychanalyse*, 42. Lacan pursues his analysis of the way in which, in Freud, "the foreign, the hostile, [which] appears in the first experience of reality for the human subject, is the scream" (68).

42. Plato, *Lysis*, 219a. In the *Republic*, Plato asks the following question: "Who then is the most able when they are ill to benefit friends and harm enemies," *echthroi*, "in respect to disease and health?" The answer: "the physician" (*Republic*, 332e) Arguing for the medical meaning of *stasis*, Kostas Kalimtzis writes that Socrates gave "a medical analysis of the operations of bile in the human body in terms of *stasis* and images taken from political strife." Hence, "the man who takes care of his health 'will not allow enemy placed by the side of enemy to stir up wars and disorders in the body, but he will place friend by the side of friend, so as to create health'" (Kalimtzis, *Aristotle*, 195 n. 6; quoting Plato's *Timaeus*, 88e–89a).

43. Plato, *Lysis*, 219a. See also Plato's *Republic*, where Socrates asks whether it is not "the mark of a womanish and petty spirit to deem the body of the dead an enemy" (469d). In the *Timaeus*, food is said to have the potential to make "the whole [human] race an enemy to philosophy and culture" (73a). As we have seen, the potential for enmity appears inherent to the body itself. Thus, were anyone to repeat the work of "the foster mother and nurse of the universe" in order to assemble a body, they would "not allow enemy placed by the side of enemy to stir up wars and disorders in the body, but he will place friend by the side of friend, so as to create health" (88e).

44. Cf. Aristotle, *On the Soul*, 431b.

45. Plato, *Republic*, 335a.

46. *Trading with the Enemy Act*, Public Law 65-91, 65th Cong, 1st sess. (October 6, 1917), ch. 106, 40 stat. 411. Susan Buck-Morss briefly discusses the relevance (and lack thereof) of the separation between the economic and the political in relation to the enemy (Buck-Morss, 15–23).

47. Nietzsche, *The Gay Science*, # 169.

48. Derrida, *Politiques de l'amitié*, 416–17. An English translation of these last chapters of *Politique de l'amitié* can be found in Derrida, "Heidegger's Ear." For this particular quote, see 214.

49. Arendt, *Eichmann in Jerusalem*, 240. The phrase "a new type of criminal" appears on page 253. Kant had offered the notion of the "enemy of humanity," *Menschenfeind*, as an ethical category, "someone for whom it is well only when things go badly for others" (Kant, *Metaphysics of Morals*, "Doctrine of Virtue," §26, §200). Schmitt briefly discusses the genealogy of notions such as "public enemy, *hostis publicus*," and "enemy of the human species, *Feind des Men-*

schengeschlechts, hostis generis humani" in Schmitt, *Ex Captivitate Salus*, 71–72.; see also Schmitt's *Nomos der Erde*, published in the same year.

50. Arendt, *Eichmann in Jerusalem*, 253. Schmitt links the historical appearance of the category *hostis generis humani* to the emergence of great sea empires in antiquity (Schmitt, *Nomos der Erde*, 15). See also Arendt, *Origins*, esp. 377, 424–27, 471–74.

51. Derrida, *Politics of Friendship*, 67.

52. Deleuze and Guattari, *A Thousand Plateaus*, 422/F526. Deleuze and Guattari spend very little time on the enemy, yet through their analysis of the "war machine" they contribute much to an understanding of what I have been calling, after their manner, the "becoming-enemy." Earlier, for example, Deleuze and Guattari identify something like a permanent feature of this "matter-movement, this matter-energy, this matter-flow, this matter in variation that enters assemblages and leaves them," a "region of *vague and material* essences (in other words, essences that are vagabond, anexact and yet rigorous)" (407) which begins to describe the enemy. Thus, the enemy "is assumed to have no other determination [than being the target of war], with no political, economic, or social considerations entering in" (420). For an important and relevant elaboration of "whatever" or "whichever" (French *quelconque*, Latin *quodlibet*, Italian *qualunque*), see Agamben, *Coming Community*.

53. On what "declaring" means in this context, see Derrida, *Politics of Friendship*, 72–73, and see Genet, *L'ennemi*.

54. Plato, *Republic* 468a. The ensuing discussion suggests that it is "illiberal and greedy to plunder a corpse," that it is perhaps "the mark of a womanish and petty spirit to deem the body of the dead an enemy when the real foeman," *echthros*, "has flown away and left behind only the instrument with which he fought? Do you see any difference between such conduct and that of the dogs who snarl at the stones that hit them but don't touch the thrower?" (469d–e). Adi Ophir illuminates this section of the *Republic* in his *Plato's Invisible Cities*, 39–40. See also Arendt, *Origins*, 452.

55. "Wer ist denn mein Feind?" asks Carl Schmitt. "Who is, then, my enemy?" Schmitt repeats the phrase "my enemy," *mein Feind*, a number of times in this paragraph; see Derrida's discussion of this text in *Politics of Friendship*, 161–67.

56. Nietzsche, *Genealogy of Morals*, essay 1, section 10.

57. Genet, *L'ennemi*, 9.

58. "Men are not naturally enemies for the simplest reason that men living in their original state of independence do not have sufficiently constant relationships among themselves to bring about either a state of peace or a state of war. It is the relationship between things and not that between men that brings about war" (Rousseau, *On the Social Contract*, 1.iv ["On Slavery"] 21/F520). As was noted by Schmitt, Rousseau recognizes only something like a state of nature, a state of war, between states. "War is not therefore a relationship between one man and another,

but a relationship between one state and another," and men are only enemies when they are at war. "In war private individuals are enemies only incidentally: not as men or even as citizens." (Cf. Spinoza, who writes that "an enemy is one who lives apart from the state and does not recognize its authority either as a subject or as an ally. It is not hatred which makes a man an enemy, but the rights of the state." Spinoza, *A Theologico-Political Treatise*, 209.) The humanity of the enemy already appears fragile—or at least restricted—insofar as "enemy" constitutes, for Rousseau, an attribute that is added to "man" when citizenship is absent or stripped from him. Confining the enemy to its martial dimension, Rousseau also articulates the space beyond the enemy as criminal: "The foreigner (be he king, private individual, or a people) who robs, kills or detains subjects of another prince without declaring war on the prince is not an enemy but a brigand" (ibid./F521).

59. Rousseau, *On the Social Contract*, 2.v ("On the Right of Life or Death") 35/F529.

60. Rousseau, *On the Social Contract*, 2.v, 36/F529; and compare, 3.xiv: "and the person of the humblest citizen is as sacred and inviolable as that of the first magistrate" (73/F556).

61. Although attached to the human, Rousseau also considered enemies *of* the human, enemies that, strictly speaking, had little to do with war. Strikingly enough, if not necessarily surprisingly, Rousseau included childhood on his enemy list. "Other, more formidable enemies against which man has not the same means of defense are the natural infirmities, childhood, old age and illness of every kind," (Rousseau, *Discourse on the Origin and the Foundations of Inequality Among Men* 1, 136/F216).

62. Hegel, *Philosophy of Right*, §338. Carl von Clausewitz argues along the same line that, although war and combat are essentially "an expression of *hostile feelings*, " it is also the case that "there are usually no hostile feelings between individuals." Clausewitz acknowledges that "modern wars are seldom fought without hatred," but this hatred is located "between nations," something that "serves more or less as a substitute for hatred between individuals " (Clausewitz, *On War*, 137–38/G285–86).

63. Hegel, *Philosophy of Right*, §330.

64. Schmitt, *Concept of the Political*, 63. Schmitt was right, of course, as can be witnessed in discussions that engage both Hegel and Schmitt. William Kluback, for example, quotes Schmitt quoting Hegel, but does not elaborate on Hegel's *Sittlichkeit* text (Kluback, "A Man of Dark Thoughts"), and Richard Dean Winfield's treatment of Schmitt with Hegel entirely ignores the theory of the enemy shared by the two thinkers (Winfield, "Rethinking Politics: Carl Schmitt vs. Hegel").

65. Clausewitz, *On War*, 161/G320. Clausewitz uses the term *Gegner*, "opponent," interchangeably with *Feind*, "enemy." The English translation has "enemy" for both. Note also that with his emphasis on the concrete or effective, *wirklich*, Clausewitz announces Schmitt's emphasis on the "concrete enemy."

66. Clausewitz, *On War*, 75/G191–92. "In war," Clausewitz writes later on, "the will is directed at an animate object that *reacts*" (149/G303).

67. Hegel, *System of Ethical Life*, 147/G 470, translation modified. Schmitt quotes from this passage without reference (Schmitt, *Concept of the Political*, 63). It should be noted, however, that in the German, Schmitt's text quoting Hegel never mentions "negated otherness" as the English translation has it. The enemy, says Hegel as paraphrased by Schmitt, is "ethical difference as an alien to-be negated," *ein zu negierendes Fremdes*, "in his living totality" (Schmitt, *Concept of the Political*, 62/G62).

68. Ibid., 28.

69. Hegel, *System of Ethical Life*, 141/G463.

70. Ibid., 142/G464. Hegel later attributes a comparable movement and production of the enemy to the unhappy consciousness. In this case, mutual indifference is impossible, and consciousness is engaged in "a contradictory movement in which one opposite does not come to rest in *its* opposite, but in it only produces itself afresh as an opposite. Here, then, we have a struggle against an enemy to vanquish whom is really to suffer defeat" (Hegel, *Phenomenology of Spirit*, 127/G164). A few pages later, Hegel will speak of the "return of consciousness into itself" as a moment in which "the enemy is met with in his most characteristic form" (135/G173). Consciousness "takes its own reality to be immediately a nothingness, its actual doing thus becoming a doing of nothing." Consciousness remains closed upon itself while turning toward no more than nothing. It produces nothingness, reproduces itself, *erzeugt*, as nothing and as its enemy. "This enemy," Hegel continues, "renews himself in his defeat, and consciousness, in fixing its attention on him, far from freeing itself from him, really remains for ever in contact with him" (136/G174). Hegel returns to the enemy and to the oscillating movement that occurs when entering a conflict with him when he discusses "the virtuous consciousness" and its conflict with the "way of the world." This conflict, Hegel writes, "can only be an oscillation between preserving and sacrificing" (232/G287).

71. Hegel, *System of Ethical Life*, 148/G470. Franz Rosenzweig underscores this aspect of the enemy for Hegel in *Hegel und der Staat* I: 136. In the *Philosophy of Right*, Hegel translates this impossibility ("the enemy can only be . . .") into a prescriptive. War must not be "waged against domestic institutions, against the peace of family and private life, or against persons in their private capacities" (§338).

72. Plato, *Laws*, book 12, 955b.

73. Hegel, *System of Ethical Life*, 149/G471.

74. Plato, *Lysis* 215c, in *Collected Dialogues*, 158.

75. Benveniste, *Indo-European Language*, 76/F92. Further quotations will be made parenthetically in the text.

76. See, of course, Derrida's "Hostipitality," in *Acts of Religion*, 356–420.

77. For a discussion of the enemy as brother and the brother as enemy, see, of

course, Derrida, *Politics of Friendship*, especially, in connection to Schmitt, 161–62; see also Loraux, *Divided City*, esp. 208–13 and 222–28.

78. Plutarch, "How to Profit by One's Enemies," 88a. This line of argument is maintained throughout Plutarch's treatise. Another example: "thus also your enemy, by taking up and diverting to himself your malice and jealousy, will render you more kindly and less disagreeable to your friends in their prosperity," 92b. On "whether a man can be his own friend or foe," see Aristotle, *Eudemian Ethics*, 1240a.

79. Adorno, *Negative Dialectics*, 10/G20.

80. Ibid., 10. Adorno returns to the "incapacitation of the subject," joining again Hegel's description of the role of the community in breaking down the "happiness of the family." Adorno thus denounces the subject as "an ideology, a screen for society's objective functional context and a palliative for the subject's suffering under society" (66–67/G72–73). The difference of tone is related, of course, to Adorno's critique of Hegel's "siding with the universal."

81. Hegel, *Phenomenology*, 288/G352. In reading this passage, I am indebted to Derrida's discussion in *Glas*, where Derrida notes that "in its head, the government *must become the enemy* of just what it governs, must suppress the family not only as natural singularity but in the judicial system proper to it" (Derrida, *Glas*, 146a; Derrida returns to this passage in more details at 187a–188a).

82. Hegel may have been thinking of Aristotle's claim that "Spartan women were very harmful" during the Theban invasion of Sparta. They "were no use at all, like women in other city-states, but caused more confusion than the enemy," *polemios* (Aristotle, *Politics*, 1269b).

83. Hegel, *Phenomenology*, 288/G352. Hegel uses the verb *erzeugen* again when claiming, in the *Philosophy of Right*, that "the state is an individual and individuality essentially implies negation" (Hegel, *Philosophy of Right*, §324). "Hence," Hegel continues, "even if a number of states make themselves into a family, this group as an individual must engender an opposite and create an enemy," *einen Gegensatz kreieren und einen Feind erzeugen*. The state must produce and reproduce—an enemy.

84. Adorno, *Negative Dialectics*, 66–67/G72–73.

85. Thanks in part to Luce Irigaray, of course, who called attention to this passage by dedicating to it an entire section of her *Spéculum: De l'autre femme*. Although she mentions the enemy, Irigaray does not elaborate on that moment of Hegel's text. Alexandre Kojève had, earlier, acknowledged the passage (Kojève, *Introduction à la lecture de Hegel*, 105). Kojève comments on the "curious" fact that woman is the agent of ruin, the particularity "that is hostile to Society as such" (188). Jean Hyppolite quotes only the "everlasting irony" moment, skipping over the internal enemy (Hyppolite, *Genèse et structure*, 352). André Glucksmann attends to both Sophocles and to Hegel under the heading of "enemy brothers," focusing most particularly on Eteocles and Polynices. From Antigone—or wom-

ankind—as enemy, there seems to be little to learn (Glucksmann, *Discours de la guerre*, 110–13).

86. Hegel, *Phenomenology*, 288/G352.

87. Ibid., *Phenomenology*, 288/G353. This is consistent, of course, with the place that Hegel attributes to war and to conflict as an essential moment of "the rational process of *the very constitution of singularity*" (see Malabou, "Naissance de la mort—Hegel et Freud en guerre," 320).

88. Freud, "Inhibitions, Symptoms and Anxiety," *The Standard Edition*, 20: 132/G273. Further references will be made parenthetically in the text.

89. Freud, *Totem and Taboo*, *The Standard Edition*, 13: 148/G431. Further references will be made parenthetically in the text.

90. See Freud, *Totem and Taboo*, 14–16, 49–51, 62–63, 142–46, 160–61.

91. Freud, "Inhibitions," 102.

92. Freud, *Totem and Taboo*, 160.

93. Freud, "Inhibitions," 129; further references will be made parenthetically in the text.

94. Freud, "Inhibitions," 106/G250. Note that in Freud's German, there is no other subject than the father.

95. This is why the enemy participates in a seeming tautology: the enemy is the enemy, or, as Adorno and Horkheimer put it in their own version of "Anti-Semite and Jew," "the person chosen as enemy is already perceived as enemy" (Adorno and Horkheimer, *Dialectic of Enlightenment*, 154/G168). It also explains why, independently of all empirical history, the enemy must always oscillate between activity and passivity, subject and object of hostility and persecution. "Those impelled by blind murderous lust have always seen in the victim the pursuer who has driven them to desperate self-defense, and the mightiest of the rich have experienced their weakest neighbor as an intolerable threat before falling upon him. The rationalization was both a ruse and a compulsion. The person chosen as enemy is already perceived as enemy" (154, translation altered).

96. Freud later on addresses the way in which a "loss of object" gives rise to even more anxiety (Freud, "Inhibitions," 138–43).

APPENDIX I

1. Glazer, *Franz Rosenzweig*, xxii–xxiii.

2. Rosenzweig, *Star of Redemption*, 156/G 174. Further references will be made parenthetically in the text, first to the English translation (which I sometimes modify slightly), and second to the German, indicated by the letter G.

3. Derrida, "Interpretations at War: Kant, the Jew, the German," 180. Olivier Mongin also asked whether the writing of the *Star* in wartime "has any other sense than a contingent one" (Mongin, "Entrer dans le vingtième siècle," 223). In spite of this opening, Mongin does not dwell much on Rosenzweig's theory of war, but

considers instead the relevance of Jan Patocka's work on the ethical dimension of war.

4. With this conflation of history and war, and notwithstanding his well-known opposition to Hegel, Rosenzweig is being here strictly Hegelian, of course ("It is only out of the opposition of autonomous states that history grows, and history alone is the bond that links these 'individuals,'" Rosenzweig, *Hegel und der Staat,* 2: 183–84), but Schmittian lines are also being installed here—six years before the publication of the early version of Schmitt's *Concept of the Political* in 1927: "Thus war and revolution are the only reality known to the state; it would cease to be a state at the moment when neither the one nor the other were to take place—even if it be only in the form of a thought of war or revolution. The state can at no moment lay down the sword" (Rosenzweig, *Star,* 333–34/G370). And compare also with the *Star,* where Rosenzweig pointedly opposes the Jewish people ("we were the only ones who separated what lived within us from all community with what is dead") to "all the peoples of the world": "Whenever a people loves the soil of its native land more than its own life, it is in danger—as all the peoples of the world are—that, though nine times out of ten this love will save the native soil from the foe," *gegen den Feind,* "and, along with it, the life of the people, in the end the soil will persist as that which was loved more strongly, and the people will leave their lifeblood upon it" (299/G332). As Stéphane Mosès and others have argued, the history from which Rosenzweig extirpates Judaism is the very same history he learned and endorsed from Hegel (Mosès, *Système et revelation,* 209–11).; see also Funkenstein's emphasis on the "warring temporality" that defines the historical world—a world defined by nation-states: For Rosenzweig, "the nation-state revealed itself as nothing but the incarnation of the *libido dominandi.* Its peace was unstable and ephemeral in the best case" (Funkenstein, *Perceptions,* 300).

5. Barbara E. Galli notes that "the discussions and views with regard to Eastern and Asian philosophies and religions in the *Star* are both colored by the times and problematic in themselves" (Galli, "'The New Thinking': An Introduction" in *Franz Rosenzweig's "The New Thinking,"* 186 n. 22). And yet, aside from Shlomo Pines's study, very little attention has been given to the subject of Islam. (See Pines, "Islam According to the *Star of Redemption.*" Pines's text is also available in German as "Der Islam im 'Stern der Erlösung'. Eine Untersuchung zu Tendenzen und Quellen Franz Rosenzweigs" in *Hebräische Beiträge zur Wissenschaft des Judentums* 3–5 (1987–89): 138–48.) Gesine Palmer's work, most notably her introduction to the Rosenzweig collection she edited (Rosenzweig, *'Innerlich bleibt die Welt eine'*), will of course, change this state of affairs as to the reception history of Rosenzweig on Islam. Yet up to now, at least, the general attitude has been to consider Rosenzweig's view on Islam as "an embarrassing prejudice" (Robert Gibbs, quoted in Galli, 186 n. 22), a contingent aspect "colored by the times." Such a claim has yet to be philosophically or rhetorically established through a reading of the *Star.*

6. "Messianic politics" is the title of the section of the *Star* to which I am here

attending. In "The New Thinking," Rosenzweig explains that "messianic politics, that is, a theory of war, thus closes the first book of the volume, and Christian aesthetics, that is, a theory of suffering, closes the second book" (Rosenzweig, "The New Thinking," in *Franz Rosenzweig's "The New Thinking,"* 95).

7. The syntax is, of course, ambiguous. The self "confirmed in its place" may equally be that of "man" or that of the "neighbor." Unlike Levinas, Rosenzweig is therefore not abolishing the symmetry between self and other. Rather, he is insisting on their distinction. "The world is not thrown in [man's] face as an endless melee, nor is he told, while a finger points to the whole melee: that is you. That is you—therefore stop distinguishing yourself from it, penetrate it, dissolve in it, lose yourself in it. No, it is quite different" (240/G267).

8. Translation slightly modified. A few pages later, Rosenzweig revisits the distinction between one neighbor and the next, the possibility of which is inherent to the love of neighbor. "With apparently devastating effect, love reaches into this composite structure [of the world] and detaches now here and now there a component for a life of its own which threatens to shatter the cohesion of the whole. In reality, however, it is not up to love which member it thus seizes with its power and delivers out of the context of life into its eternity. . . . [Man] only knows that he is to love, and to love always the nighest and the neighbor" (241/G269).

9. Funkenstein, *Perceptions*, 264.

10. For a parallel account of Paul's *adiaphora* as "an operation that divides the divisions of the law and renders them inoperative," see Agamben, *Il tempo che resta*, 54–55.

11. Meineke, "A Life of Contradiction," 470. Meineke emphasizes that for Rosenzweig "the Jew," war "must not acquire any existential significance." This is the consistency to which I am referring above. Yet in the particular instance commented upon by Meineke, Rosenzweig writes: "I deny that war makes any real impact on any man" (quoted in Meineke, 470).

12. As Eduard Strauss had already noted in his 1922 review of the *Star*, "the theology of the second part [of the *Star*] finds its counterexample in each case in Islam" (Eduard Strauss, "The Star of Redemption," in *Franz Rosenzweig's "The New Thinking,"* 129).

13. Quoted in Funkenstein, *Perceptions*, 264.

14. Rosenzweig had written earlier that "while Mohammed took over the concepts of revelation externally, he necessarily remained attached to paganism," *Heidentum*, "in the basic concept of creation" (*Star*, 117/G129). And consider the following, as well: "For all that it proceeds vigorously and arrogantly behind the idea of the unity of God, Islam thus slips into a monistic paganism," *monistisches Heidentum*, "if one may use the expression. God himself competes with God himself at every moment, as if it were the colorful, warring heaven of the gods of polytheism" (123/G137). Finally, Islam "remains stuck to the untransformed figures which the pagan world pointed out to it and supposes that it can set them in motion, just as they are, with the concept of revelation" (173/G193).

15. Pines, "Islam According to the *Star of Redemption*," 303. In this context, it might be important to consider that Rosenzweig recasts Hegel's "Judaization" of Kant. As Peter Gordon remarked in a discussion that followed an oral presentation of this material, whereas Hegel considered Kant's rapport with the law (and subsequent lack of love) as Jewish, Rosenzweig concludes his discussion of "the way of Allah" by recalling Kant, making Kant into a Muslim, as it were (Rosenzweig, *Star*, 217/G243; see also Derrida, "Interpretations at War").

16. One could equally justifiably claim that, for Rosenzweig, Islam is nothing but religion. Yet this would maintain the same structure of opposition and exclusion I have been describing: on the one hand, Judaism and Christianity, on the other, Islam. Hence, in "The New Thinking," Rosenzweig claims that Judaism and Christianity "would have been most highly astonished also to be addressed" as religions. "Only their parody, Islam, is religion from the very start and does not at all want to be otherwise" ("The New Thinking," in *Franz Rosenzweig's "The New Thinking,"* 92). The meaning of "religion" in Rosenzweig, as Gesine Palmer argues, is a difficult and highly determined one, and the possibilities of misunderstanding are numerous, perhaps most pointedly around the issue of Islam (Palmer, "Einleitung").

17. Rosenzweig, *Hegel und der Staat*, 172.

18. For a magisterial demonstration of the Christian genealogy of Rosenzweig's political theology, see Funkenstein, *Perceptions*, esp. 298–301. One should perhaps consider as well Jacob Taubes's no less magisterial *coup de force* when he turns things around and reads Paul's political theology through Rosenzweig, all but claiming that Paul finds his sources in the very rhythm of Jewish liturgy as Rosenzweig read it (Taubes, *Politische Theologie*, 50–55). Ironically, perhaps, both readings—Funkenstein's and Taubes's—could be construed as polemicizing against each other. They were both published in their final form in 1993.

CHAPTER 4

I thank Shaul Bassi for sharing the wonderful letter from John Keats to Thomas Keats with me.

1. Shakespeare, *Hamlet* 4.2.

2. Notwithstanding the distinct kind of articulation, rather than interpretation, proposed by Jacques Lacan in 1959: "up till now," Lacan says before offering his own reading, Hamlet's words "have remained as good as sealed to the commentators" (Lacan, "Desire and the Interpretation of Desire in *Hamlet*," 52). The "making sense" I am referring to above was offered by Jerah Johnson, "The Concept of the 'King's Two Bodies' in *Hamlet*."

3. Ernst Kantorowicz's book, *The King's Two Bodies: A Study in Medieval Political Theology* has been hailed as "perhaps the most important work in the history

of medieval political thought." After a short introductory chapter on "the problem," Kantorowicz turns to Shakespeare and thus locates the dramatist at the crux of a history of political theology. Hence, recalling Carl Schmitt, "political theology, too." Further references will be made parenthetically in the text.

4. "Political Shakespeare" and its derivations ("Shakespeare's Politics," or "Political Criticism of Shakespeare") is a common title in Shakespeare scholarship, but it is one that often enough indicates an interest not so much in political theory as in issues that have since been "politicized." To use Shaul Bassi's description, "political Shakespeare" has thus meant an emphasis on "the micropolitics of class, gender, and race," rather than the "macropolitics of kings and cardinals" (Bassi, "Mixed Marriages, Mixed Philosophies, and Mixed Criticisms: *Othello* and *Nigredo*," unpublished paper, 2001). By way of the two bodies, I want to try to address both of these dimensions, cultural and philosophical.

5. I will refer to the following editions of Shakespeare's plays: *The Merchant of Venice*, ed. Jay L. Halio (Oxford: Oxford University Press, 1993), hereafter abbreviated *MV*; and *Othello*, ed. E. A. J. Honigmann (London: The Arden Shakespeare, 1997), hereafter abbreviated *O*. For reasons that will become clearer, I am here borrowing the words of Emily Bartels in her discussion of the Moors that were invented by Shakespeare (Bartels, "Making More of the Moor," 442). As to the term "stranger," which is used in both plays (*MV*, 1.3.115; *O*, 1.1.134), James Shapiro points out that it operates historically as an "offensive word" (Shapiro, *Shakespeare and the Jews*, 185). One might say today that "stranger" is a "fighting word." In the same way, and for the specific purposes of this chapter, which engages once again the work of Carl Schmitt, one can take "hate" to be less the personal expression of an affect than a "fighting word," a public and decisive assertion of enmity that functions so as to invent, constitute, and/or confirm the existence of a political community. And that of an enemy.

6. Christopher Marlowe, *The Jew of Malta*, 2.3.215–18

7. "It is worth remarking that in the dramatist's own lifetime the play seems to have been universally known not as *Othello* but as *The Moor of Venice*" (Barbara Everett, "'Spanish' Othello: The Making of Shakespeare's Moor," 65).

8. The separation of the two plays has gone so far as to place them on distinct epochal sides. "The moderns," for example, at least as they are followed by Richard Halpern, would appear to have had almost nothing to say about *Othello* (with the short, but significant exception of Joyce, who certainly bears relevance here), whereas the "Jewish question" has been more "modern" (Halpern, *Shakespeare among the Moderns*). Judging from a recent collection entitled *Shakespeare and Modernity*, which includes three (out of ten) articles on Shylock, it would again seem that, for the scholars, *The Merchant of Venice* bears more of an essential relation to modernity than *The Moor of Venice*. Whatever the empirical validity of this state of affairs, it remains surprising, given the more explicitly "religious" dimension of *The Merchant* and given the Arab, African-American, colonial, post-

colonial, and other appropriations of *Othello*. This discourse could easily have been invoked, for example, by Eric S. Mallin, who begins his inquiry with a parallel between Shakespeare and the movie *Independence Day*, a movie that "features two heroes . . . an African American and a Jew" (Mallin, "Jewish Invader and the Soul of State: *The Merchant of Venice* and Science Fiction Movies," 142).

9. Bloom, *Shakespeare's Politics*, 64.

10. Greenblatt, *Shakespearean Negotiations*, 134.

11. There is much material to dispute this assertion, of course, and yet one might consider for now, and by way of example, that the recently republished collection *Shakespeare as Political Thinker*, edited by John E. Alvis and Thomas G. West, although it is indebted to the work of Alan Bloom (who does consider the political significance of *Othello* and of *The Merchant of Venice*), does not devote any of its chapters to *Othello*. But the "depoliticization" of *Othello*, its becoming a "domestic tragedy," already finds its early sources, as Shaul Bassi has demonstrated, in the Romantic deracialization of Othello (Bassi, *Le metamorfosi di Otello*).

12. Cavell, *Disowning Knowledge*, 129.

13. Cohen, *Anti-Mimesis*, 42. It is important to note, of course, that Tom Cohen seeks to correct the fact that Othello's lack of sovereignty (a term that is central to Schmitt's political theology) is consistently "overlooked." The attribution of sovereignty to Othello, the political (*and* therefore also apolitical) perspective within which he is seen, "is itself an *aesthetic* image" (ibid.). As Carl Schmitt writes, "any decision about whether something is *unpolitical* is always a *political* decision, irrespective of who decides and what reasons are advanced" (Schmitt, *Political Theology*, 2).

14. Honigmann, introduction to *Othello*, 107.

15. Danson, *The Harmonies of the Merchant of Venice*, 16.

16. I am thinking here of Julia Lupton, whose reading of Othello's theological significance also reinscribes in *Othello* the importance of the struggle of Christendom with Islam (Lupton, "*Othello* Circumcised"). Such a "theological" reading already has a history in the tradition of "Christian" readings of *Othello* (that is to say, readings that emphasize the relevance of Christian, theological categories for an understanding of the play), a tradition in which Stanley Cavell also partakes when he writes that Othello places "a finite woman in the place of God" (Cavell, *Disowning Knowledge*, 126). G. K. Hunter's formulation of the Christian, theological reading which he defends, is quite representative—parenthetical additions included: "Modern scholars often labour to document the exact racial background of Shylock (or Othello) . . . but the evidence of the plays suggest that the old framework of assumptions about Jews, Turks, and Moors—and this means theological assumptions—provided the controlling image in [Shakespeare's] mind" (Hunter, "Elizabethans and Foreigners," 49).

On the other Abrahamic end of this tradition, Daniel Vitkus sees *Othello* as having first and foremost a religious significance (the play is a "drama of conversion") because what takes precedence in it are anxieties over *Islam* as a religious threat (Vitkus, "Turning Turk," 145). However, Vitkus had elsewhere noted the "tendency to ignore" the "religious identity" of Muslims "in favor of a label that signified a 'barbaric ethnicity," the "curious reluctance to call the Muslims by any name with a religious connotation" (Vitkus, "Early Modern Orientalism," 216). As I will argue below, this reluctance is found in *Othello*, in the play itself.

On the other side of a theological reading, and aside from Alan Bloom's undeniable, if irritating contribution to a political reading of *Othello*, the contemporary state of a political reception and of cultural appropriations of Shakespeare provides ample testimony to the ways in which the play itself constitutes a stage for an unspoken or textually silent dispute between theology and politics (here again, recalling Schmitt on the *political* decision that claims that something is political or unpolitical). As Martin Yaffe has documented, a similar state of affairs can be witnessed regarding *The Merchant of Venice*. Yaffe offers a wonderful summary and a fascinating expansion of the theologico-political issues at work in and around *The Merchant of Venice* (Yaffe, *Shylock and the Jewish Question*).

17. Kantorowicz, *The King's Two Bodies*, 216.

18. Rolls, *The Theory of the King's Two Bodies*, 73.

19. Rolls here attends to the kind of association linking Othello to Desdemona (Rolls, *The Theory of the King's Two Bodies*, 157–58). A few pages later, Rolls discusses the "fashioning" of a "corporate body" in their relationship and then seamlessly moves on to discuss "a transformation in Shakespeare's understanding of the function of the body politic (186–87). Rolls does not elaborate further on this, which is why I write that he only "suggests" the link to political theology. Clearly, Rolls sees a political and theologico-political significance in *Othello*, though he leaves much unsaid about it. As I have noted above, writing from a very different perspective, Stanley Cavell underscores the same issues when he locates "Othello's placing of a finite woman in the place of God" as the "pivot" of his interpretation of the play (Cavell, *Disowning Knowledge*, 126). Finally, Harry Morris's claim that "Christian tragedy is possible" (though there is only one, and it is Shakespeare's *Othello*) hinges on a reading of the play that interestingly follows, if slightly differently, the Paul I quoted earlier: "Since all mortals are the body of the church, Christ the bridegroom (Desdemona) is wedded to the church (Everyman-Othello), and He (Desdemona) goes about his Father's business, which is the salvation of men (Othello)" (Morris, *Last Things in Shakespeare*, 85). For a refreshingly different perspective that bears on my discussion, consider James McPherson's (sole) remark comparing the Venice of Shylock with that of Othello: "This is much the same Venice that Othello inhabits, except that the Christian tradition in this tragedy seems to play no significant role" (James A. McPherson in Kaul, ed., *Othello: New Essays by Black Writers*, 49).

20. "The 'state' that presents a unified aesthetic image in the codes of Venet-

ian courtship, martial splendor, political adjudication, revenge, and love, relies on public 'reputation' (as Cassio notes) for power. In his contradictions, Othello represents the martial violence of this aesthetic state that must imprint its law on the anonymous Ottomite hordes (whose double-O reflects his own)" (Cohen, *Anti-Mimesis*, 20).

21. The question of how to read Othello's assertion of "discord" becomes highly relevant here ("And this, and this the greatest discords be—*They kiss*" 2.1.196). Is he figuring the relationship as a pleasant discord, prefiguring the "broken joint" that is to come, or, as Shaul Bassi suggests, ironically calling "discord" the *concordia discors* of the relationship? Whatever it may be, the Neoplatonic dimension argued for by Bassi (who follows here the work of Gilberto Sacerdoti) highlights the theologico-political dimension that is crucial to an understanding of the relationship between Othello and Desdemona (Bassi, "Mixed Marriages").

22. The syntax and the ambiguous genitive leave productively undecided whether Othello would here be admitting to being married to "Venice the whore" or to Desdemona, "the whore of Venice." The city's morality (and its embodiment in the female population) had after all already provided Iago with a crucial element in his deceit of Othello: "I know our country disposition well—/In Venice they do let God see the pranks/They dare not show their husbands" (3.3.204–6). Otherwise put, the city did have a "reputation for sexual licentiousness" (Honigmann, "Introduction," 11). Daniel Vitkus, though emphasizing another image, the "conventional comparison of Venice with virginity," still points out that the perception at the time was of "the Turk cuckolding the impotent Venetian patriarchs or raping the Venetian virgin." Hence, it is because of the "desperate lack of manly leadership" that Othello is "given charge." To English audiences, Vitkus continues, such reliance on a stranger "would have been almost as shocking as the elopement and miscegenation permitted by the Venetian state" (Vitkus, "Turning Turk," 163–64; cf. also Virginia Vaughan, *Othello: A Contextual History*, esp. 16 and 33).

23. Bloom, *Shakespeare's Politics*, 36. Further references will be made parenthetically in the text.

24. Earlier, Bloom had also asked: "what can possibly be the basis of their love?" (41). It is again quite striking that the introduction to *Shakespeare as a Political Thinker*, a book that claims as its "nearest progenitor" Bloom's *Shakespeare's Politics*, very little room is made for Othello. Commenting in his introduction on the fact that "erotic love in Shakespeare embraces all the colors [sic] of passion," John Alvis lists every character who has loved or been loved in Shakespeare's plays (including Desdemona) except for Othello. Aside from the reception of the two plays within traditions of reappropriations, as can be summarized under the headings of "Shakespeare and the Jews" and "African" or "Postcolonial Othello" (each of which massively ignoring the other), the exclusion or marginalization of *Othello* and of *The Merchant of Venice* from political discussions of Shakespeare is quite general, regardless of "political" or "theoretical" commitment. Pierre Sahel places

both plays outside of his inquiry into Shakespeare's political thought by focusing on the historical plays (Sahel, *La pensée politique dans les drames historiques de Shakespeare*; see also George W. Keeton, *Shakespeare's Legal and Political Background*; Alan Hager's *Shakespeare's Political Animal*; and Robin Headlam Wells's *Shakespeare, Politics and the State*, with the exception of an important comment Wells makes comparing the Venice of *The Merchant* to that of *Othello* as the site of a "battle between civilization and unreason," 58). Finally, see the counterpoint now provided by Ania Loomba in her *Shakespeare*.

25. Although I take a different and somewhat critical perspective, it should already be clear that my argument is not only indebted to but closely parallels Lupton's "*Othello* Circumcised." Lupton emphasizes, for example, the importance of Paul and of a discourse of law and justice. Such is, in fact, the basis for her reconsideration of *Othello* in the context of theological categories. In relation to the political meaning of the matrimonial relation, Lupton crucially points out that "whereas studies of race in the play tend to emphasize the movement of paganization, feminist critics have noted Othello's increasing association with justice, usually understood as the masculinist tenets of Judeo-Christian patriarchy. My point is somewhat different: Othello's justice, like that of Shylock, serves to separate the Semitic strands out of the Judeo-Christian synthesis even while grotesquely reinforcing the authority of the husband; although Othello's increasing alliance with the law is indeed patriarchal, I would insist on the Abrahamic (Judeo-Islamic) connotations of the word *patriarch*" (Lupton, "Othello Circumcised," 80).

26. Augustine, *The City of God*, 6, 5. There is some debate as to the origins of the phrase and its pertinent genealogy in regard to Schmitt's work (see Hent de Vries, "Autour du théologico-politique," and see also Heinrich Meier, "Was ist Politische Theologie? Enführende Bemerkungen zu einem umstrittenen Begriff"). In his introduction to Kantorowicz's book, William Chester Jordan does not trace the history of the phrase, but he states almost at the outset that the phrase "political theology" was "associated with the German and Nazi-leaning jurist Carl Schmitt" (*The King's Two Bodies*, x). For a discussion of Kantorowicz's link to arch-conservative circles in Germany, see Alain Boureau, "Kantorowicz, or the Middle Ages as Refuge"; Jean-François Courtine, "A propos du 'problème théologico-politique,'" and see also Agamben, "Sovereign Body and Sacred Body" in *Homo Sacer*, esp. 91–94. It may be important to note here that Kantorowicz's earliest work was conspicuously left out of the rest of his career. As Boureau points out, "the thesis that he defended at Heidelberg, the subject of which is prudently left out of the notice in *Speculum*, was concerned with Muslim corporations and was written in the context of comparative historical sociology" (Boureau, "Kantorowicz," 357).

27. Schmitt, *Political Theology*, 36/G43.

28. I am referring here to Alan Bloom and the Straussian "school," Rolls, Yaffe.

29. Schmitt, *Concept of the Political*, 26.

30. Ibid., emphasis added.

31. As I explained in Chapter 1, this crucial question was raised by Jacob

Taubes, whose formidable work points toward the momentous place of the "enemy" in Romans 11:28 (against Carl Schmitt's assertion that the New Testament does not deploy a political notion of the enemy). It is worth nothing again that although the importance of the friend-enemy distinction does not explicitly figure in Schmitt's *Political Theology*, Schmitt himself does conclude his main critique of liberalism with the charge that liberalism "wants to dissolve metaphysical truth in a discussion." With such discussions and with endless negotiations, Schmitt continues, liberalism defers "the decisive bloody battle" and, more gravely, "permit[s] the decision to be suspended" (Schmitt, *Political Theology*, 63). The decision is postponed along with the decisive bloody battle, but with the bloody battle, the question of enmity begins perhaps to emerge within *Political Theology* itself. It would take a few more years for Schmitt to place the enemy at the center of his political theory in *The Concept of the Political*. Insofar as he was continuing to reflect on sovereignty and putting the emphasis on a sovereign decision, however, Schmitt may not have felt the need to make it explicit that the sovereign decision (a decision over the "state of exception," or, as *Political Theology* famously puts it: "Sovereign is he who decides on the exception," 5) had been translated into a decision over the enemy (*Concept of the Political*, 38). At any rate, as we discussed earlier, Schmitt never made explicit the connection between political theology and the concept of the enemy.

32. Gillies, *Shakespeare and the Geography of Difference*, 32.

33. Bloom, *Shakespeare's Politics*, 42.

34. Lupton, "*Othello* Circumcised," 73; see also Honigmann's comment that "we cannot prove Othello to be a Christian convert" (introduction to *Othello*, 23) and Emily Bartels's assertion that "Othello's religious past is unclear" (Bartels, "Making More of the Moor," 436; see also Danson, "England, Islam").

35. Lupton, "*Othello* Circumcised," 74.

36. Ania Loomba, "'Delicious Traffick': Racial and Religious Difference on Early Modern Stages" in *Shakespeare and Race*, 206; see also James Shapiro, "Race, Nation, or Alien?" in his *Shakespeare and the Jews*, and Michael Neill, "'Mulattos,' 'Blacks,' and 'Indian Moors': *Othello* and Early Modern Constructions of Human Difference."

37. The "turns" of Samuel Marochitanus, the "blessed Jew of Morocco," already tell the story of "a blackamoor turned white," of a Jew turned Muslim, but also turned Christian. In this story, which was translated from Arabic into Latin in the thirteenth century, the Jew who had turned Muslim "turns" again and now "translates" into a Jew turned Christian. What Norman Daniel refers to as the "'Rabbi Samuel' literature" seems to have originated in an anti-Jewish polemical treatise called in the original Arabic *Ifham al-Yahud* and written by Rabbi Samuel the Moroccan (Samawal al-Maghribi), who had converted to Islam (Daniel, *Islam and the West*, 189). In the Latin translation of his treatise (and subsequently in the numerous translations into Western European languages), Samuel turns, therefore, white, that is to say, Christian. There is, as of yet, no study of "his" book, a heav-

ily edited translation of which appeared in English in the seventeenth century un-
der the title: *The Blessed Jew of Marocco: Or, A Blackmoor made White. Being a
Demonstration of the true Messias out of the law and prophets, by Rabbi Samuel, a
Jew turned Christian.* The book's "curious title" is mentioned by G. K. Hunter,
"Elizabethans" and surprisingly ignored by Karen Newman, "'And Wash the
Ethiop White': Femininity and the Monstrous in *Othello.*" After I completed this
chapter, a new collection on Othello appeared that includes important discussions
engaging the common discourse of "race" as it applied to Jews and Moors in the
two plays; see most particularly James R. Andreas, Sr., "The Curse of Cush: Othello's Judaic Ancestry."

38. As will become clearer, the distinction between Shylock and Othello, between Jew and Moor, is already breaking down as the image of the black ram begins to loom. Julia Lupton explains that "even Iago's infamous image of bestial
cross-coupling, 'an old black ram/Is tupping your white ewe' (1.1.90–91), echoes
Merchant's most egregious pun, that between 'ewes' and "Iewes'" (Lupton, "Othello Circumcised" 77). Shylock's excessive love of gold, moreover, was already announced by Morocco's failure to stay away from it, or, as Barbara Lewalski writes,
"This defeat and lessoning of Morocco . . . foreshadows the defeat and conversion
of Shylock, for he represents in somewhat different guise these same antichristian
values of worldliness and self-righteousness" (Lewalski, "Biblical Allusion and Allegory in 'The Merchant of Venice,'" 337). For an illuminating comparison of Shylock and Morocco (one that remain oblivious to its own originality in the scholarly landscape) that credits Shakespeare for "the juxtaposition of Moor and Jew"
so as to "rewrite the categories of exclusion," see Alan Rosen, "The Rhetoric of Exclusion: Jew, Moor, and the Boundaries of Discourse in *The Merchant of Venice.*"
(Clearly, the internal comparison between the two plays is already announced at
the outset of *Othello.* Indeed, Brabantio's "distracted lamentations after Desdemona's elopement [*O*, 1.1.158–81] are disturbingly similar to Shylock's after Jessica's
flight [*MV*, 2.8.12–22]," Honigmann, introduction to *Othello*, 77. Not surprisingly, a "Jewish" association follows with a mention of "the bitter letter" of the
"bloody book of law," promptly invoked by the duke in response to Brabantio [*O*,
1.3.68–69].) In this context, it is important to note that by emphasizing "competing notions of Jewishness circulating in early modern England," Mary Metzger
downplays the comparison with *Othello* she herself suggests in small asides. This
comparison suggests (apparently unwittingly) that "ethnic difference" could be a
"Jewish question" (Metzger, "'Now by My Hood, a Gentle and No Jew': Jessica,
The Merchant of Venice, and the Discourse of Early Modern English Identity").
And consider also James Shapiro, who strangely asserts that the discourse of race
is (or becomes?) empirical: It is "accumulated experience" that "convinced Europeans that some of the accepted stereotypes of Jewish racial otherness . . . needed
to be qualified." In this case, the enduring belief that "Portuguese Jews" were black
appears not to have needed qualification (Shapiro, *Shakespeare and the Jews*, 171).

39. It is interesting to note that Alan Bloom and others see here a regrettable

failure of Shylock, rather than the result of a historical identification of Jews with carnality. Bloom writes that "sadly, if one looks at the list of similar characteristics on which Shylock bases his claim to equality with his Christian tormentors, one sees that it includes only things which belong to the body; what he finds in common between Christian and Jew is essentially what all animals have in common" (Bloom, *Shakespeare's Politics*, 23; see also Yaffe, *Shylock and the Jewish Question*).

40. Yaffe, *Shylock and the Jewish Question*, 61.

41. Cavell, *Disowning Knowledge*, 10.

42. Bloom, *Shakespeare Politics*, 53.

43. Ibid., 53.

44. Ibid., 54.

45. Ibid., 55.

46. Lupton, "*Othello* Circumcised," 80.

47. See, for example, Cavell's interpretation of *Othello*, which situates Othello as "other" to and as "separate" from Desdemona's "flesh and blood" (Cavell, *Disowning Knowledge*, 138). Bloom goes so far as to call Othello "curiously insubstantial" (Bloom, *Shakespeare's Politics*, 58).

48. The "often" is, of course, quite unwarranted, because the two plays are almost never discussed together except to point out that they both take place in Venice. It is significant that Lupton, who leaves the "often" hanging without a footnote, admitted to having no other study to mention than that of Leslie Fiedler, *The Stranger in Shakespeare* (personal communication). Note, however, that Jean-Pierre Petit wrote what is perhaps the most striking exception to the lack of comparison of the two plays. In an article that is four pages long, he simply juxtaposes the discussion of Othello and Shylock, discussing one after the other. Like Lupton and Vitkus, Petit minimizes the importance of "race" and sees in the two plays stories of conversion (Petit, "Deux étrangers shakespeariens").

49. Lupton, "*Othello* Circumcised," 75. The centrality of marriage echoes, of course, the reading of *Othello* as a "domestic tragedy." In this context—and in direct connection with the political meaning of the husband-wife relation—it is striking to consider that, according to Linda Rozmovits, one aspect of the reception of *The Merchant of Venice* has been "most obscured by the passage of time," namely, the fact that *The Merchant of Venice* was a play, "first and foremost" about marriage, and specifically "about the marriage prospects of a wealthy orphaned young woman with a subplot about a Jewish moneylender hovering in the background" (Rozmovits, *Shakespeare and the Politics of Culture*, 5–6).

50. Bloom, *Shakespeare's Politics*, 14.

51. Ibid., 21.

52. Fiedler, *Stranger in Shakespeare*, 141; emphasis in the original.

53. Metzger, "'Now by My Hood, a Gentle and No Jew'" 52; see also Loomba, "'Delicious traffick.'"

54. Shapiro, *Shakespeare and the Jews*, 172. In his book, Shapiro himself never

discusses *Othello*. And see the novel argument made by Ania Loomba in her *Shakespeare*.

55. Ibid., 173.

56. That the merchant may not be Shylock has been argued often enough, if only on the basis of Portia's own famous query "Which is the merchant here, and which the Jew?" (*MV*, 4.1.171). But this uncertainty does not diminish—instead it increases—the distance between the two strangers and between the two plays. Such distance, in fact, mutually determines the two plays—and the two enemy bodies.

57. "This passage has not been explained; it might be an outcrop of a lost source, or a topical allusion. Perhaps it was introduced simply for the sake of the elaborate pun of Moor/more" (J. R. Brown, quoted in Eldred Jones, *Othello's Countrymen*, 71).

CHAPTER 5

This chapter could not have been written without the kind and diligent assistance of Jacques Fredj, director, Sara Halperyn, head librarian, and the staff of the Centre de Documentation Juive Contemporaine, Paris.

1. Blumenthal, "On the Nature of the Nazi Idiom [*ʿal tivah shel lashon ha-natzim*]," 55.

2. This should not be taken to mean that one can dispense with a rigorous linguistic and philological perspective, of course (consider, aside from Blumenthal's work, Klemperer's, which inspired Blumenthal, and, more recently, Christopher Hutton, *Linguistics and the Third Reich* and Anna-Vera Sullam Calimani, *I nomi dello sterminio*). Rather, as Giorgio Agamben—to whom this chapter is very much indebted—explains, it is a matter of the way in which "all disciplinary barriers are destroyed and all embankments flooded" by the "subject" of the Holocaust (Agamben, *Remnants of Auschwitz*, 48).

3. Agamben, *Remnants of Auschwitz*, 48/143.

4. S. Yizhar, "Ha-shavui," in *Shivʿa sipurim*, trans. as "The Prisoner" in *Modern Hebrew Literature*. References will be made parenthetically in the text.

5. Robert Alter, in *Modern Hebrew Literature*, 292.

6. The shift here from *voix* to *voies*, "voices" to "ways," is meant to recall the expression *voies d'eau*, "waterways," and so parting and partaking of the waters—the Red Sea, for example, where ancient Egyptians and Hebrews are dissymmetrically bound to the "same" waterway.

7. Almog, *Sabra*, 206.

8. As Barbie Zelizer has compellingly argued, the "haunting visual memories of the Holocaust and war atrocities were *produced* by the photographic record" (Zelizer, *Remembering to Forget*, 1; emphasis added).

9. Böll, *And Where Were You, Adam?* Interestingly enough, this story, as if citing Yizhar, includes a painting of "a flock of sheep . . . and in the middle of them a shepherd" (14), later described again as "the flock of sheep and the stupid shepherd" (17/G22).

10. Hever, *Producing the Modern Hebrew Canon*, 113.

11. I do not know whether Idith Zertal meant to recall, as I do, the phrase made famous by Christopher Browning (and, opposite Browning, by Daniel Jonah Goldhagen), but be that as it may, "Ordinary People" is the title of her chapter on the Mossad, another of "the key factors in building consciousness and forging self-identity" in Israel (Zertal, *From Catastrophe to Power*, 153).

12. Immediately after discussing Yizhar's story, but without elaborating on the connection he thus makes, Almog writes that "presumably, the Sabra soldiers' attitude toward the Arab refugees was also affected, even if indirectly, by the anti-Diaspora ethos in which the Sabras were educated. The tendency to look down on the 'bowed heads' and 'bent backs' of Holocaust refugees to a certain extent dulled the sensitivity to the suffering of the Palestinian refugees" (Almog, *Sabra*, 207).

13. The relation of stupidity to the human and the inhuman is explored in ways that are crucial to the questions I am addressing throughout in Ronell, *Stupidity*.

14. Deleuze, *La philosophie critique de Kant*, 74.

15. Enthusiasm (*Enthusiasm*, to be distinguished from *Begeisterung*) is perhaps the best known among the sublime emotions. Yet, as Jean-Luc Nancy points out, it is neither "all nor the nexus of the sublime." Rather, "the only true nobility of the sublime" is "apathia, the absence of affect and of tone" (Nancy, *Le discours de la syncope*, 110–11).

16. Arendt, *Lectures on Kant's Political Philosophy*, 7. Arendt's contribution is essential here, of course, because she put the emphasis on the political dimension of the *Critique of Judgment*. Yet she made little room for the "Analytic of the Sublime" in her reading (52–53), which, according to John Llewelyn, may have something to do with a certain forgetting: "Arendt forgets that one expects others to share not only our feelings regarding the beautiful, but also our feelings regarding the sublime." The "Analytic," therefore "might have a more important role to play in a *Critique of Political Judgement*" (Llewelyn, *HypoCritical Imagination*, 146).

17. De Man, "Hegel on the Sublime," in *Aesthetic Ideology*, 106. Although unsatisfying, it seems quite clear that Adorno's accusation that Kant's discussion of the sublime was politically charged (it "betrayed an unmitigated complicity with domination") also implies a recognition of its political dimension (Adorno, *Aesthetic Theory*, 284).

18. For a discussion of the different, political, legal, and natural meanings of the word *Gewalt*, see Derrida's reading of Walter Benjamin "Zur Kritik der Gewalt" in "Force of Law: The 'Mystical Foundation of Authority.'"

19. Paul de Man—perhaps the most insistent *political* commentator on Kant's

aesthetic theory—points out that "the kinetics of the sublime are treated at once, and somewhat surprisingly, as a question of *power*" (de Man, *Aesthetic Ideology*, 78). Through his discussion of language as a system of tropes, de Man shows how Kant's text accounts for "the occurrence of the sublime" as well as for "the empiricization of force into violence and battle" (79; see also 122–23 and 133: "there is history from the moment that words such as 'power' and 'battle' and so on emerge on the scene. . . . History . . . is the emergence of a language of power out of a language of cognition." Derrida commented at length on this statement by de Man in "Typewriter Ribbon: Limited Ink (2) ('Within Such Limits')," esp. 302 and 319–20). In *The Critique of Judgment*, nature returns as a site for political thinking in section 83 ("Of the Ultimate Purpose of Nature as a Teleological System"). Moments such as this one enable, if rarely, a reading of Kant's aesthetic theory in political terms: "Here the issue is nature and politics or, better, whether nature can be understood as organized and thus purposive or whether it must be seen as hostile to man, formless and violent in its exertions" (Ronald Beiner and William J. Booth, introduction to *Kant and Political Philosophy*, 4).

20. Alternative understandings would include reflections on the political after Kant, beginning with the "concept" or "fact" of freedom, which, Kant says, is "the *keystone* of the whole architecture of the system of pure reason." As Nancy comments, this implies that freedom exceeds the political, that the political is "carried" by the fact of freedom. In other words, as Nancy puts it, "perhaps the political should be measured against the fact that freedom does not wait for it" (Nancy, *Experience of Freedom*, 77). Reading the political (and the political lexicon) of Kant would also have to include Jean-François Lyotard's assertion that "the philosophy of the political, i.e., the 'free' critique or reflection upon the political, reveals itself as political by discriminating between family of heterogeneous phrases that present the political universe" (Lyotard, *L'enthousiasme*, 9).

21. To translate *Gemüt* as "mind" is of course to circumvent the difficulty of a word that might as legitimately be translated "affect," thus opening onto the entire lexicon of affection, affectivity, emotions, and sentiments deployed by Kant. As Paul de Man asks: "But what exactly is affectivity in Kant? It is easier to say what it is not" (de Man, *Aesthetic Ideology*, 123). Earlier, de Man had expressed his doubts as to whether Hegel, for example, ever did "justice . . . to Kant's concept of affect (*Gemüt*)" (109).

22. This (lack of) accord, constitutive of the sublime, thus participates in what Judith Butler calls "the paradox of subjection" (Butler, *The Psychic Life of Power*). Insofar as Butler reinscribes a discourse of affect ("passionate attachments") into the workings of power, political and other, my discussion of Kant is an attempt to follow her important gesture.

23. Consider the way in which enthusiasm only "seems to be sublime," how it can "in no way deserve the approval of reason" and yet, "nevertheless," can be said

to be sublime: "aesthetically, enthusiasm is sublime" (Kant, *Critique of Judgment*, section 29).

24. It is in the context of such conflicting forces that Kant recurrently pointed out the "analogy" between nature and politics, between physics and politics, focusing specifically on "attraction and repulsion." This use of analogy as a pathway to exploring the political dimension of Kant was famously invoked by both Hans Saner (in his *Kant's Political Thought*, esp. 65–68) and by Lyotard: "The philosophical sentence is, according to Kant, an analogue of the political sentence" (Lyotard, *L'enthousiasme*, 12).

25. This is the recurring question of the sublime, of course. Echoing here is Lyotard's "why are there two sensations when there is just one feeling, the sublime?" (Lyotard, *Lessons on the Analytic of the Sublime*, 109/F138). But as Lyotard goes on to explain in his commentary on the "Analytic," the two distinct, even contradictory sensations have everything to do with the possibility (and impossibility) of *one* subject: Both the beautiful and the sublime, as judgments, "are united in the same subject" (Kant, *Critique of Judgment*, section 29). The sublime produces (and undoes) what remains *one* "subjective finality." If, as Lyotard writes, "the 'subjective' can and must persist as the sensation of itself that accompanies any act of thinking the instant it occurs" (Lyotard, *Lessons on the Analytic of the Sublime*, 23/F38), what of the moment when two sensations, two feelings occur? What of "enthusiasm" and "pride," then? What, in other words, would a subject of both Judaism and Islam be? What would a subject be that would "feel" for both Judaism and Islam? And would such "subject" be *comparable* to the no less impossible "subject" of the sublime? Reading, then, "the Jew, the Arab."

26. Derrida, *The Truth in Painting*, 137/F157.

27. "The various kinds of belief among peoples seem to give them, after a time, a character, revealing itself outwardly in civil relations, which is later attributed to them as though it were universally a temperamental trait. Thus Judaism in its original economy, under which a people was to separate itself from all other peoples by means of every conceivable, and some arduous, observances and was to refrain from all intermingling with them, drew down upon itself the charge of *misanthropy*. Mohammedanism is characterized by *pride* because it finds confirmation of its faith not in miracles but in victories and subjugation of many peoples, and because its devotional practices are all of the spirited sort" (Kant, *Religion Within the Limits of Reason Alone*, 172/G858). Kant is certainly pursuing the train of thought begun in *Critique of Judgment*, including his reflections on subjection.

28. Slavoj Žižek may provide a most obvious example for this absence of commentary, in the gesture he makes of quoting the very passage I am discussing here and cutting it precisely before Islam is mentioned. Hence, "Kant himself pointed out the connection between such a notion of Sublimity and the Jewish religion"— and presumably, no other religion (Žižek, *The Sublime Object*, 204. Most commentators simply quote the passage in its entirety, yet do not comment at all on Islam as it appears in the Kantian text). I should add that the so-called

"iconoclasm"—what Hermann Cohen called "the iconoclastic turmoil in which Islam and, in the background, the Jews take part"—is indeed a "turning point" of the "history of Christianity." (Note that, like Kant, Cohen distinguishes between, on the one hand, the Jews, who have a religion, and Islam, the subject of whom is irrelevant: It is only and fully a religion.) This "iconoclasm," however, may begin to account for the comparison, but does not suffice to explain the particular site of its occurrence, nor does it explain the incomparability that is asserted at the same time. Finally, what of the lack of exegetical energy here? (see Cohen, *Religion of Reason,* 54).

29. Hans Reiss, introduction to *Kant: Political Writings,* 29 n. 1.

30. From Kant's use of the term, it is clear that "despotism" has yet to coagulate into a stable political category. As a figure of domination, *Beherrschung,* it is joined in an exclusive pair by the republic (although Kant will write of Cromwell's "despotic republic"). At times an adjective, at times the name of a regime, at times a mode of government (democratic or not), despotism is being invented (see *Kant: Political Writings* and Lyotard, *L'enthousiasme*). It is also the case that fanaticism (which "must always be distinguished from enthusiasm," Kant had written in the *Observations*), although associated with religion, was not yet so heavily linked with Islam (Kant, *Observations on the Feeling,* 108 n). In the *Critique of Judgment* itself, Kant speaks of "freeing the will from the despotism of desire" (section 83). As I will try to show below, it would take the combination of Kant and Montesquieu in Hegel for the absolute subjection that despotism entails to be articulated under the figure of the Muslims. And the Jews.

31. As Mladen Dolar writes in his introduction to the English translation, there are "numerous intersections" between Grosrichard's book and Edward Said's *Orientalism* (ix). It should become obvious that both books are equally essential here.

32. Grosrichard, *Sultan's Court,* 19.

33. Asli Çirakman follows the descriptions that collapse the difference between "despotism and slavishness" and concludes that the two are "interchangeable or oscillating qualities" (Çirakman, "From Tyranny to Despotism," 62). But however widespread that collapse, it demands to be interrogated, and the differences read that it covers over.

34. Grosrichard, *Sultan's Court,* 44.

35. Montesquieu, *Spirit of the Laws,* book 24, 3, quoted in Grosrichard, 88. When quoting the French original, I have used the Pléiade edition of Montesquieu, *Oeuvres completes,* vol. 2.

36. These are complicated matters, of course, because religion also appears to be the "one thing" that "may be sometimes opposed to the prince's will" (3,10).

37. Grosrichard, *Sultan's Court,* 32.

38. Ibid., 47.

39. Later, much later, it is of Asia that Montesquieu will speak explicitly, 17.6.

40. For an expression of Hegel's admiration for Montesquieu, see e.g., *Philosophy of Right,* 177. See also H. S. Harris's comment that "there can, of course, be

no question of the enormous influence of Montesquieu upon Hegel's political and social thought from 1794 onward" (H. S. Harris, *Hegel's Development*, 424 n. 2).

41. Hegel "The Spirit of Christianity," in Hegel, *Early Theological Writings*, 194/G286–87. The French translation gives *passivité totale* for *durchgängige Passivität* (Hegel, *Premiers écrits*, 192). Alain David discusses the analogies between Judaism and slavery as it appears in the *Phenomenology* (David, *Racisme et antisémitisme*, 188–89).

42. Hegel, "The Spirit of Christianity," 194/G286.

43. The English translation has "genius of hatred."

44. Hegel, "The Spirit of Christianity," 195/G287.

45. Ibid., 195 n. 15 (translator's note).

46. Hegel, *Premiers écrits*, 194 n. 1. The same point is made again regarding a passage where Hegel attends to the "Oriental spirit," *Geist der Orientalen*.

47. Hegel, "[Fragmente historischer und politischer Studien aus der Berner und Frankfurter Zeit]," in *Werke* 1: 428.

48. See, for example, *Early Theological Writings* 94, 260. Further citations will be made parenthetically in the text.

49. Hegel, *Philosophy of Right*, 213; *Werke* 7: 499.

50. Hegel, *The Philosophy of History*, 355–56; *Werke* 12: 428.

51. As we have seen briefly, there are two different words already in Kant, *Enthusiasm* and *Begeisterung*. The valence accorded to either word, however, seems as unstable as any precise sense. "Fanaticism" is only slightly more clearly marked in terms of its (negative) excesses. In *Lectures on the History of Philosophy*, Hegel remarks Muslim fanaticism while crediting (or blaming) it from the spread of Islam: "As quickly as the Arabians with their fanaticism spread themselves . . ." We have seen how this Hegel found its compelling way into Rosenzweig's *Star of Redemption*.

52. Hegel, *Lectures on the Philosophy of Religion*, 3: 218; *Vorlesungen* 5: 149.

53. Ibid., 2: 158; *Vorlesungen* 4: 64.

54. An editorial note already asserted that Islam's monotheism is "derived from the Jewish religion" (ibid., 2: 500 n. 706).

55. Ibid.,3: 242–43; see also how Islam is described as "being cleansed of nationalism," 2: 158.

56. The editors of the *Lectures* assert that "the only significant discussion of Islamic religion in the lectures" occurs in the section from which I am about to quote. Andrew Shanks concurs and expands by asserting that Islam is "a religion he [Hegel] scarcely discusses at all elsewhere, except in passing" (Shanks, *Hegel's Political Theology*, 66). Then again, the heavy Christianocentrism of Shanks, as well as his remarkable omission of the history of the phrase "political theology," may account for the problem.

57. Just earlier Hegel had said: "This religion has in general the same content as the Jewish religion" (242/G171).

58. *Lectures on the Philosophy of Religion*, 2: 243.

59. Ronell, *Dictations*, 4.

60. Freud, *The Psychopathology of Everyday Life*, in *The Standard Edition*, 6.

61. Freud, *Psychopathology*, 3/G15. Further citations will be made parenthetically in the text.

62. This remarkable phrase attributed to the Czar Nicholas I quickly became a commonplace in referring to the Ottoman Empire throughout Europe. A corrupt version of the phrase speaks of "the dying man of Europe." It is still widely used in scholarly discourse. Norman Itzkowitz, for example, recently used it matter-of-factly (Itzkwowitz, "The Problem of Perception," 32; and see illustration on 31). I have been unable to find a critical discussion of the history of this phrase, which haunts this entire chapter.

63. Freud, *Beyond the Pleasure Principle*, in *The Standard Edition*, 18: 53.

64. Benslama, "La répudiation originaire," 139.

65. Freud reinscribes the Abrahamic configuration in *Moses and Monotheism* (a book that, he says, "tormented me like an unlaid ghost" Freud, *Moses and Monotheism*, in *The Standard Edition*, 23: 103) and he opened the *Psychopathology* with it, as well. Implying a complex process of memory and forgetting concerning the church (Freud, *Moses*, 55–56), Freud also rewrites the Abrahamic, the Turk, and the Jew by exploring what Moses shared with the Turks. On the basis of Moses's Egyptian identity, Freud compares the Turk's attitude toward circumcision, or rather noncircumcision, with that of Moses and other Egyptians: "Even to this day a Turk will abuse a Christian as an 'uncircumcised dog'. It may be supposed that Moses, who, being an Egyptian, was himself circumcised, shared this attitude" (30, see also the reference to borrowings from "Arabian tribes," 34). Jan Assmann underscores the momentous division Freud is struggling to undo here, arguing against "the map of memory": "on the map of memory Israel and Egypt appear as antagonistic worlds" (Assmann, *Moses the Egyptian*, 6).

66. To Kafka's Abrahams one should perhaps add Kafka's "Savages," who actualize in more ways than one the promise made to Abraham that his descendants will be "as numerous as the stars of heaven and the sands on the seashore" (Genesis 22:17). Kafka's prophetic parable indeed gives pause as it reproduces the rhythmic repetition carrying yet "another Abraham," punctuating the repetition, this time, with the words "or rather," *oder vielmehr*. Kafka describes the ghostly and disappearing figure of those "of whom it is recounted that they have no other longing than to die, or rather, they no longer have even that longing, but death has a longing for them, and they abandon themselves to it, or rather, they do not even abandon themselves, but fall into the sand of the shore and never get up again. . . . Anyone who might collapse without cause and remain lying on the ground is dreaded as though he were the Devil, it is because of the example, it is because of the stench of truth that would emanate from him. Granted nothing would happen; one, ten, a whole nation might very well remain lying on the ground and nothing would happen" (Kafka, "The Savages," 121). I return to Kafka's text in Appendix 2, "Corpse of Law."

67. Levi, *Survival in Auschwitz [If This Is a Man]*, 81/181. Compare also the tes-

timony of Stanislaw Sterkowicz, who writes that "the Muslims died, without arousing even a trace of compassion in our hearts already reduced to ashes" (Zdzislaw Ryn and Stanislaw Klodzinski, "An der Grenze," 95).

68. Quoted in Lanzmann, *Shoah*, 139, in Inge Clendinnen, *Reading the Holocaust*, 40 n.

69. See Clendinnen, *Reading the Holocaust*, 39–41, who, like many, also took note of these terms. As I mentioned earlier, the first issue of *Yad Vashem Studies*, published in Jerusalem in 1957, included the article by Nahman Blumenthal discussed at the beginning of this chapter (Blumenthal, "On the Nature of the Nazi Idiom (in Hebrew, ʿAl tivah shel lashon ha-natzim"). Blumenthal's article, which opens with a quote from Talleyrand as an epigraph ("La parole a été donnée à l'homme pour déguiser sa pensée," speech was given to man to disguise his thoughts), includes a discussion of the colloquial character of LTI (Blumenthal mentions Klemperer's work in a footnote), as well as a note on how unusual it is. "In no [linguistic] style, except for the Nazi style, would such a high number of terms be used as readiness for self-sacrifice, love and faith, loyalty and honesty, the motherland," *moledet*, "and the people" (Blumenthal, "On the Nature," 41). Blumenthal focuses on a language that would have been used exclusively by the perpetrators. and he announces, perhaps, some of the recent debates surrounding Daniel Goldhagen's argument, going so far as to suggest, at the end of the article, that this "use," *shimush*, of the Nazi-language raises a legal question: "we might be able to reach a conclusion as to the dissemination of the Nazi language in the German people. And since this language is the language of criminals, the legal question emerges of the criminal responsibility of those who used it" (55).

In a later issue of *Yad Vashem Studies*, in Shaul Esh's "Words and their Meaning: 25 Samples from the Nazi-Idiom," this language, *lashon*, here translated as "idiom," functions on many levels: renewal (these are new words or older words with a new meaning: *blutlich, Eindeutschung, Entjudung, Vernichtungstelle*, etc.), hiding and obscuring (these are the words that Hillberg also mentions: *Abwanderung, Ausscheidung*, etc.), and so on. Esh includes other functions that seem to come down to some form of other of concealment (*Endlösung, Sonderbehandlung*, etc.). Joining Blumenthal in emphasizing the novelty and even uniqueness of the Nazi language (e.g. *Sternträger, besternter*), Esh nonetheless points out the continuity that exists between the "previous" German language and Nazi German (the word *Untermensch*, for example, was not only in usage long before the Nazis, but began its renewed career within Nazi circles as a word against "inner" enemies such as the SA. Esh also points out that Jews and *Untermenschen* were not linked in SS publications until 1935).

70. Canada ("A name given by Polish prisoners to the section in the camp where the belongings of deported Jews were sorted and stored. There almost anything could be *organized*. Obviously the Poles imagined Canada to be a country of unlimited wealth") and "Mexico" ("The name *Mexico* originated in the spring of 1944 when prisoners were quartered in this not quite completed camp without any

clothing whatsoever. They wrapped themselves in coloured blankets which made them look rather like Mexican Indians") are terms that may not precisely "belong" to LTI to the extent that they appear to have been used only by the camp inmates, rather than by the SS or German soldiers (I am quoting from the glossary provided at the end of Filip Müller's *Eyewitness Auschwitz: Three Years in the Gas Chambers.* One should note that there are also names that, apparently, still lack any discursive reference. *Piepel* or *Pipel,* a "function" most terribly described by Ka-Tzetnik is such a name. I return to Ka-Tzetnik below.

71. Levi here performs the claims he is making, because German would be the only language of precision, the only precise language to describe what occurred to language—yet it is German *still* spoken, out of context.

72. Levi, *The Drowned and the Saved,* 97/176.

73. Young, *Writing and Rewriting the Holocaust,* 105, quoted in Sullam Calimani, *I nomi dello sterminio,* 60. On the "death of the German language," see Steiner, *Language and Silence,* 117. Berel Lang writes that "language was at once victim of the genocide and one agent of many among its causes." In its becoming instrumentalized, language is "detached from history and nature and finally also from moral judgment" (Lang, *Act and Idea in the Nazi Genocide,* 81–84, quoted in Sullam Calimani, 62).

74. The citations of Pius XI's encyclical are from Blumenthal, "On the Nature of the Nazi Idiom," 43–44.

75. With this phrase, Clendinnen seeks to account for what she calls some of the "most effective imagined evocations of the Holocaust," which function "by invocation, the glancing reference to an existing bank of ideas, images and sentiments." When we are not shown what we expect to see, Clendinnen continues, "we flick to the identikit image of 'the Holocaust' we carry in our heads." Such a technique "essentially . . . still draws on existing capital" (165). As my use of the phrase is meant to suggest, there is more at stake than the subsequent "artistic" representation. Rather, as Agamben has shown, literature (Dostoevski, Rilke, and Kafka may all have been "good prophets"), one could perhaps say language, was already setting itself in motion.

76. Sullam Calimani explains that the phrase quickly gained currency—and clarity as to its meaning—among the different echelons of the Nazi bureaucracy (*I nomi,* 67).

77. Mieczyslawa Chylinska, quoted in Ryn and Klodzinski, "An der Grenze," 98.

78. Ryn and Klodzinski write that the word appears "in the German or Polish form" (89). Primo Levi alternates between the Italian and the German form.

79. I will insist on translating rather than transliterating the German terms *Muselmann* and *Muselmänner* (Muslim, Muslims), much as I use the thoroughly and scandalously catachrestic term "Holocaust" throughout for its convenience in terms of cultural currency. I simply do not know whether it is for me to agree or disagree with the use of a term that is both widespread and marked with the singularity of the event it has come to signify. Precisely the same things could, of

course, be said of the Hebrew word *shoah*, which, as Agamben notes, "often implies the idea of a divine punishment" (Agamben, *Remnants of Auschwitz*, 31). *Shoah* does not seem, therefore, any more—or any less—appropriate, except that invoking it in English might run the risk of erasing (successfully or not) the added weight of the word's participation in the appropriation of the Holocaust by a national project, Political Zionism (see Arendt, *Eichmann*, Segev, *Seventh Million*, Massad, "Palestinians," Finkelstein, *Holocaust Industry*). This chapter addresses such an erasure, the difficult sedimentation and contamination of history in and as language, the very possibility of a historical rupture in language. Hence, it hardly seems necessary (if perhaps nonetheless unavoidable), while writing in English, to take on without ambivalence the not yet fully globalized term *Shoah*, the added weight of what thus remains a Hebrew and, by now, Israeli word.

80. Clendinnen, *Reading the Holocaust*, 35.

81. Quoted in Ryn and Klodzinski, "An der Grenze," 94; see also Hermann Langbein, "Der Muselmann," in his *Menschen in Auschwitz*, 111–28. Langbein quotes the important testimony of Wladislaw Fejkiel: "During this time, the sick were indifferent to what happened around them. They were closed to all those surrounding them. They could barely move, and ever so slowly, unable to bend their knees. . . . When you saw them from afar, you could think they were Arabs praying. Hence the name of the hunger-stricken in the camp, 'Muslims,'" *Muselmänner* (114).

82. Wiesel, "Stay Together, Always," 58.

83. Levi, *Survival*, 82/181–82.

84. Rousset, *L'univers concentrationaire*, 51.

85. Kogon, *Der SS-Staat: Das System der deutschen Konzentrationslager*, trans. Heinz Norden as *The Theory and Practice of Hell: The German Concentration Camps and the System Behind Them*. In a detailed chapter on the psychology of the prisoners, Kogon wonders about what is, for him, a singular psychological enigma or puzzle, "eine einzige psychologisch rätselhafte," that people led to their death "never fought back!" (Kogon, *Theory and Practice*, 284/G372). This fact, Kogon writes, is "quite understandable" in some cases—first, for political prisoners "who felt a sense of political responsibility." Second, it is also understandable for those "who had long since lost any real will to live." "In the camps they were called "Moslems," *Muselmänner*, men of unconditional fatalism, *Leute von bedingungslosem Fatalismus*, men whose wills were broken" (ibid.). (The German text continues, although the translation does not, emphasizing the utter passivity in which everything happened to them was never as a result of their agency: no will, no power, no ability any more: "they simply couldn't any more": "Ihren Untergangsbereitschaft war aber nicht etwa ein Willensakt, sondern Willensgebrochenheit. Sie ließen mit sich geschehen, was eben geschah, weil alle Kräfte in ihnen gelähmt oder bereits vernichtet waren. Widerstand von ihnen erwarten, hätte geheißen, ihren seelischen Zustand verkennen; sie konnten einfach nicht mehr.") What is important to note is that it is not the Muslims that Kogon finds mysteri-

ous or puzzling. Rather, it is the thousands who did not defend themselves. Why? he asks, and wishes: If only religion could explain it! "If at least it had been the spirit of religion that enabled them to accept their fate, inwardly resolute, outwardly serene. In the face of inevitable death, the man of religion, surrendering mortal life to step before the divine master and judge, has no desire for the toils of conflict with the earthly enemy he leaves behind. . . . But there is no inkling that the masses cut down by the SS were religious in this sense" (284–85/G372).

86. Wiesel, *La nuit*, 78; note that Wiesel says "as *we* said," *comme* nous *disions*.

87. There are exceptions, of course, to the dissemination of the word "Muslims." Raul Hillberg, among prominent examples, does not speak of them, nor does Sidra de Koven Ezrahi, and major new encyclopedias of the Holocaust do not include an entry on the Muslims (often preferring to discuss at length the politics of the Mufti of Jerusalem). As Agamben puts it, "it is a striking fact that although all witnesses speak of him as a central experience, the *Muselmann* is barely named in the historical studies on the destruction of European Jewry" (Agamben, *Remnants of Auschwitz*, 52). But this remains true also of literary, philosophical, and other scholarly studies.

88. Fackenheim, "Holocaust," in Morgan, ed., *A Holocaust Reader*, 125.

89. Fackenheim, "The Holocaust and Philosophy," in ibid., 255.

90. Agamben, *Remnants of Auschwitz*, 52.

91. Ibid., 44.

92. Ibid., 45.

93. I thank Hélène Contant for telling me about this song, which her mother learned in kindergarten in Germany in the 1930s. This song belongs to a long and well-known tradition, of course. Interestingly, Nabil Matar documents how, in seventeenth-century England, there were those who "warned the English public that they should be alert to coffee's magical power: it was an 'ugly Turkish Enchantress' which put the English drinker under the 'power of this Turkish Spell.' Even if coffee-drinkers did not want to 'turn Turke', the secret ingredient of coffee would overpower their Protestant faith and convert them to a Levantine religion: for coffee makes the drinker 'faithless as a Jew or infidell.'" (Matar, *Islam in Britain*, 113; Matar further discusses the complex associations that link Turk with Jew in the following paragraph, and see also 148–51 and 167–83).

94. Agamben, *Remnants of Auschwitz*, 45.

95. According to Ryn and Klodzinski, it is difficult to determine whether the invisibility of the word stems from its unequivocality or from its equivocality ("An der Grenze," 89). Agamben also remains cautious regarding its recent visibility: "*Perhaps*," he writes, "only now, almost fifty years later, is the *Muselmann* becoming visible" (Agamben, *Remnants of Auschwitz*, 52).

96. Anatol Adamczyk, quoted in Ryn and Klodzinski, "An der Grenze," 111.

97. Cixous, "We Who Are Free, Are We Free?" 208.

98. Ronell, *Dictations*, 3.

99. Levi, *Survival in Auschwitz*, 80–81.

100. Tadeusz Borowski, quoted in Cixous, "We Who Are Free," 208 n. 6. Borowski is among the few writers who make explicit the instability of the Muslim as more than a terminal stage. Indeed, the Muslim can still and always turn or "convert." The Muslim can turn ghost, Jew, but most importantly, the Muslim can turn back: "In Auschwitz one man knows all there is to know about another: when he *was* a Muslim, how much he stole" (Borowski, "Auschwitz, Our Home [A Letter]," in *This Way for the Gas*, 102, emphasis added). This inscription of the past tense resonates with the "Ich war ein Muselmann" registered by Ryn and Klodzinski and, most strikingly, by Agamben, though one should note that one survivor— Edward Sokól—strikingly writes in the present tense: "Ich bin ein Muselmann," Ryn and Klodzinski, "An der Grenze," 122. "Muslim," the noun, can thus also turn verb, or at least participle: "The following day, when we were again driven out to work, a 'Muslimized' Jew from Estonia who was helping me haul steel bars tried to convince me all day that human brains are, in fact, so tender you can eat them absolutely raw" (Borowski, "The Supper," in *This Way for the Gas*, 156). See Ryn and Klodzinski on the Polish verb "to become a Muslim, *muzulmanie*," 100. Finally, "Muslim" (already an analogy?) is carried further by the force of analogy and simile: "What a goddam nuisance for a healthy man to be rotting in bed *like* a 'Muslim'" (Borowski, "A True Story," in *This Way for the Gas*, 158).

101. Levi, *Survival in Auschwitz*, 81.

102. Ryn and Klodzinski, "An der Grenze," 102.

103. Stanislawa Piaty, quoted in Ryn and Klodzinski, "An der Grenze," 105; see also the following testimony: "The Muslim was always waiting for something, as long as he was still conscious . . . later . . . he was convinced that his fate was sealed and that it must be so. For the most part, he did not believe in freedom and had no hope of surviving the camp" (Roman Grzyb in ibid., 117).

104. Agamben, *Remnants of Auschwitz*, 51.

105. Czeslaw Ostankowicz, quoted in Ryn and Klodzinski, "An der Grenze," 96. In another testimony, however, prayer, as well as belief, seems to come to an end: The Muslim "even leaves behind prayer and loses his belief in God, in the existence of Heaven and Hell" (Bronislaw Goúcinski in Ryn and Klodzinski, "An der Grenze," 135).

106. Ibid., 109, cf. also 121.

107. Kafka, "The Savages," 121.

108. Levi, *Survival in Auschwitz*, 82/182.

109. Ryn and Klodzinski, "An der Grenze," 98.

110. Kogon, *Der SS-Staat*, 372, quoted in Agamben, *Remnants of Auschwitz*, 53.

111. Agamben, *Remnants of Auschwitz*, 47–48.

112. Levi, *Survival in Auschwitz*, 90/182. The notion of the "divine spark" raises in a peculiar way the question of theology, otherwise absent from Levi's text. It also echoes Kabbalistic accounts, one of which was made famous by another Jew turned Muslim, Sabbatai Sevi. In 1947, Gershom Scholem had only began to write his account of this "false Messiah," who revealed himself and proceeded to convert

to Islam in order to "raise the sparks out of the husks" of evil in 1666 (Scholem, *Sabbatai Sevi*). I expand on this matter in Appendix 2, "Corpse of Law." To the best of my knowledge, the theological (if not Kabbalistic) dimension of Levi's "divine spark" was only recently noted by Fethi Benslama in an important article on the *Muselmann* (Fethi Benslama, "La représentation et l'impossible"). Although my reading takes another course than his, I have greatly benefited from Benslama's essential contribution to the question.

113. The Muslims further appear as sites of a military-theological configuration. Indeed, while researching this chapter, I was unable to find any sustained discussion of Nazi racial policy toward the "Semites" as an *inclusive* category, that is, as a category that included Jews *and* Arabs in the first half of the twentieth century. There are two books that address Nazi *foreign* policy in the Middle East. Only one of the two, Lukasz Hirszowicz's *The Third Reich and the Arab East*, addresses some of the difficulties associated with the topic.

The other book on this topic is Francis Nicosia, *The Third Reich and the Palestine Question*. Hirszowicz writes that "not only the Jews, but the people of Asia and Africa generally occupied a very low rung in Hitler's racial ladder. A contemptuous attitude to the Arabs, aversion to their character and political behavior, disbelief in their state-forming capacity and their loyalty as allies are expressed by many statements of German leaders and officials" (315; see also 45–47. Faced with a diplomatic problem in his struggle against Britain and British colonialism, "Hitler even proposed to omit his racial-ladder theory from the forthcoming Arab translation of *Mein Kampf*," 46).

Another study underscores some of the discrepancies in terms of racial theory and the rapport to Arabs and Muslims. In the process, it clarifies the use of the word *Muselmann* in German and partially explains that pragmatic concerns did not always reflect racist doctrine. I am referring here to George H. Stein's *The Waffen SS*. Stein describes how "the first major Waffen SS formation to be recruited without regard for racial and ethnic factors was ordered into existence by Adolf Hitler in February 1943" (180). This formation was "sometimes referred to as the Kroatischen SS-Freiwilligen-Division and at other times it was called the Muselmanen-Division" (181; the division was later renamed). It was composed "of Moslems from Bosnia and Herzegovina" (180). "Each battalion had its *imam*, each regiment its *mullah*, and with Hitler's consent the Moslems were given the same privileges they had had in the old Imperial Austro-Hungarian Army" (182). The continued and complex racism that nonetheless operated (Stein writes of the Waffen SS having "compromised its racial exclusiveness," 185) only adds to the difficulty of reading this history, as well. Bernard Lewis also cover some of this matter, but he does little to render it more legible, insisting as he does that the Nazis simply found in "most Arabs" unified followers of Hajj Amin al-Husayni and thus their best allies (Lewis, *Semites and Anti-Semites*; for a more balanced account of this last issue, see Philip Mattar, *The Mufti of Jerusalem*, and see Massad, "Palestinians and Jewish History").

114. Sofsky, *Order of Terror*, 200. Further references will be made parenthetically in the text.

115. The epigraph above is the title of Yitzhak Laor's essential and provocative work of Israeli literary and cultural criticism, *Anu kotvim otakh moledet* (We write you, motherland) which engages, among other issues, the suppression of Palestinian existence in, or rather from Israeli literature. Laor himself offers a more idiomatic and no less relevant translation of his own title into English: "Narratives Without Natives."

116. I am referring here to the work of critics such as Gila Ramras-Rauch, Fouzi El Asmar, Ehud Ben-Ezer, and others.

117. For lack of courage and ability, I have not addressed here the question of sexual difference that marks the discourse on the Muslims. Ryn and Klodzinski, however, make abundantly clear that even women were called "Muslims, *Muselmänner*" in the masculine form (sometimes, but not always, with an addition as in "weibliche Muselmänner" (Langbein, *Menschen in Auschwitz*, 114). Many of the testimonies on Muslims are written by women and on women. Yet here, too, the question of recognizability and readability emerges no less imperatively.

118. On Shilansky's participation in Jewish and Israeli political terrorism, see Segev, *Seventh Million*, 236–39.

119. Shilansky, *Muzelman*, trans. by Katie Kaplan as *Musulman*.

120. Ryn and Klodzinski, "An der Grenze," 117.

121. Ka-Tzetnik's *House of Dolls*, for example, was first published in Hebrew in 1953. The first English translation (New York, 1955) was followed by sixteen printings in England between 1956 and 1959. By 1958, the book had been translated into Danish, Swedish, Japanese, Italian, Yiddish, Spanish, French, Bulgarian, Czech, and German. It now exists in sixteen languages.

122. Bartov, *Mirrors of Destruction*, 189.

123. Ka-Tzetnik, *Kar'u lo piepel*, trans. by Moshe Kohn as *Piepel* (London, 1961) and later as *Moni: A Novel of Auschwitz* (Secaucus, N.J., 1963). It is from this last edition that I will quote here. It makes no mention of it, but it is Moshe Kohn's translation. This edition also states that the novel was previously published under the title *Atrocity*. The "map" of the Auschwitz hierarchy is not found in the Hebrew edition I have used. For the sake of consistency, I continue to replace the various spellings ("Mussulman," "Mussulmen") of the word that occupies me throughout this chapter with "Muslim" or "Muslims."

124. The word "stinking" is not in the Hebrew, something that may be balanced by the subsequent translation of the word *tzo'ah*, "excrement," as "Mussulman" (Ka-Tzetnik, *Moni*, 103/H89).

125. There is no lapse that I know of in Hebrew regarding the spelling and transliteration of the word "Muslim" that English translations awkwardly render as "Mussulman." It is always and only of the *Muzelman* that one reads—and one does read—whatever reading means. I have found no discussion of any possible

connection between this now Hebrew word and the word "Muslims" (Hebrew: *Muslemim*). Writing his *Mirrors of Destruction* in English about Ka-Tzetnik and others, Omer Bartov explains that *mussulmen* is a word "originating in the German word for Moslem [sic], this term was commonly used by Nazi-concentration camp inmates to describe the most emaciated among them" (Bartov, *Mirrors of Destruction*, 14). In the rest of the book, Bartov continues to use the spelling "Mussulman" and "Mussulmen." The index of his book has two distinct entries: one for "Muslims" (page 140: "The heroes and martyrs of days gone by reappear on late twentieth-century battlefields, reenacting the sacrifices and atrocities of their forefathers. Thus the Croats describe the Serbs as 'Chetniks,' the Serbs call the Croats 'Ustashe,' and the Muslims are seen as 'Turks'"), and one for "Mussulmen" (pages 14, 174, 178, 186, 193, 195–96, 199, 279 n. 94, and 287 n. 29). Had Bartov used a different spelling regarding the German origins of the word "Mussulmen," on page 14 ("Muslim" instead of "Moslem"), would the two entries have shared a page number? With what consequences, finally?

126. Ka-Tzetnik, *Moni*, 116–17/H100.

APPENDIX 2

1. Agamben, "The Messiah and the Sovereign," in Agamben, *Potentialities*, 161/I11.

2. The phrase "zone of indistiguishability" is a recurring one in Agamben's work.

3. Agamben, "The Messiah, 163.

4. Ibid., 161.

5. The link between law and theology is, of course, a privileged site of the reflections of Carl Schmitt. The renewed and productive interest in the question of the theologico-political in the works of Walter Benjamin, Franz Rosenzweig, Gershom Scholem, Leo Strauss, Ernst Kantorowicz, Jacob Taubes, Hans Blumenberg, and others can in fact be described as one of the major effects of Schmitt's writing. Agamben is at the forefront of a continued reflection on the issues raised by Schmitt, as is apparent throughout his work.

6. Agamben, *Homo Sacer*, 80.

7. With the word *Urzelle* I am referring to Franz Rosenzweig's own description of his 1917 letter as the origin from which evolved *The Star of Redemption* (see *Franz Rosenzweig's "The New Thinking"*). Prior to *Il tempo che resta*, Agamben had offered two extended readings of the messianic as it relates to the state of exception, to "law and life," in the context of Kafka's work and its interpretations by Walter Benjamin, Gershom Scholem, and Jacques Derrida. The first reading, the 1992 lecture delivered in Jerusalem from which I have been quoting, is entitled "The Messiah and the Sovereign." The second reading is found in *Homo Sacer* in the chapter entitled "Form of Law." The two "versions" complement each other in a way that exceeds any simple sense of development while expressing distinct ar-

gumentative gestures. It is to the disctintiveness of the Jerusalem lecture as it affects a reading of the figure and history of *homo sacer* that I attend in this chapter.

8. Agamben, "The Messiah," 162. As Agamben explains, messianism entails a relation between the divine and human spheres, even if that relation is thought of as one of interruption. In "the days of the Messiah," judgment is pronounced and the law realizes itself. What then comes to light is "the hidden foundation of the law" insofar as the status of the law of this world comes into question (Will the Messiah confirm the law? Will he bring a new one?). Hence, Agamben continues, the Messiah is "the figure through which religion confronts the problem of the Law, decisively reckoning with it" ("The Messiah," 162–63).

9. Benjamin, "Franz Kafka," 135. The shift from future to present in Benjamin's sentence is most important to consider, of course.

10. Agamben, "The Messiah," 167.

11. Ibid., 169.

12. Wilhelm Müller, *Werke (Gedichte I)*, 186.

13. 14. In Kafka's *Nachgelassene Schriften und Fragmente*, this late parable, found on an isolated sheet of paper among those gathered by Max Brod, bears no title. The Schocken bilingual edition provides a title—"The Savages, *Die Wilden*"—that I use for purposes of convenience (Kafka, *Parables and Paradoxes*, 120–21). Except for one comma, the text found in the Fischer edition is identical to the American edition (Franz Kafka, *Zur Frage der Gesetze und andere Schriften aus dem Nachlaß*, 84–85).

14. Agamben, "The Messiah," 174.

15. On "messianic music," see Jacob Taubes, "The Price of Messianism," 596.

16. Agamben, *Il tempo che resta*, 45.

17. Agamben, "The Messiah" 168.

18. The text ends without final punctuation. Clearly, Derrida's remarks very much apply here: "as you know, among the works we have inherited there are those in which unity, identity, and completion remain problematic because nothing can allow us to decide for certain whether the unfinished state of the work is a real accident or a pretence, a deliberately contrived simulacrum by one or several authors of our time and before" (Derrida, "Before the Law," 185/F102).

19. There is little, no doubt, to authorize the slippage and upgrade of "die Ewigkeit in eigener Person" into a divine power. And yet, the quasi-theological debates that have surrounded the question of theology in Kafka since the beginning could hardly come under interrogation without explicitly attending to this question. Such attention would be precisely in keeping with the indistinguishability raised by Agamben's reading, in his reading of Kafka in particular, as I am trying to follow it here.

20. Benjamin, "Franz Kafka," 112. Benjamin refers to those "holders of power first as *Gewalthaber*, then as *Machthaber*, thus recalling the difficult relations between *Gewalt* and *Macht* that he traced in his "Critique of Violence," "Zur Kritik

der Gewalt." Derrida addresses these two terms in details in his reading of Benjamin in "Force of Law: The 'Mystical Foundation of Authority.'"

21. Eternity is thus in the structural position of the sovereign who, "having the legitimate power to suspend the law, finds himself at the same time outside and inside the juridical order" (Agamben, "The Messiah," 161/112). Benjamin remarks that "for Kafka music and singing are an expression or at least a token of escape, a token of hope which comes to us from that intermediate world . . . in which the assistants are at home" (Benjamin, "Franz Kafka," 118). Earlier in this essay, he describes these assistants as "neither members of, nor strangers to, any of the other groups of figures" (117).

22. Agamben, "The Messiah," 168.

23. Kafka, "On Parables," in *Parables and Paradoxes*, 10.

24. Agamben, "The Messiah," 167. And see also Eric Santner's informative discussion of Agamben's reading in the context of the messianic (Santner, *The Psychotheology of Everyday Life*, 40–44).

25. On this undoing of interpretation and literature, see Avital Ronell, "Doing Kafka in *The Castle*."

26. Benjamin, quoted in "The Messiah," 171.

27. Agamben, "The Messiah," 169–71.

28. Agamben, *Il tempo che resta*, 45

29. Note that the doorkeeper of "Before the Law" is described as *mächtig*, recalling the might or power of "das mächtige Leben."

30. Agamben, "The Messiah," 164.

31. For a discussion of how the "as if" structures the rapport with law as law, see Derrida on Kant in "Before the Law," 190. On the importance of the "as if" in Kafka, see Alan Udoff's "Introduction: Kafka's Question."

32. Agamben, "The Messiah," 172/120.

33. Ibid., 169.

34. Agamben, *Homo Sacer*, 53.

35. Ibid.

36. *The Correspondence of Walter Benjamin and Gershom Scholem, 1932–1940*, 123; *Walter Benjamin/Gershom Scholem: Briefwechsel 1933–1940*, 154. Agamben quotes from Scholem's letter in "The Messiah," 169.

37. The little hunchback who hides under the table, guiding "a puppet in Turkish attire and with a hookah in its mouth," serves as the famous figure for "theology, which today, as we know, is wizened and kept out of sight," in the attic, as it were (Benjamin, "Theses on the Philosophy of History," in *Illuminations*, 253). In the Kafka essay, the hunchback who "will disappear with the coming of the Messiah" is said to be "at home in distorted life" (134). It is this disappearance (and this life) that must be read.

38. Benjamin to Scholem, July 20, 1934 in *Correspondence*, 128; *Briefwechsel*, 159.

39. Benjamin to Scholem, June 12, 1938 in *Correspondence*, 225; *Briefwechsel*, 272.

40. Keeping to the theologico-political configuration elaborated by Kafka, one would have to follow Derrida's suggestion on Kafka's "Before the Law" when reading "The Savages," as well ("It is the origin of literature at the same time as the origin of law—like the dead father, a story told, a spreading rumor, without author or end, but an ineluctable and unforgettable story," 199/F117) and attend to *Totem and Taboo*, of course, and to "those whom we describe as savages," *die sogennante Wilden*, "the tribes," *jene Völkerstämme*, "which have been described by anthropologists as the most backward and miserable of savages," *die zurückgebliebensten, armseligsten Wilden* (Sigmund Freud, *Totem and Taboo*, in *The Standard Edition*, 13: 1). And to the Darwinian "band of brothers," *die Bande des Brüderclan*, which Freud recasts in his account.

41. Benjamin, "Franz Kafka," 133.

42. Agamben, *Homo Sacer*, 60.

43. Ibid., 60/I70.

44. Ibid., 61.

45. On punctuation, see Agamben on Deleuze and the colon, on the "nonrelation" produced by the *agencement* of the colon. Agamben notes that "only a comma can take the place of a colon," *Potentialities*, 222.

46. Genesis 22:17. On Kafka's Abraham, see Ronell, *Stupidity*.

47. The new "corps de connaissance" to which Freud claimed to have given birth involved, as Derrida describes, an account of a rapport with law (and the categorical imperative), a discovery of the "source of morality," which Freud understood as an "elevation," itself a turning away from the body, "from the zones of the body that are malodorous and must not be touched. The turning away is an upward movement." It seeks to escape the rising "stench" and parallels the downward movement of the "savages." (Derrida, "Before the Law," 193–94/F111–12). Derrida also discusses the question of exemplarity as the site-nonsite of the inaccessibility of the law, the way in which the law cannot provide a law that would determine when and in which case to apply it.

48. See Derrida, *Politics of Friendship*.

49. Benjamin, "Franz Kafka," 113.

50. Ronell, "Doing Kafka," 218.

51. Ibid., 216.

52. On the "weak messianic force," see Benjamin, "Theses on the Philosophy of History" in *Illuminations*, 253. Derrida emphasized the importance of this notion for an understanding of messianicity in *Specters of Marx*.

53. Agamben, "The Messiah," 174.

54. Agamben, *Homo Sacer*, 82/I91.

55. "We shall give the name *relation of exception* to the extreme form of relation by which something is included solely through its exclusion" (Agamben, *Homo Sacer*, 18). Compare Derrida on "the man from the country" who, before the law, "is a subject of the law" and at the same "is also outside the law (an outlaw). He is neither under the law nor in the law," *il n'est pas sous la loi ou dans la loi*. "He is

both a subject of the law and an outlaw," *sujet de la loi: hors la loi* ("Before the Law," 204/F122). Derrida goes on to refer to Ernst Kantorowicz and to the theory of sovereignty he elaborated.

56. Agamben, *Homo Sacer*, 59.

57. Ibid., 181. See also Agamben's *Coming Community*, where the question raised is "what could be the politics of whatever singularity, that is, of a being whose community is mediated not by any condition of belonging, . . . not by the simple absence of conditions . . . but by belonging itself?" (Agamben, *Coming Community*, 85/I58).

58. Agamben, *Homo Sacer*, 184–85/I206.

59. Kafka, "The Savages," quoted above. Compare Kafka's words to those of Karol Talik, who reproduces a continuous grammatical breakdown when testifying that, becoming a Muslim, "you became so indifferent to your fate that you no longer wanted anything from anyone. You just waited in peace for death. They no longer had the strength or the will to fight for daily survival" (quoted in Agamben, *Remnants of Auschwitz*, 167).

60. Agamben, *Homo Sacer*, 185.

61. Ibid., 53/I61.

62. Ibid., 185/I207.

63. Levi, *Survival in Auschwitz*, 80/I80.

64. Ibid., 80–81/I80–81.

65. Ibid., 81.

66. Ibid., 82/I81

67. Ibid., 82; Agamben quotes this passage in *Remnants of Auschwitz*, 43–44.

68. Levi, *Survival in Auschwitz*, 82/I82, quoted in Agamben, *Remnants of Auschwitz*, 55.

69. Scholem, *Messianic Idea*, 45. On the Lurianic Kabbalah, its doctrine of the divine sparks, and its appropriation in Sabbateanism, see Gershom Scholem, *Sabbatai Sevi: The Mystical Messiah*.

70. Scholem, *Messianic Idea*, 61.

71. Ibid., 145.

72. Ibid., 145.

73. Ibid., 98.

74. Lenowitz, *Jewish Messiahs*, 149.

75. Scholem, *Messianic Idea*, 145. Compare how Taubes writes about Zevi: "and now the catastrophe occurred," in Taubes, *Politische Theologie*, 19.

76. It is indeed striking to consider that having broken new ground in turning critical attention to the *Muselmann*, the Muslim, and having significantly participated in the renewed discussion of the theologico-political, Agamben summarizes the spheres that are abandoned by the Muslim onto a new indistinguishability in the following terms: "At times a medical figure or an ethical category, at times a political limit or an anthropological concept, the *Muselmann* is an indefinite being in whom not only humanity and non-humanity, but also vegetative existence and

relation, physiology and ethics, medicine and politics, and life and death continuously pass through each other" (Agamben, *Remnants of Auschwitz*, 48). There would be, then, no *theological* zone of indistinguishability, nothing between the Jew and the Muslim. As to the status of Islam in the scholarly literature, Paul Fenton's assertion about Gershom Scholem's work remains relevant: "The impression gathered is that the whole of this intriguing episode in Jewish history could well have taken place outside of the Muslim realm and that its unhappy hero did not end up by converting to Islam" (Paul B. Fenton, "Shabbatai Sebi and His Muslim Contemporary Muhammad An-Niyazi," 81).

77. Idel, *Messianic Mystics*, 206.

78. Lenowitz, *The Jewish Messiahs*, 149.

79. Agamben, "The Messiah," 166.

80. Liebes, *Studies in Jewish Myth and Jewish Messianism*, 106/H18.

81. Quoted in Liebes, *Studies*, 100/H14.

82. See Amarillo, "Sabbatean Documents," 250.

83. Scholem, *Messianic Idea*, 146.

84. Levi, *Survival in Auschwitz*, 81/I81.

85. Derrida, "Before the Law," 210.

86. Agamben, "the Messiah," 174/I21.

87. Ibid., 164.

88. Derrida, "Before the Law," 212/F130.

Bibliography

Abelard, Peter. *Collationes.* Ed. and trans. J. Marenbon and G. Orlandi. Oxford: Clarendon Press, 2001.

———. *Expositio in Epistolam ad Romanos.* Ed. and trans. Rolf Peppermüller. Freiburg: Herder, 2001.

Adorno, Theodor W. *Aesthetic Theory.* Trans. C. Lenhardt. London: Routledge, 1984.

Adorno, Theodor W. *Negative Dialectics.* Trans. E. B. Ashton. New York: Continuum, 1973. *Negative Dialektik.* Frankfurt am Main: Suhrkamp, 1966.

———, and Max Horkheimer. *Dialectic of Enlightenment: Philosophical Fragments.* Trans. Edmund Jephcott. Stanford: Stanford University Press, 2002. *Dialektik der Aufklärung: Philosophische Fragmente.* Frankfurt am Main: Fischer Taschenbuch Verlag, 1971.

Agamben, Giorgio. *The Coming Community.* Trans. Michael Hardt. Minneapolis: University of Minnesota Press, 1993. *La communità che viene.* Turin: Einaudi, 1990.

———. *Homo Sacer: Sovereign Power and Bare Life.* Trans. Daniel Heller-Roazen. Stanford: Stanford University Press, 1998. *Homo sacer: Il potere sovrano e la nuda vita.* Turin: Einaudi, 1995.

———."The Messiah and the Sovereign: The Problem of Law in Walter Benjamin." In Agamben, *Potentialities: Collected Essays in Philosophy.* Ed. and trans. Daniel Heller-Roazen. Stanford: Stanford University Press, 1999, 160–74. "Il Messia e il sovrano: Il problema della legge in W. Benjamin." In *Anima e paura: Studi in onore di Michele Ranchetti.* Ed. Bruna Bocchini Camaiani and Anna Scattigno. Macerata: Quodlibet, 1998, 11–22.

———. *Potentialities: Collected Essays in Philosophy.* Ed. and trans. Daniel Heller-Roazen. Stanford: Stanford University Press, 1999.

———. *Remnants of Auschwitz: The Witness and the Archive.* Trans. Daniel Heller-Roazen. New York: Zone Books, 1999. *Quel che resta di Auschwitz: L'archivio et il testimone (Homo sacer III).* Turin: Bollati Boringhieri, 1998.

———. *Il tempo che resta: Un commento alla Lettera ai Romani.* Turin: Bollati Boringhieri, 2000.

Alcalay, Ammiel. *After Jews and Arabs: Remaking Levantine Culture.* Minneapolis: University of Minnesota Press, 1993.

Allaire, Gloria. "Noble Saracen or Muslim Enemy? The Changing Image of the Saracen in Late Medieval Italian Literature." In *Western Views of Islam in Medieval and Early Modern Europe.* Ed. David Blanks and Michael Frassetto. New York: St. Martin's Press, 1999, 173–84.

Allouche-Benayoun, Joëlle and Doris Bensimon. *Juifs d'Algérie hier et aujourd'hui: Mémoires et identités.* Toulouse: Privat, 1989.

Almog, Oz. *The Sabra: The Creation of the New Jew.* Trans. Haim Watzman. Berkeley: University of California Press, 2000.

Alter, Robert, ed. *Modern Hebrew Literature.* West Orange, N.J.: Behrman House, 1975.

Alvis, John E., and Thomas G. West, eds. *Shakespeare as Political Thinker.* Wilmington, Del.: ISI Books, 2000.

Amarillo, Abraham. "Sabbatean Documents from the Saul Amarillo Collection" (in Hebrew). In *Sefunot* 5 (1961): 235–74.

Andreas, James R., Sr. "The Curse of Cush: Othello's Judaic Ancestry." In *Othello: New Critical Essays.* Ed. Philip C. Kolin. New York: Routledge, 2002, 169–87.

Anidjar, Gil. "Jewish Mysticism Alterable and Unalterable: On Orienting Kabbalah Studies and 'the *Zohar* of Christian Spain.'" *Jewish Social Studies* 3 (fall 1996): 89–157.

Aquinas, Thomas. *Opera omnia.* Ed. S. E. Fretté. Paris: Ludovic Vives, 1876.

———. *Summa contra Gentiles.* Trans. A. C. Pegis et al. Notre Dame: University of Notre Dame Press, 1975.

———. *Summa theologiae.* Trans. Thomas Gilby et al. New York: Blackfriars/ McGraw-Hill/Eyre and Spottiswoode, 1975.

Arendt, Hannah. *Eichmann in Jerusalem: A Report on the Banality of Evil.* New York: Viking, 1963.

———. *Lectures on Kant's Political Philosophy.* Ed. Ronald Beiner. Chicago: University of Chicago Press, 1982.

———. *Love and Saint Augustine.* Ed. and trans. Joanna Vecchiarelli Scott and Judith Chelius Stark. Chicago: University of Chicago Press, 1996.

———. *The Origins of Totalitarianism.* New York: Meridian Books, 1958.

Aristotle, *Nichomachean Ethics.* Trans. H. Rackham. Cambridge, Mass.: Harvard University Press, Loeb Classical Library, 1962.

———. *Politics.* Trans. H. Rackham. Cambridge, Mass.: Harvard University Press, Loeb Classical Library, 1959.

————. *Rhetoric.* Trans. John Henry Freese. London: William Heinemann, Loeb Classical Library, 1926.

————. *On the Soul.* Trans. W. S. Hett. Cambridge, Mass.: Harvard University Press, Loeb Classical Library, 1957.

Aristote Politique: Etudes sur la Politique *d'Aristote.* Ed. Pierre Aubenque and Alonso Tordesillas. Paris: Presses Universitaires de France, 1993.

Assmann, Jan. *Moses the Egyptian: The Memory of Egypt in Western Monotheism.* Cambridge, Mass.: Harvard University Press, 1997.

Augustine. *Augustine on Romans: Propositions from the Epistle to the Romans, Unfinished Commentary on the Epistle to the Romans.* Ed. Paula Fredriksen Landes. Chico, Ca.: Scholars Press, 1982.

————. *On Christian Teaching.* Trans. R. P. H. Green. Oxford: Oxford University Press, 1997. *De doctrina Christiana.* Vol. 34 of *Patrologia Latina.* Ed. J. P. Migne. Paris, 1844–65.

————. *The City of God.* Trans. Henry Bettenson. London: Penguin, 1984. *De civitate Dei contra paganos.* Vol. 41 of *Patrologia Latina.* Ed. J. P. Migne. Paris, 1844–65.

Badiou, Alain. *Saint Paul: La fondation de l'universalisme.* Paris: Presses Universitaires de France, 1997.

Baer, Yitzhak F. *Galut.* Trans. Robert Warshow. New York: Schocken, 1947.

Balibar, Étienne. "Subjection and Subjectivation." In *Supposing the Subject.* Ed. Joan Copjec. London: Verso, 1994, 1–15.

Barber, Malcom. "Lepers, Jews and Moslems: The Plot to Overthrow Christendom in 1321." *History: The Journal of the Historical Association* 66 (1981): 1–17

Barrett, C. K. *A Commentary on the Epistle to the Romans.* New York: Harper and Brothers, 1957.

Bartels, Emily. "Making More of the Moor: Aaron, Othello, and Renaissance Refashionings of Race." *Shakespeare Quarterly* 41, no.:4 (1990): 433–54.

Bartlett, Robert. *The Making of Europe: Conquest, Colonization and Cultural Change 950–1350.* Princeton: Princeton University Press, 1993.

Bartov, Omer. *Mirrors of Destruction: War, Genocide, and Modern Identity.* Oxford: Oxford University Press, 2000.

Bassi, Shaul. *Le metamorfosi di Otello: Storia di un'etnicità immaginaria.* Bari: B. A. Graphis, 2000.

————. "Mixed Marriages, Mixed Philosophies and Mixed Criticisms: *Othello* and *Nigredo.*" Unpublished paper, 2001.

Bauer, Walter. "Das Gebot der Feindesliebe und die alten Christen." *Zeitschrift für Theologie und Kirche* 27 (1917): 37–54.

Beiner, Ronald and William J. Booth, eds. *Kant and Political Philosophy: The Contemporary Legacy.* New Haven: Yale University Press, 1993.

Benjamin, Walter. *The Correspondence of Walter Benjamin and Gershom Scholem, 1932–1940.* Trans. Gary Smith and Andre Lefevere. Cambridge, Mass.: Harvard University Press, 1992. *Walter Benjamin/Gershom Scholem: Briefwechsel 1933–1940.* Ed. Gershom Scholem. Frankfurt am Main: Suhrkamp, 1980.

———. *Illuminations: Essays and Reflections.* Ed. Hannah Arendt. New York: Schocken, 1969.

———. "Franz Kafka." Trans. Harry Zohn. In *Illuminations: Essays and Reflections,* 111–45.

———. "Theses on the Philosophy of History." Trans. Harry Zohn. In *Illuminations: Essays and Reflections,* 253–64.

Bennington, Geoffrey. *Legislations: The Politics of Deconstruction.* London: Verso, 1994.

Benslama, Fethi. "La représentation et l'impossible." *Le genre humain* ("L'art et la mémoire des camps: Représenter exterminer") (December 2001): 59–80

———. "La répudiation originaire." In *Idiomes, Nationalités, Déconstructions— Cahiers Intersignes.* Pari: L'aube-Toubkal, 1998, 113–53.

Benveniste, Emile. *Indo-European Language and Society.* Trans. Elizabeth Palmer. London: Faber andFaber, 1973. *Le vocabulaire des institutions indo-européennes 1: Économie, parenté, société.* Paris: Minuit, 1969.

Blanchot, Maurice. *L'entretien infini.* Paris: Gallimard, 1981.

Bloom, Alan. *Shakespeare's Politics.* Chicago: University of Chicago Press, 1986.

Blumenkranz, Bernard. *Les auteurs chrétiens latins du moyen âge sur les juifs et le judaïsme.* Paris: Mouton, 1963.

Blumenthal, Nahman. "On the Nature of the Nazi Idiom." (In Hebrew: ʿAl tivah shel lashon ha-natzim). *Yad Vashem Studies* 1 (1957): 41–55

Böll, Heinrich. *And Where Were You, Adam?* Trans. Leila Vennewitz. Evanston: Northwestern University Press, 1994. *Wo wärst du, Adam.* Opladen: Friedrich Middelhauve, 1951.

Boureau, Alain. "Kantorowicz, or the Middle Ages as Refuge." In *Medievalism and the Modernist Temper.* Ed R. Howard Bloch and Stephen Nichols. Baltimore: Johns Hopkins University Press, 1996, 355–67.

Borowski, Tadeusz. *This Way for the Gas, Ladies and Gentlemen.* Trans. Barbara Vedder. New York: Penguin, 1967.

Boyarin, Daniel. *A Radical Jew: Paul and the Politics of Identity.* Berkeley: University of California Press, 1994.

———. *Unheroic Conduct: The Rise of Heterosexuality and the Invention of the Jewish Man.* Berkeley: University of California Press, 1997.

Brossollet, Guy. *Essai sur la non-bataille.* Paris: Belin, 1975.

Bryan, Christopher. *A Preface to Romans: Notes on the Epistle in Its Literary and Cultural Setting*. Oxford: Oxford University Press, 2000.

Buck-Morss, Susan. *Dreamworld and Catastrophe: The Passing of Mass Utopia in East and West*. Cambridge, Mass.: MIT Press, 2000.

Butler, Judith. *The Psychic Life of Power: Theories in Subjection*. Stanford: Stanford University Press, 1997.

Camille, Michael. *The Gothic Idol: Ideology and Image-Making in Medieval Art*. Cambridge: Cambridge University Press, 1989.

Cardini, Franco. *Europe and Islam*. Trans. Caroline Beamish. Oxford: Blackwell, 2001.

Carpenter, Dwayne E. "Minorities in Medieval Spain: The Legal Status of Jews and Muslims in the *Siete Partidas*." *Romance Quarterly* 33 (1986): 275–87.

Cattin, E., et al., eds. *Figures du théologico-politique*. Paris: Vrin, 1999.

Cavell, Stanley. *Disowning Knowledge in Six Plays of Shakespeare*. Cambridge: Cambridge University Press, 1987.

Charles-Saget, Annick. "Guerre et nature: Etude sur le sens du *Polémos* chez Aristote." In *Aristote politique: Etudes sur la* Politique *d'Aristote*. Ed. Pierre Aubenque and Alonso Tordesillas. Paris: Presses Universitaires de France, 1993, 93–117.

Chazan, Robert. *Daggers of Faith: Thirteenth-Century Christian Missionizing and Jewish Response*. Berkeley: University of California Press, 1989.

Chouraqui, André N. *Between East and West: A History of the Jews of North Africa*. Trans. M. M. Bernet. New York: Atheneum, 1973.

Cicero. *On Friendship*. Trans. W. A. Falconer. Cambridge, Mass.: Harvard University Press, Loeb Classical Library, 1927.

Çirakman, Asli. "From Tyranny to Despotism: The Enlightenment's Unenlightened Image of the Turks." *International Journal of Middle East Studies* 33, no. 1 (2001): 49–68.

Cixous, Hélène. *Benjamin à Montaigne: Il ne faut pas le dire*. Paris: Galilée, 2001.

———. "We Who Are Free, Are We Free?" Trans. Chris Miller. *Critical Inquiry* 19, no. 2 (winter 1993): 201–19.

Clausewitz, Carl von. *On War*. Ed. and trans. Michael Howard and Peter Paret. Princeton: Princeton University Press, 1989. *Vom Kriege*. Ed. Werner Hahlweg. Bonn: Ferd Dümmlers, 1980.

Clendinnen, Inge. *Reading the Holocaust*. Cambridge: Cambridge University Press, 1999.

Cohen, Hermann. *Religion of Reason Out of the Sources of Judaism*. Trans. S. Kaplan. Atlanta: Scholars Press, 1995.

Cohen, Jeremy. *Living Letters of the Law: Ideas of the Jew in Medieval Christianity*. Berkeley: University of California Press, 1999.

Cohen, Tom. *Anti-Mimesis from Plato to Hitchcock.* Cambridge: Cambridge University Press, 1994.

Contamine, Philippe. *La guerre au moyen âge.* Paris: Presses Universitaires de France, 1992.

Corn, Georges. *L'Europe et l'Orient: De la balkanization à la libanisation—Histoire d'une modernité inaccomplie.* Paris: La découverte, 1989.

Courtine, Jean-François. "A propos du 'problème théologico-politique.'" In *Droits* 18 (1993): 109–18.

Craig, Leon H. *The War Lover: A Study of Plato's* Republic. Toronto: University of Toronto Press, 1994.

Cutler, Allan Harris, and Helen Elmquist Cutler. *The Jew as Ally of the Muslim: Medieval Roots of Anti-Semitism.* Notre Dame: University of Notre Dame Press, 1986.

Dahan, Gilbert. *La polémique chrétienne contre le judaïsme au Moyen Age.* Paris: Albin Michel, 1991.

Daniel, Norman. *Islam and the West: The Making of an Image.* Edinburgh: Edinburgh University Press, 1960.

Danson, Laurence. "England, Islam, and the Mediterranean Drama: *Othello* and Others." *Journal for Early Modern Cultural Studies* 2, no. 2 (fall–winter 2002): 1–25.

———. *The Harmonies of the Merchant of Venice.* New Haven: Yale University Press, 1978.

Darwish, Mahmoud. *The Adam of Two Edens.* Ed. Munir Akash and Daniel Moore. Syracuse: Jusoor and Syracuse University Press, 2000.

David, Alain. *Racisme et antisémitisme: Essai de philosophie sur l'envers des concepts.* Paris: Ellipses, 2001.

Davis, Norman, ed. *Non-Cycle Plays and Fragments.* London: The Early English Text Society and Oxford University Press, 1970.

Deleuze, Gilles *La philosophie critique de Kant.* Paris: Presses Universitaires de France, 1963.

———, and Félix Guattari. *A Thousand Plateaus: Capitalism and Schizophrenia.* Trans. Brian Massumi. Minneapolis: University of Minnesota Press, 1987. *Mille Plateaux: Capitalisme et Schizophrénie.* Paris: Minuit, 1980.

de Man, Paul. *Aesthetic Ideology.* Ed. Andrzej Warminski. Minneapolis: University of Minnesota Press, 1996.

Derrida, Jacques. "Above All, No Journalists!" Trans. Samuel Weber. In *Religion and Media.* Ed. Hent de Vries and Samuel Weber. Stanford: Stanford University Press, 2001, 56–93.

———. *Acts of Religion.* Ed. Gil Anidjar. New York: Routledge, 2002.

———. *Adieu: To Emmanuel Levinas.* Trans. Pascale-Anne Brault and Michael B.

Naas. Stanford: Stanford University Press, 1999. *Adieu: A Emmanuel Levinas*. Paris: Galilée, 1997.

———. "Before the Law." Trans. Avital Ronell. In *Acts of Literature*. Ed. Derek Attridge. New York: Routledge, 1992, 181–220. "Préjugés: Devant la loi." In *La faculté de juger*. Paris: Minuit, 1985, 87–139.

———. "Circumfession." Trans. Geoffrey Bennington. In Jacques Derrida and Geoffrey Bennington, *Jacques Derrida*. Chicago: University of Chicago Press, 1993, 3–315. "Circonfession." In Jacques Derrida et Geoffrey Bennington. *Jacques Derrida*. Paris: Seuil, 1991, 7–291.

———. "The Crisis in the Teaching of Philosophy." In *Who's Afraid of Philosophy?: Right to Philosophy I*. Trans. Jan Plug. Stanford: Stanford University Press, 2002, 99–116. "La crise de l'enseignement philosophique." In *Du droit à la philosophie*. Paris: Galilée, 1990, 155–79.

———. *The Ear of the Other: Otobiography, Transference, Translation*. Trans. Peggy Kamuf. New York: Schocken, 1985. *L'oreille de l'autre*. Montreal: VLB, 1977.

———. "Faith and Knowledge: The Two Sources of 'Religion' at the Limits of Reason Alone." Trans. Samuel Weber. In Derrida. *Acts of Religion*, 40–101. "Foi et savoir: Les deux sources de la 'religion' aux limites de la simple raison." In *Religion*. Ed. Jacques Derrida and Gianni Vattimo. Paris: Seuil, 1996, 9–86.

———. "Force of Law: The 'Mystical Foundation of Authority.'" Trans. Mary Quaintance. In Derrida. *Acts of Religion*, 228–98. *Force de loi*. Paris: Galilée, 1994.

———. *The Gift of Death*. Trans. David Wills. Chicago: University of Chicago Press, 1995. *Donner la mort*. Paris: Galilée, 1999.

———. *Glas*. Trans. John P. Leavey Jr. and Richard Rand. Lincoln: University of Nebraska Press, 1986. *Glas: que reste-t-il du savoir absolu?* Paris: Denoël/Gonthier, 1981.

———. *Of Grammatology*. Trans. Gayatri Chakravorty Spivak. Baltimore: Johns Hopkins University Press, 1976. *De la grammatologie*. Paris: Minuit, 1967.

———. "Heidegger's Ear: Philopolemology." Trans. John P. Leavey, Jr. In *Reading Heidegger: Commemorations*. Ed. John Sallis. Bloomington: Indiana University Press, 1993, 163–218.

———. "How to Avoid Speaking: Denials." Trans. Ken Frieden. In *Derrida and Negative Theology*. Ed. Harold Coward and Toby Foshay. Albany: State University of New York Press, 1992, 73–142. "Comment ne pas parler: Dénégations." In *Psyché: Inventions de l'autre*. Paris: Galilée, 1987, 535–95.

———. "Interpretations at War: Kant, the Jew, the German." Trans. Moshe Ron. In Derrida, *Acts of Religion*, 135–88. "Interpretations at War: Kant, le Juif, l'Allemand." In *Phénoménologie et politique: Mélanges offerts à Jacques Taminiaux.* Brussels: Ousia, 1989, 209–91.

———. "Lettres sur un aveugle: *Punctum caecum.*" In Jacques Derrida and Safaa Fathy, *Tourner les mots: Au bord d'un film.* Paris: Galilée/ARTE, 1999.

———. *Memoirs of the Blind: A Self-Portrait and Other Ruins.* Trans. Pascale-Anne Brault and Michael Naas. Chicago: University of Chicago Press, 1993. *Mémoires d'aveugle: L'autoportrait et autres ruines.* Paris: Editions de la réunion des musées nationaux, 1990.

———. *Monolingualism of the Other, or, the Prosthesis of Origin.* Trans. Patrick Mensah. Stanford: Stanford University Press, 1998. *Le monolinguisme de l'autre, ou la prothèse de l'origine.* Paris: Galilée, 1996.

———. *The Other Heading: Reflections on Today's Europe.* Trans. Pascale-Anne Brault and Michael B. Naas. Bloomington: Indiana University Press, 1992. *L'autre cap.* Paris: Minuit, 1991.

———. "Politics of Friendship." Trans. Gabriel Motzkin, Michael Syrotinski, and Thomas Keenan. *American Imago* 50, no. 3 (1993): 353–91.

———. *Politics of Friendship.* Trans. George Collins. London: Verso, 1997. *Politiques de l'amitié.* Paris: Galilée, 1994.

———. *The Post Card: From Socrates to Freud and Beyond.* Trans. Alan Bass. Chicago: University of Chicago Press, 1987. *La carte postale: De Socrate à Freud et au delà.* Paris: Flammarion. 1980.

———. *The Truth in Painting.* Trans. Geoffrey Bennington and Ian McLeod. Chicago: University of Chicago Press, 1987. *La vérité en peinture.* Paris: Flammarion, 1978.

———. "Typewriter Ribbon: Limited Ink (2) ('Within Such Limits')." Trans. Peggy Kamuf. In *Material Events: Paul de Man and the Afterlife of Theory.* Ed. Tom Cohen et al. Minneapolis: University of Minnesota Press, 2001, 277–360.

———. "What is a 'Relevant' Translation?" Trans. Laurence Venuti. *Critical Inquiry* 27, no. 2 (2001): 169–200.

———. *Writing and Difference.* Trans. Alan Bass. Chicago: University of Chicago Press, 1978. *L'écriture et la différence.* Paris: Seuil, 1967.

Desmond, William. "Enemies." *Tijdschrift voor Filosofie* 63 (2001): 127–51.

Djaït, Hichem. *Europe and Islam: Cultures and Modernity.* Trans. Peter Heinegg. Berkeley: University of California Press, 1985.

Dunn, James D. G. *Word Biblical Commentary 38A (Romans 1–8).* Dallas, TX: Word Books, 1988.

Encyclopedic Dictionary of Roman Law. Ed. Adolf Berger. Transactions of the American Philosophical Society, new series 43, no. 2 (1953).

Esh, Shaul. "Words and their Meaning: 25 Samples from the Nazi-Idiom" (in Hebrew). In *Yad Vashem Studies* 5 (1962): 109–33.

Everett, Barbara. "'Spanish' Othello: The Making of Shakespeare's Moor." In *Shakespeare and Race*. Ed. Catherine M. S. Alexander and Stanley Wells. Cambridge: Cambridge University Press, 2000, 64–81.

Fenton, Paul B. "Shabbatai Sebi and His Muslim Contemporary Muhammad An-Niyazi." In *Aproaches to Judaism in Medieval Times*. Vol. 3. Ed. David Blumenthal. Atlanta: Scholars Press, 1988.

Fiedler, Leslie. *The Stranger in Shakespeare*. New York: Stein and Day, 1972.

Finkelstein, Norman G. *The Holocaust Industry: Reflections on the Exploitation of Jewish Suffering*. London: Verso, 2000.

Fitzmyer, Joseph A. *Romans: A New Translation with Introduction and Commentary*. New York: The Anchor Bible/Doubleday, 1993.

Foucault, Michel "Il faut défendre la société." In *Dits et écrits III (1976–1979)*. Paris: Gallimard, 1994, 124–30

———. *"Il faut défendre la société": Cours au Collège de France (1975–1976)*. Paris: Seuil/Gallimard, 1997.

Fraisse, Jean-Claude. *Philia: La notion d'amitié dans la philosophie antique. Essai sur un problème perdu et retrouvé*. Paris: Vrin, 1974.

Frassetto, Michael. "The Image of the Saracen as Heretic in the Sermons of Ademar of Chabannes." In *Western Views of Islam in Medieval and Early Modern Europe*. Ed. David Blanks and Michael Frassetto. New York: St. Martin's Press, 1999, 83–96.

Freud, Sigmund. *Beyond the Pleasure Principle*. Trans. James Strachey. In *The Standard Edition of the Complete Psychological Works of Sigmund Freud*. Vol. 18, 7–64. *Jenseits des Lustprinzips*. In *Studienausgabe*. Vol. 3, 213–72.

———. *Civilization and its Discontents*. Trans. Joan Riviere. In *The Standard Edition*. Vol. 21, 59–145. *Das Unbehagen in der Kultur*. In *Studienausgabe*. Vol. 9, 191–270.

———. *The Future of an Illusion*. Trans. W. D. Robson-Scott, In *The Standard Edition*. Vol. 21, 5–56. *Die Zukunft einer Illusion*. In *Studienausgabe* 9, 135–89.

———. "Inhibitions, Symptoms and Anxiety." Trans. Alix Strachey. In *The Standard Edition*. Vol. 20, 87–174."Hemmung, Symptom und Angst." In *Studienausgabe* 6, 227–308.

———. *Moses and Monotheism: Three Essays*. Trans. James Strachey. In *The Standard Edition*. Vol. 23, 3–137. *Der Mann Moses und die Monotheistische Religion: Drei Abhandlungen*. In *Studienausgabe* 9, 455–581.

———. *The Psychopathology of Everyday Life*. Trans. Alan Tyson. In *The Standard*

Edition. Vol. 7. *Zur Psychopathologie des Alltagslebens.* Frankfurt am Main: Fischer Taschenbuch, 1954.

―――. *The Standard Edition of the Complete Psychological Works of Sigmund Freud.* Ed. James Strachey. London: The Hogarth Press and the Institute of Psycho-Analysis, 1961.

―――. *Studienausgabe.* Ed. Alexander Mitscherlich et al. Frankfurt am Main: S. Fischer, 1974.

―――. "Thoughts for the Times on War and Death." Trans. E. C. Mayne. In *The Standard Edition.* Vol. 14, 275–302. "Zeitgemässes über Krieg und Tod." In *Studienausgabe* 9, 33–60.

―――. *Totem and Taboo.* Trans. James Strachey. In *The Standard Edition.* Vol. 13, 1–161. *Totem und Tabu.* In *Studienausgabe* 9, 287–444.

Funkenstein, Amos. *Perceptions of Jewish History.* Berkeley: University of California Press, 1993.

Galison, Peter. "The Ontology of the Enemy: Norbert Weiner and the Cybernetic Vision." *Critical Inquiry* 21, no. 1 (autumn 1994): 228–66.

García y García, Antonio. "Jews and Muslims in the Canon Law of the Iberian Peninsula in the Late Medieval and Early Modern Period." In *Jewish History* 3, no. 1 (spring 1988): 41–50.

Gasché, Rodolphe "The Debt of Europe." In *Future Crossings: Literature Between Philosophy and Cultural Studies,* Ed. Krzysztof Ziarek and Seamus Deane. Evanston: Northwestern University Press, 2000, 123–46.

Gaston, Lloyd. "Israel's Enemies in Pauline Theology." *New Testament Studies* 28 (1982): 400–23.

Gauss, Julia. "Die Auseinandersetzung mit Judentum und Islam bei Anselm." *Analecta Anselmiana* 4 (1975): 101–9.

Genet, Jean. *L'ennemi déclaré: Textes et entretiens.* Paris: Gallimard, 1991.

Gillies, John. *Shakespeare and the Geography of Difference.* Cambridge: Cambridge University Press, 1994.

Ginzburg, Carlo. *Ecstasies: Deciphering the Witches' Sabbath.* Trans. Raymond Rosenthal. New York: Pantheon, 1991.

Guibert de Nogent. *Autobiographie.* Ed. E.-R. Labande. Paris: Les belles lettres, 1981.

Glancy, Jennifer. "Israel vs. Israel in *Romans* 11: 25–32." *Union Seminary Quarterly Review* 45, nos. 3–4 (1991): 191–203.

Glazer, Nahum. *Franz Rosenzweig: His Life and Thought.* New York: Schocken, 1974.

Glucksmann, André. *Le discours de la guerre.* Paris: L'herne, 1967.

Goiten, Shlomo Dov. *Jews and Arabs: Their Contacts through the Ages.* New York: Schocken, 1974.

Graboïs, Aryeh. "Un chapitre de tolérance intellectuelle dans la société occidentale au XIIe siècle: Le 'dialogus' de Pierre Abélard et le 'Kuzari' d'Yehudah Halévi." In *Pierre Abélard, Pierre le Vénérable: Les courants littéraires et artistiques en Occident au milieu du XIIe siècle.* Paris: Editions du Centre National de la Recherche Scientifique (Colloques Internationaux du Centre National de la Recherche Scientifique, no. 546), 1975, 641–54.

Greenblatt, Stephen. *Shakespearean Negotiations: The Circulation of Social Energy in Renaissance England.* Berkeley: University of California Press, 1988.

Griffith, Sydney H. "Jews and Muslims in Christian Syriac and Arabic Texts of the Ninth Century." In *Jewish History* 3, no. 1 (spring 1988): 65–94.

Grosrichard, Alain. *The Sultan's Court: European Fantasies of the East.* Trans. Liz Heron. London: Verso, 1997. *Structure du sérail: La fiction du despotisme asiatique dans l'Occident classique.* Paris: Seuil, 1979.

Guénoun, Denis. *Hypothèses sur l'Europe: Un essai de philosophie.* Belfort: Circé, 2000.

Hager, Alan. *Shakespeare's Political Animal: Schema or Schemata in the Canon.* London: Associated University Presses, 1990.

Halevi, Ilan. *A History of the Jews: Ancient and Modern.* Trans. A. M. Berrett. London: Zed Books, 1987.

Halpern, Richard. *Shakespeare among the Moderns.* Ithaca: Cornell University Press, 1997.

Hardt, Michael and Antonio Negri. *Empire.* Cambridge, Mass.: Harvard University Press, 2000.

Harle, Vilho *The Enemy with a Thousand Faces: The Tradition of the Other in Western Political Thought and History.* Westport, CT and London: Praeger, 2000.

————, ed. "Concepts of the 'Enemy' in European Thought." A special issue of *History of European Ideas* 13, no. 4 (1991).

Harris, H. S. *Hegel's Development: Toward the Sunlight. 1770–1801.* Oxford: The Clarendon Press, 1972.

Harshav, Benjamin. *Language in Time of Revolution.* Stanford: Stanford University Press, 1999.

Hart, Mitchell B. *Social Science and the Politics of Moden Jewish Identity.* Stanford: Stanford University Press, 2000.

Hays, Richard B. *Echoes of Scriptures in the Letters of Paul.* New Haven: Yale University Press, 1989.

Hegel, George Wilhelm Friedrich. *Hegel's Philosophy of Right.* Trans. T. M. Knox. London: Oxford University Press, 1967. *Grundlinien der Philosophie des Rechts.* In *Werke.* Vol. 7.

————. *Hegel's System of Ethical Life and First Philosophy of Spirit.* Trans. H. S. Harris and T. M. Knox. Albany: State University of New York Press, 1979.

System der Sittlichkeit. In *Sämtliche Werke.* Ed. Georg Lasson. Leipzig: Felix Meiner, 1913.

—————. *Lectures on the History of Philosophy.* Trans. E. S. Haldane and F. H. Simson. Lincoln: University of Nebraska Press, 1995. *Vorlesungen über die Geschichte der Philosophie.* In *Vorlesungen.* Vol. 9. Ed. Pierre Garniron and Walter Jaeschke. Hamburg: Felix Meiner Verlag, 1986.

—————. *Lectures on the Philosophy of Religion.* Ed. Peter Hodgson. Trans. R. F. Browne et al. Berkeley: University of California Press, 1985. *Vorlesungen über die Philosophie der Religion.* In *Vorlesungen.* Vols. 4–5. Ed. Walter Jaeschke. Hamburg: Felix Meiner Verlag, 1984.

—————. *The Philosophy of History.* Trans. J. Sibree. Buffalo, N.Y.: Prometheus Books, 1991. *Vorlesungen über die Philosophie der Geschichte.* In *Werke.* Vol. 12.

—————. *Phenomenology of Spirit.* Trans. A.V. Miller. Oxford: Oxford University Press, 1977. *Phänomenologie des Geistes.* In *Werke.* Vol 3.

—————. *Premiers écrits (Francfort 1797–1800).* Ed. Olivier Depré. Paris: Vrin, 1997.

—————. "The Spirit of Christianity and its Fate." Trans. T. M. Knox. In *Early Theological Writings.* Philadelphia: University of Pennsylvania Press, 1971, 182–301. "Der Geist des Christentums und sein Schicksal." In *Werke.* Vol. 1, 274–418.

—————. *Werke.* Ed. Eva Moldenhauer and Karl Markus Michel. 20 vols. Frankfurt am Main: Suhrkamp, 1969–71.

Heng, Geraldine. "The Romance of England: *Richard Coer de Lyon,* Saracens, Jews, and the Politics of Race and Nation." In *The Postcolonial Middle Ages.* Ed. J. J. Cohen. New York: Palgrave, 2000, 135–71.

Heschel, Susannah. "Revolt of the Colonized: Abraham Geiger's *Wissenschaft des Judentums* as a Challenge to Christian Hegemony in the Academy." *New German Critique* 77 (spring/summer 1999): 61–85.

Hever, Hannan. *Producing the Modern Hebrew Canon: Nation Building and Minority Discourse.* New York: New York University Press, 2002.

Hirszowicz, Lukasz. *The Third Reich and the Arab East.* London: Routledge, 1966.

Hobbes, Thomas. *De cive.* Ed. Howard Warrender. Oxford: Clarendon Press, 1983. Trans. Charles T. Wood et al. as "The Citizen." In *Man and Citizen.* Ed. Bernard Gert. Indianapolis: Hackett, 1991, 87–388.

—————. *Leviathan.* Ed. Richard Tuck. Cambridge: Cambridge University Press, 1996.

Hobson, Marian. *Jacques Derrida: Opening Lines.* London: Routledge, 1998.

Hölderlin, Friedrich "The Ground for 'Empedocles.'" In *Essays and Letters on Theory.* Ed. and trans. Thomas Pfau. Albany: State University of New York Press, 1988.

Huber, Wolfgang. "Feindschaft und Feindesliebe: Notizen zum Problem des 'Feindes' in der Theologie." *Zeitschrift für Evangelische Ethik* 26 (April 1982): 128–58.

Hunter, G. K. "Elizabethans and Foreigners." *Shakespeare Survey* 17 (1964): 37–52.

Hutter, Horst. *Politics as Friendship: The Origins of Classical Notions of Politics in the Theory and Practice of Friendship.* Waterloo, Ontario: Wilfrid Laurier University Press, 1978.

Hutton, Christopher. *Linguistics and the Third Reich.* London: Routledge, 1999.

Hyppolite, Jean. *Genèse et structure de la phénomenologie de l'esprit de Hegel.* Paris: Aubier Montaigne, 1946.

Idel, Moshe. *Messianic Mystics.* New Haven: Yale University Press, 1998.

Iogna-Prat, Dominique. *Ordonner et exclure: Cluny et la société chrétienne face à l'hérésie, au judaïsme et à l'islam 1000–1150.* Paris: Aubier, 1998.

Irigaray, Luce. *Spéculum: De l'autre femme.* Paris: Minuit, 1974.

Itzkwowitz, Norman "The Problem of Perception." In *Imperial Legacy: The Ottoman Imprint on the Balkans and the Middle East.* Ed. L. Carl Brown. New York: Columbia University Press, 1996.

James, William, *The Varieties of Religious Experience: A Study in Human Nature.* New York: Modern Library, 1999.

John of Salisbury [Ioannis Saresberiensis], *Policraticus.* Ed. K. S. B. Keats Rohan. Turnholti: Brepols, 1993. Trans. Cary J. Nederman as *Policraticus: Of the Frivolities of Courtiers and the Footprints of Philosophers.* Cambridge: Cambridge University Press, 1990.

Johnson, Jerah. "The Concept of the 'King's Two Bodies' in *Hamlet.*" *Shakespeare Quarterly* 18, no. 4 (1967): 430–34.

Johnston, David. *The Rhetoric of Leviathan: Thomas Hobbes and the Politics of Cultural Transformation.* Princeton: Princeton University Press, 1986.

Jones, Eldred. *Othello's Countrymen: The African in English Renaissance Drama.* London: Oxford University Press, 1965.

Ka-Tzetnik. *Kar'u lo piepel.* Tel-Aviv: 'Am ha-Sefer, 1961. Trans. Moshe Kohn as *Moni: A Novel of Auschwitz.* Secaucus, N.J.: Citadel Press, 1963.

Kafka, Franz. *Zur Frage der Gesetze und andere Schriften aus dem Nachlaß.* Frankfurt am Main: Fischer Taschenbuch Verlag, 1994.

———. *Parables and Paradoxes.* New York: Schocken, 1961.

Kalimtzis, Kostas. *Aristotle on Political Enmity and Disease: An Inquiry into Stasis.* New York: State University of New York Press, 2000.

Kant, Immanuel. *Critique of Judgement.* Trans. J. H. Bernard. New York: Hafner, 1951. *Kritik der Urteilskraft.* In *Werkausgabe* Vol. 10. Ed. Wilhelm Weischedel. Frankfurt am Main: Suhrkamp, 1974.

———. *Metaphysics of Morals.* Trans. Mary Gregor. Cambridge: Cambridge Uni-

versity Press, 1996. *Die Metaphysik der Sitten.* In *Werkausgabe.* Vol. 8. Ed.
Wilhelm Weischedel. Frankfurt am Main: Suhrkamp, 1993.

―――. *Observations on the Feeling of the Beautiful and the Sublime.* Trans. J. T.
Goldthwait. Berkeley: California University Press, 1965.

―――. *Religion Within the Limits of Reason Alone.* Trans. Greene and Hudson.
New York: Harper Torchbooks, 1960. *Die Religion innerhalb der Grenzen der
bloßen Vernunft.* In *Werkausgabe.* Vol. 8. Ed. W. Weischedel. Frankfurt am
Main: Suhrkamp, 1993.

―――. *Political Writings.* Ed. Hans Reiss. Cambridge: Cambridge University
Press, 1991.

―――. *Eine Vorlesung Kants über Ethik.* Ed. Paul Menzer. Berlin: Pan Verlag Rolf
Heise, 1924.

Kantorowicz, Ernst. *The King's Two Bodies: A Study in Medieval Political Theology.*
Princeton: Princeton University Press, 1997.

Käsemann, Ernst. *Commentary on Romans.* Trans. G. W. Bromiley. Grand Rapids,
Mich.: Eerdmans, 1980.

Kaul, Mythili, ed. *Othello: New Essays by Black Writers.* Washington, D.C.:
Howard University Press, 1997.

Kavka, Gregory S. *Hobbesian Moral and Political Theory.* Princeton: Princeton
University Press, 1986.

Keats, John. *The Letters of John Keats.* Ed. Maurice Buxton Forman. London: Oxford University Press, 1947.

Kedar, Benjamin Z. *Crusade and Mission: European Approaches toward the Muslims.* Princeton: Princeton University Press, 1984.

Keeton, George W. *Shakespeare's Legal and Political Background.* London: Sir Isaac
Pitman andSons, 1967.

Klassen, William. "'Love Your Enemies': Some Reflections on the Current Status
of Research." In *The Love of Enemy and Nonretaliation in the New Testament.*
Ed. W. M. Swartley. Louisville, Ky.: Westminster/John Knox, 1992, 1–31.

Klemperer, Victor. *LTI: Notizbuch eines Philologen.* Leipzig: Reclam Verlag, 1975.

Kluback, William. "A Man of Dark Thoughts: Carl Schmitt." In *The Owl of Minerva* 19, no. 2 (spring 1988): 183–90

Kogon, Eugen. *The Theory and Practice of Hell: The German Concentration Camps
and the System Behind Them.* Trans. Heinz Norden. New York: Farrar,
Straus, 1950. *Der SS-Staat: Das System der deutschen Konzentrationslager.*
Frankfurt am Main: Verlag der Frankfurter Hefte, 1946.

Kojève, Alexandre. *Introduction à la lecture de Hegel.* Ed. Raymond Queneau.
Paris: Gallimard, 1947.

Krell, David Farell. *The Purest of Bastards: Works of Mourning, Art, and Affirmation in the Thought of Jacques Derrida*. University Park: Pennsylvania State University Press, 2000.

Kritzeck, James. *Peter the Venerable and Islam*. Princeton: Princeton University Press, 1964.

Kruger, Steven F. "Medieval Christian (Dis)identifications: Muslims and Jews in Guibert of Nogent." *New Literary History* 28, no. 2 (1997): 185–203.

Lacan, Jacques. "Desire and the Interpretation of Desire in *Hamlet*." Trans. James Hulbert. In *Literature and Psychoanalysis, The Question of Reading: Otherwise*. Ed. Shoshana Felman. Baltimore: Johns Hopkins University Press, 1982, 11–52.

———. *Le séminaire VII: L'éthique de la psychanalyse*. Paris: Seuil, 1986.

Lang, Berel. *Act and Idea in the Nazi Genocide*. Chicago: University of Chicago Press, 1990.

Langbein, Hermann. *Menschen in Auschwitz*. Vienna: Europa Verlag, 1972.

Laor, Yitzhak. *Narratives Without Natives (Anu Kotvim Otakh Moledet): Essays on Israeli Literature*. Tel Aviv: Ha-kibbutz Ha-me'uhad, 1995.

Lenowitz, Harris. *The Jewish Messiahs: From the Galilee to Crown Heights*. Oxford: Oxford University Press, 1998.

Levi, Primo. *Survival in Auschwitz [If This Is a Man]*. Trans. Stuart Woolf. New York: Collier Books, 1961. *Se questo è un uomo*. 1947. Turin: Einaudi, 1989.

———. *The Drowned and the Saved*. Trans. R. Rosenthal. New York: Vintage International, 1989. *I sommersi e i salvati*. Turin: Einaudi, 1986.

Levinas, Emmanuel. "Ethics and Politics." Trans. Jonathan Romney. In *The Levinas Reader*. Ed. Seán Hand. Oxford: Basil Blackwell, 1989.

———. *Otherwise than Being or Beyond Essence*. Trans. Alphonso Lingis. Pittsburgh: Duquesne University Press, 1998. *Autrement qu'être ou au-delà de l'essence*. The Hague: Martinus Nijhoff, 1974.

———. *Totality and Infinity: An Essay on Exteriority*. Trans. Alphonso Lingis. Pittsburgh: Duquesne University Press, 1961. *Totalité et infini: Essai sur l'extériorité*. The Hague: Martinus Nijhoff, 1961.

Lewalski, Barbara K. "Biblical Allusion and Allegory in 'The Merchant of Venice.'" *Shakespeare Quarterly* 13, no. 3 (1962): 327–43.

Lewis, Bernard. *Semites and Anti-Semites: An Inquiry into Conflict and Prejudice*. New York: W. W. Norton, 1999.

Liebes, Yehuda. *Studies in Jewish Myth and Jewish Messianism*. Trans. Batya Stein. Albany: State University of New York Press, 1993. A partial translation of *Sod ha-emunah ha-shabta'it: kovetz ma'amarim*. Jerusalem: Bialik Institute, 1995.

Llewelyn, John. *The HypoCritical Imagination: Between Kant and Levinas*. London and New York: Routledge, 2000.

Lomax, John Phillip. "Frederick II, His Saracens, and the Papacy." In *Medieval Christian Perceptions of Islam*. Ed. John Tolan. New York: Routledge, 2000, 175–97.

Longenecker, Richard N. "The Focus of Romans: The Central Role of 5:1–8:39 in the Argument of the Letter." In *Romans and the People of God: Essays in Honor of Gordon D. Fee on the Occasion of His 65th Birthday*. Ed. S. K. Soderlund and N. T. Wright. Grand Rapids, Mich.: Eerdmans, 1999, 49–69.

Loomba, Ania. "'Delicious Traffick': Racial and Religious Difference on Early Modern Stages." In *Shakespeare and Race*. Ed. Catherine M. S. Alexander and Stanley Wells. Cambridge: Cambridge University Press, 2000, 203–24.

———. *Shakespeare, Race, and Colonialism*. Oxford: Oxford University Press, 2002.

Loraux, Nicole. *The Divided City: On Memory and Forgetting in Ancient Athens*. Trans. Corinne Pache and Jeff Fort. New York: Zone Books, 2002.

Lupton, Julia Reinhard. "*Othello* Circumcised: Shakespeare and the Pauline Discourse of Nations." *Representations* 57 (winter 1997): 73–89.

Luther, Martin. *Luther's Works*. Ed. Helmut T. Lehmann. Saint Louis: Concordia Publishing, 1972.

———. *Lectures on Romans: Glosses and Scholia*. Trans. Walter G. Tillmanns and Jacob A. O. Preus. In *Luther's Works*. Vol. 25. Ed. Hilton C. Oswald. Saint Louis: Concordia Publishing, 1972. *Vorlesung über den Römerbrief*. Ed. Eduard Ellwein. Munich: Chr. Kaiser Verlag, 1927.

———. "On War Against the Turk." Trans. Charles M. Jacobs and Robert C. Schultz. In *Luther's Works*. Vol. 46. Ed. Robert C. Schultz. Philadelphia: Fortress Press, 1967, 155–205.

Lyotard, Jean-François. *L'enthousiasme*. Paris: Galilée—Le livre de poche, 1986.

———. *Lessons on the Analytic of the Sublime*. Trans. Elisabeth Rottenberg. Stanford: Stanford University Press, 1994. *Leçons sur l'analytique du sublime*. Paris: Galilée, 1991.

———, and Eberhard Gruber. *The Hyphen: Between Judaism and Christianity*. Trans. Pascale-Anne Brault and Michael Naas. Amherst, N.Y.: Humanity Books, 1999. *Un trait d'union*. Sainte-Foy, Quebec: Editions du griffon d'argile, 1993.

Malabou, Catherine. *L'avenir de Hegel: Plasticité, temporalité, dialectique*. Paris: Vrin, 1996.

———. "La naissance de la mort. Hegel et Freud en guerre?" In *Autour de Hegel: Hommage à Bernard Bourgeois*. Ed. François Dagonnet and Pierre Osmo. Paris: Vrin, 2000, 319–31.

———. "Ouverture: Le voeu de plasticité." In *Plasticité.* Ed. Catherine Malabou. Paris: Léo Scheer, 2000, 6–25.

Mallin, Eric S. "Jewish Invader and the Soul of State: *The Merchant of Venice* and Science Fiction Movies." In *Shakespeare and Modernity: Early Modern to Millennium.* Ed. Hugh Grady. London: Routledge, 2000, 142–67.

Mamdani, Mahmood. *When Victims Become Killers: Colonialism, Nativism, and the Genocide in Rwanda.* Princeton: Princeton University Press, 2001.

Marlowe, Christopher. *The Jew of Malta.* Ed. N. W. Bawcutt. Manchester: Manchester University Press, 1978.

Marochitanus, Samuel. *The Blessed Jew of Marocco: Or, A Blackmoor made White. Being a Demonstration of the true Messias out of the law and prophets, by Rabbi Samuel, a Jew turned Christian.* York: T. Broad, 1648.

Marrati-Guénoun, Paola. *La genèse et la trace: Derrida lecteur de Husserl et Heidegger.* Dordrecht: Kluwer Academic Publishers, 1998.

Martin, Ralph P. "Reconciliation: Romans 5:1–11." In *Romans and the People of God: Essays in Honor of Gordon D. Fee on the Occasion of His 65th Birthday.* Ed. S. K. Soderlund and N. T. Wright. Grand Rapids, Mich.: Eerdmans, 1999, 36–48.

Massad, Joseph. *Colonial Effects: The Making of National Identity in Jordan.* New York: Columbia University Press, 2001.

———. "Palestinians and Jewish History: Recognition or Submission?" *Journal of Palestine Studies* 30, no. 1 (autumn 2000): 52–67.

———. "On Zionism and Jewish Supremacy." *New Politics* 7, no. 4 (winter 2002): 89–99.

Mastnak, Tomaz. *Crusading Peace: Christendom, the Muslim World, and Western Political Order.* Berkeley: University of California Press, 2002.

Matar, Nabil. *Islam in Britain, 1558–1685.* Cambridge: Cambridge University Press, 1998.

Mattar, Philip. *The Mufti of Jerusalem: Al-Hajj Amin al-Husayni and the Palestinian National Movement.* New York: Columbia University Press, 1988.

Mayer, Hans. *Outsiders: A Study in Life and Letters.* Trans. Denis M. Sweet. Cambridge, Mass.: MIT Press, 1982.

Meier, Heinrich. "Was ist Politische Theologie? Enführende Bemerkungen zu einem umstrittenen Begriff." In Jan Assmann, *Politische Theologie zwischen Ägypten und Israel.* Munich: Carl Friedrich von Siemens Stiftung, 1995, 7–19.

Meineke, Stefan. "A Life of Contradiction: The Philosopher Franz Rosenzweig and His Relationship to History and Politics." *Leo Baeck Institute Yearbook* (1991): 461–89.

Metzger, Mary J. "'Now by My Hood, a Gentle and No Jew': Jessica, *The Mer-*

chant of Venice, and the Discourse of Early Modern English Identity."
PMLA 113, no. 1 (1998): 52–63

Mongin, Olivier. "Entrer dans le vingtième siècle: La guerre et ses arrières-pensées." *Les cahiers de la nuit surveillée 1: Franz Rosenzweig* (1982): 223–32.

Montesquieu. *The Spirit of the Laws.* Trans. Thomas Nugent. New York: Hafner, 1949. *L'esprit des lois.* In *Oeuvres completes.* Vol. 2. Ed. Roger Caillois. Paris: Gallimard, La pléiade, 1951.

Moore, R. I. *The Formation of a Persecuting Society: Power and Deviance in Western Europe, 950–1250.* Oxford: Blackwell, 1990.

Morgan, Michael L., ed. *A Holocaust Reader: Responses to the Nazi Extermination.* New York: Oxford University Press, 2001.

Morris, Harry. *Last Things in Shakespeare.* Tallahassee: Florida State University Press, 1985.

Mosès, Stéphane. *Système et revelation: La philosophie de Franz Rosenzweig.* Paris: Seuil, 1982.

Mosse, George L. *Fallen Soldiers: Reshaping the Memory of the World Wars.* New York: Oxford University Press, 1990.

Müller, Filip. *Eyewitness Auschwitz: Three Years in the Gas Chambers.* Trans. Susanne Flatauer. Chicago: Ivan R. Dee, 1999.

Müller, Wilhelm. *Werke (Gedichte I).* Ed. Maria-Verena Leistner. Berlin: Gatza, 1994.

Nancy, Jean-Luc. *Being Singular Plural.* Trans. Robert D. Richardson and Anne E. O'Byrne. Stanford: Stanford University Press, 2000. *Etre singulier pluriel.* Paris: Galilée, 1996.

———. "The Deconstruction of Christianity." Trans. Simon Sparks. In *Religion and Media.* Eds. Hent de Vries and Samuel Weber. Stanford: Stanford University Press, 2001, 112–30.

———. *Le discours de la syncope 1. Logoadaedalus.* Paris: Aubier-Flammarion, 1976.

———. *The Experience of Freedom.* Trans. Bridget McDonald. Stanford: Stanford University Press, 1993. *L'expérience de la liberté.* Paris: Galilée, 1986.

———. *Le partage des voix.* Paris: Galilée, 1982.

Nederman, Cary J., and Kate Langdon Forhan, eds. *Medieval Political Theory—A Reader: The Quest for the Body Politic, 1100–1400.* London: Routledge, 1993.

Neill, Michael. "'Mulattos,' 'Blacks,' and 'Indian Moors': *Othello* and Early Modern Constructions of Human Difference." *Shakespeare Quarterly* 49, no. 4 (1998): 361–74

Neufeld, Thomas R. Yoder. *'Put on the Armour of God': The Divine Warrior from Isaiah to Ephesians.* Sheffield: Sheffield Academic Press, 1997.

Newman, Karen. "'And Wash the Ethiop White': Femininity and the Monstrous in *Othello*." In *Shakespeare Reproduced: The Text in History and Ideology*. Ed. Jean E. Howard and Marion F. O'Connor. New York: Routledge, 1990, 143–62.

Nicosia, Francis R. *The Third Reich and the Palestine Question*. New Brunswick: Transaction, 2000.

Niditch, Susan. *War in the Hebrew Bible: A Study in the Ethics of Violence*. New York: Oxford University Press, 1993.

Nietzsche, Friedrich. *The Anti-Christ*. In *Twilight of the Idols and the Anti-Christ*. Trans. R. J. Hollingdale. London: Penguin, 1990. *Der Antichrist*. In *Sämtliche Werke*. Vol. 6. Ed. Giorgio Colli and Mazzino Montinari. Munich: Deutscher Taschenbuch, 1988.

———. *The Gay Science*. Trans. Walter Kaufmann. New York: Vintage, 1974. *Die Fröhliche Wissenschaft*. In *Sämtliche Werke*. Vol. 3.

———. *On the Genealogy of Morals*. Trans. Walter Kaufmann. New York: Vintage, 1967. *Zur Genealogie der Moral*. In *Sämtliche Werke*. Vol. 5.

Nirenberg, David. *Communities of Violence: Persecution of Minorities in the Middle Ages*. Princeton: Princeton University Press, 1996.

Olender, Maurice. *The Languages of Paradise: Race, Religion, and Philology in the Nineteenth Century*. Trans. Arthur Goldhammer. Cambridge, Mass.: Harvard University Press, 1992. *Les langues du paradis. Aryens et Sémites: Un couple providentiel*. Paris: Gallimard/Le seuil, 1989.

Ophir, Adi. *Plato's Invisible Cities: Discourse and Power in the Republic*. London: Routledge, 1991.

Origen, *Commentary on the Epistle to the Romans, Books 1–5*. Trans. T. P. Scheck. Washington, D.C.: The Catholic University of America Press, 2001.

Palmer, Gesine. "Einleitung." In Franz Rosenzweig, *'Innerlich bleibt die Welt eine': Ausgewählte Texte von Franz Rosenzweig über den Islam*. Ed. Gesine Palmer. Bodenheim: Philo Verlag, 2002.

Pelagius. *Pelagius's Commentary on St. Paul's Epistle to the Romans*. Trans. Theodore De Bruyn. Oxford: Clarendon Press, 1993.

Petit, Jean-Pierre. "Deux étrangers shakespeariens." In *Regards européens sur le monde anglo-américain: Hommage à Maurice-Paul Gautier*. Paris: Presses de l'université de Paris-Sorbonne, 1992, 127–30.

Pines, Shlomo. "Islam According to *The Star of Redemption*: Toward a Study of Franz Rosenzweig's Sources and Biases" (in Hebrew). *Bar-Ilan Yearbook* 22–23 (1987–88): 303–14.

Piper, John. *'Love Your Enemies': Jesus' Love Command in the Synoptic Gospels and in the Early Christian Paraenesis. A History of The Tradition and Interpretation of its Uses*. Cambridge: Cambridge University Press, 1979.

Plato. *Collected Dialogues of Plato*. Ed. Edith Hamilton and Huntington Cairns. Princeton: Princeton University Press, 1961.

———. *Laws*. Trans. R. G. Bury. Cambridge, Mass.: Harvard University Press, Loeb Classical Library, 1968.

———. *Republic*. Trans. Paul Shorey. Cambridge, Mass.: Harvard University Press, Loeb Classical Library, 1937.

Plutarch. "How to Profit by One's Enemies." Trans. Frank Cole Babbitt. in *Moralia*. vol. II. Cambridge, Mass.: Harvard University Press, "Loeb Classical Library," 1928, 3–41.

Powell, James M. "The Papacy and the Muslim Frontier." In *Muslims under Latin Rule, 1100–1300*. Ed. J. M. Powell. Princeton: Princeton University Press, 1990, 175–203.

Rasmussen, Tarald. *Inimici Ecclesiae*. Leiden: E. J. Brill, 1989.

Raz-Krakotzkin, Amnon. "Between 'Brit-Shalom' and the Temple: Redemption and Messianism in Zionist Discourse through the Writings of Gershom Scholem" (in Hebrew). *Theory and Criticism* 20 (spring 2002): 87–112.

———. "Binationalism and Jewish Identity: Hannah Arendt and the Question of Palestine." In *Hannah Arendt in Jerusalem*. Ed. Steven Aschheim. Berkeley: University of California Press, 2001, 165–80.

———. "Exile Within Sovereignty: Toward a Critique of the 'Negation of Exile' in Israeli Culture" (in Hebrew). *Theory and Criticism* 4–5 (1993): 23–56, 113–32.

———. "A Few Comments on Orientalism, Jewish Studies, and Israeli Society" (in Hebrew). *Jama'a* 3 (1998): 34–61.

———. "A National Colonial Theology—Religion, Orientalism, and the Construction of the Secular in Zionist Discourse." *Tel Aviver Jahrbüch für deutsche Geschichte* 30 (2002): 312–26.

———. "A Peace Without Arabs: The Discourse of Peace and the Limits of Israeli Consciousness." In *After Oslo: New Realities, Old Problems*. Ed. George Giacaman and Dag Jorund Lonning. London: Pluto Press, 1998. 59–76.

———. "'Without Accounting for Others': The Question of Christianity in Scholem and Baer" (in Hebrew). *Mada'e ha-Yahadut* 38 (1998): 73–96.

———. "The Zionist Return to the History of Redemption: Or What is the 'History' to Which the 'Return' in the Phrase 'the Zionist Return to History' Refers?" (in Hebrew). In *Zionism and the Return to History: A Reevaluation*. Ed. S. N. Eisenstadt and M. Lyssak. Jerusalem: Ben-Zvi Institute, 1999. 249–79.

Robbins, Jill. "Circumcising Confession: Derrida, Autobiography, Judaism." *diacritics* 25:4 (winter 1995): 20–38.

———. *Prodigal Son/Elder Brother: Interpretation and Alterity in Augustine, Petrarch, Kafka, Levinas.* Chicago: University of Chicago Press, 1991.

Rodinson, Maxime. *La fascination de l'islam.* Paris: La découverte, 1989.

Rodrigue, Aron. *Images of Sephardi and Eastern Jewries in Transition: The Teachers of the Alliance Israélite Universelle, 1860–1939.* Seattle: University of Washington Press, 1993.

Rolls, Albert. *The Theory of the King's Two Bodies in the Age of Shakespeare.* Lewiston: Edwin Mellen Press, 2000.

Ronell, Avital. *Dictations: On Haunted Writing.* Lincoln: University of Nebraska Press, 1993.

———. "Doing Kafka in *The Castle.*" In *Kafka and the Contemporary Performance.* Ed. Alan Udoff. Bloomington: Indiana University Press, 1987, 214–35.

———. *Stupidity.* Champaign, Ill.: University of Illinois Press, 2001.

———. "True Lyotard." Textscript, 2001.

Rosen, Alan. "The Rhetoric of Exclusion: Jew, Moor, and the Boundaries of Discourse in *The Merchant of Venice.*" In *Race, Ethnicity, and Power in the Renaissance.* Ed. Joyce Green MacDonald. Cranbury, N.J.: Fairleigh Dickinson University Press, 1997, 67–79.

Rosenzweig, Franz. *Franz Rosenzweig's "The New Thinking."* Ed. and trans. Alan Udoff and Barbara E. Galli. Syracuse: Syracuse University Press, 1999.

———. *Hegel und der Staat.* Munich: R. Oldenburg, 1920.

———. *'Innerlich bleibt die Welt eine': Ausgewählte Texte von Franz Rosenzweig über den Islam.* Ed. Gesine Palmer. Bodenheim: Philo Verlag, 2002.

———. *The Star of Redemption.* Trans. W. W. Hallo. Notre Dame: University of Notre Dame Press, 1985. *Der Stern der Erlösung.* The Hague: Martinus Nijhoff, 1976.

Rousset, David. *L'univers concentrationaire.* Paris: Editions du Pavois, 1946.

Rozmovits, Linda. *Shakespeare and the Politics of Culture in Late Victorian England.* Baltimore: Johns Hopkins University Press, 1998.

Rousseau, Jean-Jacques. *Discourse on the Origin and the Foundations of Inequality Among Men.* Trans. Victor Gourevitch. Cambridge: Cambridge University Press, 1997. *Discours sur l'origine et les fondements de l'inégalité parmi les hommes.* In *Oeuvres complètes.* Vol. 2. Ed. Michel Launay. Paris: Seuil, 1971. 204–67.

———. *On the Social Contract.* Trans. Donald A. Cress. Indianapolis: Hackett, 1987. *Du contrat social ou Principes du droit politique.* In *Oeuvres complètes.* Vol. 2. Ed. Michel Launay. Paris: Seuil, 1971, 518–85.

Russell, Frederick H. *The Just War in the Middle Ages.* Cambridge: Cambridge University Press, 1975.

Ryn, Zdzislaw, and Stanislaw Klodzinski. "An der Grenze Zwischen Leben und Tod. Eine Studie über die Erscheinung des 'Muselmanns' im Konzentrationslager." Trans. (from Polish) Olaf Kühl. *Auschwitz-Hefte* 1 (1987): 89–154.

Sahel, Pierre. *La pensée politique dans les drames historiques de Shakespeare.* Paris: Didier Edition, 1984.

Said, Edward. *Orientalism.* New York: Vintage, 1979.

Saner, Hans. *Kant's Political Thought: Its Origins and Development.* Trans. E. B. Ashton. Chicago: University of Chicago Press.

Santner, Eric L. *The Psychotheology of Everyday Life: Reflections on Freud and Rosenzweig.* Chicago: University of Chicago Press, 2001.

Schmidt, Christoph. "The Political Theology of Gershom Scholem" (in Hebrew). *Theory and Criticism* 6 (spring 1995): 149–60.

Schmitt, Carl. *Ex Captivitate Salus: Erfahrungen der Zeit 1945/47.* Cologne: Greven Verlag, 1950.

———. *The Concept of the Political.* Trans. George Schwab. Chicago: University of Chicago Press, 1996. *Der Begriff des Politischen.* 1932. Berlin: Dunker & Humblot, 1996.

———. *The Leviathan in the State Theory of Thomas Hobbes: Meaning and Failure of a Political Symbol.* Trans. George Schwab and Erna Hilfstein. Westport, Conn.: Greenwood Press, 1996. *Der Leviathan in der Staatslehre des Thomas Hobbes: Sinn und Fehlschlag eines Politischen Symbols.* Hamburg: Hanseatische Verlagsanstalt, 1938.

———. *Der Nomos der Erde im Völkerrecht des Jus Publicum Europaeum.* Cologne: Greven Verlag, 1950.

———. *Political Theology: Four Chapters on the Concept of Sovereignty.* Trans. George Schwab. Cambridge, Mass.: MIT Press, 1985. *Politische Theologie: Vier Kapitel zur Lehre von der Souveränität,* 1922. Berlin: Duncker and Humblot, 1996.

———. *Roman Catholicism and Political Form.* Trans. G. L. Ulmen. Westport, Conn.: Greenwood Press, 1996. *Römischer Katholizismus und politische Form.* 1925. Stuttgart: Klett-Cota, 1984.

Scholem, Gershom. *The Messianic Idea in Judaism.* New York: Schocken, 1971.

———. *Sabbatai Sevi: The Mystical Messiah.* Trans. R. J. Zwi Werblowsky. 1957. Princeton: Princeton University Press, 1973.

Schollmeier, Paul. *Other Selves: Aristotle on Personal and Political Friendship.* Albany: State University of New York Press, 1994.

Segev, Tom. *The Seventh Million: The Israelis and the Holocaust.* Trans. Haim Watzman. New York: Hill and Wang, 1994.

Sénac, Philippe. *L'occident médiéval face à l'Islam: L'image de l'autre*. Paris: Flammarion, 2000.

Shakespeare, William. *The Merchant of Venice*. Ed. Jay L. Halio. Oxford: Oxford University Press, 1993.

———. *Othello*. Ed. E. A. J. Honigmann. London: The Arden Shakespeare, 1997.

Shanks, Andrew. *Hegel's Political Theology*. Cambridge: Cambridge University Press, 1991.

Shapiro, James *Shakespeare and the Jews*. New York: Columbia University Press, 1996.

Shilansky, Dov. *Muzelman*. Tel-Aviv: Hotza'at 'Ed, 1961. Trans. Katie Kaplan as *Musulman*. Tel-Aviv: Menora Publishing House, 1962.

Shohat, Ella. "Sepharadim in Israel: Zionism from the Standpoint of its Jewish Victims." *Social Text* 19–20 (1988): 1–35.

Smith, Robert. *Derrida and Autobiography*. Cambridge: Cambridge University Press, 1995.

Sofsky, Wolfgang. *The Order of Terror: The Concentration Camp*. Trans. William Templer. Princeton: Princeton University Press, 1997.

Southern, Richard. *Western Views of Islam in the Middle Ages*. Cambridge, Mass.: Harvard University Press, 1962.

Soyinka, Wole. "Shakespeare and the Living Dramatist." In *Shakespeare and Race*. Ed. Catherine M. S. Alexander and Stanley Wells. Cambridge: Cambridge University Press, 2000, 82–100.

Spinoza. Benedict de. *A Theologico-Political Treatise*. Trans. R. H. M. Elwes. New York: Dover, 1951.

Spivak, Gayatri Chakravorty. *A Critique of Postcolonial Reason: Toward a History of the Vanishing Present*. Cambridge, Mass.: Harvard University Press, 1999.

Stein, George H. *The Waffen SS: Hitler's Elite Guard at War, 1939–1945*. Ithaca: Cornell University Press, 1966.

Steiner, George. *Language and Silence*. London: Faber and Faber, 1967.

Stern-Gillet, Suzanne. *Aristotle's Philosophy of Friendship*. Albany: State University of New York Press, 1995.

Sullam Calimani, Anna-Vera. *I nomi dello sterminio*. Turin: Einaudi, 2001.

Taubes, Jacob. *Ad Carl Schmitt: Gegenstrebige Fügung*. Berlin: Merve, 1987.

———. *Die Politische Theologie des Paulus*. Ed. Aleida Assmann and Jan Assmann. Berlin: Wilhelm Fink, 1993.

———. "The Price of Messianism." *Journal of Jewish Studies* 33, nos. 1–2 (1982): 595–600.

Taylor, Mark. *Nots*. Chicago: University of Chicago Press, 1993.

Theological Dictionary of the New Testament. Ed. G. Kittel. Trans. G. W. Bromiley. Grand Rapids, Mich.: Eerdmanns, 1964.

Theological Lexicon of the New Testament. Ed. Ceslas Spicq. Trans. James D. Ernst. Peabody, Mass.: Hendrikson, 1994.

Tolan, John. "Muslims as Pagan Idolaters in Chronicles of the First Crusade." In *Western Views of Islam in Medieval and Early Modern Europe.* Ed. David R. Blanks and Michael Frasseto. New York: St. Martin's Press, 1999, 97–117

Trachtenberg, Joshua. *The Devil and the Jews: The Medieval Conception of the Jews and Its Relation to Modern Antisemitism.* 1943. Philadelphia: Jewish Publication Society, 1983.

Triki, Fathi. *Les philosophes et la guerre.* Tunis: Publications de l'Université de Tunis, 1985.

Udoff, Alan. "Introduction: Kafka's *Question.*" In *Kafka and the Contemporary Critical Performance.* Ed. Alan Udoff. Bloomington: Indiana University Press, 1987, 1–14.

Vaughan, Virginia M. *Othello: A Contextual History.* Cambridge: Cambridge University Press, 1994.

Vitkus, Daniel. ""Early Modern Orientalism: Representations of Islam in Sixteenth and Seventeenth-Century Europe." In *Western Views of Islam in Medieval and Early Modern Europe.* Eds. David R. Blanks and Michael Frasseto. New York: St. Martin's Press, 1999, 207–30.

———. Turning Turk in *Othello*: The Conversion and Damnation of the Moor." *Shakespeare Quarterly* 48, no. 2 (1997): 145–76.

Voelke, André-Jean. *Les rapports avec autrui dans la philosophie grecque d'Aristote à Panétius.* Paris: Vrin, 1961.

Vries, Hent de. "Autour du théologico-politique." In *Judéités: Question pour Jacques Derrida.* Ed. Joseph Cohen and Raphaël Zaguri-Orly. Paris: Galilée, 2003.

———. *Philosophy and the Turn to Religion.* Baltimore: Johns Hopkins University Press, 1999.

———. *Religion and Violence: Philosophical Perspectives from Kant to Derrida.* Baltimore: Johns Hopkins University Press, 2002.

Waardenburg, Jean-Jacques. *L'islam dans le mirroir de l'occident.* Paris: Mouton, 1963.

Wallmann, Johannes. "Luther on Jews and Islam." In *Creative Biblical Exegesis: Christian and Jewish Hermeneutics through the Centuries.* Ed. Benjamin Uffenheimer and Henning Graf Reventlow. Sheffield: Journal for the Study of the Old Testament, Supplement Series 59, 1988, 149–60.

Wasserstrom, Steven M. *Between Muslim and Jew: The Problem of Symbiosis under Early Islam.* Princeton: Princeton University Press, 1995.

Weber, Samuel. *Institution and Interpretation.* Minneapolis: University of Minnesota Press, 1987.

———. "Wartime." In *Violence, Identity, and Self-Determination.* Ed. Hent de Vries and Samuel Weber. Stanford: Stanford University Press, 1997, 80–105.

Wells, Robin Headlam. *Shakespeare, Politics and the State.* Houndmills: Macmillan, 1986.

Westermann, Claus. *The Promises to the Fathers: Studies on the Patriarchal Narratives.* Trans. D. E. Green. Philadelphia: Fortress Press, 1976.

Wiesel, Elie. *La nuit.* Paris: Minuit, 1958.

———. "Stay Together, Always." *Newsweek,* January 16, 1995: 58.

Winfield, Richard Dean. "Rethinking Politics: Carl Schmitt vs. Hegel." In *The Owl of Minerva* 22, no. 2 (spring 1991): 209–25.

Wyschogrod, Edith. "Derrida, Levinas, and Violence." In *Derrida and Deconstruction.* Ed. Hugh J. Silverman. New York: Routledge, 1989, 182–200.

Yaffe, Martin. *Shylock and the Jewish Question.* Baltimore: Johns Hopkins University Press, 1997.

Yerushalmi, Yosef Hayim. *Zakhor: Jewish History and Jewish Memory.* Seattle: University of Washington Press, 1982.

Yizhar, S. "The Prisoner." Trans. V. C. Rycus. In *Modern Hebrew Literature.* Ed. Robert Alter. West Orange, N.J.: Behrman House, 1975, 294–310. "Hashavui." In *Shiv'a sipurim.* Tel-Aviv: Ha-Kibbutz ha-Me'uchad, 1971, 91–108.

Young, James. *Writing and Rewriting the Holocaust.* Bloomington: Indiana University Press, 1988.

Zabus, Chantal. "Encre blanche et Afrique originelle: Derrida et la postcolonialité." In *Passions de la littérature: Avec Jacques Derrida.* Ed. Michel Lisse. Paris: Galilée, 1996, 261–73.

Zahn, Theodor. *Der Brief des Paulus an die Römer.* Leipzig: A. Deichert, 1910.

Zelizer, Barbie. *Remembering to Forget: Holocaust Memory Through the Camera's Eye.* Chicago: University of Chicago Press, 1998.

Zertal, Idith. *From Catastrophe to Power: Holocaust Survivors and the Emergence of Israel.* Berkeley: University of California Press, 1998.

Žižek, Slavoj. *The Sublime Object of Ideology.* London: Verso, 1989.

Cultural Memory | *in the Present*